LS

POTESTAS

Ohio University Press
Athens, Ohio
1968

CLAVIUM

Lev
SHESTOV

*Translated, with an
introduction by
Bernard Martin*

TO NATHALIE BARANOFF AND TATIANA RAGEOT

TABLE OF CONTENTS

A THOUSAND AND ONE NIGHTS

PART I

Part II

Part III

On the Roots of Things

Part IV

Memento Mori

X CONTENTS

Introduction

Most of the essays and aphorisms collected in Lev Shestov's *Potestas Clavium*, which was not published in book form until 1923 when it appeared in Russian in Berlin, where written during the war years and originally printed in various journals in Moscow in 1916 and 1917.[1] The war itself was a deeply shattering experience for Shestov. In "A Thousand and One Nights," which he was to put at the head of *Potestas Clavium*, he ventures the suggestion that the tragedy of the world conflict, and indeed all of the horrors of the Twentieth Century, may be seen as God's answer to "Christian" Europe and its sacrilegious attempts to reach the heavens through rational, mechanical means, and he offers the hope that these horrors may destroy that presumptuous self-assurance which has led men to deify themselves and their own reason instead of the living God.

The concern to restore men's faith in the God of the Bible, which for some years had been growing in Shestov's mind, is here prominent but not yet as massively dominant as in his later books, especially in *In Job's Balances* and *Athens and Jerusalem*.

[1] See the note at the end of this volume, p. 405. For a general survey of Shestov's life and thought see my introduction to Shestov's *Athens and Jerusalem*, Ohio University Press, Athens, 1966.

In a sense, *Potestas Clavium* may be regarded as a transition between these works, in which his mature religious philosophy is expressed, and such earlier books as *Good in the Teaching of Tolstoy and Nietzsche: Philosophy and Preaching*, *Dostoevsky and Nietzsche: The Philosophy of Tragedy*, and *The Apotheosis of Groundlessness*,[2] in which he had begun clearing the way for his religious message by a bold assault on rationalism, philosophic idealism, scientism and autonomous morality. Here the polemic is continued and intensified, and Shestov brings to it the resources of the ironic and elegantly simple literary style that he had by now perfected, as well as his thorough familiarity with the whole range of European philosophy and literature.

In *Potestas Clavium* Shestov takes up once again the defense of the living individual whose uniqueness, spontaneity and freedom, he feels, have been denied by the rationalistic tradition that has dominated Western philosophy from the time of the pre-Socratics and by the scientism that has, especially in modern times, put forth such boundless pretensions. Philosophy and science have been concerned with abstractions, with generic concepts, seeing in them true, necessary and eternal being. The fact, however, Shestov wishes to insist, is that these are ghosts and that reality inheres only in the living individual. "The general and the necessary are non-being *par excellence*. And it is only when it will recognize this that philosophy will redeem the sin of Adam and arrive at the ῥιζώματα πάντων, the roots of life, at that τιμιώτατον, that "most important" of which men have dreamt for so many thousands of years."[3]

By the time he wrote the essays contained in *Potestas Clavium*, Shestov had already become persuaded that reason and knowledge do not liberate but enslave men, and had arrived at that interpretation of the Biblical legend of Adam, the serpent and

---

[2] Published in English translation under the title *All Things Are Possible,* Robert M. McBride and Co., New York, 1920.
[3] "On the Roots of Things," below, p. 286.

the tree of the knowledge of good and evil that he was to expound so passionately and insistently in his later years. "God forbade plucking the fruits of this tree not out of fear that man would obtain more than what had been granted to him and not out of jealousy. The accursed serpent deceived Eve, deceived Adam, deceived Anaximander, and blinds all of us to this day. The tree of knowledge does not increase our powers but, on the contrary, diminishes them. We must choose between the tree of the knowledge of good and evil and the tree of life." [4]

Years before, Shestov had already undertaken a vigorous attack on the fundamental presuppositions of positivistic science, especially the principle of regularity in the sequence of the phenomena of nature and the idea of causal necessity that is assumed to govern them. In a work published in 1905 he had argued that the causal relationships between natural phenomena which science is concerned to discover and describe are—despite the fact that they exude an air of regularity, permanence and necessity—in an ultimate sense completely arbitrary and ungrounded. The truth is that the universe may be so constituted as to permit at any moment the most fantastic metamorphoses: "... we are forced to admit that anything whatsoever may result from anything whatsoever ... from our own minds and our own experience we can deduce nothing that would serve us as a ground for setting even the smallest limit to nature's own arbitrary behavior. If whatever happens now had chanced to happen quite differently, it would not, therefore, have seemed any the less *natural* to us." [5] In the present work Shestov reiterates his conviction that what appears "natural" to the mind lulled into slumber by routine and habit is really profoundly enigmatic and mysterious. Such is the constancy of natural phenomena. "Why for millions of years," he demands, "has no light ray ever traced a curve, no stone floated on water, and no

[4] "The Labyrinth," below, p. 157.
[5] *All Things Are Possible*, pp. 23–24.

beet seed produced pineapples? Say what you will, I find this strange and monstrous, and only the inertia of our stupid and cocksure reason has found for this order of things the epithet 'natural.' " [6] Shestov here extends his challenge of "necessary" and "natural" explanations in the realm of physical phenomena to such explanations in the realm of history, concentrating his attack on the Marxist theory of history, to which he refers as "economic materialism." [7]

In his earlier work Shestov had already initiated his life–long polemic against what he regarded as the unjustified claims made on behalf of logic and logical principles. In the view of the rationalist tradition it is admitted that empirical facts may be arbitrary and contingent but the basic axioms of logic, e.g., the principle of identity and the principle of non-contradiction, are regarded as necessary, universal and eternal. This Shestov emphatically denied. That "A = A" is not a necessary, but an empirical truth. It is true only for our phenomenal world; other worlds are conceivable in which it is false.[8] Shestov did not wish completely to discard logic; what he did wish to insist upon is that it is not the only or primary road to truth. "Against this one must fight, even if he has against him all the authorities of thought beginning with Aristotle." [9]

In *Potestas Clavium* the challenge to the absolute claims of logic is renewed.[10] Shestov here further affirms that men have come to look upon logical contradictions as "the *pudenda* of the human mind," just as they regard certain physical organs as the *pudenda* of the body, and concludes, "thus, the demands of logic finally have for their source simply a deep-rooted human prejudice." [11] Indeed, rationalism as such is similarly rooted,

[6] "Sursum Corda," below, p. 174.
[7] See "The Philosophy of History," below, pp. 69–76.
[8] *All Things Are Possible*, pp. 128–29.
[9] *Ibid.*
[10] See "Magna Charta Libertatum," below, pp. 113–14.
[11] "Pro Domo Mea," below, p. 167.

Shestov urges, in an arbitrary preference for order, fixity, limitation: "the pretensions of reason to all-inclusiveness take their rise in our taste for the limited, which encloses itself in artificial bounds and feels such extreme fear before all that is unknown." [12] The acceptance of the kind of rationalism exemplified *par excellence* by the philosophy of Edmund Husserl is explicable, Shestov suggests, only by "the desire not to escape outside the limits of positivism, a desire dependent not on metaphysical considerations but on the profoundly inculcated habit of living and thinking in certain conditions of existence already well-known and comfortable." [13] We wish to sleep, and it is when we "know" and "understand," when our judgments are "clear and distinct," that we sleep most soundly.[14]

Shestov offers no theory of knowledge and explicates no theory of truth. His concern, he insists, is not with "the problem of knowledge" but with "knowledge as a problem." However, one might not improperly characterize the theory of metaphysical truth implicit in *Potestas Clavium* as negating the descriptions of truth commonly given in the rationalist philosophic tradition. Truth is not what is logically necessary. It is not what is recognized and acknowledged everywhere, always, and by everyone. It denies self-evidence and affirms contradiction. It is manifold, not one; private and individual, not public and common; essentially incommunicable, not transmissible to all.

Shestov regards Husserl, who sought to make philosophy a rigorous science and, against relativist doctrines, to develop a theory of truth as something that all beings—men and monsters, angels and gods—must recognize as truth,[15] as the greatest and most brilliant modern representative of the rationalist tradition. A large part of *Potestas Clavium* is devoted to a trenchant

---

[12] "The Philosophy of History," below, p. 71.
[13] "Memento Mori," below, p. 316.
[14] "De Profundis," below, p. 197.
[15] See "Memento Mori," below, p. 305.

critique of Husserl's philosophy.[16] Shestov sees Husserl's opposition of "scientific philosophy" to "wisdom" or "profundity of thought" and his charge of the philosophers who were interested in the latter with faithlessness to their true mission as evidence that Husserl was carrying on the work of Kant. Just as Kant concluded that metaphysics is impossible, so Husserl, who identifies metaphysics with wisdom, also concluded that it is impossible.[17] But metaphysics or wisdom is, in Husserl's view, unnecessary; all that is required is science and, in philosophy, the application of the phenomenological method to every problem. These will yield truths that are universal and eternally unshakeable. Shestov's critique, in "Memento Mori" and "What is Truth?: On Ethics and Ontology," of Husserl's rationalism, a critique which also serves as an occasion for the presentation of his own views and those of others in the history of philosophy —notably, Plotinus—who dared "to soar beyond reason and knowledge," is an incisive one and constitutes one of the most valuable parts of *Potestas Clavium*.

No less intense than Shestov's attack on rationalism in *Potestas Clavium* is his attack on autonomous ethics. Here also the polemic had been inaugurated long before. As early as 1900, in the second book that he wrote, *Good in the Teaching of Tolstoy and Nietzsche: Philosophy and Preaching*, Shestov had exposed the hollowness of the ancient tendency to identify "the good" with God, a tendency represented most prominently in the late Nineteenth Century in Tolstoy's moralistic preaching, and had recounted Nietzsche's shattering discovery, after serving the good with all his heart and soul for years, that it could

16 Despite, or perhaps because of, the radical differences between them, the two philosophers enjoyed a warm friendship over a period of years. Shestov reports Husserl as having said of him "No one has ever attacked me so sharply as he—and that's why we are such close friends." (Shestov, "In Memory of a Great Philosopher: Edmund Husserl," translated by George Kline, *Philosophy and Phenomenological Research*, Vol. XXII, June, 1962, p. 449).
17 "Memento Mori," below, p. 295.

not save him or any other man. If God is the good, then, indeed, as Nietzsche proclaimed, "God is dead." The closing sentences of the book had summed up its message as well as the thought that was to obsess Shestov for the rest of his life: "Good —we now know it from the experience of Nietzsche—is not God. 'Woe to those who live and know no love better than pity.' Nietzsche has shown us the way. We must seek that which is *above* pity, *above* good. We must seek God." In *Potestas Clavium* Shestov returns to the fray. Socrates, who first propounded the idea of the good, he here suggests, "wished to become like God, indeed to transcend God. God created the universe, Socrates created the good which is more valuable than the whole universe. And ever since Socrates all reasonable beings, mortal or immortal, have been seeking the sources of the real in the good. The universe is transitory, the good is eternal." [18] Not only for Socrates but also for the Cynics, the Stoics, Spinoza, Kant, and even many Christian and Jewish philosophers and theologians up to our own day, the good has replaced God. If a sense of the reality of God and of human freedom is to be recovered, it can only be through a refutation of the claims of autonomous reason and autonomous morality.

In *Potestas Clavium* Shestov seeks to show that the logical and moral universe in which modern man lives and which, as he believes, bars his way to God, is the product of a long historical development whose beginnings he traces to the very dawn of Greek thought, to Anaximander. It was the Greek philosophers—particularly Socrates and his disciples, and then the Stoics—who identified God with, or subordinated him, to the rule, moral and logical. It was they who elevated the idea of law to the status of the supreme principle of the universe, promising men, through knowledge and obedience, possession of the keys to the kingdom of heaven.

The idea of the *potestas clavium* was first proclaimed "by the

---

[18] "Sancta Superbia," below, p. 35.

great prophet of a small people, Socrates." [19] Christianity only tore the power away from the hands of the pagan philosophers in order to claim it for itself, and for long centuries the pretension of Catholicism to the capacity for opening and closing the gates of heaven was not challenged. But now science, in its turn, is claiming the *potestas clavium*. " 'Scratch' any European, even if he be a positivist or a materialist, and you will quickly discover a medieval Catholic who holds frantically to his exclusive and inalienable right to open for himself and his neighbor the gates of the kingdom of heaven." [20]

The history of Christianity is understood by Shestov as the history of the progressive Hellenization and consequently, distortion, of the biblical message. The God of the Bible was gradually transformed from the Omnipotent One who stands beyond and above all rules and principles into the guardian of the law. The result was not man's promised liberation, but his enslavement.

It was Shestov's proclaimed mission and his life–long endeavor to reverse this trend, to restore to man his right to the God revealed in the Bible and to the primordial freedom bestowed upon man by this God. In this endeavor *Potestas Clavium*, which is here presented for the first time in English translation, played a major role.

BERNARD MARTIN

Case Western Reserve University
Cleveland, Ohio
July, 1968

[19] "Potestas Clavium," below, p. 48.
[20] *Ibid.*, p. 47.

A Thousand and One Nights

(By Way of a Preface)

> *The good is not God. We must seek that which is higher than the good. We must seek God.*
>
> —L. Shestov

> *Qu'on ne nous reproche donc plus le manque de clarté, puisque nous en faisons profession.*
>
> —Pascal

Has there ever been even a single philosopher who recognized God?

Aside from Plato, who recognized God only in part, all the others sought nothing but wisdom. How strange! The golden age of Greek philosophy coincides with the decay of Athens. Now, one would think that periods of decay would teach man to question, that is, to direct his thinking toward God. Obviously from the fact that man is miserable and that states, peoples, and even ideals perish, it does not by any means "follow" that an omnipotent, omniscient, absolutely good Being, to whom one can address prayers in the hope of being heard, exists. But if the existence of such a Being could be deduced from facts, one would have no need of faith and could be satisfied with science, to whose domain all "it follows" belong.

The "logic" of the religious man, however, is quite different from the logic of the scientist. The psalmist says, *de profundis ad te, Domine, clamavi* (out of the depths I cried unto Thee, O Lord). What relationship is there between *de profundis* and *Dominus*? If we were to put this question to a scientist, he would not "understand" it; he would say that between these two terms there is not and can not be any relationship, any more than between the howling of the night wind in the chimney and the

movement of my pen on paper. At best, he would appeal to
Aristotle's classic argument about the necessary and the contingent: "The causes from which lucky results might happen are
indeterminate; and so luck is obscure to human calculation and
is a cause by accident but, in the unqualified sense, a cause of
nothing. It is good or bad luck when the result is good or evil,
and prosperity or misfortune when the scale of the results is
large. Since nothing accidental is prior to the essential, neither
are accidental causes prior. If, then, luck or spontaneity is a
cause of the material universe, reason and nature are causes before it" (Aristotle, *Met. XI, 8, fin.*).

The relationship between *de profundis* and *Dominus* is certainly an accidental one: reason which knows the fundamental
causes of things proclaims this without any hesitation, and nature
in this case takes the part of reason. For nature *Dominus, clamare,*
and *de profundis* are three ideas which have no inner connec-
tions among themselves. I can make Aristotle's words still clearer
by quoting Hegel who, more than Aristotle himself, was permeated with the spirit of the Stagyrite's philosophy. "The movement of the solar system follows immutable laws: and these laws
are its reason." What more could one wish? It is completely
Aristotelian. The supreme principle—"reason" and "nature"—is
finally nothing other than the laws of motion. Spinoza with his
geometric method was even more daring and rigorous than Aristotle and Hegel. He was, indeed, not afraid to declare openly:
*De natura rationis non est res, ut contingentes, sed ut necessarias
contemplari,** thus making everything contingent necessary. In
our example, *de profundis* as well as *clamare* and *Dominus* must,
according to Spinoza, be changed from contingent to necessary,
that is, lose all the shadings of good and of bad (ἀγαθὴ καὶ κακὴ
τύχη) that Aristotle had still believed it possible to preserve. And
still less can good and ill luck (εὐτυχία καὶ δυστυχία) constitute a

---

* The nature of reason is not to contemplate things as contingent but as
necessary.

philosophical problem for him. I do not wish here, naturally, to defend eudemonistic or even utilitarian theories, though I must confess that in comparison with the mechanistic world-view the most vulgar hedonism appears singularly profound. Furthermore, we must not lose sight of the fact that in Aristotle himself good and ill luck are not to be taken in the sense of ordinary success or failure. He says that luck or accident (τύχη καὶ αὐτόματον) was the cause of the appearance of the world. A "success" such as the appearance of the world is credited to luck!

And yet this is perfectly correct: from the point of view of reason the appearance of the world is a matter of pure chance. To put it differently, reason is compelled to admit that the world might have arisen but that it also might not have arisen. If one wishes to know the whole truth, reason itself finally admits the possibility neither of the rise nor the existence of the world—so that the world arose and exists contrary to reason and to all possibilities. And when Aristotle declares that luck is obscure to human calculation, he expresses himself inexactly or, rather, he does not tell all. Not only is luck obscure to human calculation —luck does not at all exist and can not exist for human reason and it can not, of course, be the object of scientific cognition. "The accidental, then, is what occurs, but not always nor of necessity, nor for the most part. Now we have said what the accidental is, and it is obvious why there is no science of such a thing; for all science is of that which is always or for the most part, but the accidental is in neither of these classes." (*Met., XI, 1065a*).

Indeed, chance or the accidental exists neither always nor most of the time. It irrupts brutally and, as some think, illegitimately into well-regulated and organized unity. But if knowledge has for its purpose, as it did among the ancients, to find the πρῶται ἀρχαί, the fundamental principles, and to arrive at the ῥιζώματα πάντων, the roots of everything, has it the right to push chance or luck out of the field of its investigations? Chance does not occur always, it occurs only rarely—but does this mean that it is less important, less essential? Aristotle, it is true, unhesitatingly declared that preference must be given to that which occurs always and often rather than to that which occurs rarely and only from time to time. But this is merely an arbitrary statement that has no foundation and no value as an argument. If Aristotle could find nothing other than this to defend his ideas, it is that he really had nothing more to say.

For it is very clear that the significance, the meaning, and even the reality of a thing does not at all depend on its frequency. Genius is met with very rarely while there are multitudes of mediocre people; yet it is genius that attracts our attention. Revelations occur once in a hundred or even a thousand years, but if only one single revelation had occurred since the beginning of the world up to our time, it would have for us infinitely more value than the phenomena that repeat themselves every hour or even every minute. It will be objected that phenomena which repeat themselves can be verified and even reproduced artificially (experimentation) while accidental facts can not be verified. We confirm every day the fact that a stone sinks in water, but it was once only, on Mount Sinai and in the absence of all witnesses, that God revealed Himself to man. How shall we know with certainty whether this really happened or not?

It appears that the only essential and decisive argument that can be offered against the accidental is not that it is devoid of importance, but that it cannot be seized and recorded. Everything that is accidental is, by its very nature, capricious and arises only for an instant. That is why Plato, in formulating the fundamental thought of Greek philosophy, distinguished (*Timaeus* 27D) τί τὸ ὂν ἀεί, γένεσιν δὲ οὐκ ἔχον, καὶ τί τὸ γιγνόμενον μὲν ἀεὶ, ὂν δὲ οὐδέποτε, that is, "that which always is and has no becoming, and that which is always becoming but never is."

That which always is, is conceived by reason, by thought, as always equal to and identical with itself. As for that which arises and disappears—how is it to be seized and fixed? Reason is absolutely incapable of seizing it. In our example, *de profundis ad te, Domine, clamavi,* man implores God from the depths of an abyss of horror and despair. Here everything is only "accidental." When there was no abyss or horror or despair, man did not see God and did not call upon Him. But it also sometimes happens that the abyss as well as the horror and despair are there, but there is no one to call—God is absent. God is not always present. He also appears and disappears. One cannot even say of God that He is frequently present. On the contrary, ordinarily, most often, He is not. It follows then that He cannot be the object of scientific knowledge. And Aristotle's *primum movens immobile,* that *primum movens* which Aristotle calls God, is not at all worthy of being so called or, more exactly, *primum movens* is the direct opposite of God—so that if this is the πρώτη ἀρχή, the first principle, we must say frankly that God is not. For whatever be the abyss into which man finds himself thrown, whatever be the horror and despair in which he founders, he will never implore a "prime mover," even if it were self-evident to him that this mover has always been and will be eternally. Such a God would never have inspired the psalmist, and if there had been only this God, we would never have had psalms or prophets or apostles. In brief, apart from Plato—who, as I have said, could never decide between reason which conceives what is always equal to and identical with itself and the irrational but powerful tendency that drew him toward the ancient myths—all the other philosophers were firmly convinced that God exists only for the people, only for the mob.

II

Plato recognized ἀνάμνησις * and believed in ideas, and it certainly was not reason that led him to this. Thus he fully de-

* Recollection.

served the harsh reproaches that Aristotle threw at him. It would, however, be naïve to imagine that Aristotle himself was free of all reproach in this matter and that he succeeded in securely establishing his philosophy. In regard to the fundamental problem of philosophy, the object of knowledge, he is quite as hopelessly confused as his teacher. He does not admit the existence of ideas; only particular objects are real for him. But the object of knowledge is, according to him, not the particular but the general, that is—contrary to the goal he had set for himself—not what exists but what does not exist. Even Aristotle's greatest admirers, such as Zeller and Schwegler, are obliged to recognize this.

Unfortunately, neither asks himself how it happened that so tremendous a genius, so great a scientist, could allow such a flagrant contradiction in his system, and why this very Aristotle, who had shown such great perceptiveness when it was a matter of discovering Plato's contradictions, became so blind and careless in regard to his own ideas. One would think that he, to whom truth was dearer than friendship, than Plato, than anything in the world, would have shown himself more demanding toward himself than toward his teacher. Furthermore, how does it happen that contradictions so essential, which should presumably have taken away all value from the philosophical work of these brilliant Greeks, did not and do not at all even today prevent these thinkers from remaining the guides of all who seek truth? As far as the fundamental problem of philosophy is concerned we are, indeed, still at the same point as the Greeks. Still today he who holds with Aristotle has a science of the nonexistent "general," while he who holds with Plato is condemned to a mythology that is completely unacceptable to the modern intelligence. Yet, both wished that philosophy have for its object that which exists and that it be a "rigorous science."

Listen with what assurance the modern Aristotle, Hegel, speaks of philosophy: *Das Wahre gelangt aber nicht nur zur Vorstellung und zum Gefühle, wie in der Religion, und zur*

*Anschauung, wie in der Kunst, sondern auch zum denkenden Geist; dadurch erhalten wir die dritte Gestalt der Vereinigung (des Objektiven und Subjektiven)—die Philosophie. Diese ist insofern die höchste, freieste und weiseste Gestaltung.**

Such, in fact, is the philosophic tradition: all the philosophers always tried to exalt their work as much as possible. And Aristotle himself is, in this respect, in no way inferior to Hegel. But Aristotle lived more than two thousand years ago. Philosophy was then only beginning its work. The cultured world then still did not know those two particular "cases" of revelation, each unique, that the Old and New Testaments were. But Hegel did know them; he spoke often of these "particular cases" and boasted that the German people to which he belonged understood these revelations more deeply than all other peoples.

Or were these perhaps only words? Of course they were only words. Hegel was too close in spirit to Aristotle seriously to admit any mythology—whether the Homeric or the Biblical. *Denkende Geist* was everything for him, and that which did not find place in the thinking spirit was rejected as transitory, useless, meaningless. Like Aristotle, he wished above all that philosophy be a science, and science was for him, before everything else, that kind of knowledge which can be communicated and transmitted to others. The master had said: σημεῖον τοῦ εἰδότος τὸ δύνασθαι διδάσκειν ἐστίν (the distinctive sign of knowledge is that it can be taught to others). And no one can any longer renounce these words. The distinctive sign of knowledge consists in the fact that it can be learned always and by all. Therefore, the philosophers, insofar as they were and are obliged to take account of revelation, always tried—contrary to the perfectly clear meaning of the Biblical account—to transform revelation into an ἀεὶ ὄν, to make of a historical fact, that is, that which happened only

* Truth, however, belongs not only to idea and feeling, as in religion, and to intuition, as in art, but also to the thinking spirit: thereby we receive the third form of unification (of the objective and the subjective)—philosophy. This is the highest, freest, and wisest form.

once and which (like every historical fact) was swallowed up by time, a permanent and unchanging thing. Even the Fathers of the Church, who had entirely assimilated the Greek philosophy, expounded the Holy Scriptures in such a way as to harmonize them with the first principles, πρῶται ἀρχαί, discovered by reason (*lumen naturale*). The birth of the Son, the Incarnation, the death of Christ were conceived not as particular events which happened once but as existing eternally. In connection with this there arose and developed the doctrine of the λόγος, outlined for the first time by the Hellenized Jew Philo, even though the λόγος is spoken of in the Bible only once, in the first chapter of the Fourth Gospel. The idea of the λόγος was elaborated by Greek philosophy, and minds with philosophic, that is atheistic, tendencies, minds that trusted only themselves, joyfully took advantage of the possibility that was thus given them of connecting revelation with reason, that is, the *lumen naturale* with the *lumen supernaturale*. It is unnecessary to say that it is the *lumen naturale* that profited and still profits from all the advantages of this union. Catholicism understood this very well and the Vatican Council decreed that *Dei existentiam naturali ratione posse probari.**

But, I repeat, we must not deceive ourselves. One can obviously demonstrate the existence of God by means of rational arguments, and we have more than enough of this kind of proofs. But these can only hurt the cause that they are supposedly defending. Every time reason set about proving the existence of God, it required as a first condition that God be ready to submit Himself to the fundamental principles that reason prescribed to Him. The God proved by reason, whatever predicates the latter granted Him—omnipotence, omniscience, goodness—, was God only by the grace of reason. And then He was quite naturally deprived of the predicate of life, because reason, even if it wished to, is completely incapable of creating anything whatsoever that is alive; this is not its affair. Furthermore, reason,

* The existence of God can be proved by natural reason.

by its very nature, hates life more than anything in the world, feeling it instinctively to be its irreconcilable enemy. Since reason appeared in the arena of history, its chief task has always been to struggle against life. And never perhaps has this burst forth with such self-evidence as in our day when, to the unanimous applause of the civilized world, panlogism and even—*sit venia verbo* *—panepistemism loudly proclaimed their right to universal domination. Such was the final result of the millennial struggle between the Jewish and the Greek genius, as it is commonly expressed. In philosophy it was Hegel who triumphed. In theology it was the Vatican Council which proclaimed, as I have already said, *Dei existentiam naturali ratione posse probari.*

It must be said that this thesis, proclaimed in 1870 by the Vatican Council, was actually developed and affirmed throughout the historical development of Catholicism and was already in fact a dogma in the Middle Ages. It could not be otherwise, considering the alliance that was concluded between the Jewish spirit and the Greek genius. Christianity was born in Galilee. It was Renan, I think, who said that at the beginning of our era Judaea was the most ignorant country of the ancient world, Galilee the most ignorant region of Judaea, and in Galilee the carpenters and fishermen in the midst of whom the new doctrine was born formed the most ignorant part of the population of the region. How, then, could it have happened that the *lumen naturale*, which for centuries had been carefully nurtured in the lands of Greek culture, suddenly found itself in the possession of the uneducated carpenters and fishermen of Galilee? The Greeks were persuaded that reason was not only capable of demonstrating the existence of God and of explaining everything but that it could also fulfill all human aspirations. How, then, could they admit that the *ratio naturalis* which they possessed in the highest degree must bow down before the *ratio supernaturalis* of the Jews, that it was the Jews and not the Greeks who possessed the

* If one may use the expression.

λόγος ἐν ἀρχῇ (in the beginning was the word)? How could they admit that when an ignorant Jew cried from the depths of the abyss (*clamabat de profundis*), God answered him, while when a cultivated Greek reasoned, his reflections led to nothing?

It is clear that neither the Greeks nor the Romans, Jesus' contemporaries, nor the Europeans, our own contemporaries, ever seriously admitted that *clamare de profundis* could, as far as the search for truth is concerned, have any advantages whatsoever over dialectical thought. But I express myself too weakly: educated men of all times have known perfectly well that to cry—whether from the depths of an abyss or from the height of a mountain—is a completely useless and absurd thing, and that cries and entreaties have absolutely no connection with truth. This is the final meaning of Hegel's thoughts, quoted above, on the relationship between "religion" and "philosophy." He says that the truth is accessible in religion through imagination and feeling and in art through contemplation, but that it is in philosophy alone that it appears to the thinking spirit. And it is only in philosophy that it reaches its freest, wisest, most perfect expression.

At first blush, it may seem that Hegel is only trying to be just and to render each its due. Religion, art, philosophy—each, in its own way, attains truth. But, in reality, it is not a matter of justice when Hegel declares openly that all advantages are with the thinking spirit; the other forms of perceiving the truth have great positive value, but this value attains superlative degree only in the case of the thinking spirit. Why is this? Why is the thinking spirit higher, freer and—into the bargain—wiser than any other form of the spirit's activity? Obviously Hegel could give us only one reason: such is the philosophical tradition. But Hegel is not content with these advantages. The pretensions of the thinking spirit are much more serious and important. It wishes to be the final court of appeal, it wishes to arrogate to itself the right to pronounce final decision over all the first and last questions of being. When man *clamat de profundis,* the thinking spirit *knows* that, no matter how desperate his cries may be, they will lead to nothing. You will succeed, if you take great pains, in deceiving your senses and perhaps imagining that you have seen God and that God has heard you. But this will be only a "religious" truth which, before the tribunal of the thinking spirit, will not show itself to be the highest, freest and wisest. *Dei existentiam naturali posse probari ratione.*

III

In other words, we must again turn to the ontological argument for the existence of God, an argument which Descartes developed so brilliantly in modern times and which Hegel believed possible to re-establish despite its "refutation" by Kant.

We must observe that already Descartes, as the preface to his *Meditations* shows, not only assumed that it was possible to prove the existence of God by means of the *lumen naturale* but also that he was convinced, like Hegel, that only what is confirmed by the natural reason is true and that everything else is false. How strange it is to read these lines from Descartes, who had such complete confidence in reason: "Everything that the atheists generally bring forward in objection to the existence of God rests either on the fact that human emotions are ascribed to God or that our minds pretend to such power and wisdom that they undertake to understand and determine what God can and must do; thus, as soon as we are aware that our minds are to be considered finite but God incomprehensible and infinite, all these difficulties disappear of themselves."

I think one can say without fear of error that every time a rationalist appeals to the incomprehensibility of God he is concealing behind this his conviction that the questions that have been put to him demand no answer or, rather, are not worthy of an answer. As far as Descartes is concerned, this supposition is all the more admissible inasmuch as he still remembered very well the trial of Galileo. Descartes could not answer with his real thought the customary arguments of the "atheists" who say that God allows evil to rule on earth, that he is indifferent to the sufferings of the righteous and the triumph of the wicked, etc. Even Spinoza could not speak with complete freedom, though he was more audacious and resolute than Descartes. Yet Spinoza was not afraid to write:

> Though daily experience shows us by countless examples that the useful and the harmful fall without distinction on the pious and the impious, men can not for all this renounce the deeply rooted prejudice (that God is good and just). They have found it easier to explain such phenomena by reference to similar phenomena of whose meaning they are ignorant, and thus to remain in their actual and native state of ignorance, than to overthrow all this scaffolding and build another. Therefore they proclaim as indubitable truth that the decrees of God far surpass the understanding of men. This alone would have been able to bring it about that the human species should forever remain ignorant of the truth if mathematics, which is concerned not with ends but solely with the essences and properties of figures, had not brought before men another norm of truth.

It is clear that Spinoza says what Descartes thought. Only he who wishes forever to hide the truth from men can say that the decrees of the gods are incomprehensible to human reason. But did not Descartes try to attain the truth? And did not Spinoza follow in Descartes' footsteps? Can it be assumed that Descartes did not see quite as clearly as Spinoza that recourse to the incommensurability of human and divine reason is only a dangerous and harmful method of hiding the truth? Descartes' method already contained in germ what Spinoza said. Or, to speak in more general fashion, the scientific method admits nothing in common between God and man and simply eliminates God from the field of human vision. For God's reason and will differ absolutely from our reason and will, even though we use the same terms to designate them. So we use the same word to designate the dog, the domestic quadruped that barks, and the constellation in which Sirius shines. And the most honest and truthful testimony on this matter is once again furnished us by Spinoza: *Nam intellectus et voluntas, qui Dei essentiam constituerent, a nostro intellectu et voluntate toto coelo differre deberent, nec in ulla re, praeterquam in nomine convenire possent; non aliter scilicet, quam inter se conveniunt canis, signum coeleste, et canis, ynimal latrans* * (*Eth. I, XVII, Scholium*).

With the magnificent power of expression that his simple language possesses, Spinoza here reveals the final, hidden thought of every scientific method and knowledge. Descartes did not dare to proclaim it openly for he feared, as I have said, Galileo's fate. Hegel also did not say everything for certain reasons which, even if they are not commonplace, are in any case alien to science. Among modern philosophers only Schopenhauer and Feuerbach declared openly and loudly that God is not. Indeed, if God's will and reason resemble man's will and reason only as the constellation of the Dog resembles the dog that barks, anything whatsoever can be called God. Then the matter of the materialists may also be God. In other words, between God and man there is nothing in common.

Spinoza, it is true, assumes that even though God is completely indifferent to man, man must nevertheless love God. Furthermore, Spinoza also assumes that the God whom he presents is worthy of love and is an absolutely perfect being. However, this is no longer an "objective" judgment but a value judgment, that is, the particular opinion, to be sure, of an extremely

---

* Now the intellect and will which constitute the essence of God must differ from our intellect and will as does heaven from earth. Nor can they be the same in any way except that a common term denotes them both. Clearly they agree in no other way, just as the single term *canis* signifies the heavenly constellation of the Dog and the animal that barks.

remarkable man but still an opinion that it is impossible to demonstrate either *more geometrico* or by any other means. Here ends, in short, the domain of "strict knowledge," so that we can confidently pass over the ethical and religious ideals of Spinoza. What alone is important for us is that, according to Spinoza, God does not exist and that not only is this no great misfortune but, on the contrary, a great good. And what is still more important is that *such was the thought of all the philosophers without exception from the most ancient times to our own day.*

Basically the doctrine of the Cynics and the Stoics had for its chief object to show men that they could obtain everything they need solely through the power of their own creative will. Virtue, as the supreme goal which gives life its value and meaning, is precisely the substitute that must, according to the doctrine of these schools, replace God. And, if the philosophers are to be believed, it is a perfectly acceptable substitute. In this respect the Cynics and especially the Stoics have played a very important role in the history of philosophy. It is generally assumed that "theoretical" problems interested them only very slightly and that scientific philosophy passed them by. This is a great mistake. Through his moral preaching Socrates already determined the fate of the philosophic endeavors that followed him. The Cynics and especially the Stoics expressed with the boldest relief and clarity, though "narrowly," as the manuals say, the fundamental principles on which philosophy had to build itself up. Philosophy is possible only on the condition that man be prepared to renounce and destroy himself. In other words, the "moral" perfection of man is the beginning of all philosophy. He who cannot rise above his particular, personal existence, his "accidental" individuality, is not a philosopher. Hegel proclaims this openly in his *Logic.* The virtue of the theoretical thinker consists in renouncing himself, in ceasing to be a man who has needs and becoming a being who is only a knowing subject,

*Bewusstsein überhaupt, denkender Geist.** This condition was
perhaps not formulated so nakedly and not with the words that
I use here. But words are of no importance; the essential thing
is that all the philosophical systems without exception are permeated with the Stoic spirit.

It will perhaps not seem paradoxical now if I say that Stoicism
is the brother of skepticism. Stoicism is the fruit of despair. In
the place of the living, real being was set the idea, since men had
lost all hope of preserving the rights of the living being. All that
is born—and all that lives, as experience shows, is born—must
perish. Hegel frankly admits that "natural death is only an absolute right that nature exercises over man." And this philosopher
is so entirely convinced of death's rights that one does not feel
even the least tension in the tone of his declaration. Completely
in the spirit of Spinoza, he speaks of life and death, of nature
and man, as if it were a question of perpendiculars and triangles.
And, just as he feels neither joy nor sorrow at the thought that
the sum of the angles of a triangle is equal to two right angles,
he hands man over to the absolute power of nature with complete
indifference. Man, for him, is only a moment in the history of the
Spirit, but, in the Spirit, man is already overcome. I repeat and
emphasize: all the philosophers have thought and still think thus.
They sacrifice the living man and the living God with the
same indifference, persuaded that once science exists there is no
need of anything else whatsoever—obviously without even suspecting that science is still not in possession of the truth.

The only exception to this general rule in modern times is
Nietzsche. When he became convinced that God did not exist,
he was seized with so mad a despair that, despite his extraordinary literary talents, he could never succeed in adequately expressing what men had done in killing God. But Nietzsche was
not heard. Everyone believes, as in the past, that the existence of

* Consciousness in general, thinking spirit.

God—whether he is or is not—is of no importance whatsoever. It suffices that one continue to name Him such, but one could also do without the name and replace it with words such as *natura, substantia*, etc.

It is perhaps not important in the end that men either admit or deny God. This neither adds nor takes away anything from His existence. Even if one admitted that among the hundreds of millions of men who have confessed God in words only a few have truly felt His presence, there would be nothing terrible in this: the *consensus omnium* plays no role here. That God exists is the chief thing, even if no one had ever heard anything of Him. And, conversely, if all men on earth believed in God but He did not exist, it would be necessary to curse this faith, no matter how sweet and consoling it may be.

IV

And yet men cannot and do not wish to stop thinking of God. They believe in Him, they doubt, they lose their faith, they return to Him. The so-called "proofs" for the existence of God show themselves to be finally only a kind of philosophical ballast; they are certainly very interesting and instructive but completely useless for the purpose they set themselves. If one reads Anselm, Descartes, Spinoza, Hegel—whatever may be the glory of these names, whatever may be the depth and wisdom of their reflections—one has the very clear impression that these men did not believe in God. Or, more exactly, that what they called God is not God. The Greek philosophers already were firmly convinced, as I have said, that God does not exist, that God is in virtue, that is, in the capacity man possesses of renouncing the real world and confining himself within the world of ideas, the ideal world, the only world that is forever protected against all attacks. One can take away my father, my mother, my children, my wealth, my fatherland even—but who can take away from me the realm of ideas? In the Middle Ages realism triumphed among the Catholic philosophers mainly because the "general" (the ideal), not knowing γένεσις (birth, beginning), was not subject to φθορά (death, end). And in modern times everyone rushed to idealism—this we must never forget—only because ideas, even the simplest ideas, are indestructible. It is easy to kill a living rabbit or a ladybird, but who can kill "the rabbit in general" or a geometrical truth? Idealism is the only refuge of those who have lost all hope of saving living beings.

But is this a way out? Would it not be better, following Schopenhauer and the Hindu wisdom that Schopenhauer valued so highly, openly to renounce God and admit that human life is evil and continuous suffering and that, consequently, our final task consists in destroying in ourselves "the will to live"? Obviously not, from the practical point of view; practically, idealism is justified. But it would be better for those who thirst for the supreme truth, for those in whose eyes practical considerations retreat into the background because of certain (perhaps exceptional) circumstances of their eixstence.

Schopenhauer's disciple Nietzsche was the first philosopher who was seized with terror at the idea of what men had done in killing God. It may be that if Nietzsche had been brought up on Hegel he would never have suspected that Hegel's God is only masked atheism. Only because Schopenhauer taught him to speak the truth about the God of the philosophers was it given him to feel the meaning of the crime that men had committed in creating the cult of general ideas (the ideal). Nietzsche himself says that men do not realize to this day what they have done. That is true. We are only beginning little by little to discover the abyss into which we have fallen. And in the measure that the reality becomes revealed, our horror at the crime that has been committed and is still being committed grows.

Even external events have, as if they were doing it purposely, mysteriously developed in such a way that even the blind must see that cultivated mankind has entered a period of insanity. The war that has been unleashed over mankind has taken on such proportions and made so many victims that there is no one, it seems, in all of Europe who has not been affected in what is dearest to him. The representatives of the Allied Powers, assembled in congress to divide the spoils of crushed Germany, are hoping thus to heal their own wounds, but everyone realizes that this method of treatment must fail. The bleeding wounds will not close; on the contrary, they will spread still more. And the cries of men tortured to death will rise again, and again they will ask why men have killed, why men still kill God.

Then finally, perhaps, men will turn away from the methods of the "natural" explanation of life. Perhaps ancient memories will suddenly reawaken, and from the secret depths of the human soul will escape the ancient but ever-living *de profundis ad te, Domine, clamavi.* And then men will discover as "self-evident truth" that history is not at all the self-unfolding of the "idea," that Judaea was not—as Hegel thought—one of the moments of this self-unfolding, that the Greeks did not possess all truth, and that contemporary Germany is not at all the completion and crown of the ancient civilization. The inhabitants of the most ignorant region of the ancient world knew much more than the cultured lands of the modern world. They knew, for example, that, even if God is not envious, He is still jealous and not at all disposed, at least for the present, to authorize anyone whomsoever—even if he be a scientist—to penetrate His secrets. To be sure, Aristotle said that all this is only foolishness and falsehood: πολλὰ ψεύδονται οἱ ἀοιδοί (the poets lie a great deal). And Hegel, Aristotle's disciple, was angry at the very possibility of such a thought: *Denn warum sollte er (das heisst Gott) uns nicht offenbaren, wenn wir einigen Ernst mit ihm machen wollen.** Exactly:

* For why should not He (i.e., God) reveal Himself to us, if we are willing to be serious with Him?

wenn wir einigen Ernst mit ihm machen wollen. . . . O holy simplicity! How they must have laughed on Olympus when Hegel wrote these lines! And do you not hear with your human ears that there is in these words of Hegel and in all his writings not the least, even distant, hint of that seriousness which would be necessary to bring nearer the moment of revelation? Do you recall what happened when men set themselves to build the Tower of Babel? And yet, when they undertook this colossal work, they certainly wished *einigen Ernst mit ihm machen!* If we wish to obtain the word of God, it is not the serious people, the practical people of affairs, who can help us. On the contrary God answers these "serious" people with confusion of tongues. Men who had agreed so completely on all the points of their undertaking suddenly, without visible cause, stopped understanding each other.

Now what is presently happening is just that of which the Bible tells. Not more than five years ago [i.e., 1913] men appeared to understand each other so well and were building in such complete agreement that majestic tower, called modern culture, which was to unite all men and establish paradise on earth. And the paradise would certainly have been realized if an incomprehensible madness had not suddenly darkened men's minds and pushed them to destroy, with a rage of which history does not know any other examples, the product of centuries-old efforts and labors. The proud tower of European culture is now in ruins. We must begin again the painful work of Sisyphus. And there is no longer any Hegel whose philosophy of history could console men by explaining to them that *was wirklich ist, sei vernünftig,** that Germany had to be crushed because its historic role had ended, or even that it is time for all of Europe to return to the shadow, that is, cease to live historically in order to give its place to the Land of the Rising Sun, to the United States, to the young Australian republics, or to still others.

* What is real is rational.

You think that Hegel would have preferred to renounce his philosophy of history rather than thus console Germany and Europe? But he would, in that case, have had to renounce his whole philosophy, for his philosophy of history forms the essential part of his system. You think that he would have agreed, that he would have been prepared to admit that God is neither the Absolute Idea nor the Spirit, that God is—as the Bible teaches —a personal God, and that the present war is God's answer to all of "Christian" Europe and its sacrilegious attempt to reach the heavens by mechanical, "rational" means?

It may be. Yes, it may very well be. For Hegel was not only a scholar but also a man and consequently capable, at the sight of the misfortunes of his fatherland, of repeating after the Psalmist, "Let my tongue cleave to the roof of my mouth if I forget thee, O Jerusalem!" But if it be so, if even Hegel would have been capable of renouncing his grandiose constructions and admitting that the moving element in history is not the "inner dialectic" of the Spirit, but certain mysterious, inconceivable, and terrible forces—what, then, must we do and say in face of the events that unroll before our eyes? For the moment it would perhaps suffice to recall the Biblical story and declare ourselves ready not *einigen Ernst mit ihm zu machen* but to accept it with all that seriousness and extraordinary tension of the soul with which man awaits the fateful events of his existence, events such as the approach of death.

If the horrors of these last years bring about the fall of our presumptuous self-assurance, then the misfortunes and sufferings that have broken over our heads will perhaps have served some useful purpose. But it is hardly likely that this will happen. We must believe that men—those eternal Sisyphuses—will begin again in five, ten, or twenty years patiently to roll the immense rock of history and try, just as before, to push it in torment to the top of the mountain, in order that the catastrophe and all the misfortunes of which we have been the witnesses may repeat themselves once more. The philosophy of history does not at all resemble the description which Hegel has given us with such enviable assurance and such weighty carelessness. Mankind does not live in the light but in the bosom of darkness; it is plunged into a perpetual night. No! Not in one or two or ten but in a thousand and one nights! And "history" will never lead "man" to the light. Furthermore, the light is not accessible to "man." "Man" may build an immense tower but he will not reach God. The only one who can reach God is "this man" (all Hegelian terminology), this single, particular, accidental, but living man, whom up until now philosophy, as well as the entire "empirical" universe, has so carefully and methodically pushed outside the limits of "consciousness in general." This is perhaps the moment to recall Pascal's words, too much forgotten by the creators of the great philosophical systems: *L'homme n'est qu'un roseau le plus faible de la nature, mais c'est un roseau pensant. Il ne faut pas que l'univers entier s'arme pour l'écraser. Une vapeur, une goutte d'eau suffit pour le tuer. Mais quand l'univers l'écraserait, l'homme serait encore plus noble que ce qui le tue, parce qu'il sait qu'il meurt et l'avantage que l'univers a sur lui, l'univers n'en sait rien.* (Man is only a reed, the weakest in nature, but he is a thinking reed. It is not necessary that the whole universe arm itself to crush him. A vapor, a drop of water, suffices to kill him. But when the universe will have crushed him, man will still be more noble than that which kills him, because he knows that he dies and the advantage which the universe has over him; the universe knows nothing of this.) Do you hear in this the echo of the same psalm: *De profundis ad te, Domine, clamavi?* How strange: Pascal remained outside the highroad of philosophy. Or is there perhaps nothing strange in this? This setting of a reed, so weak and small, over against all the immense mass of the universe, of a particle of the All over against the whole of it—is this not too absurd for reasonable men to pay any attention to it? Yes, we must believe that is so. The classical philosophy has accustomed our minds to mathematical methods of reasoning and to proofs. Two is always more than one. One and one always make two. If we give up these propositions, we shall go astray in a forest of contradictions and forever lose the highroad.

But it is only in mathematics that one and one always make two; in reality it also happens that the sum is three or even zero. When nature united the stonecutter Sophroniscus and the midwife Phaenarete, the result was three and not two and the third, namely Socrates, proved himself greater than the sum of the two. Or was Socrates, according to you, not a "greatness"? Was he only a thinking reed?

Here is where the entire difficulty of the problem appears. Must a thinking reed really be for philosophy a *quantité négligeable*? I am prepared, like Pascal, to consider the reed as small and weak as anyone might wish, just as I am prepared to admit that the voice of the psalmist who cried from the depths of the abyss was lost in the infinite spaces of the universe. But the enigma remains no less an enigma; the mystery remains a mystery. Even the most positive of the scientists will not deny that for one ray of light to stray from its rectilinear route would be enough to overthrow the whole scientific theory of light. But when living beings are united, one and one constantly make three, four, five, and even more.

Arithmetic has power only in the "ideal" world subject to man, chiefly and perhaps even exclusively because this world was created by man himself and consequently obeys its author. But in the real world a different hierarchy prevails: there that which in the ideal world is smaller is "greater." The laws in general are different there; it may even be that there cannot be any question of laws there, that one wishes to know nothing about our laws there. St. Paul teaches: "Though I speak with the tongues

ot men and of angels, and have not charity, I am become as
sounding brass, or a tinkling cymbal. And though I have the gift
of prophecy, and understand all mysteries, and all knowledge;
and though I have all faith, so that I could remove mountains,
and have not charity, I am nothing. . . . Charity never faileth:
but whether there be prophecies, they shall fail; whether there
be tongues, they shall cease; whether there be knowledge, it shall
vanish away" (I Cor.: 13).

You feel offended that I set over against scientific theories the
words of an ignorant Jew? Very well, if you absolutely must
have a scientific authority, listen to what was said by Plato who,
five hundred years before St. Paul, expressed almost the same
thought in the same terms: "Who then among us would wish
to live if he possessed all wisdom, all reason, all science, but on
condition of never feeling any joy, great or small, as well as any
pain, great or small, or in general any sentiment of this kind?"
(*Phil. 21d*).

Like St. Paul, Plato renounces wisdom, reason, knowledge, if
these must be acquired at the cost of renouncing joy and sorrow,
that is, the "accidents" of his particular, individual, "accidental"
being.

It will perhaps be objected that this was, on Plato's part, only
an accidental lapse, that one can oppose to it many quotations
from his other writings. Yes, certainly, one can. But the goal of
these reflections consists precisely in seizing and saving from
oblivion the "accidental". It will be further objected that all this
is very obscure and that I have not observed Descartes' rule
which demands that our judgments be clear and distinct. I shall
not reply to this at all. I shall content myself with recalling the
point of departure of Descartes' conceptions: *apud me omnia
fiunt mathematice in Natura.** This explains his entire method-
ology. But Pascal, who was also a mathematician of genius,
thought differently: *Je n'aime que ceux qui cherchent en gémis-*

* With me all things in Nature become a question of mathematics.

*sant.** In accordance with this, he sees the universe and knowledge under a different aspect. *L'homme cherche partout avec inquiétude et sans succès dans les ténèbres impénétrables.*† This is our fate, this is our destiny. Therefore, *Qu'on ne nous reproche donc plus le manque de clarté, puisque nous en faisons profession.*‡

Kiev, January, 1919   Lev Shestov

* I love only those who seek with lamentation.
† Man searches everywhere with anxiety and without success in impenetrable darkness.
‡ Do not reproach us with lack of clarity, for we make it our profession.

PART I

*But Isaiah is very bold and saith:
I was found of them that sought me
not; I was made manifest unto them
that asked not after me.*

Rom. 10:20 (*Isa.* 65:1)

Sancta Superbia

In deep antiquity the Greek philosophers already sought to penetrate the final riddle of life. Almost immediately they felt that the problem which they had raised could be resolved only on one condition: if it be found that life is subject to a stable, immutable order. One might think that polytheism excluded the possibility of such an assumption. The gods of the Greeks were many and diverse. And these gods, like men, were unstable, capricious, impulsive beings who allowed themselves to be dominated by passions and never stopped arguing among themselves. How could one speak of a stable order, susceptible to knowledge, under these conditions? But already in Herodotus we find a thought which obviously expressed the ancient Greeks' conception of the universe: τὴν πεπρωμένην μοίρην ἀδύνατά ἐστιν ἀποφυγέειν καὶ θεῷ, that is, even a god cannot escape the decrees of fate. The ancient Greeks were already obviously afraid to leave the universe to the sole will of the gods, for this would have been equivalent to admitting absolute arbitrariness as the fundamental principle of life. Every fixed order, whatever it may be, is better than arbitrariness. "Fate," in Herodotus, assuredly serves to designate such an eternal and perhaps irrational order, but Herodotus, it seems, is completely satisfied with it. It suffices for him that the gods, like men, should be bound by something, by anything whatsoever. For what man fears above all else is that his fate, or even the fate of the universe, should be the plaything of chance.

But later philosophy could not long be content with the ancient *Moîpa*, fate. It transformed *Moîpa* little by little into λόγος, reason. I shall not concern myself here with the progressive development of the idea of λόγος. Instead I shall pass immediately to Socrates, for the work of Socrates attained, it seems, the limit of human possibilities. Up to the present day, in any case, every attempt to get rid of the Socratic heritage has always been considered by mankind as an attack on its most sacred treasures.

In one of Plato's early dialogues the question that concerns us is formulated by Socrates in this way: Is what is holy so because it is beloved of the gods or, on the contrary, is it beloved of the gods because it is holy? It is readily seen that Socrates' fundamental thought is identical with Herodotus'. Socrates naturally declares that the gods are not at all free to love what they wish, that the gods—like men—are subject to the law, which excludes all arbitrariness. The good is, as it is expressed today, autonomous. Mortals and immortals equally obey the commandments of the good.

We see that the years of spiritual work which elapsed between the epoch in which the conception formulated by Herodotus arose and that in which Socrates' philosophy developed did not pass in vain. For Socrates, blind faith was replaced by the good that sees perfectly well. Herodotus, who subordinates both the gods and himself to an eternal law, bows down before a painful alternative: a law, no matter how puzzling and heavy it may be, is—as I have said—always better than arbitrariness. But Socrates' attitude toward his law, the law of the good, is completely different. He accepts this law not because it is imposed upon him by force but freely and willingly; *Moîpa* is transformed in Socrates into λόγος, fate becomes the reason that is common to gods and men. He no longer submits to an ineluctable destiny, and destiny no longer destroys his life with its inexorable prescriptions. On the contrary, reason gives him wings; reason is the chief and only source of his powers. Whatever man has, whatever he does, has in and of itself no value so long as it lacks the sanction of reason. Reason, to employ a comparison of Nietzsche's, is the swollen udder which man sucks to obtain milk for his nourishment. Reason is the source of the good and it is only the good that makes the life of mortal men and immortal gods worth living. Plato remained faithful to his teacher when he later hypostatized the good by making it the supreme idea, which is absolutely autonomous and exists independently of everything, and which is our spiritual bread, the sole nourishment that gives us true life.

One recalls the famous discussion between Socrates and Callicles in Plato's *Gorgias*. The question is to determine which is better: to do injustice or to suffer injustice. Socrates affirms without any hesitation that, if one had to choose, it would certainly be better to suffer injustice than to commit it oneself. This restriction, "if one had to choose," of course puzzles the attentive reader a bit. But for the moment, let us pass over it. However that may be, Socrates definitely prefers to suffer injustice himself than to be unjust toward anyone. Callicles delivers a violent and impassioned speech in which he expresses his indignation that Socrates should be ready, in the name of an illusory "good," to surrender slavishly before force. Callicles will not admit that a weak, conquered man can find any feeling of satisfaction. The conquered man is miserable, and there is no talisman in the world that can transform the ugliness of a conquered, crushed person into beauty. A popular Russian fable tells of a certain miraculous elixir with the mysterious power of reuniting the parts of a body that has been cut into bits and restoring life to it. But Callicles does not believe in fables and scornfully rejects the "babblings" of Socrates about justice as a source of great power. Despite all the cleverness of Socrates' demonstrations, Callicles does not allow himself to be persuaded. He believes that man's goal on earth consists in finding the means of realizing his own will. Precisely like Nietzsche in our time, he wishes to obtain the high prerogative of proclaiming what pleases him as good and what displeases him as bad. Not only for the gods but for men and for himself he demands complete freedom: he wishes to be free of every previously established law, free—as we see—not only of blind *Moîpa* but also of the moral law that Socrates proclaims. Freedom for Callicles is incompatible with obedience. He consents to depend neither on a general law nor on the will of any other man. He wishes to be himself law-giver in all domains, he wishes his own words and commandments to be engraved on the tablets of the law.

But ardent and daring as Callicles was, history did not recognize him as the conqueror. Only once in his dialogues, in the *Gorgias*, did Plato give complete and definitive expression to the conception of life which Callicles represents. In his other works he leaves the field free to Socrates. None of his interlocutors ever succeeds in saying anything even slightly significant in defense of Callicles' ideas. Socrates seizes Plato's undivided attention as well as that of all of his future readers. And this is quite understandable. Socrates set himself a tremendous goal that was unique of its kind. It is not correct to see in Socrates chiefly the ancestor and master of dialectic and the creator of general ideas. His lifework consisted in searching out for himself and for mankind (perhaps only for mankind?) a new source of the elixir of life. Socrates wished to accomplish the greatest of miracles and succeeded in doing so.

The task Callicles set himself was certainly difficult: to develop all his mental and physical powers to such a point that it would be possible for him to harm and do injustice to others without himself running the risk of suffering any injustice. But, first of all, Callicles did not succeed in accomplishing this task. At most he, like his disciples, succeeded in avoiding defeats for a certain time. Moreover, his own powers were not sufficient for this. No matter what he says, no matter how great his eloquence, it is certain that without the help of chance, without a concurrence of favorable circumstances, man is incapable of always succeeding and of protecting himself against defeats. It is very probable that toward the end of his life Callicles, following the example of the Asiatic despot, had occasion sorrowfully to remember Solon. Furthermore, it must be said that Callicles built with materials already prepared. To attain his goals he used what men already possessed, with the difference only that he acted more daringly and cleverly.

Quite different was the work of Socrates. Socrates set himself the goal of *creating something out of nothing*. He went where everything had previously been destroyed without leaving a trace. Even more: if he found some traces or vestiges of an ancient reality, before beginning to build he first finished destroying and threw down what was still standing. He sought a "good" in which there would no longer be a single atom of the human values that Callicles glorified and in which the latter saw the content of his life. All that troubled Callicles, made him joyous or sad, left Socrates completely indifferent; it simply did not exist for him.

In Oscar Wilde's *Salome* the pagans, speaking of the Jews, say: "These people believe in what they do not see and do not believe in what they see." The same thing could be said of Socrates. In Socrates' "good" Plato's ideas, as well as their hypostatized character, are already completely found. Socrates, if we may so express ourselves, drinks his "good" as ordinary men drink water. He sees it with spiritual eyes, he touches it with spiritual hands. It has for him, as have the things of the external world for us, real existence. If you asked him what would be better—to suffer hunger and cold, to be imprisoned, etc., but to be just, that is, to participate in the good, or, on the contrary, to be separated from this life-giving source and possess all the riches of the earth—he would answer without hesitation that it is better to be just. And his power did not consist in the cleverness with which he forced people, by means of his dialectical method, to give to the questions he had posed precisely the answers he himself believed correct. It is told of Socrates that he once remained immobile for twenty-four hours in the same place, reflecting on a question that was not clear to him. We should grossly deceive ourselves were we to imagine that during that time Socrates "was speaking to himself." It is much more probable that during these twenty-four hours he was inwardly silent, just as he was outwardly. He was not inventing speeches or objections against possible adversaries. He needed this long, absolute silence and this inward tension in order to invoke and call into existence a new reality that had never yet appeared in the world. If he spoke any words during this time they were certainly incantations: let the new reality, the world of the good, be born, let the old sensible world disappear forever! And it is certain that he was more than once inwardly silent while the people who surrounded him imagined that he was speaking to himself. He would never have been able to see anything of what he did see if he had not himself first created what he needed.

And, indeed, from Socrates' hands there came into the world a completely new reality which had not existed before, and its creator, Socrates, himself gave it a name which men before him did not know. Or, if you prefer, the name already existed; Socrates was unwilling for men to think that he introduced into the world something new, something which not only had no one ever seen before but which did not even exist before. Nevertheless, the name for it was found. It is not astonishing that young people of brilliance like Plato and Alcibiades listened so eagerly to Socrates' teachings and sought to catch every one of his words with such awe. They adored in him the creator. It is also not astonishing that οἱ πολλοὶ (the mob) felt such animosity toward the wise man whom the oracle had praised; they perceived and hated in him the terrible destroyer. For in declaring that the good is everything he was at the same time saying that everything outside the good is only illusion. Plato's doctrine of ideas is merely the brilliant development or, to put it better, the admirably executed translation of Socrates' work. If Plato had not lived mankind would never have known that, in addition to matter and other essences once created one knows not by whom, there is still another essence more real than all that previously existed— the good; and that all other realities are finally illusory and that the good alone is real.

It is in this that the immense, incomparable value of Socrates' work, which was later attributed to all of Hellenism, consists. Socrates wished to become like God, indeed to transcend God. God created the universe, Socrates created the good which is more valuable than the whole universe. And ever since Socrates all reasonable beings, mortal or immortal, have been seeking the sources of the real in the good. The universe is transitory, the good is eternal.

Plato was obviously wrong when, replying to Diogenes, he said to him, "You have eyes to see the horse but you have no organ to see 'horse-ness' (the idea of the horse, the horse in itself)." It is not a question of an organ. To see the world of ideas, to penetrate—in other words—into the kingdom of the good, it is not at all necessary to obtain a new organ. Plato was likewise wrong when he argued that all men before their appearance in the world already contemplated the ideas in all their purity, and that man need only make an effort to re-establish the past in his memory. No one had ever seen the good in his past life because *before Socrates the good did not exist anywhere in the universe.* Socrates and Plato themselves showed that the only way which leads to the good is καθαρσις, purification.

To enter the universe created by Socrates it is necessary to renounce the universe created by God. One must find in himself the power to do without everything, to feel no need of anything. It may be that in this respect the Stoics, and especially the Cynics, showed more rigor in developing Socrates' thought than did Plato and Aristotle. The Cynics and the Stoics sought only the good; for them all of life was identified with the good. In Plato Socrates, as I have noted above, says that *if it is impossible to do otherwise* he would prefer suffering injustice to committing it. In his opinion, then, it would be better still not to suffer injustice. Injustice is, all the same, painful for him to bear. But in the Cynics the fear of suffering and outrage completely disappeared; they were afraid only of joy. Antisthenes says that he would prefer losing his reason to experiencing pleasure—μανείην μᾶλλον ἤ ἡσθείην. It was among the Cynics that the theme which was later the delight of the medieval monks resounded for the first time. St. Theresa's *Pati, Domine, aut mori* is only a free translation of the Greek saying of the father of the Cynic school.

To be sure, mankind could not decide to accept Socrates' good in all its fullness and with its exclusive character. Plato, who established a compromise between God and Socrates, suited men's taste better. The ancients called Diogenes a Socrates gone mad, and they were certainly right. Is there any greater madness than the desire to surpass God himself? The desire to become like God is already daring enough! But men could no longer renounce Socrates. Only at rare intervals in history do we find attempts to rebel against the power of Socrates.

What strange creatures men are. Once the mob saw in Socrates, precisely because he tried to create a new world, an extremely dangerous person, and it was not afraid to poison him as mad dogs are poisoned. But a very short time passed and Socrates was elevated to the rank of saint. Those who later rose against Socrates always called down upon themselves anger and indignation. Indeed, the "good" that Socrates created appears to men more lovable and even more real than all other values.

When in our time Nietzsche introduced the formula "beyond good and evil" he aroused general horror at the first moment. Even more: for Nietzsche himself the most terrible and saddest thing was to renounce Socrates' world. He felt then what the first man must have felt when God drove him out of paradise. Nietzsche thought that he had to renounce Christianity, but this was hardly so; he had to renounce the Hellenistic elements of Christianity, that is, what had been introduced into the doctrine derived from the Orient by Greek philosophy, which had already at the time attained its full flowering. Nietzsche was far from being the first who tried to free himself from the enchantment of Greek thought. Even in the bosom of Catholicism such attempts were many times made and occasionally even achieved very resounding success. It is sufficient, for example, to recall the controversy between Pelagius and St. Augustine. Though Catholicism took the side of St. Augustine, it did not repudiate Socrates. Catholicism venerated St. Paul but lived according to Socrates as the most moderate of his disciples, Aristotle, expounded him. Indeed, can men renounce the idea of the good? Unlike the world created by God, in which the possibilities for realizing human desires are so limited, in Socrates' world all desires are fulfilled. Man needs only to penetrate into this world, that is, be ready to renounce God's world, and he immediately finds himself free to possess the innumerable riches of which Plato speaks so eloquently in his dialogues. This world knows no limits; it gives shelter to millions of individuals and with its spiritual nourishment will satisfy them completely. All who wish to enter it are received as welcome guests. All will find a place there—slaves and kings, the strong and the weak, persons of genius and those who lack all talent. There miraculous transformations take place: the weak become powerful, workmen become philosophers, the ugly become beautiful. How could mankind be deprived of such a world? Is it not thanks to Socrates, indeed, that a miserable day-laborer can become the master of the world? The tyrant can be unjust to the slave; he can take away from him his last ewe, but it is impossible for him to take away his virtue. The tyrant will be wicked; his victim will remain, despite everything, virtuous. And not only a tyrant but the gods themselves can do no evil to a simple and weak mortal. Fate itself, which rules over the gods, must bow down before the good. The righteous man can look to the future with courage, pride and assurance; he has no need of anything other than his virtue. But virtue—that is indispensable to him and he will not give it up to anyone.

It is not for nothing that Mill said that men must never forget that among them there once lived a being such as Socrates—Socrates, who was himself righteous and who taught men to be righteous also; who, while only a man, created a universe more valuable than God's. Man will never renounce Socrates and the world that he created! Never? We speak decisive words too readily, we are inclined to believe that we can predict not only the near but even the most distant future. It is so tempting to imagine that we already know everything and that nothing of the unexpected can come to us any more. But apparently Nietzsche was only the precursor of coming events. It seems likely that the reign of Socrates is approaching its end and that mankind will renounce the truth and the good of the Greek world and return to the God whom it has forgotten.

Destroying and Building

Everyone knows that the final goal of man is to build and that destruction is in itself a terrible thing that can be justified only if it is a temporary step leading to new building. Why is everyone so sure of this? The rationalist philosophers—and where is one to find a philosopher who is not a rationalist?—believe that this absolute truth, like all absolute truths, is furnished us directly by reason and is self-evident. I am almost in agreement with this. In truth destruction is hateful and construction beautiful. But it is necessary to add a restrictive clause and say "as far as we know." And this restriction leads to unexpected results.

First of all, once we admit it, our statement forfeits its right to residence in the domain of philosophy. We are obliged to drive it out of philosophy and banish it to ethics or sociology or even political economy. There it will gladly be accepted, but philosophy is philosophy precisely because it will not admit conditional truths into its domain. Common sense, which rules autocratically in the positive sciences, declares with assurance: one of the most monstrous of crimes is the crime of Herostratus. Without any reason this man destroyed the Temple of Diana, one of the great marvels of art. People like Herostratus must be put into chains in order not to be able to destroy. Ethics, sociology, political economy all echo, "put into chains." And the philosopher? The philosopher is silent. He remembers: did not Gogol throw the second volume of *Dead Souls*, which was also a marvelous work of art and worth more than the Temple of Diana, into the flame? Must we also chain this writer? Indeed, not Gogol alone! Look at what nature does—with what carelessness, what ease, it deforms or destroys the most beautiful of works, its own as well as those of man. Did Mount Vesuvius take pity on Herculaneum and Pompeii? Was the fire afraid to destroy the library of Alexandria? Far more: nature systematically destroys everything that it creates. Alexander the Great and Plato, Pushkin and Gogol, and so many others who could have built so many beautiful temples—all these it has pitilessly annihilated. Did it make d'Anthès' hand tremble when he coldly directed his pistol against Pushkin in the duel? Why did it not then intervene? Why does it systematically destroy everything that it creates and everything that men create? Why must it send men old age, which transforms the most wondrous beauty into ugliness, weakens the minds of the most intelligent, and ruins the most active will? Why death, which puts an end to the most daring enterprises? Destruction, death—this is the inevitable end of all nature's works. The moralist and sociologist can forget this. But the philosopher does not forget it. He can not and, if you wish, must not forget it.

Do you know how the philosopher defines the problem of philosophy, not for the mob but for himself and for the initiates? If you wish to know, do not open one of the numerous introductions to philosophy that offer you in two or three pages a list of customary definitions but look into the works of the divine Plato. There you will read these doubly mysterious words: for the non-initiate this is a secret, but philosophy is a preparation for death and a gradual dying. This is almost a literal translation; here is the original: κινδυνεύουσι γὰρ ὅσοι τυγχάνουσιν ὀρθῶς ἁπτόμενοι φιλοσοφίας λεληθέναι τοὺς ἄλλους, ὅτι οὐδὲν ἄλλο αὐτοὶ ἐπιτηδεύουσιν ἢ ἀποθνῄσκειν τε καὶ τεθνάναι.

As you see, it is clearly said that philosophy is an apprenticeship for and anticipation of death, and that for the non-initiate this is a secret. And the most extraordinary thing is that the secret has remained a secret to this day, even though it was revealed to men twenty-five hundred years ago and even though the *Phaedo* (64A), where the quoted words appear, is one of the best known and most admired of Plato's dialogues. And even today, do you think that if these words of Plato were traced in letters a meter high on all walls this would in any way change the situation? Not in the least. Nothing would be changed, and the manuals of philosophy would continue to explain that philosophy is a science, etc., that before beginning to philosophize it is necessary to provide prolegomena to every future metaphysics, etc. It is well known what the introductions to philosophy cover. Even in works especially devoted to Plato the definition I have just quoted is passed over in silence or even not noticed at all. Resolve this great enigma, O you wise Oedipuses! How did it happen that the mystery revealed to Plato remained a mystery? And it will always remain such—this I declare in all certainty.

Man needs what has positive value or, to put it differently, what can be immediately utilized. He does not need truth. Error and illusion can be quite as useful to man as truth. Plato with his dying and preparation for death, however, does not build up but destroys. Even for himself his definition was not always useful. Most of the time he was obliged to have recourse to other definitions, definitions that were later introduced into the manuals of philosophy for the use of those beginning and ending their studies. Since I have gone thus far, I shall go to the end. Even Plato himself was not always capable of understanding the secret he had revealed. But of this he tells us nothing. It was a very simple man, the shoemaker Jacob Boehme, who told us this two thousand years later. He did not hold any social position; he could permit himself the luxury of being frank. In a fit of frankness he admitted that he himself did not always understand what he had once said. When God withdrew his hand from him, his own works appeared incomprehensible to him. Plato naturally could not say this. Aristotle had already found too much confusion and too many contradictions in his writings. Can there be any knowledge whatsoever if not only do men fail to understand each other but if I myself cannot understand today what I said yesterday? But we know that the task of men consists in building, in constructing positive works. Yes, obviously, positive—as the pupils of Plato and even the faithful disciples of Jacob Boehme demand.

It seems to me that the preceding sufficiently clarifies the question. However, if these clarifications are insufficient, it is no great misfortune. We must believe that it is the fate of philosophy to begin and not finish, to raise questions to which there is not and can not be any answer. This is precisely what ἀποθνῄσκειν τε καί τεθνάναι * means.

* To die and to be dead.

The Classical Argument

Since the most ancient times philosophers have been divided into two quantitatively unequal groups. The first—and these always form the large majority—wished to believe and did believe that they knew a great deal. The others believed that they knew very little. It will be recalled that Socrates declared that he knew nothing. But this was only a pretense on his part, a methodological trick similar to Descartes' *de omnibus dubitandum*, a pretext to establish the propositions destined forever to deliver us from all doubts. In any case, it is precisely from Socrates on that the philosophers began to claim the capacity of omniscience. Even the skeptics, as becomes evident when we carefully examine the problems they raised, never renounced knowledge entirely. They said only that our knowledge was probable, not certain. But they were nevertheless convinced that they possessed criteria permitting them to distinguish the probable from the improbable. Further, if we examine the matter more closely, skepticism with its probable judgments does not differ so very much from dogmatism with its certain judgments. When it is a question of choosing between two probable judgments that are opposed to each other, the skeptic relies on a determinate criterion. But from where did he take it? Does not the totality of his criteria finally form a certain system of knowledge that is very little distinguished from the systems of the dogmatists? We could establish a series of judgments as acceptable to skeptics as to dogmatists, but it seems hardly necessary. In the domain of empirical knowledge you will not find any more profound divergences between the representatives of two points of view as different as those of the skeptics and the dogmatists than between the diverse representatives of one and the same point of view. The certain judgments of the dogmatists will be accepted by the skeptics, but qualified by the latter as probable. And then there is this also: the dogmatist, having attained certitude, feels calm and declares that he has achieved the supreme goal, for tranquility of mind is the highest goal of every reasonable being in general and of the philosopher in particular. But the skeptic will not make any different use of his probable knowledge. He celebrates his ἀταραξία which, if one does not show a philological scrupulousness that would be here inappropriate, can be translated by the term "tranquility of mind." In brief, certain knowledge and probable knowledge are hardly distinguishable from one another.

But when it is a question of ignorance, it is quite different. When the dogmatists attacked the skeptics, they set out from the supposition that their adversaries did not admit any knowledge. And then they pushed forward their classical argument like a destructive battering ram: he who says that knowledge is impossible contradicts himself, for he knows that he does not know; therefore, knowledge is possible. And he arrives at his knowledge that knowledge is impossible by employing the same methods of judgment that everyone else employs. Why, then, does this man who recognizes the methods of searching for truth acknowledged by all, after arriving at a certain limit, suddenly renounce and reject them as useless? Why can not the method which served to obtain the knowledge that one can not know furnish the knowledge that one can know? These arguments, as you see, are irresistible. As the dogmatists have loved to put it since the most ancient times, they silence the most obstinate of opponents. The dogmatists have always triumphed over their opponents, for an opponent reduced to silence is no longer dangerous, no longer an opponent.

This naturally holds only so long as we set ourselves the modest aim of getting rid of an opponent. But what if we admit the possibility of other aims? What if we aim not at confusing our opponent in the eyes of the mob but at convincing him? Or what if we trust our opponent, respect him, and do not assume that he involves himself in contradictions because he is foolish or blind or—what is still worse—because, unlike us, he is indifferent to the truth and sets for himself only "practical" or "finite" goals—what, I say, if we admit this? The opponent is as intelligent, clear-headed, sincere and conscientious as we or—*horribile dictu*—even surpasses us in all these respects; and if he expresses judgments whose contradictory character he himself perceives, it is because they impose themselves upon him with that necessity which, according to our own judgment, is inherent in truth. Yes, it was and still is so. In the reality of the everyday contradictions are absent, or they are less conspicuous. A is always equal to A, the whole is greater than its parts, there is no action without a cause, each of us sees what the others see, *Deus impossible non jubet,** etc. One can employ general methods that are obligatory upon all, and these methods yield excellent results. And our opponent himself, as has been said, uses these methods so long as, together with other men, he stands in full light. But there are places where the light of the sun does not penetrate—under the earth, at the bottom of the sea. There, there is no light, there darkness rules, but are life and the truth of life impossible there? May it not be that our opponent, who has lived in those regions where few beings have ever descended, tries to reveal to us the deepest, most unknown secrets? And that it is precisely because that rigorous logic to which we have be-

* God does not command the impossible.

come accustomed here is unknown there, in those obscure regions, that he embroils himself in contradictions and his tongue stammers? We can certainly force him to silence. We can, like Aristotle, say that he is only pronouncing empty words that have no sense even for him. This will surely give us peace, the supreme good, or ἀταραξία (tranquility) which is also the supreme good. For shall we not thus be certain of possessing the final truth?

In this respect the classical argument is above all praise. But what if our curiosity awakens, what if life shakes in us the Aristotelian assurance, and we ask ourselves: may not this man who contradicts himself be in communion with some mysterious reality? May not this confusion, this mass of inextricable contradictions hide in themselves that precisely which is indispensable, most significant, and most meaningful for us? Will it not then occur to us that the pride of the conqueror is less desirable than the humility of the conquered? And that our classical argument, like all mechanical means of constraint, is not at all as seductive as it seems to us? All the more so since those who have perceived the contradictory nature of reality are not ordinarily very disputatious. There is no need to force them to silence by means of the classical argument, for they do not generally attach any very great importance to the triumph of their "truths." If you wish them to be silent and not contradict you, you need not demonstrate anything to them. Tell them simply that you do not wish to listen to them and that you wish to be conquerors. This will act on them as effectively as your arguments. They will of themselves be silent, depart and leave you a free field.

Potestas Clavium

Do you know what these words, *potestas clavium*, mean? Yes, no doubt, but probably not exactly, for who, apart from specialists, is nowadays concerned with Catholic dogmatic? But there is every reason to believe that we are wrong in imagining that Catholic dogmatic is alien to us. "Scratch" any European, even if he be a positivist or a materialist, and you will quickly discover a medieval Catholic who holds frantically to his exclusive and inalienable right to open for himself and his neighbor the gates of the kingdom of heaven. The materialists and atheists claim this right quite as much as do the faithful sheep of the great herd of St. Peter's followers. Referring to the well-known verse of the Gospel of St. Matthew (16:19), "and I will give unto thee the keys of the kingdom of heaven; and whatsoever thou shalt bind on earth shall be bound in heaven; and whatsoever thou shalt loose on earth shall be loosed in heaven," the Catholics declare that God delegated His power to St. Peter who, in turn, delegated it to his successors up to the present Pope. From this it follows that the decisions of the Pope or of duly consecrated Catholic priests are unassailable to all eternity. God Himself, as the Catholic theologians put it *literally*, cannot change the decisions of the priests appointed by Rome. For He declared that He delegated His power to the Apostle; but God cannot contradict Himself just as, by reason of His invariability, He cannot change any of the decisions He Himself has taken. I emphasize that this line of reasoning reproduces almost literally the reflections of the Catholic theologians. I believe that I have even succeeded in preserving their tone, the positive tone of practical men breathing a healthy assurance. I do not cite any texts because I have no books at hand but, in short, quote from memory.

So, then, spoke the Catholic theologians; so for centuries has the Catholic Church thought. Evidently Catholic theology could not feel at peace so long as it had not obtained that fullness of power which would guarantee it domination over human souls for all eternity.

It would, however, be a mistake to believe that the idea of the *potestas clavium* was born at the beginning of our era and that it was Catholicism that invented it. No, it was not Christianity that invented this doctrine; long before the rise of Christianity it was proclaimed by the great prophet of a small people, Socrates. If we are to believe Plato, Socrates was the first to discover that man has at his disposal this immense and terrible power, the keys to the kingdom of heaven. Already in that distant time when human thought was still being formed, he declared that the keys of the kingdom are found not in heaven but on earth and that he who wishes to cross the threshold of paradise must concern himself with the keys while he is still on earth. Later, when he will have left our earth, it will be irremediably too late. The Catholics needed only to seize the talisman held by the pagans. "The keys exist and are found on earth, but in our temples and not in yours," Catholicism declared to the pagans with finality. Do you believe that your philosophy with its κάθαρσις (purification) will open for you the gates of paradise? Never. *Virtutes gentium splenida vitia sunt.** Even though Denifle has demonstrated recently that this phrase is not found in St. Augustine, it is certain that he said almost the same thing

* The virtues of the pagans are only splendid vices.

and in almost the same terms. Consider the complete formula of Pope Innocent III: *Corde credimus et ore confitemur unam Ecclesiam non haereticorum sed sanctam, Romanam, catholicam et apostolicam, extra quam neminem salvari credimus.**

Catholicism, I repeat, only raised the question whether the philosophers had legally taken possession of the *potestas clavium*. But the idea of the limitless power that man possesses over heaven and earth came from Socrates' head. And this idea still lives today; it lives in each of us, no matter what our philosophical convictions may be. Each of us imagines that he has in his possession that great truth which opens for him the way leading to the final mystery and to eternal blessedness. Even Luther, who revolted against the Roman Church and whom the Roman Church condemned, claimed assuredly the right to final judgment. When Zwingli died, Luther said that his soul would be condemned and that if God saved him it would be *extra regulam*. Luther, as you see, does not grant much. Still more: it seemed to Luther that certainty was the very essence of Christianity. *Nihil apud Christianos notius et celebratius quam assertio. Tolle assertiones et Christianismum tulisti.†* And each of us imagines that his truth is the real truth and that his keys are the real keys. And further, *Carpe diem!* Make haste while you are still alive to find the keys, the talisman, for afterwards it will be too late.

Socrates and the Catholics speak of all this openly, making use of almost the same fantastic expression that I have employed here. Positivist minds, men of science, naturally avoid these expressions and use words that conform better to the modern taste for the "everyday," for the things of current life, which are called—one knows not why—"natural," while everything that is fantastic is

---

* With our heart we believe and with our lips confess one church, not of heretics but holy, Roman, catholic and apostolic, outside of which we believe no man can be saved.
† Nothing is better known and more celebrated with Christians than the assured statement. Take away these statements and you have taken away Christianity.

called—again only God knows why—"unnatural." But this in no way changes the matter. Just as Catholicism once wrested the *potestas clavium* from paganism, so in our day positive science tries to wrest this so enviable prerogative from the hands of Catholicism. We wish to have these miraculous keys in our hands. We will not renounce for anything in the world the right to pronounce the eternal condemnation or justification of men. We judge what is good and what is bad, what should be and what should not be, with the same assurance as did our predecessors, the Catholic theologians.

Look closely at any philosophical system. What is the spirit that animates it? The philosopher who would be modest enough voluntarily to renounce the *potestas clavium* would become the object of deepest scorn: *Tolle potestatem clavium, sapientiam tulisti.** Even if he should agree to hand this immense power over to the Creator. If you do not have this miraculous talisman, be silent! Hide your shameful poverty from the world! Men are so accustomed to the idea that they possess and must possess this limitless power over earthly reality as well as over all possible realities that they could not bear the idea that they do not have and could never have this power. If God Himself announced from heaven that the *potestas clavium* belongs not to men but to Himself alone, even the gentlest would rebel.

The legend of the Grand Inquisitor in Dostoevsky makes us see this in striking fashion. With a perceptiveness that bordered on clairvoyance and appeared completely incomprehensible to his contemporaries, Dostoevsky laid bare in this legend the secret of Catholicism's pretensions. Catholicism believes not in God but in itself. If Christ descended to earth a second time, the Grand Inquisitor would have him burned, as he dealt with all heretics, i.e., all those who dared believe that power over heaven and earth does not belong entirely to the successors of St. Peter, for *credimus et confitemur unam Ecclesiam Romanam, extra quam*

* Take away the power of the keys and you have taken away wisdom.

*neminem salvari.** And the Grand Inquisitor would have acted very justly, that is, logically. No one can doubt—can he?—that rigorous logic is not only the condition but the very essence of truth. Indeed, once God delegated His rights to the Bishop of Rome, how could He Himself act on earth as judge and legislator? This would be equivalent to His renouncing His attributes of invariability and immutability! It is true that these predicates, as well as all the others, were attributed to God by men themselves. But despite this or, better, because of this, men will never permit God to renounce them. For if God renounced invariability and immutability He could end by renouncing the other predicates as well and appearing one fine day to the eyes of men under a completely different aspect from that under which they represented Him when they decided to believe in Him.

God, says the Grand Inquisitor, has granted to men the right to bless in His name what they themselves will make and invent. God is only the supreme sanction of the order established by men. If He pretends to more, we must reject Him. It was thus that Dostoevsky understood the essence of Catholicism. One could, in formulating briefly the content of the legend of the Grand Inquisitor, say, making use of the terms not of Dostoevsky but of his great predecessor Luther, who lived four centuries before: the Pope is the Antichrist.

So Luther said. The dispute between Luther and the Pope reduced itself finally to this: that Luther, after a long period of hesitation and torturing doubt, suddenly discovered that the head of the Roman Church, of which he himself was a part, had installed himself and his reason in the place of God. Luther's dispute with Rome burst forth four hundred years before the Vatican Council in which the dogma of papal infallibility was proclaimed for the first time. But in fact this dogma had existed since the Middle Ages under the form of the dogma of the

* We believe and confess one Roman Church outside of which no man is saved.

infallibility of the Roman Church. For the Church was embodied, even in this period, in the person of the Pope—at least when the papal throne was occupied by a man sufficiently strong and daring to take upon himself the burden of representing God on earth. Conversely, in our day, after the Vatican Council, the spiritual power of the Pope over the Catholic world is much less formidable when the Pope does not dare or does not know how to make use of it. In brief what Dostoevsky tells us in his legend was discovered by Luther four hundred years ago. And if I have said that Dostoevsky's perceptiveness bordered on clairvoyance, as far as Luther is concerned one can speak of revelation. Luther himself was profoundly convinced of this. Dostoevsky stood outside Catholicism, and so it was relatively easy for him to discover in the eyes of his neighbor, and moreover of a neighbor whom he did not like, not only an enormous beam but even a splinter. His legend astonished the whole world, as if he were the first to reveal the goal to which the Roman Catholic Church's efforts tended.

Imagine to yourself Luther's situation. He was a faithful and devoted Catholic. He was a monk and a priest. He became a monk only because he was convinced that the monastic life permitted him to serve God better. And this very Luther, after having spent ten years in a monastery, had to admit that he belonged to the army of the Antichrist, that it was not God whom he was serving but His eternal enemy.

Having made vows of poverty, chastity and obedience, despite the advice of his friends and against his father's wishes, he hoped that he would accomplish a work pleasing to God; and lo, suddenly he discovered, as he later recounted, that in pronouncing his vows he was denying God. *Ecce, Deus, tibi voveo impietatem et blasphemiam per totam meam vitam* *—so Luther later formulated the true significance of his vows. I shall not examine here when Luther was right—whether when, crossing the threshold of

* Behold, God, I vow to you impiety and blasphemy for my whole life.

the monastery, he imagined that he was entering upon a painful, sorrowful way but one which must lead him directly toward salvation or whether when, later on, it was suddenly "revealed" to him that what he considered the way to salvation led him to his ruin. I shall not raise this question for, despite all its importance and meaningfulness, it recedes to a secondary place before another no less terrible and difficult question.

When Luther entered the monastery he was sincerely persuaded of the righteousness of his way; when he left the monastery he was no less clearly convinced that by remaining there he would be damning himself.

It seems to us men of the twentieth century that in both cases Luther exaggerated considerably. Still more: the very idea that the accomplishment of this or that act can have the consequence of eternal salvation or eternal damnation appears to us fantastic, sick, almost insane. But it is precisely for this reason, it seems to me, that we should more often look back to those times when such thoughts could be born in the minds of men. In the Middle Ages man considered his existence—no, he did not "consider" it, it is we who "consider," but to characterize this epoch we must find other terms—in the Middle Ages man felt, experienced, lived his existence under the aspect of the Last Judgment. The meaning and importance of this or that particular action were not limited to their visible results. He always believed that somewhere, in another world, each of his actions acquired a value absolutely independent of the significance it had on earth. Human life is not simply a bubble which suddenly rose only to burst almost immediately afterward among millions of other bubbles on the surface of the earth. Human life has a mysterious meaning, and each of us bears the weight of a terrible responsibility. All the sorrows and joys of our earthly existence are nothing beside the sorrows and joys of the other life. Here on earth we can only have a weak presentiment of what this other, real life will be. Only in rare instants of inward illumination can we participate in this other, divine, no longer human reality. Nowadays we behave badly or well and can pretty well foresee the consequences of our acts, whereas then these consequences were regarded as infinite. Eternal damnation, eternal blessedness—these words that have almost lost their meaning for modern consciousness still shone for the man of the Middle Ages with a vivid light. When Luther entered the monastery he fled eternal damnation and hoped for salvation; when he left the monastery it was again for his salvation and in order to escape damnation.

If one admits that man does not, indeed, live only amidst passing sorrows and joys, as is believed today, if one admits that it was our ancestors who knew the truth and that a terrible judgment, the Last Judgment, awaits us and that each of our actions can throw us into the depths of Hell—then one can imagine what the monk Luther must have felt when suddenly he discovered that the vows he had pronounced condemned him to *impietatem et blasphemiam per totam vitam* and that the Roman Church to which he was completely devoted was the church of the Antichrist. Such errors are possible, and no sincerity, no purity of soul, can protect man from them.

Luther's own experience forced him to that confession which resounds in our ears like a blasphemous paradox: *Hic est fidei summus gradus, credere illum esse clementem, qui tam paucos salvat, tam multos damnat, credere justum, qui sua voluntate nos necessario damnabiles facit, ut videatur, referente Erasmo, delectari cruciatibus miserorum et odio potius quam amore dignus. Si igitur possem ulla ratione comprehendere, quomodo si Deus sit misericors et justus qui tantam iram et iniquitatem ostendit, non esset opus fide* (*De servo arbitrio*, ed. Weimar, I, XVIII, p. 633). That is, "the highest degree of faith is to believe that He is merciful who saves so few and damns so many men, that He is righteous who by His own will has necessarily made us guilty so that, according to Erasmus, it seems that He rejoices in the suffering of the miserable and is more worthy of being hated than loved. If I could understand with my reason how such a God can be righteous and merciful, faith would not be necessary."

I cannot here quote other confessions of Luther's, but he who has understood the horror that a man forced to such confessions must have felt will also understand the meaning of Catholicism's *potestas clavium*.

Yes, Dostoevsky was right. Catholicism has indeed taken the place of God. But what could the Grand Inquisitor do when he confronted experiences like those that assailed Luther? What could the father confessor say in answer to the monk's doubts? If there is not on earth—the heavens are so far away—a person or institution which has full power to resolve finally the torturing doubts of those who have the gift of suffering from their doubts as the men of the Middle Ages suffered, existence would be a perpetual torture. The thing must be decided: either we must transfer the power of the keys to a person or institution, whether this be the visible Roman Catholic Church with its successors of St. Peter or a council of theologians; or we must accustom men to consider life in a more calm and positive spirit in order that the problems that are posed to them may not transcend their individual powers; or, finally, we must admit that the inward struggle that was imposed on Luther and on many others beside him is inevitable and even desirable, even though it will lead to no result that is comprehensible to us. But men cannot admit the last alternative or do not wish to do so (who can say what we can and cannot do?). No, those who have lived through these struggles have no need of our authorization; they do not expect it and, I would even say, do not wish it. We must then choose between the first two solutions or a combination of them. It is this, in short, that has been done. The *potestas clavium* still exists, but it is now found simultaneously both in the hands of the Catholics and unbelieving philosophers. The flock of both the former and the latter, that is, the immense majority of men, are accustomed to a life of regular, placid work whose consequences are evaluated in heaven almost in the same way as on earth. The Pope has found a compromise with philosophy. Philosophy, even Protestant philosophy, has ceased to argue with the Pope; it is almost ready to consider him its ally. Those, however, who await the Last Judgment are abandoned to themselves. Is this terrible? No, it is not terrible. It is in this that their immense and perhaps only prerogative consists—*sit venia verbo.**

* If one may use the expression.

The Fixed Stars

"Poetry, God forgive me, must be a bit foolish," said one of the most intelligent, perhaps even the most intelligent of the Russians —Pushkin. But he continued, nevertheless, to write verses and to introduce into these verses that portion of foolishness without which poetry, like food without salt, becomes unbearable. One can, then—if one wishes—simulate foolishness and do it in such a way that everyone takes this simulated foolishness to be sincere and true. I should say even more: one can also simulate intelligence and do it so well that it will not occur to anyone to see simulation in it. And we must say that the majority of writers, unlike Pushkin, need to concern themselves not so much with appearing foolish as with appearing intelligent. The facts prove that their efforts are crowned with brilliant success. It is probable that the very essence of literary talent consists in skillfully playing intelligence, nobility, beauty, daring, etc. For intelligent, noble, daring men are very rare, while there are ever so many talented writers. People succeed in counterfeiting even sincerity so well that the most expert eye is easily deceived. Perhaps Pushkin acts so strongly upon us precisely because he has no desire to be intelligent, because he understands how little intelligence is worth.

In practical life, whether one wishes it or not, one must obviously obey the commandments of reason. The only privilege of poetry—and it is not a negligible one—is that it does not oblige anyone to think what he speaks. Say what ever comes to your mind, provided only that it be melodious and charming. Pushkin wrote: "We are born not for the tribulations of existence nor for gain nor for struggle, but for higher aspiration, gentle song and prayer."

So sang Pushkin. But read his letters and his biography: cares, continual tribulations, petty struggles and always—without respite—worry about money, money, money. One wonders how he could find moments to create, to surrender himself to inspiration, to compose prayers and sweet songs. For this he was obviously forced to reduce his hours of sleep. This is why true poets work at night, for daytime life does not permit them to maintain relationships and "foolishness." During the day they must plunge into the cares of existence, win their bread, take part in the struggles of life. How cruelly fate mocked Pushkin, who dreamed of a poet's existence free of all struggle! For he died in fighting, in fighting a duel with an insignificant man who knew how to handle a pistol well. How could Pushkin bare his breast to the blows of the first simpleton who came along—he who, from his youth, understood men so well?

Vladimir Soloviev, our famous philosopher, tried to decipher the secret of Pushkin's fate and explain his death. Naturally he did not explain anything, and thank God for that. There are things that it is better not to understand, not to explain. Strange as it may be, it is often better to weep, curse, and laugh than to understand. It does no harm not only for poetry but for prose as well to be, at times, not too intelligent and not to know everything. There is no spectacle more disagreeable and more repugnant than that offered us by the man who imagines he understands everything and can give an answer to everything. That is why a philosophy that is consistent with itself and rigorously logical ends at length by becoming unbearable. If one must philosophize, let it at least be from day to day—without taking into account today what one said yesterday. If poetry must not be too intelligent, then philosophy must be insane, like our entire existence. For in a rational philosophy lies quite as much malice and treachery as in ordinary common sense. Look at it a little closer: under its opulent garments the most common appetites are distinguishable. It aspires to what is indubitable and to the certainty that two is more than one, and it wishes always to obtain possession of two in order to be stronger than him who possesses one. Poor Pushkin with his sweet songs and prayers! He sang and prayed, but d'Anthès took aim and naturally killed the poet. Rational philosophy must certainly take the side of d'Anthès, in that—as always—it sends before its judgments a regiment of noble phrases. For philosophy, like d'Anthès, wishes to strike a sure, unfailing blow by orienting itself through the fixed stars.

Eros and the Ideas

All men seek the truth, and all are certain that in seeking the truth they know perfectly well what it is they are seeking. Many also are those who have already found the truth and who are surprised or even indignant that others are unwilling to share their joy in this happy discovery. Indeed, why is this? Why is it that I see so clearly that I am right while others believe that I possess no truth that is particularly precious and that my "convictions" offer no advantage over those of others? And, above all, why is it that I am so stubbornly bent on making others recognize that I am right? Is this "recognition" really indispensable to me? Probably it is not so indispensable as all that. For since the world has been in existence no one has ever succeeded in making himself "recognized" by everyone. And yet men continue to live and to believe in themselves. It is not only Catholicism, which counts hundreds of millions of faithful followers, that has proclaimed *quod semper ubique et ab omnibus creditum est.** We often see that a man who has succeeded in gathering around himself a small group of faithful disciples enjoys, thanks to them, complete satisfaction and imagines that his little world is all of humanity—indeed, not only humanity but the entire universe; it

* What is believed always, everywhere, and by all.

is not some dozen poor human beings who have consecrated him a prophet but all men, all reasonable beings—and only the obstinate enemies of the light and the truth refuse to recognize him.

How is such blindness to be explained? Does it not come from the fact that man finally does not at all need to be unanimously recognized, as the philosophers imagine, and that by its very nature the truth not only can not but does not even wish to be a "truth for all"? I know that such a supposition will be judged unacceptable; I know also that it contains an insoluble contradiction. But I have already indicated more than once—and I repeat again—that if a judgment is contradictory, this does not suffice to overthrow it. Obviously one can not invert this statement and say that the contradiction which a judgment contains is the proof of its truth. It may be, if you please, that contradiction is one of the signs that make us recognize that we are approaching the final truth, for it shows that man no longer feels the fear which ordinary criteria inspire in him. In any case, it is certain that one cannot say that every judgment that carries a contradiction in itself is altogether superfluous for us. If men believed that, half at least—and the more beautiful, the more interesting half—of human thoughts would never have been expressed and humanity would be spiritually much poorer than it is.

Many "truths," and the most important ones, cannot obtain recognition by all, and most often do not even pretend—this is the most significant point—to this recognition. An example will make my thought clearer. In his *Metaphysics of Sexual Love* Schopenhauer brilliantly develops the idea that love is only a fleeting illusion. The "will" desires to realize itself once more in an individual, and so it suggests to John that Mary is a rare beauty and to Mary that John is a great hero. As soon as the goal of the "will" is achieved, as soon as the birth of a new being is assured, the will abandons the lovers to themselves and they then discover with horror that they have been the victims of a dreadful mistake. John sees the "real" Mary—that is, a dense, stupid, and ill-natured woman; Mary, on her side, discovers the real John—a dull, banal, and cowardly fellow. And now, after the delusions of love have been dissipated, the judgments Mary and John pronounce on each other agree perfectly with the judgments of all, with what *semper ubique et ab omnibus creditum est*. For everyone always thought that Mary was ugly and stupid and John cowardly and foolish. Schopenhauer does not doubt in the least that Mary and John saw true reality precisely when they saw what everyone else saw. And not only Schopenhauer thinks so. This is again *quod semper ubique et ab omnibus creditum est*. But it is precisely because this truth appears so unquestionable that there is good reason to raise the question of the legitimacy of its pretensions. Did John and Mary really deceive themselves during the short time when, the "will" having kindled its magic flame in them, they abandoned themselves to the mysterious passion that drew them together and they saw each other as so beautiful? May it not be that they were right precisely when they were alone in their opinion and appeared to all others as poor idiots? May it not be that at that time they were in communion with true reality and that what their social natures oblige them to believe is only error and falsehood? Who knows!

When their judgments are accepted by everyone, when they become understandable, accessible, self-evident and consequently indisputable—is it, perhaps, then precisely that they become flat, poor, empty, and of further use only to statistics or to some other positive science that takes its origin from mathematics and for this reason calls itself "royal"? You do not agree to admit this? But your agreement is of no consequence here. Whether or not you admit this supposition in no way changes the matter, and it will not make the white and uniform light of daily life more brilliant or alluring than the brief and enchanting flame that is kindled in us from time to time by an incomprehensible force—whether this be Schopenhauer's "will" or some other mysterious power. And when such a flame burns in the soul of a man, it is completely indifferent to him whether or not others agree with him and whether his truths are justified by such or such a theory of knowledge.

Darwin and the Bible

The Bible recounts to us the fall of our progenitor Adam, the first man. You believe that this is only an invention of ignorant Jews? You believe that the discovery of an English scientist is closer to the truth and that man is descended from the ape? Well, permit me to tell you that the Jews were closer to the truth, that they were indeed very close to it.

You will perhaps ask me why I take the side of the Jews with such assurance. Was I present at the creation of the world? Did I see Eve eat the apple and offer it to Adam? I certainly was not there, and I did not see anything. I do not even have at my disposal the moral proofs that Kant invoked for the defense of his postulates. In general, I do not have any proofs at all. But I think that proofs in such cases are superfluous and even very irksome ballast. Try to admit, if you are capable of it, that in certain cases one can, one must, do without proofs—and look a little at man. Does one not discern even now the fig-leaves under which he once hid his nakedness when he suddenly felt the horror of his fall? And his perpetual anxiety, his inextinguishable thirst? It is idle chatter to say that men have always been able to find on earth what they need. They seek agonizingly but do not find anything—not even those who are considered the teachers and guides of mankind. What great art they must display to give themselves the appearance of "those who have found"! And in the end, despite their genius, they succeed at most only in deceiving and blinding others. For no one can be a light to himself. It is not without reason that it has been said of the sun that it gives light and joy to others but for itself is dark. If man were descended from the ape he would be able to find what he needs in the manner of the ape. I shall be told that such people exist and that they are even very numerous. Certainly. But it follows from this only that Darwin and the Jews were equally right. One part of mankind is really descended from the fallen Adam, feels in its blood the burn of its ancestor's sin, suffers pangs from it and aspires to the paradise lost, while the others really spring from the ape that is free of all sin; their consciences are at peace, nothing tortures them, and they do not dream of impossible things. Will science agree to such a compromise with the Bible?

Exercitia Spiritualia

Those who talk much of righteousness rarely call themselves righteous, but this does not mean that they do not consider themselves such. On the contrary, to believe that righteousness is the supreme goal of man and not to consider oneself righteous or, at least, closer to this perfection than the majority of men—who would willingly accept this? Ordinarily those who seek righteousness sooner or later find it. The seeking itself quickly convinces them of their own merits and gifts: "all those other people live without thinking about anything whatever, while I suffer and seek . . . therefore I am superior to the mob." There is probably not a single preacher who does not censure the mob and who does not draw a certain spiritual satisfaction from the knowledge of his right to censure others. Even men like Tolstoi, Nietzsche, and Dostoevsky were incapable of renouncing the right they had arrogated to themselves of correcting and reproving their neighbors. Now this is, generally speaking, no great misfortune. The existence of these men was filled with such painful labors that no one would have the heart to reproach them with living, from time to time, like everyone else and enjoying a certain consolation and rest in the knowledge of their relative perfection. What is unfortunate is that often their readers—and not the worst of these—allowed themselves to be tempted by their weakness, by what was in them "human, all too human." It is not for nothing that Pushkin said, "When Apollo does not call the poet to perform the holy sacrifice, he is, among the miserable children of the world, perhaps the most miserable."

Nietzsche and Tolstoi felt especially how important moral perfection is for men and how unimportant it is in the eyes of God. Nietzsche wrote *Beyond Good and Evil*. Tolstoi, in his last works, does not stop repeating how his thirst for moral perfection and his desire to feel himself morally superior to other men tormented him and prevented him from living. And yet just those who need to believe in their exclusive virtue, as starving men need bread, seek support in Nietzsche and Tolstoi. When Nietzsche and Tolstoi noticed a straw in the eye of their neighbor, this reminded them of the beam in their own eyes. Their readers and disciples allow themselves to be infected by their indignation against the mob, their pathetic tone and invectives, and imagine that is where the source of their prophetic gift lies. They strain themselves to see the straw in their neighbor's eye in order not to see the beam in their own. Perhaps I am wrong, but it seems to me that it is a long time already since men and especially writers, have felt a need as sharp as that of our contemporaries to believe in their absolute righteousness. And this, after Tolstoi and Nietzsche! Almost every writer is persuaded of his providential role or, to put it differently, that he possesses the "truth," while he mocks his colleagues who believe, with just as much assurance, in their own role and their own truth. This spectacle, to one who contemplates it without participating in it, produces the impression of a veritable Bedlam, a madhouse each of whose inhabitants believes himself to be Ferdinand VIII, King of Spain, and is surprised, irritated or even indignant that his neighbors—all with the same assurance and solemnity—pretend to the throne of Spain. Has it always been so, or is this situation special to our epoch? Perhaps it must be so.

Are the gods perhaps unwilling for men to know the final mystery, and do they develop in them that self-love which impels them to take the first illusion that comes along for the supreme truth and also that special blindness which does not permit us to see ourselves in a mirror but does not prevent us from seeing our neighbors as they are? Or is there some other mystery here? May it not be that the time has come for us to awaken from common sense and to admit, instead of a reality identical for all, that our natural environment is constituted by a collection of illusions that intersect and mutually exclude each other?

In any case, I believe that the ceaseless and attentive contemplation of the spectacle of innumerable Ferdinands all pretending to the single throne of Spain—the truth—would be very useful to philosophers as a kind of *exercitia spiritualia*.

The Philosophy of History

It is said that St. Augustine founded the philosophy of history. It is also said that the philosophy of history is already found in the Old Testament, which served St. Augustine as a guide in his reflections on the destinies of mankind. The Old Testament is not content to relate the history of the Jewish people but also explains it, and it is precisely in this that the philosophy of history consists. This statement seems at first sight very close to the truth. But the unfortunate thing, to my way of thinking, is that we have amassed in our mind a great number of judgments that seem to approach the truth. We men are altogether too undemanding and too lazy creatures: as soon as we obtain only the appearance of success we fold our arms. And often, just to have the right to fold our arms, we are ready to consider an unquestionable defeat a victory. Not for nothing do the Italians say, *Se non è vero è ben trovato.** We are very little concerned with the truth, provided what we are told is interesting and witty. The so-called proofs with which men support their statements are not proofs at all in the majority of cases but mere declarations that are as little convincing as the theses they are designed to support. That is why most books are so bulky, monotonous, and boring. A writer has some idea that he could express in ten

* If it is not true, it is well said.

to twenty pages, but instead he writes an enormous volume, crammed three-quarters full with commonplaces that everyone has known for a long time and that therefore say nothing new. The commonplaces seem all the more to come close to the truth precisely because they are repeated at every turn with the air of assurance which would be appropriate to the expression of the truth if we possessed it, with a tone admitting of no dispute. On the subject of the philosophy of history quite as many commonplaces have been expressed as on other subjects. It is worthwhile to examine them a little more closely. Let us begin with the Old Testament, which serves as a model for the philosophy of history, and with St. Augustine, the forefather—if one may so express it—of the philosophers of history. The Old Testament recounts the history of the Jewish people and explains its fate. That is undeniable. The Jews lived in Egypt, escaped from it, wandered forty years in the wilderness, finally reached the Promised Land, etc. All the events of this history had a deep significance that Scripture illuminated. And it was precisely this that led St. Augustine astray. If the fate of the Jewish people was disclosed to us, it must then be, St. Augustine concluded, that the destinies of other peoples and of all humanity can also be disclosed. St. Augustine remained too long at the school of Greek thought and, as we see, could not, despite all his hatred of paganism, give up the right to draw conclusions. Socrates, Plato, Aristotle—all the best representatives of ancient wisdom—declared that the truth must be sought in the general and not in the particular. The purposes of God can also be discovered for, as we recall, τήν πεπρωμένην μοίρην ἀδύνατά ἐστιν ἀποφυγέειν καὶ θεῷ.* If the history of the Jewish people can be explained by its particular destiny, it must then be that each people, mankind in its entirety, must have its particular destiny; one need only "discover" the mission God has assigned it. This is so clear, so understandable, so agreeable to the Greek method

* Not even a god can escape the decrees of fate.

of seeking and discovering the truth. It is, therefore, indubitable! We see here, perhaps, one of the most curious examples of what is false in the fundamental procedure of Greek thought and how greatly inapplicable it is beyond certain obvious limits. And we see here also how dearly our desire to "understand" everything costs us. For how often, in order to "understand," do we consent not to know—and not to know precisely what is most important for us? It is said in the Bible that God chose the Jewish people in order to realize His great purpose. And He made this known to the world through the mouth of His prophets. But does this give us the right to say that God assigns to each of the peoples a certain mission and informs the philosophers and historians, the successors of the ancient prophets, of His designs? Examine the meaning of this passage from the particular to the general and you will understand that the generalization is made only because we are unwilling to admit the free action of God, only because we have faith in ourselves alone and are afraid to put our faith in the Creator, and because we feel at peace only when we are guaranteed the possibility of verifying in advance what Heaven prepares for us.

It is better to admit *Moîpa*, fate fixed once for all, than God. Such is the true meaning and goal of rationalism which has always loved to boast of its advantages vis-à-vis empiricism, which contents itself with experience. What can limited experience mean in the sight of all-embracing reason? But the pretensions of reason to all-inclusiveness take their rise in our taste for the limited, which encloses itself in artificial bounds and feels such extreme fear before all that is unknown. If you have not noticed this until now, perhaps the example I have just cited will make you think about it.

By its very nature reason cannot help being limited. At most it is capable of speaking boastfully of the limitless character of the problems it raises: in the Bible the prophets speak of the mission of the Jewish people alone; well, I shall not remain behind them but go even further, I shall make still more astonishing discoveries. The prophets spoke of one people only; I shall speak of all peoples and all mankind, I shall speak of what was and what will be, I shall know what is beyond the heavens and under the earth! Of course, poor, miserable human reason will discover nothing. But it is not at all necessary for it to recognize anything really new, hitherto unknown, which would not find a place in the prepared framework of its concepts. It is enough for it to persuade men that it can make them know, that it can explain. Does not economic materialism represent the philosophy of history for many minds, even very intelligent minds? Does this theory not also take pride in having left the Bible very far behind? The Bible swarms with miracles, contradictions, scientifically uncontrolled facts. And many people are convinced that economic materialism is incomparably deeper and truer than the Bible. And indeed, we must agree, there is no trace whatsoever of the miraculous in economic materialism. Everything in it is "natural." But I cannot for the life of me understand why this is considered so great an excellence; for the natural presents no advantage over the supernatural. Not even from the point of view of approaching the truth. On the contrary, we have every reason to believe that natural explanations remove us from the truth, and it seems that even the representatives of positive science are today beginning to realize this.

Listen to the voice of the contemporary mathematician and physicist: in it is perceptible an anxiety that is not customary to the representatives of positive thought. To be sure, many of them continue to believe that mathematics must serve as the model for all existing and possible sciences, even for philosophy. That is probably why historical materialism, which uses methods that are almost mathematical—it counts, weighs, measures—appears to many people as one of the loftiest triumphs of the human spirit. They know, of course, that it is flat, dull, and even—excuse the expression—stupid, but, on the other hand, its method is rigorous.

Do not think, however, that I am here raising objections to that kind of philosophy of history which calls itself economic materialism. I began with it because it is the most perfect, i.e., the most rigorous and consistent, philosophy of history. It is a little more boring, a little more lifeless, a little more stupid than its brothers, but from the scientific point of view these are not at all defects. Truth is not obliged to be brilliant and lively. No one even, as far as I know, has tried to establish that it must be intelligent. But it is considered proven that truth does not admit any contradictions and is consistent with itself. In this respect one can ask nothing better than economic materialism, which leaves other philosophies of history far behind. Furthermore—and this is the most important thing—this philosophy actually gives ready-made answers to all questions. The other philosophies try to do the same but, in fairness, we must say that they are very far from successful. They know how to answer many, almost all questions, but this "almost" has a decisive importance, for the whole task of philosophy finally consists in getting rid of a certain residue of insoluble questions which the positive sciences have transmitted to it. So that an almost complete explanation is, in philosophy, equivalent to total renunciation of explanation.

One can say, it seems to me, without fear of being imprecise that the philosophy of history strives for omniscience. The modern St. Augustines, particularly Hegel, have tried to accomplish just this task. It is known that economic materialism derives completely from Hegel, i.e., from the conviction that we can draw out of our reason everything we need—obviously by means of the dialectical method. St. Augustine was still quite modest, compared to Hegel. He drew his knowledge not only from reason but also from the Bible. For Hegel the Bible no longer existed. Striving for omniscience, he disdained all sources of knowledge except his own head. Methodologically he was certainly right. For omniscience is possible only on the condition of establishing in rigorous fashion the source of knowledge to which one will have recourse. This is Hegel's head and the reason it contains—no more and no less. The head is capable of producing only thoughts, that is, universal concepts; consequently, thought is the only thing that exists. I repeat once more that it was not Hegel who invented this. Hegel only developed with very Germanic methodicalness and perseverance the ideas he had received from ancient philosophy. The methodological principle of Plato, as the inscription on the front of his Academy declared, was, "Let no one ignorant of geometry enter here."

Plato already was obliged to transform his living ideas into inanimate numbers and into equally inanimate concepts. Hegel only developed rigorously what the Greeks had brought to mankind. Hegel and all of us after him are sincerely convinced that the twenty-five hundred years which have elapsed since Plato have not passed in vain for mankind. According to Hegel, it could not be otherwise. For history is "development." No one doubts this today; it is considered proven. Many learned books that have appeared in the course of the last century apply themselves to demonstrating and supporting this idea, even though it has no need at all of being supported and even fears all support, for it is finally itself which claims to support everything and it cannot, consequently, admit the least doubt concerning its rights. Without this idea of development, modern philosophy could not understand history at all. History would become for it a variegated, meaningless kaleidoscope. The idea of development is therefore true, for it is completely impossible to admit that history has no humanly understandable meaning. This is impossible, just as it is impossible that what has once been should not have been, etc.

But now that we have arrived at an absolute impossibility, it will do no harm to stop for a moment and recall certain things. This, for example: that there lived in the Middle Ages a certain Peter Damian who declared that it is possible for God to make that which has already been not to be. And I think it is not a bad idea to throw this stick into the wheels of philosophy's swift-moving chariot. That is why I shall not here examine whether Peter Damian was right or even whether his words have any meaning. My object is to stop the course of thought, of that thought concerning which a popular Russian song says that it is swifter than a swift horse. Whether we stop it by means of rational arguments or through the raving cry of the medieval monk is of no importance. If you wish to know the truth, I shall even say that in my opinion the monk is here more in place than the *raisonneur*, because the former permits himself to shout at the truth and to trample arguments underfoot without letting himself be impressed by their noble origin, reason itself. The *raisonneur* will not dare to leave the familiar rut and turn to methods not sanctified by tradition. Rational arguments are the fixed stars by which he has determined his orientation. Can he rebel against them? He would rather rebel against God Himself, if God should extend His power so far as to put the fixed stars in motion. But the vision of the divine omnipotence ravished the monk's heart. The psalms and the prophets had nourished his soul, which was exalted by the thought that the fixed stars themselves would move at the breath of the Almighty. If God be with me, whom else do I still need? God's ways and designs are inscrutable; the prophets themselves knew only what was revealed to them. Will he then deplore the failure of Hegel's attempt to penetrate the mystery of the divine decisions? Or that the little tower of Babel constructed by philosophy turns out to be so like a doll's house? The monk blesses the day he was born when he remembers that all of Hegel's and his disciples' thick volumes fall into dust under the influence of time, and his heart rejoices at each new breach that appears in the edifice built by the philosophers.

Hegel did not guess right, Hegel created confusion, Hegel deceived men—is this a misfortune? No, it would have been a misfortune—a terrible, irremediable misfortune—if Hegel and those who derived from him had guessed right, if they had spoken the truth, if history had a "meaning," and if their absolute marked out the limits of human "possibilities." But fortunately it is not so. The great and little Hegels are only false pretenders to the seat of the prophets, and their "absolute" which proclaims its power so loudly is subject to decomposition and death, like everything that comes of human hands.

The mystery of the Creator is impenetrable, and human destinies begin and end in spheres where the rational investigation of men cannot enter. To study the past, i.e., to try to understand the life of beings who are no longer in our midst, is most important and most necessary. But we must study the past not to justify the present and convince ourselves of our superiority over our ancestors or, to put it differently, not to establish in history the idea of development. Human life is so complex that it cannot fit into the framework of any of the ideas we have invented. The present does not at all occupy a level superior to that of the past, just as Liguori or Harnack do not, as religious thinkers, surpasse the prophet Isaiah or the apostle Paul. Philosophy as Hegel understood it prevents us from truly seeing history, and history as science hides from us the past of men. We must renounce self-admiration, we must renounce omniscience, and then those ways, now closed, which will lead us to discover at least the smaller mysteries of life will be opened to us.

De Novissimis

You have probably not seen it with your own eyes but you have undoubtedly heard that sometimes a man's hair turns white in one night: someone who had black hair on lying down to sleep finds himself completely white on waking. We have grounds to believe that the opposite at times also happens: old men are transformed overnight into young people—only their hair does not regain its original color. But if this is so, if such transformations are possible on earth, how can we speak of the immuntable principles of thought? Of what value then are the foundations on which Kant's famous postulates rest? Kant explains that he cannot renounce his postulates, "for in that case my moral principles would be overthrown—those principles which I cannot renounce without becoming contemptible in my own eyes."

Here the Russian proverb is proven true: "Do not ask an old man but one who has experienced much." Kant was almost sixty years old when he published his *Critique of Pure Reason*, but it seemed to him impossible that his moral principles could ever be shaken and that he could, consequently, become an object of hatred and disgust to himself. But if he had read the lives of certain saints—the writings of St. Theresa, St. Bernard—or even looked at Luther's works, he would have become convinced that what appeared to him unbelievable, inconceivable even, nevertheless actually happened. St. Theresa, St. Bernard, and Luther many times recognized themselves in their own consciousness as the least, the vilest, the most miserable of human beings. And if Kant had been able to read Nietzsche or had reflected on the epistles of St. Paul, he would have discovered that his moral principles were not at all as solid as he imagined: it requires only a strong subterranean shock for any earthly stability to be thrown down completely. But Kant did not in the least suspect this. A page further he repeats that his postulate is so strictly bound to his moral disposition that, just as he runs no danger of losing the latter, so he does no fear that the former can ever be taken away from him (*Kr. d. R. V. 857, II Aufl.*). Whence comes this unconcern of Kant's? Kant, this scholar *par excellence* accustomed to extraordinary caution in his judgments, who advanced his reflections with extreme deliberateness, and who permitted himself to take a step forward only after having first carefully studied the terrain on which he proposed to set his foot, suddenly showed an almost child-like trust. And his case is not unique. Look, for example, at Plato. Having established that the soul which aspires to unity and universality in the human and divine scorns all pettiness, he asks: "Do you think that the great soul which is the spectator of all time and all existence can think much of human life?" (*Republic 486A*)

To his own question Plato responds negatively and with the same assurance with which Kant responds to his. And—what is particularly important—Plato's question and Kant's play a decisive role in the systems of the two philosophers. If it turns out that Kant's morality is not at all as solid as it seemed to its author or if, despite Plato, a great soul which has long wandered in the most distant realms of cosmic being discovers that a single human life has no less value than all human lives together—what will remain of Plato's and Kant's systems?

I have already said, in speaking of Kant, that if he had consulted men who had lived and experienced much, they would have made him see that there are many things on earth and in heaven of which the most learned of the scholars do not even dream. And he would then have felt what appeared to him entirely inconceivable—he would have felt a great disgust for himself! But may it not be that it is not necessary to fear this feeling so greatly and to avoid it? May it not be that it is the condition of important revelations? St. Theresa, St. Bernard, Luther, Shakespeare, Dostoevsky, Tolstoi—I could continue the list indefinitely —all felt a disgust for themselves and all repeated with terror the words of the psalmist: *de profundis ad te clamavi, Domine.* Why then did Kant conclude that everything that leads man to a horror of himself must be rejected? Why consider respect for oneself the sign of truth and the reward of truth?

Note that Plato's statement is also based on the assumption that the normal and natural attitude of the soul toward itself is respect and not disgust. Plato speaks of a great soul—that is, of a soul that respects itself and for which the whole world must have respect, respect that it obtains not as *gratia gratis data* * but for its merits. One can even generalize and say that every philosopher proceeds from the assumption that the soul, if it wishes, can obtain its own respect as well as that of others. Without this supposition no philosophical system could subsist even for a moment. It is the dogma *stantis et cadentis philosophiae.*†

But just here it would be well to recall the testimony of those men of different type that I have set opposite Plato and Kant. Through the mouth of his Hamlet, Shakespeare admits that if one acted toward people according to their merits, no one could avoid a box on the ear. Notice that Hamlet himself did not always speak thus. There was a time when Hamlet declared, and with no less assurance than Plato or Kant, that he would never put himself in the situation of feeling disgust for himself. I think that it is not necessary to prove what I put forward, i.e., to quote

---

* Grace freely given.
† On which philosophy stands or falls.

passages of Shakespeare's work prior to *Hamlet*. Anyone who has read even only his historical chronicles will easily remember the phrases. For a long time Shakespeare knew contentment and mental equilibrium and believed that it was perfectly natural and normal for man to love and respect himself. The point of departure for his philosophy prior to *Hamlet* was the conviction that equilibrium of the soul is the supreme good for man. However, the word "conviction" is not altogether exact. It may be, it is certain even, that Shakespeare did not even guess that he had this conviction, just as a strong and healthy man has no idea that health and strength are precious. He learns this only later, after having lost them. But this does not change the situation in the least. Man may not realize the importance he ascribes to equilibrium of the soul and yet strain all his powers to secure it for himself.

Of course, at the first threats of fate reason will become excited and do all that its nature prescribes to avoid the misfortunes preparing to break over man. When the natural ground begins to disappear under our feet, reason tries to create through its own powers an artificial ground. And this is what is ordinarily called "philosophy." Man asks himself: "How can I bring it about that fate return to me what it has taken away from me?" He does not doubt in the least that it is absolutely necessary to obtain the return of what has been taken away from him. To entrust his existence to fate, to admit that the fate which has taken away his equilibrium is just as righteous as the fate which only a while ago granted him this "supreme good"—this, man, especially the man of reason who is persuaded that he knows everything better than anyone else, is incapable of doing. He knows that equilibrium of the soul is happiness, a good, and that its loss is unhappiness, an evil. He knows this through his own experience, you will say. Yes, certainly, but there is something else here besides. For if it were a question only of experience, neither Kant nor Plato could have clothed their statements in the form they did. They could have spoken only of themselves and, moreover, of the past. That is, Kant could have said: "When I happened to think for a moment that my moral principles could be proven false or stripped of their value, I experienced a feeling of disgust for myself of which I tried to get rid." This confession would have been the statement of a fact, nothing more. But Kant's pretensions extend infinitely further. He assures us that not only he, Kant, but every man, every reasonable being, is aware and will always be aware of an indissoluble relationship between his existence and his moral principles, and that every man wishes to respect himself and is afraid above everything else of feeling disgust for himself. I ask, who gave Kant the right to proceed to all these generalizations and anticipations which constitute, as is known, the very essence of his critiques? How does he know what every man feels? How does he know what he himself will feel tomorrow? May it not be that tomorrow he will experience disgust for these very feelings of his worthiness whose sweetness he savors today? Is it not possible that he could be forced to say, like Antisthenes, μανείην μᾶλλον ἤ ἡσθείην (I would prefer losing my reason to experiencing pleasure) and go still further than Antisthenes by understanding ἡσθείην as including not only physical pleasures (eating, drinking, etc.) but also moral pleasures? Or even to realize that the most repugnant and vilest pleasures are not at all those which eating and drinking give but precisely those that are aroused by a good conscience, the feeling of moral worth, of acting well—the things of which he speaks as the foundation of his philosophy and his ethical system? This, you will say, cannot be. I expected this answer. For we must finally uncover the invisible prompter who whispers such categorical statements to man. Who says this cannot be? Obviously, our reason—that reason which proudly considers itself capable of guiding us in all the difficult circumstances of life, that reason which has convinced us that it "enlarges" our poor and miserable experience. But consider for once exactly what it does. With all its generalizations and its anticipations it does not enlarge but, on the contrary, infinitely restricts our already sufficiently impoverished experience. Reason knows the single case of Kant and from it immediately "concludes" that it knows all possible cases. And it does not any longer itself wish or permit us to see, to hear, to seek. Kant was frightened by the idea that he could come to feel disgust for himself, and he cried out pathetically, "Hold fast to the pillars of your morality, else you will perish!" It is as if one tried to restrain Christopher Columbus at the moment of his departure upon unknown seas by conjuring him not to abandon his familial hearth, for it is only in the bosom of his own family and under the roof of his own house that can can be happy, while the seas hide terrible dangers. Certainly it is dangerous to roam the seas—no one denies it. But Christopher Columbus did not listen to the objections of his familial Kants and threw himself into his adventure. And likewise ὁ ἀνθρώπινος βιός—the individual human soul—does not listen to Plato. It aspires to freedom, it wishes to escape, to throw itself into infinite space, far from the familial *penates*, the work of famous philosophers with clever hands. Often it has not the time even to think of this. It does not recognize that reason, which transformed its poor experience into a doctrine of life, has deceived it. The gifts of reason—calmness, peace, pleasures—suddenly disgust it. It aspires to what reason is not even capable of imagining. It can no longer live according to the general rules established for all. All knowledge is painful to it precisely because it is knowledge, i.e., a generalized poverty. It does not wish to know, it does not wish to understand, in order not to find itself bound and limited. Reason is a siren; it knows well to speak of itself and its works in such a way that it seems its doctrines and its knowledge do not bind but deliver. It speaks only of freedom. And it heaps up the most amazing promises. It promises everything except what it cannot conceive, what it cannot even suspect. But we already know what it can conceive and foresee. It promises us all the postulates—

those of which Kant spoke, and Plato's also—on condition that we prostrate ourselves before it and worship it. But it does not go beyond promises. If this is enough for you, take reason for your guide, generalize and anticipate experience and continue to believe that this is a most important and useful thing. If not, abandon your calculations and generalizations and go daringly, without looking backward, toward the unknown where God will lead you—and then, come what may! You have no desire for this? That is your affair.

The Irrefutability
of Materialism

I shall say it openly and right from the start: no one has ever refuted materialism. All the objections the opponents of materialism have raised relate not to materialism itself but to the arguments invoked for its defense. To be sure, it is not difficult to destroy these arguments. But are other metaphysical systems in a better position in this respect? It is true that materialism takes the fate of its arguments very much to heart, being convinced—no one knows why—that it must share their fate. In general, it is too scrupulous and, despite its apparent robustness, more nervous than is appropriate to a philosophical theory. It suffices for its opponents to call it "metaphysical" for it immediately to blanch with fear; it believes that all is lost. Not at all! Even if materialism should be called metaphysical, this would not in any way change its nature. And I do not think that the idealists would have an easier job if materialism made use of its rights as a metaphysics.

But the chief argument against materialism is that it admits the possibility of miraculous transformations, in the genre of Ovid's metamorphoses. Inanimate matter is suddenly transformed into spirit. This objection greatly troubles the materialists, more so than the former objection; they try to escape the reproach of credulity that is thrown at them, and for this purpose seek to replace "suddenly" with "gradually." To be sure, the defense is a sorry one. Their perceptive opponents very easily discover the fatal "suddenly" which the "gradually" conceals. But if I were a materialist, sudden transformations would not embarrass me at all. On the contrary, I would myself insist upon them and so disarm my opponents. Yes, there are sudden metamorphoses, perhaps not of every kind but of a certain kind only. It may also be that anything whatsoever can come from anything whatsoever. What follows from this? Reason does not understand the suddenness? But has materialism bound itself to everything comprehensible to reason? Does the fact that a thing is incomprehensible or even irrational give us the right to refuse to recognize it? Many of the things that in fact exist are incomprehensible to reason. It also does not understand how atoms coming together can form an ape or a rational man.

So materialism could answer. But the materialists, I am certain, will never speak thus. They also woo reason, which they consider to have been born of atoms and regard as perishable; and they flatter it just as much as their opponents, the idealists, who believe reason to be a primal and eternal principle. And that is why the materialists lay quite as much value on the possibility of demonstrating their truth by rational arguments as on the truth itself. It is clear that under these conditions they can arrive at nothing. To demonstrate the truth of materialism is impossible; and if one admits that demonstrability constitutes the *conditio sine qua non* * of truth materialism finds itself in a bad way. Its opponents understand this very well, and that is why they speak not of materialism but of the rights of materialism before the tribunal of reason. But this procedure is obviously inadmissible and even dishonest. Before the tribunal of reason every metaphysic, whether it be idealist or materialist, will be in the wrong, for at a certain moment in its development it must rely on the incomprehensible—i.e., what is unacceptable to reason—as on

* Necessary condition.

something given. So, then, if materialism would be invulnerable, it must renounce all argumentation whatsoever.

Sic volo, sic jubeo, stat pro ratione voluntas.* It is time to understand that only that philosophy which dares to be arbitrary will succeed in breaking its way through.

Will the materialists follow my advice? I think not. It is probable that they will prefer to meet the idealists halfway, for the effort of the idealists, who try to root out of reality all miracles and everything unexpected, is much closer to them than the conceptions of materialism. Freedom always terrifies men who have become accustomed to thinking that their reason is above everything in the world. I would also certainly not be mistaken in making the contrary assumption: if the idealists were obliged to choose, they would surely agree to accept matter rather than arbitrariness as the supreme principle of the universe.

---

* Thus I wish, thus I command, my will is reason enough.

Reason

Like all the philosophers, Epictetus tries to demonstrate that always and under every circumstance man must preserve the equilibrium of his soul. A misfortune has come to you: your father has died—you weep, you despair, and there is not, it seems, any remedy in the world capable of restoring peace of heart to you. But this is only apparently so. In reality a remedy exists. Try to reflect rationally. What would you have said if it had been your neighbor's father who had died? You would have said that it is completely natural. Every man must die—such is the law of nature. Why then are you so agitated and inconsolable at your father's death? Reflect a moment and you will understand that your father's death is an event as natural, as right, as the death of all other men and that, consequently, you have no more reason to lament today, when you father is no more, than yesterday, when you still had your father.

At first blush this reasoning is impeccable. Unfortunately, it can be turned around. One can say, "My neighbor has lost his father, and this leaves me quite indifferent. But is this right? If it were my father, I should be in despair. Why does not the death of a stranger produce in me the same painful impression? This is an 'error': I ought to lament the death of any man just as I lament the loss of my dear ones."

Compare these two reasonings: which is the more rigorous and logical? They are, it is clear, equally good, and if Epictetus gave preference to the first, this was not because it was more "rational" but because it led him more surely and rapidly to the supreme goal of the Stoic philosophy, to ἀταραξία, the complete independence of man vis-à-vis external circumstances. The Stoic wished to be master of the world. *Si vis tibi omnia subjicere, te subjice rationi,** said Seneca. but in reality neither with the help of reason nor without it could he subject everything to his wishes. There was then only one thing to do—to say that man has no need of the universe at all. Man and the universe have nothing in common. If one's father, following the laws of nature, has died—this concerns neither Epictetus nor any other wise man. For the wise man knows very well that external events, being independent of his will, must not concern him if he does not wish to become the slave of a senseless power. This is the fundamental thought of the Stoic philosophy. The Cynics were certainly more logical. They testified with much more daring, by their life as well as their doctrine, to their scorn for that universe which they could not subject but to which they no longer wished to be subordinate. If ἀταραξία is the supreme goal of man, he must obviously be indifferent to everything, to his own sufferings as well as to those of others.

But "reason" has nothing to do with this, and the reflections of Epictetus have nothing to do with it either. One can get along very well without reason and reflections: one can say once and for all that he does not wish to admit any power over himself. I refuse either to rejoice over the joys or to grieve over the sorrows that may accidentally come to me. If fate should grant me the genius, beauty, and power of Alexander of Macedon, I shall, following the example of Diogenes, decline them. If, on the contrary, I am plunged into tortures, I shall endure them without tears. I do not wish to rejoice or despair so long as I

* If you wish to subject all things to yourself, subject yourself to reason.

shall not have acquired the power to laugh and weep not according to the caprice of fate but of my own will. That is why the Stoics talked so much of the vanity of terrestrial goods. What are the gifts of fate worth if it can presently take them back and make misfortunes rain on our heads? Ἔχαι οὐκ ἔχομαι * was the favorite adage of the Stoics, and it was from this that all their interminable reflections, presumably founded on reason, flowed. But they could have gotten along very well without reasoning and argumentation.

Reason supports the Stoics quite as well as it supports their opponents. As long as A = A, as long as their resolution not to submit to nature remains unshakable, the Stoics will succeed in solving the problems they pose: they will not weep or rejoice, whatever be the gifts and trials the gods send them; they will sing under torture and pour out tears when empires are offered them. But if their resolution weakens, if it suddenly appears to them that it is better to be the least of slaves in the universe created by the gods than king in that empire of shadows which they have themselves invented—farewell, then, to all reflections, arguments, appeals to reason! And then they may come to prefer the divine arbitrariness to the harmony and order imagined by men.

* I hold, I am not held [i.e., I hold my own fate, it is not forced on me].

Synthesis

Synthesis is highly honored not only in Europe but also in Russia, despite the fact that we have for many years been straining all our efforts to rid ourselves of the "spiritual yoke" of the West. When synthesis is anywhere involved, everyone pursues it. It is imagined that synthesis is what is best and that we must always synthesize. It was not only Spencer, when he thought to make room in his system of synthetic philosophy for the most puzzling facts of human life, who sought general ideas; there are today many very believing philosophers who follow Spencer's method in their researches.

They begin with fetishism and end with the most developed religions. According to these philosophers, the savage who worships a cow, a serpent or a piece of wood "believes," and in his belief one can find true faith *in nuce*. I have found similar statements in books which even bore the imprimatur and, moreover, these books are known to everyone.

As far as Spencer is concerned, these actions are very understandable: for him religion is a social phenomenon which can be studied and explained like all other natural phenomena. From his point of view the savage who strikes his idol to force it to come to his aid; the Arab or Turk who hurls himself into combat convinced that if he succeeds in killing many infidels he will know the joys of paradise with its gardens, fountains, and houris; the prophet Isaiah; and St. Paul are all believers, religious spirits. Such a synthesis is certainly very useful and even appears scientific, for it greatly simplifies the problem: one can do without explaining Isaiah or St. Paul and content himself with studying the savage and the Turk whose psychology lies, so to speak, at hand and seems in any case elementary and perfectly clear. But what meaning can such a synthesis have for a believer? It is enough to look a little more closely at the matter to realize that the fetishism of the savage has absolutely nothing in common with religious faith. The savage is convinced that if he strikes his idol the latter will be afraid of him and will grant him a successful hunt. It is thus that uncultivated minds believe in sorcerers and cultivated people in materialism, or deceived husbands in their wives' virtue and naïve proprietors in their managers' honesty. But what has the faith of these deceived people, who trust the word of those near to them or of persons above them, at all in common with religious faith? These sentiments that are so different from each other are designated by the same term only through accident. So it is, to use Spinoza's comparison, that one calls by the name "dog" both the constellation and the domestic animal that barks. People wish to generalize and gladly renounce the truth in order to obtain some all-embracing synthesis, for it is indubitable that he who believes that he finds a common element, faith, in the fetishist and in the psalmist can set up a comprehensible and even convincing argument but has certainly lost from view precisely the things he seeks and for the sake of which he set out on the road.

Thoughts Expressed and Not Expressed

At present Tiutchev's verse, "A thought expressed is a lie," is developed in thousands of variants; and everyone agrees that a thought expressed in words becomes false because we have at our disposal only few words, and the words that we do possess, being insufficiently supple and elastic, enchain and contract the thought.

There is a certain amount of truth in this statement, but a very small amount. Our thought becomes false when we clothe it in words not so much because we do not find adequate expression for it but, above all, because we do not dare show it to others in the form under which it was originally revealed to us. The poorest language would amply suffice to express many things about which we are today silent. We are always afraid of everything, and we are particularly afraid of our thoughts. That is why when, from time to time, a daring man appears, he always finds the words he needs. In any case, one can state without hesitation that we could say many more things than we do say and that we could lie much less than we do lie. But the truth is painful for us; we do not need it, we are not fit for it, and so we lie—timorously trying to justify ourselves by the poverty of our language.

Consider a little the ideas current among men. Are they false because those who proclaimed them did not succeed in expressing themselves accurately? Is it true that a man who declares that the supreme good is love, while he himself is filled with hatred, could not say that the supreme good for him would be to conquer and crush his enemy? He could say it very well; but he knows that if he does so, he will appear foolish and ridiculous. And one who declares that he does not accept life because he cannot become a Napoleon—could he not simply admit that he would really like to be a councillor of state? Certainly he could, but he believes that his real idea is too dull and flat and he wishes to express only brilliant ideas that sparkle like diamonds.

The philosophers declare—each obviously of himself—that their doctrines are free of all internal contradictions and that they are attached to them only because they see that they are thus free. What? Have they not the words necessary to express without mutilation their real thought—to say quite simply that they chose the doctrine that was particularly to their taste and that their goal is not so much to avoid contradiction as to hide these in the most careful way possible from the sharp looks of their opponents? There is no need of particularly profound words for these very simple thoughts not to be changed into lies. But the philosophers are unwilling to express themselves openly, out of fear of losing their reputation and appearing ridiculous and foolish. Nevertheless, in order to conform to tradition, they complain that their thought, despite all their efforts, is turned into a lie.

And the debates on absolute truth! The Catholics affirm that they teach *quod semper ubique et ab omnibus creditum est.* Could they not say, instead of *semper* "for a long time," instead of *ubique* "in many places," instead of *omnibus* "by many people"? Those who speak of absolute truth have already contented themselves for a long time, and that very well, with relative truths, but they continue to speak of absolute truth, the most absolute that can be.

Finally, not to forget one of the most widespread thoughts of the present hour, who does not now speak of his prophetic mission? Everyone today wishes to be a prophet. Napoleon is already no longer enough; he represents too modest a rank. Do you think, perhaps, that this idea is false because the prophets could not express their true thought in words? It is generally writers who proclaim their prophetic mission, and indeed writers who lose their heads at the least praise. They could explain perfectly well that they have no need in the least to be prophets and would be very happy to be endlessly praised for their talent, their intelligence, their cleverness. But they do not dare offer this truth to their readers and consider themselves obliged to lie and to explain sadly that language misrepresents their thought, which thus necessarily becomes false.

Do not think that I have in mind here only insignificant writers with mediocre minds. Not at all—this defect inheres in everyone! All lie, lie unbearably, and live in an atmosphere of falsehood in which they do not choke but content themselves with sighing sadly. In the end men prefer the traditional lofty falsehoods to the truth, whatever it may be—not only to the lowly truth but even to that of which no one knows what it finally is. And then they wonder why they never succeed in speaking the truth and why life is so filled with lies.

Rules and Exceptions

What kind of truths does man need? This question immediately implies another: How can we know what truths we need? Is there some principle from which we can deduce with assurance that certain truths are necessary to us and certain others are not? This principle does not exist. In any case, as far as I know, men are not in possession of it.

Some, it is true, declare that the truths which all men will declare themselves prepared to accept once and for all are necessary truths. But this statement appears self-evident only at first blush; in reality it is very naïve and imposes upon us only because it has been repeated constantly and because, like everything customary, it seems perfectly clear, understandable and even natural. Above all, where are there such truths that are admitted by everyone? I am not speaking, naturally, of mathematics and the exact sciences. They have nothing in common with the truths of which we are speaking here. As soon as we pass beyond the limits of the so-called exact sciences, every man goes his own way. Not only can we not unite everyone around any truth whatsoever and obtain universal agreement on any point, but it also often happens that a single individual recognizes at one time several contradictory truths. There cannot, then, be any question of indisputable principles and infallible conclusions. The Germans are still capable of relying on deductions, principles and certainties. But we others must learn how to do without these scientific ornaments and answer as the occasion arises.

It may perhaps be that people will even object to the way that I posed the first question. I shall be told that it is not at all appropriate to ask what truths we need, for we are always obliged to accept the truths that arise, whatever these may be. But I shall say again that this is only an idea inculcated in us by our German education. Men do not at all accept the truths such as they are but most of the time, almost always, choose what pleases them according to their various tastes. As the Russian people say, "One is loved not because he is lovable but he is lovable because he is loved." Consider. As a general rule, men change their convictions with age. What pleased them in their youth becomes disagreeable and unbearable when they become old. In our day people bid farewell to the convictions of their youthful years even before the appearance of their first gray hairs, and not only do they not feel embarrassed by these rapid transformations—they even glory in them. If it were a question of truth, of a truth that one could not admit so long as it had not become indubitable, this haste and these transformations would be completely impossible. But in reality, in youth as well as in maturity and old age, we are not very much concerned with the objective value of the truth, so that it is completely natural to ask oneself if men, in acting thus, do not obey an instinct inculcated by nature itself. Of course, men do not openly admit their changeability and even painstakingly seek to hide it.

Following a millennial custom, men surround each of their statements with ceremonies and solemn rites. They do not choose what pleases them according to their taste. Oh no, they commune with the absolute truth, consecrating their entire existence to it. The day before, it is true, they had similarly sworn fidelity to a truth opposed to the first, but this does not at all trouble them and they do not even suspect (men are very myopic beings and this is not an accidental trait of their nature but the fundamental predicate of their being) that tomorrow they will again change masters, just as Don Juan does not suspect that he will once more have to betray his mistress, even though he has already changed women dozens of times. Men would be bored if they had always to do with the same truth. Among human beings truths are like women—they age rapidly and lose their charm.

This time I have succeeded, it seems to me, not only in making but in proving my point. What follows will appear less convincing, but this is in the order of things. If we choose our truths, can there be any question of proofs; can one prove anything? Youth is generous, old age avaricious. The rich are generally conservative, undertaking little and thinking only of preserving what they have amassed. Misery, as is known, is inventive, etc.

At present in Russia, generosity does not enjoy any great prestige. People continue, it is true, to sing its praises and to boast of it—and particularly those who would like to take everything for themselves. No longer applicable to Russia is Rostopchin's old joke: in Europe the peasant, wishing to become a gentleman, revolts; while in Russia the gentleman, wishing to become a peasant, organizes a revolution. In this respect we are all completely Europeanized: the gentleman wishes to remain what he is and watches very carefully that the peasant not take away one bit of his belongings. We still have "noble penitents," but they repent not for having exploited the peasant but for not having taken from him everything that could have been taken. It is obvious that Russia's youth is passing away, and even though it is still far from old age it has already acquired the wisdom of ripe maturity. There was a time when we aspired only to become Europeans; today it is constantly repeated to us that we must rid ourselves of the spiritual yoke of strangers and again become ourselves. But never before have we copied the West so much as today while, on the contrary, at the time when the Western phraseology flourished among us we preserved our special char-

acter. A little while ago Europeans did not understand our young
people at all, and the speeches of Dostoevsky and Tolstoi upset
them. Today our youth is Europeanized, and Tolstoi and Dostoevsky have had to give way to the ideologues of the real—just as
in Europe. They are still a little embarrassed among us to be
Europeans and continue to employ a few old words, but this will
not last long. Soon they will speak with that cynical frankness
which is proper to mature men who accept only what they see
with their own eyes and scorn all dreams.

I have deliberately chosen, to begin with, a very simple, understandable example of transformation. Under our eyes men have
rid themselves of the old truths and substituted new ones. And
they have done this very calmly, as if the old truths had never
been truths at all but only seemed such, as if no one had ever
sworn eternal fidelity to them, while the new truths are established for the first time and forever, *in saecula saeculorum*. In
twenty or twenty-five years the new eternal truths will certainly
undergo the same fate as those that preceded them. They will be
thrown into the ditch with the refuse and yield their place and
their predicates of eternity and immutability to other, still newer
truths.

I believe that this eternal truth must be repeated as often as
possible, for it is extremely difficult to assimilate. Human "nature" protests against it with all its powers and "ever since the
world has existed" has driven it far from itself. For if one accepts
it, we are told, he must admit that there is a place where all differences between good and evil, truth and error, justice and injustice, fade completely away. No one could any longer say of
himself that he is right, that he is good, that he has the truth.

We must, however, remark that though men have been afraid
to make this admission, they have always more or less obstinately
persecuted those who have reflected, be it ever so little, on the
first and last things—*de novissimis*. Has not mankind accepted the
parable of the prodigal son and of the Pharisee and the publican?

It heard the words "Judge not!" and was obliged to accept them. But how can a man who is just and good, a man who knows the truth—a man such as the Pharisee was—not judge? Was not the publican a wicked man, knowing neither virtue nor truth? How can I not thank God for not being like the publican? One can refrain from rejoicing in his wealth, his success, the homage that he receives, but would not to refrain from rejoicing in one's virtue be a grievous sin? To admit that the publican is better than we or in any case not worse would be equivalent to renouncing truth, goodness, and that righteousness which is inseparably bound to truth and goodness. Is it possible to admit this? Is it possible to admit that a father rejoices more on the return of his prodigal son who had abandoned him than over his faithful son who had never left him? If we accept this, do we not renounce goodness and truth?

For a long time now mankind has found itself before this difficult dilemma. It seems to have tried over and over again to resolve it anew, but it always returns finally to the Socratic method. Whenever men have had to choose between the inconceivable truth of revelation and the "understandable" affirmations of Greek wisdom, they have always—not without hesitation, to be sure—inclined toward the latter. Whatever European mankind may have said about faith, whatever the passionate efforts it has made to attain faith, it has never been able to conquer its innate unbelief. It spoke of faith, but it sought knowledge and understanding.

Philo, who first tried to make Western man participate in the revelation that arose in the East, felt quite rightly that there was only one means of drawing the Greco-Roman world to the truth of the Bible: to prove that this truth was in perfect agreement with the doctrines of Greek wisdom. He knew that the Europeans would not believe in God Himself so long as He had not given them sufficient proofs of His divine rights. And Philo was the first to insist on the rationality of Biblical doctrine. The *logos* of Greek philosophy, its eternal reason, is already completely contained in the revelation given to the Jewish people on Mount Sinai. God is rational, the essence of God is reason: it was on this condition that the success of the new religion rested. The Greco-Roman world expected from revelation not a new, previously unheard-of truth but a new, authoritative, indisputable confirmation of the truth already known to it. On Mount Sinai, said Philo to the pagans, God proclaimed the same truth that your famous wise men—Socrates, Plato, Aristotle—glorified as the only rational truth. This, apparently, was the only way to bring the Bible to Europe.

Later it became necessary to say that philosophy is the handmaid of theology—*ancilla theologiae*. And people sincerely believed this. But, in fact, it was just the opposite that happened. Europe accepted the theology of the East on the express condition that the latter forever subordinate itself to the philosophy that had been created long before in Europe. It is no accident that Aristotle was called *praecursor Christi in naturalibus* * and was and still is considered by Catholics as the philosopher κατ' 'εξοχήν.† Catholicism could not and would not be content with simply believing. It was always afraid to take the wrong road, to believe in him whom it ought not to believe and not to believe in the way necessary. Before believing, it asked *cui est credendum*—who is to be believed? But of whom did it ask? Who will take upon himself so terrible a burden of responsibility, who will answer so fearful a question?

The Orient, the fatherland of religions, did not offer the Bible only. How is one to decide, and who shall decide, what books of the Orient contain the true revelation? Philo's solution appeared extremely tempting: revelation must not contradict the reason of the Greeks, the *logos*. Naturally, this solution had a fateful

* The precursor of Christ among the philosophers, aided only by natural reason [i.e., lacking the gift of faith].
† Supreme [pre-eminent].

influence on the further development of Catholicism. In reality, the Bible—the New Testament as well as the Old—did not at all comply with the demands reason imposes on truth. In these mysterious books the principle of contradiction, the first condition for the truth of any statement, is completely ignored. Even more, one can say that Greek philosophy, by its very nature, excluded the possibility of the revelation of the Old and New Testaments. In Plato and Aristotle we read that philosophy was born out of wonder—διὰ τὸ θαμάζειν—and many wished to see in this statement at least a hint of the admissibility of revelation. But this is hardly correct. Plato's and Aristotle's wonder is only curiosity, nothing more. But all curiosity is only the consequence of a certain rupture of the mind's equilibrium and is always accompanied by the desire to restore this equilibrium. Plato raises the questions in order to obtain answers. And he obtains what he needs. Hence his motto: μηδεὶς ἀγεωμέτρητος εἰσίτω *—geometry must precede philosophy. This is the fundamental thought of the Greek wisdom, which is considered sacred by all philosophers without exception to the present day. Philosophy must be a rigorous science; it must explain everything, without leaving the least residue. And theology, in this respect, never would nor could remain behind philosophy. The Vatican Council corroborated in modern times the idea that faith cannot be contrary to reason, that it must be in accord with reason: *verum etsi fides sit supra rationem, nulla tamen unquam inter fidem et rationem vera dissensio esse potest: cum idem Deus, qui mysteria revelat et fidem infundit, animo humano rationis lumen indiderit, Deus autem negare se ipsum non possit nec verum vero unquam contradicere* † (*Cap. IV, de fide et ratione*). European man chose,

---

* Let no one lacking knowledge of geometry enter here.
† But even if faith be above reason, there still can never be any real disagreement between faith and reason, since the same God who reveals mysteries and infuses faith has endowed the human soul with the light of reason. God, however, cannot negate himself, nor can truth ever contradict truth.

out of the different doctrines which came to him from the Orient, that which could meet his needs and his habits of mind, and he accepted it only after having first made it undergo a certain reworking corresponding to these needs and habits. It is in this finally that the Hellenization of Catholicism, of which modern Protestant theologians speak so much, consists. Needing to choose between the faith coming from the Orient and the reason it had itself cultivated, Europe could not long hesitate. If it accepted this faith, this was only after having first subjected it to the most severe testing. And it is natural that reason continued to dominate minds during the entire evolution of Catholicism. The latest Protestant scholars—the liberal theologians—imagine that they are less Hellenized than the monks of the Middle Ages. But this is only one of those exalted illusions with which our time, like all other eras, loves to deck itself out. Harnack, Loofs and Troeltsch, and the French modernists who are so close to the liberal German theology, are all permeated with Hellenism, and to such a degree that they have become incapable of distinguishing between Hellenism and their own human essence. It seems to them that "to be oneself" is equivalent to being a Greek. And whatever the truth that appears to them and no matter how attractive it may be, they will push it away if it offends even only slightly their second, Hellenized nature. They expect the truth to bless what they are accustomed to, what they love. And if a truth does not correspond to their hopes, they reject it and sincerely consider it a lie.

Harnack confidently declares in his *Dogmengeschichte* that mankind had to labor two thousand years to attain that conception of God which liberal Protestant theology has now accepted. It is in this that this faithful disciple of Hegel sees quite seriously "the meaning of history"! I repeat once more: one is loved not because one is lovable, but one is lovable because one is loved. We ourselves choose our truths—this is a general rule. In certain very exceptional cases we may observe that it is not we who choose the truths but the truths that choose us. These cases, however, are so rare, so exceptional, that no account is taken of them in the theory of knowledge. For the conditions of knowledge are conditions that always exist and are always unchangeable (in reality, that almost always exist and are almost always unchangeable, but we succeed very easily in ridding ourselves of this "almost"). If one wishes to follow rare exceptions, it is impossible to construct any theory.

Words and Deeds

The philosophy of the Stoics is not of especially great interest. This becomes particularly noticeable when we read the works of Seneca and Cicero. They are splendid writers, but their eloquent writings quickly tire us: we feel the artificiality and its pathos—the *honos* which, according to Cicero himself, *alit artes*.* Stoic philosophy separated from Stoic life loses all meaning. But it would be incorrect to say the opposite. One cannot say that the life of a Stoic, even if he should never try to justify himself through theoretical considerations, is devoid of a certain attractiveness and of a certain greatness. In this respect the reflections of Marcus Aurelius are particularly significant. We prize here not the art of the author, who cannot be compared either to Seneca or to Cicero in this regard, but the frankness of his confessions. Everyone has probably noticed that all of Marcus Aurelius' remarks are enveloped, as with a veil, in a certain sadness and anxiety. It is not the sadness of a spring evening or of a clear autumn day when one feels, despite everything, a certain joyous life. It is not even the melancholy of an abandoned country cemetery upon which the nearness of field and forest confer a gentle poetry. No, the sadness of Marcus Aurelius is that of a prisoner who knows that he will nevermore leave his prison or taste the

* The gift which nourishes the arts.

joys of freedom. "Live according to nature, for everything in the world is transitory": such is the constant refrain of the royal philosopher. Submit, resign yourself, for all your most desperate efforts cannot restore your freedom to you. Virtue alone is eternal, everything else is condemned to perish. So Marcus Aurelius artlessly speaks about life. And it seems that he himself does not feel any joy in his words. Perhaps he suspects that, *sub specie aeternitatis*, virtue is not worth any more than all the other goods of our existence.

Indeed, virtue is not eternal. To introduce eternity into our assumptions is the most risky kind of argumentation, for eternity, precisely because it is eternity, swallows everything up—the ordinary goods of life as well as vices and virtues. It seems that, despite everything, virtue was incapable of inspiring Marcus Aurelius. Because for virtue to transport us with enthusiasm, we must believe and feel that we have in ourselves the power required always victoriously to resist the seductions of life. In other words, to believe in virtue, it is necessary to be oneself virtuous to the end or at least to think that one can be virtuous to the end. Just as in order to be able to believe in truth, a man must think that he himself or the school to which he belongs possesses the truth. It is because of this that all the virtuous men and all the possessors of truth are ordinarily so intolerant and fanatical, so that the idea has even been established that fanaticism and intolerance are the principal predicates of truth and virtue. But this is obviously a grievous error. Fanaticism and intolerance are the fundamental characteristics of a human nature that is feeble, cowardly, and limited and, consequently, the characteristics of falsehood and evil. The true Stoic, who still lives entirely in the region of the human, all too human, needs a source whence he can draw the power necessary for a continuous struggle: he must be a fanatic. He cannot but feel himself superior to other men. But Marcus Aurelius did not have this feeling, and the Stoic philosophy was therefore unsuitable to him. He accepted Stoicism because he had found nothing better in life, not because Stoicism answered the longings of his soul. This is probably the explanation of the melancholy spirit that his book breathes.

The Stoic must be a warrior, a combatant by his very nature; that is, he must love battle and consider victory a goal in itself, even if it be a Pyrrhic victory. If you have lost your army, that is no misfortune, for if the victory were yours, you would have no more need of an army. Such were the true Stoics—not those who talked but those who fought. They did not regret anything; they sacrificed everything, only not to surrender. He who is incapable of letting himself become drunk with battle, to live for battle and victory, will not let himself be moved either by the brilliant discussions of Cicero and Seneca or the melancholy reflections of Marcus Aurelius. It is related that Epictetus, when his master broke his arm, said, "You have wronged yourself, for you have crippled your slave." Will you perhaps maintain that this is philosophy? Who can be certain that in pronouncing his proud words Epictetus was not inwardly in despair and ready to say, with the Psalmist, "My God, why hast Thou forsaken me?" In life, it is true, one often comes across moments when one envies Epictetus his power and courage. We must sometimes know how to answer the outrages of the rabble as Epictetus did. But philosophy has nothing to do with this. Philosophy begins when the powerful rabble departs and man remains alone with himself. Then his courage abandons him, and it is better so. Then despair seizes hold of him, and this is even better. Then . . . but the reader has already ceased to believe what I say. Ah well, he may be right. One must know how to stop in time.

Nature and Men

It is said that nature, like Pushkin's official copyist who grew old in office, contemplates good and evil with indifference and is insensible to all the horrible sufferings that strike man. And it is also said that it is absolutely impossible to move nature or to make it forsake its stony impassivity through any means whatsoever. Earthquakes, wars, epidemics, famines, floods—men have known all these; but nature has never allowed the least sign of comprehension or pity to escape it. The clear sky shone impassively above the battlefield at Borodino as well as in the days of the Flood. From this people conclude with assurance that nature will never leave its dismal impassivity, no matter what happens on earth.

Is this conclusion correct? May it not be that in this case also generalizations are illegitimate and only mislead men? Yes, epidemics, floods, wars have had no effect on nature. But what if man found the means of destroying it to the last living being, to the last atom even? Would nature still maintain its placidity? Would it not be moved by the prospect of the total destruction of all its creatures? Would it not deign to pay attention to man, speak to him as its equal, and agree to certain concessions?

Can one raise such questions? It seems to me that John Stuart Mill, with his conscientiousness and honesty, would have admitted the legitimacy of my questions. Now, for the moment this is enough. For once it is admitted that such questions might be raised, everyone must confess that it is probable that nature would be afraid and agree to acquaint man with its mysteries.

Caveant Consules

To contradict oneself is considered completely inadmissible. It is enough to convict someone of contradicting himself for his statements immediately to lose all authority. But it is quite natural and legitimate for men to contradict each other; this disturbs and irritates no one. Why? Why, if I affirm at one and the same moment that the universe has existed through all eternity and that there was a time when it did not exist, is this considered impudence on my part or a sign of madness, while if I declare that the world has always existed and my neighbor says that the world was born in time, does this appear quite natural, provoke no distress in anyone and seem not at all puzzling?

Yet, neither my neighbor nor I judge in the capacity of empirical subjects. The theory of knowledge has already definitely established that the subject which expresses judgments has nothing in common with the empirical subject, and that generally it is not even the psychological subject but objective reason itself. Insofar as we judge, we are all one. Consequently, there is no difference between contradicting oneself and contradicting others. I must be as much concerned with being consistent with my neighbor as with being consistent with myself, if I do not wish to arrive at that result which has always so frightened philosophic minds—namely, that it no longer be this or that empirical subject that is constrained to silence (this certainly has nothing distressing about it; most of the time one could even only rejoice in it) but *super-empirical reason* itself. The philosophers and theorists of knowledge have not thought of this; they have probably overlooked it. But it must be thought about, it is absolutely necessary that it be thought about. Carelessness in this case can have terrible consequences. For it may well be that suddenly one fine day reason, discovering the contradictions it contains, will find itself "forced to silence" and, obedient to the honesty and conscientiousness that are proper to it, forever and finally hold its peace. It is necessary, before it is too late, to fend off this threatening danger, and I am the first to cry the alarm.

The Magic Cap

Philosophy has often raised and resolved the so-called final questions: Does God exist? Is there a soul, and if there is, is it immortal or not? Is the will free?, etc. These questions appear perfectly legitimate, and the answers that are given to them, affirmative or negative, seem completely acceptable. One might believe that it is impossible, or at least senseless, to obstain from raising these questions. Is this really so?

It seems to me that it is enough to ask a man "Does God exist?" immediately to make it impossible for him to give any answer whatever to this question. And I believe that all those who have answered it, affirmatively or negatively, spoke of something quite other than that about which they were asked. There are truths that one can see but cannot show. And these are not only the truths concerning God or the immortality of the soul. There are many other truths of the same kind. I do not mean that one cannot speak of them; one can speak of them, and even very well— but precisely when they are not asked about. Strange as this may seem, they are afraid of questions. That is why one cannot show or explain them, i.e., make them self-evident. They always have with them the magic cap of Russian legendry which renders one invisible; as soon as one steals near them to seize them, they put on their cap and become invisible. And their cap is even more extraordinary than that of the legends. Not only do they vanish from our gaze but, at the same time, the very recollection of them disappears, as if they had never existed; and he who had seen them with his own eyes differs in no way from his neighbor who had never seen them.

Magna Charta Libertatum

The principles of identity and contradiction, which lie at the foundation of our knowledge and without which knowledge is said to be impossible, finally limit our knowledge narrowly. A = A; A is always equal to A; A cannot be not A. Why is this? Why is A always equal to A? Why can it not become not A? Aristotle, as is known, greatly limits the scope of these "laws." He says: in one given place and time A is always equal to A and cannot be not A. But if this limitation is necessary, it follows that the laws of identity and contradiction can be of significance only in the domain of empirical reality, for the metaphysicians brush aside time and space. To put it differently, to pass from empirical philosophy to metaphysics one must be prepared to renounce the principles of identity and contradiction. And this is very understandable: metaphysics, with its immense tasks, does not admit the limitations which the empirical sciences accept and even cultivate. Hence it is a useless enterprise to exhibit the contradictions of metaphysical constructions. The validity of a metaphysical system does not by any means consist in the harmony and concordance of its theses, but in something quite different. Thus, if it be a question of prolegomena to all future metaphysics, it is not at all necessary to seek out new sources for universal judgments; on the contrary, it is necessary to proclaim a freedom of judgment hitherto unknown. In metaphysics it is true that παντὶ λόγῳ λόγον ἀντικεῖσθαι,* and herein lies the source of its immense riches, hitherto hidden from view. "I am persuaded of this," as those who wished their judgments to obtain universal approval used to say. And I am convinced, further, that the metaphysicians who have always suffered from the impossibility of ridding themselves of contradictions will be very grateful to me for my discovery and for the great charter of freedom that I proclaim. Henceforth, indeed, he who will accuse the metaphysicians of contradictions will see himself immediately reproached for his dishonesty.

But if someone wishes to draw from my words the conclusion that henceforth every man who decides παντὶ λόγῳ λόγον ἀντικεῖσθαι † will become a metaphysician, I will not contradict him either. Is this enough? I fear not. One who acquires only the name of metaphysician will be very dissatisfied and will prefer to return to the former state of things, to Aristotle's three laws. He wishes indeed, despite all his metaphysical aspirations, that I recognize him, that you recognize him, that all men and all rational beings recognize him.

You see that freedom does not appear always and to everyone as something so ethereal, so weightless, or even so negative a quantity as is generally believed. For some it is harder to bear than the heaviest load.

It is very possible that not only the would-be metaphysicians but also the genuine ones will renounce the Magna Charta. The greatest even of the philosophers need "recognition" and hold tenaciously to the principles of identity and contradiction. They are ready to admit all objections, provided they can maintain the hope of being recognized or of obtaining at least the illusion of recognition.

---

* In opposition to any and every reason another reason can be offered.
† To offer a reason in opposition to any and every reason.

Unselfishness
and Dialectic

In Plato's dialogue *Protagoras* we see an extremely significant encounter between Socrates and Protagoras. Socrates, according to his custom, poses questions and demands of Protagoras' brief answers, almost only a "yes" and "no." As soon as Protagoras refuses to answer in monosyllables and tries to present detailed explanations, Socrates protests. He has, he pretends, a very short memory and if one tells him many things at a time he will become entirely confused.

Alcibiades, who is present at the conversation, does not take this excuse seriously: Socrates has an excellent memory and calls himself forgetful only in jest. Alcibiades is certainly right: Socrates does not have a short memory. Socrates is obviously also jesting when he humbly declares that he considers Protagoras a more skillful debater than himself. He is very well aware of his powers as a dialectician. Nevertheless, when Protagoras refuses to yield and insists on his right to conduct the discussion as seems to him more proper, Socrates gives him an ultimatum: if you do not agree to speak with me in my way, I shall leave and break off the discussion.

True, it is difficult to know to what extent Plato's dialogues faithfully reproduce the character of Socrates' conversations. But I believe that in public discussions—and he would speak, it seems, only in public places—Socrates did obstinately seek to reduce the discussion to an exchange of as brief questions and answers as possible. Why? Does this form really give us the best guarantee for the discovery of the truth? When Socrates threatened to depart, those present intervened, among them Prodicus, who said: "I beg you, Protagoras and Socrates, to argue with one another and not wrangle (ἀμφισβητεῖν μέν, ἐρίζειν δὲ μή); for friends argue with friends out of good will, but only adversaries and enemies wrangle" (*Prot. 337b*).

Even before this, the following dialogue takes place between Socrates and Protagoras. Socrates asks if justice is something holy. Protagoras, who apparently feels that Socrates wishes to trap him, hesitates and tries to preserve a possibility of retreat. "If you wish," he says, "justice is holy and holiness is just." To this Socrates replies rather sharply, "Pardon me . . . , I do not want this 'if you wish' or 'if you will' sort of conclusion to be proven, but I want you and me to be proven; I mean to say that the conclusion will be best proven if there be no 'if' " (*Ibid.*, 331c).

I have quoted these sentences in an attempt to clarify the problems that Socrates raised (if Socrates acted and spoke as Plato shows us) or the problems of Plato himself (in case his dialogues were invented by him). Did Socrates really consider Protagoras his friend, as Prodicus supposed? Did Socrates really seek the same thing as Protagoras? Or did Socrates consider Protagoras an enemy and, as is proper for an enemy, seek to conquer Protagoras —that is, not to argue with him but rather, in debating with him, to force him at all costs to submission and make him wish the same thing that he, Socrates, wished?

I am inclined to think the second assumption is the more probable one. It is no secret to anyone that Plato and Socrates considered the Sophists their enemies and were quite prepared to slander them. If even today we have still not been able to get a complete idea of the teaching of the Sophists, whose fault is this if not Plato's and his disciples? Plato tries to force his adversaries to fight with the arms that are most advantageous to himself. And he is not at all ashamed to have recourse, when he must (only I do not understand why he had to admit it so frankly), to ruses, pretenses, traps, and even physical force, as happens in war. Here Socrates pretends to be "forgetful," though he has an excellent memory; there he flatters Protagoras by praising his oratorical talents; again he assures him that they both follow a common goal, though it is quite obvious that their goals are opposed; further on, he threatens him with scandal and says that he will withdraw and break off the conversation. It is as if Plato wished expressly to emphasize that the goal of dialectic is not the search for truth but the annihilation of the enemy. This is extremely important for us.

Plato knew perfectly well that Protagoras did not wish the same thing as he himself wished. And he knew likewise that it was not possible to conquer Protagoras except by killing him, in a spiritual or intellectual sense. And ever since Plato all the philosophers up to our own day have continued to think the same. And not only to think: philosophers think of this as little as ordinary people think of their breathing or of the circulation of the blood in their bodies. All of us are persuaded that those who think otherwise than we must be treated as enemies with whom we must not discuss but wrangle. And if we continue to repeat, like Socrates, that we wish to obtain what all others likewise require, this is only a formula of politeness behind which always lies the ardent desire to conquer and annihilate our enemies. This is the heritage of the Greek wisdom which thinking mankind has assimilated.

Can it be considered eternal? Should we rejoice over the fact that, thanks to the efforts of Plato's disciples and followers, we know almost nothing of the intellectual work accomplished by the Sophists and have been able to believe that the Sophists thought only of gold and honors while Socrates and his disciples pursued nothing but truth? Following the few rare traces that Plato and Aristotle have preserved for us, modern historians have concluded that the Sophists did not seek gold only, and one could add that it was not truth alone that Socrates required.

In the Middle Ages Socrates found some faithful partisans: Catholicism showed the same ardor in destroying the heritage of pagan culture and it is a miracle, a matter of chance, or something else that I do not undertake to specify, that the works of Plato, Aristotle, and Plotinus were saved. And yet the visible vandalism of Plato and of Catholicism had a less destructive influence than their invisible theory of the sole truth. How many profound and daring thoughts have perished for the reason only that they could not be reconciled with the idea of the sole truth and could not breathe in the atmosphere saturated with this idea? Or did they, perhaps, not perish and only disappear from the sight of men and history? This may very well be assumed, for everything that does not exist for man and has not been included in history cannot, for this reason, be considered non-existent.

The Enigmas of Life

In several of his dialogues (*Gorgias 523, Phaedo 107, Republic 614*) Plato speaks to us in detail about the fate of souls after death. We shall all have to pass in our new life the tribunal of the sons of Zeus—Minos, Rhadamanthus, and Aeacus. In order that their judgments not be mistaken and that the judges not allow themselves to be led astray by the position of the souls on earth, Zeus ordained that the souls should appear in the other world not only without clothing but also without bodies. According to Plato, the naked soul would not be able to dissemble its sins in any way. He who has lived virtuously will have preserved his soul clean of all blemish; the soul of him who has sinned much will be broken, battered, covered with repugnant marks and sores—just as a body which has borne many illnesses becomes ugly and deformed. So thought Plato, who, as far as is known, never saw any souls naked and deprived of their bodies but only guessed what they would look like when their fleshly envelope fell off.

I believe that the sons of Zeus, who had to judge the dead and who saw the naked souls, would have smiled if they had somehow been able to hear Plato's conjecture. They saw the souls with their own eyes and did not need to have recourse to guesses or to judge by the analogy which holds that if sicknesses deform the body, sins likewise deform the soul. Indeed, from the very beginning, the analogy is far from flawless: certain persons become handsomer after sickness. Furthermore, it is very probable that wicked men and precisely those who have the most abominable vices, those who do not distinguish and do not wish to distinguish good from evil, possess souls that are very clean and very smooth, as if highly polished. Whatever they do, they always feel that they are in the right. The inward struggles that so painfully torment the souls of sensitive and anxious people by imposing upon them a constant tension—these are alien to them. Ideally pure souls are the property of ordinary, normal people who in their way know what is good and what bad, avoid the great evils, do good in small measure, and sleep with a tranquil conscience. The soul of a bourgeois or rentier is much cleaner and smoother than that of Socrates, Tolstoi, Pascal, Shakespeare, or Dostoevsky, just as a rentier's face is rounder and more placid, and his gaze more carefree. If Minos followed Plato's rules he would send Dostoevsky and Shakespeare to hell and populate the Field of Elysium with French rentiers and Dutch peasants. This is clear as day. Plato should not have spoken with such assurance of what he did not know.

But there is still another extremely important thing: if someone had pointed out in time to Plato that he was wrong, that it is not evil and vices but rather good and inward struggles—which in any case cannot be considered "bad"—that render the soul ugly and deformed, what would he have replied to this? The careful readers of Plato will understand the importance such a question must have for him. Indeed, let us assume that Plato could have convinced himself with his own eyes that the good does not beautify the soul but rather deforms it, that it introduces into it not harmony but disharmony—would he have, for all this, renounced the good? To put it differently, would we have advised men to wrong their neighbors or, at least, to think the least possible about justice and injustice, like those women who avoid all work and cares and refuse even to bring their children into the world in order not to lose their beauty?

But then he would have been obliged to renounce not only the λόγος but also his favorite idea of harmony: φιλοσοφίας μὲν οὔσης μεγίστης μουσικῆς, ἐμοῦ δὲ τοῦτο πράττοντος (Philosophy is the supreme music and I follow it). He would even perhaps have been obliged to become a μισόλογος (hater of reason), though he considered this the greatest of dangers and warned his disciples against it. Only a μισόλογος, indeed, would be capable of advising the soul to do that which deforms it. Not to fear either ugliness of the body or of the soul! Not to fear them—without such fearlessness being justifiable on any grounds whatsoever! Plato, the Greeks in general, and perhaps even all men will never agree to this; everyone wishes to have "sufficient reasons." And yet it must be agreed to. Tolstoi and Dostoevsky had souls that were deformed and completely broken: I saw this with my own eyes, I could not be deceived. In the case of Socrates, likewise, his soul was no more beautiful than his body; we have on this matter the authoritative testimony of Zopyrus who was much more perceptive than Alcibiades and perhaps even than Plato.

It follows from this that all the enigmas of being are still not solved. I say this only because it seems to me that it is always forgotten.

The Power of the Good in Plato

Meletus did a great wrong to Socrates, accused him falsely before the judges, and had him condemned. And Socrates answered with only one word: he called him "unrighteous." If Plato is to be believed, of the two adversaries confronting each other the loser was not Socrates but Meletus. If one accepts the judgment of the crowd, τῶν πολλῶν, Meletus did not suffer at all and it was Socrates who was overcome. And then the question arises: which is the stronger—the hemlock that poisoned Socrates, or the word "unrighteous" with which Socrates struck Meletus and Anytus?

When we today, twenty-five hundred years after the death of Socrates and his enemies, read the *Apology* or the *Phaedo* we see clearly that the moral condemnation is more powerful than the hemlock. Anytus and Meletus are quite as dead as Socrates, they survived him by only a few years. If he had not been condemned to death, Socrates would in any case have died several years later and nothing would be changed today: we would say that he died twenty-five hundred years ago. But Anytus and Meletus are forever nailed to the pillory, while the image of Socrates is surrounded with a halo. Is moral condemnation therefore stronger than poison? And is Plato right when he declares that the idea of the good is the most powerful force that exists in the universe? Did Anytus and Meletus therefore miscalculate and were they, like short-sighted and weak minds, deceived?

Let us now go further. Two thousand years more will elapse, or even twenty-five thousand years. It may be that a day will come when the earth will no longer exist or even our solar system, when time itself will no longer be. Eternity will then engulf the pillory on which Plato and history nailed Anytus and Meletus. What will then happen to the power of the good? It will be said that Socrates counted on the immortality of the soul. But he declared that even if death were complete destruction, he would nevertheless remain as he was. Was he right? It is fortunate, indeed, that the inspired Plato took up his defense and that the tribunal of history condemned Anytus and Meletus. But, in millions of cases, a legal action between the good and the wicked in no way attracts the attention of history. The wicked harms the good, he does him wrong, and that is the end of the matter. For his part the good man will, in a weak voice, call his offender "wicked": but his voice will be smothered by the loud voices of the offender's friends and flatterers and his word of condemnation will never even reach his enemy's ears. The good and its verdicts do not always have the power Plato wished to see in them. In Socrates' "case" it was history that conquered and not the good, which triumphed only accidentally. But Plato and his readers imagined that the good must always, by its very nature, triumph. No, "by nature," victory can be given to anything whatsoever—to physical force, to talent, to intelligence, to science —but not to the good.

Why do I say this? First, because it is the truth, that is, because it corresponds to reality. And secondly—but I would answer this question with another: Why must it not be spoken of, why must it be passed over in silence? To save Plato's reputation? Not to offend his disciples? Do you perhaps believe that it would be "better" to be silent? But then you believe many things. And what kind of "better" is it that may have misled you? Contemporary science is much too sure of itself, and it would do no harm to take away some of its pride.

Aurea Mediocritas

With the same simplicity and naturalness with which Horace, while still alive, rejoiced at the monument he had erected to his glory:

Exegi monumentum aere perennius
*Regalique situ pyramidum altius,**

with the kind of naturalness that almost none of our contemporary writers has, the famous Roman poet celebrated the "golden mean." I am certain that even in our day many poets adore the mean, but none of them will admit this and dare to call it "golden." So that those who would live according to Horace's prescription either do not know how to apply it or, if they do know, prefer to keep this knowledge to themselves. And surely if they decided to be frank and open, they would not dare invoke Apollo, the god of the sun and song. But Horace is not afraid to do this.

* I have erected a monument more lasting than bronze, and higher than the regal structure of the pyramids.

Quondam cithara tacientem
Suscitat Musam neque semper arcum
*Tendit Apollo.**

The *aurea mediocritas*, the golden mean, was the ideal of the ancients. And, furthermore, we also in our theories are not very far removed from this ideal. Κοινωνία τοῦ ἀπείρον καὶ πείρατος (the union of the boundless and the bounded), which is at the foundation of the philosophy of Aristotle as well as of Plato—have we found anything to replace this principle? No, we have found nothing else; he who would be honest must admit this. When we speak of relative or absolute reason, we have always in mind the golden mean or, as Plato expresses it, κοινωνία τοῦ ἀπείρον καὶ πείρατος.

We feel certain only when we can synoptically embrace every view. But where there are no limits such a view of the whole is imposisble. There one cannot know what will happen and one is obliged to assume the possibility of all kinds of metamorphoses and surprises, no matter how unacceptable these may be to us. Consequently, even though a man may resolutely turn away from the *aurea mediocritas*, if he refuses to admit that certain things that he is incapable of foreseeing even approximately may happen to him, one can have no confidence in his words. There is, then, this alternative: we must choose between the absolutely unknown or that limitation which the language of the ancients, devoid of all artifice, designated by the words the middle, the mean, moderation, etc. It will be objected that such expressions disgust us, that *aurea mediocritas* in our usage is a term of derision. Certainly. Nevertheless, we cannot get along without "measure," and the measureless is for us, as it was for the Greeks and Romans, synonymous with the monstrous.

In order that this not be so, in order that the measureless obtain

---

* Sometimes Apollo rouses his silent Muse with his lyre and does not always bend his bow.

the rights which the *mediocritas* once obtained, in order that we might apply the term "golden" to what is excessive and measureless, we would have to have that which we do not have and which we shall perhaps never have. What then? We must found our hopes on ugliness and the unknown, see in them not an end but a beginning, consider them not negative but positive. But I have expressed myself badly: the words "we must," to which we are so habituated, are not appropriate here, for every norm that guarantees the future leads us immediately back to Horace. It would be better to say that it sometimes happens that ugliness and the unknown begin invincibly to attract men. In the same poem Horace says:

> *Sperat infestis, metuit secundis*
> *Alteram sortem bene praeparatum*
> *Pectus.**

This means that an experienced man continues to hope in misfortune and does not, in good fortune, forget the variability of fate. Contrary to Horace, one could say there are misfortunes after which a man no longer wishes happiness but other still greater misfortunes. There are good fortunes and successes after which a man is not only unable but does not even wish to set any limits whatsoever to his demands. Neither in the first nor in the second case does he know what will come of his demands. But he does not even need to know. He knows, to express myself paradoxically, that all his power lies in his not knowing and also that all the weakness of mortals lies in their knowing. Indeed, have we not the right to hope that we shall be spared the cup of omniscience, not the most terrible but the most loathsome—if it be permitted to use this expression here—of the cups prepared here on earth for living beings? Schopenhauer affirms that man is

* A heart well prepared for any change in fortune has high hopes in adversity and cautious fears in prosperity.

obliged to choose between boredom and suffering: if you flee boredom you will not be able to avoid suffering, and *vice versa*. This, it seems, is correct. It seems also that those who know much or even everything (there are such people) have chosen boredom. As for the philosopher who refuses to accept boredom— the true philosopher will accept anything whatsoever except boredom—what should he do?

After all that has been said, I think it is not necessary to answer this question.

The Gods

Since the most ancient times it has been believed that the principal advantage the gods have over human beings lies in the fact that the gods lack absolutely nothing. They have everything and therefore need nothing. That is why they do not know change, while men—those wretched beings—suffer hunger, thirst, cold, heat, etc.

Surely there is a great error here. First of all, if mortals are wretched, it is not because they experience cold, hunger, fatigue. I even think that it would be a great pity if men did not know what fatigue is. And I am very sorry for the gods if it is true that they never know fatigue, heat, cold, etc. I certainly do not mean to say by this that men are happy. Oh no! Even if I said it, who would believe me? But they are not unhappy because they happen at times to be fatigued or to suffer hunger. If a tired person can rest, if a starving person can eat, what more does he need? What is distressing among men is that often one who is tired cannot rest, one who is cold does not find means of warming himself, and one who is hungry does not have anything to eat. I am even inclined to believe that the pagan gods did know fatigue, hunger, cold; their superiority over men came from the fact that they could in good time rest, eat, warm themselves, so that they did not perish from lack of heat or nourishment.

I will say even more: I think that what is terrible in our existence is not that we sometimes happen to fall into despair. We have every reason to believe that the man who has once known despair would not wish not to have had this experience. It is true that he would perhaps not willingly agree to repeat it, but he would no longer wish never to have had it. Why have men refused so positively to grant to the gods what they themselves have prized so highly? I believe they had no reason for this refusal. I believe that to represent the existence of the gods as perfect is not to understand them. But to understand the gods is necessary—though impossible. It is necessary for us to know that we do not at all know what perfection is.

On the Absolutely Perfect Being

We speak glibly of the perfect being and are so accustomed to the idea that we sincerely believe it has a determinate meaning, identical for all. But is this really so? Try to define the idea of the absolutely perfect being. Its first predicate is obviously omniscience, its second omnipotence.

For the moment this suffices. But is omniscience really a predicate of the absolutely perfect being? I say no. Omniscience is a misfortune, a downright misfortune, and one, furthermore, that is shameful and offensive. To know everything in advance, to understand everything—what could be more tiresome and more disgusting? For one who knows everything there can be no other end than to fire a bullet into his head. There are men who know everything, even on earth. To be sure, they do not really know everything and finally even know nothing or almost nothing and only simulate omniscience; but this suffices for an atmosphere of ennui to prevail about them that is so painful and so distressing that one can endure them only with great difficulty and in very small doses. No! The absolutely perfect being must not be so omniscient. To know much—that is very good, but to know everything is dreadful.

It is the same with omnipotence. He who can do everything has no need of anything. And we can verify this on earth: millionaires perish and go crazy, in the strict sense of the word, with boredom; their wealth is for them only a painful burden. And now the third predicate of the absolutely perfect being: he is always at rest. Good Lord! One would not wish such a fate on one's worst enemy. I could enumerate all the other predicates ordinarily ascribed to the absolutely perfect being; they will not prove themselves the least bit better than those that I have discussed. I shall be told perhaps that it is because of my human limitations that I cannot understand the sublime beauty of omniscience, of omnipotence, and of the eternal rest that nothing can disturb. But are not those who admire these sublime things also men and are they not limited beings? Can it not be objected against them that it is precisely because they are limited that they have contrived their absolutely perfect being and rejoice in their work? I am even inclined to believe that it is precisely human limitation that has inculcated in us the conviction that the *via superlationis vel eminentiae*, as the Catholic theologians say, is the way that leads to an understanding of perfection. Among us men on earth knowledge, power, and rest are prized very highly; if we raise all these to the superlative degree, which we likewise esteem, we obtain perfection. But this is pure childishness. It is good to have large eyes, but eyes the size of a saucer or even of a silver dollar would make the most beautiful face frightful. But the most important thing is that, in attributing to the perfect being this or that quality, men do not think of the interests of the perfect being but of their own. It is necessary for them that the absolutely perfect being be omniscient, for then they can deliver their fate into his hands without fear. And it is also necessary for them that he be omnipotent, so that he may be able to help them out of all difficulties. Furthermore, it is necessary that he be impassive, unchangeable, etc.

But what would happen to this being if he remained such as

he comes out of the hands of men? No one thinks of this. And do not think of it! I hope that he is at least powerful enough to be what he wishes to be, and not such as human wisdom would make him if its words could transform themselves into deeds.

The Last Judgment

Esse potest justitia Dei sine voluntate tua, sed in te esse non potest praeter voluntatem tuam . . . Qui ergo fecit te sine te, non te justificat sine te. Ergo fecit nescientem, justificat volentem * (*Augustine, sermo 169*).

If, in establishing this thesis, St. Augustine had based himself on the clear meaning of Scripture, one leaving no place for any other interpretation, we could dispute with him only by citing other passages of Scripture. But St. Augustine proceeds otherwise: he affirms that even for one who has not read Scripture it must be *completely obvious* that God can create man without asking his consent but, as for saving him against his will, this God cannot do. For St. Augustine this is as obvious as the truth, to use Spinoza's favorite comparison, that the sum of the angles of a triangle is equal to two right angles. According to St. Augustine, salvation must, at least in some fashion, be earned. Hence, *facienti quod in se est Deus non denegat gratiam.*† Hence,

---

* The justification of God can exist without your will, but it cannot exist in you without your willing it. Therefore he who made you without yourself does not justify you without yourself. He made you without your knowledge, but he justifies you only if you wish it.

† God does not deny grace to one who cooperates as he can.

also, the question of St. Thomas Aquinas: *utrum fides meritoria est?* *—a question to which he can answer only in the affirmative.

What St. Augustine says is so like the truth that at first blush it seems that no one could think otherwise and that he who says that he does think otherwise is only making believe. So, then, if there can be error here, we must believe that man has no possibility of distinguishing truth from error. Then it would be possible that two times two equal five, that a kilogram be lighter than a gram, that there be golden iron, hot ice, etc. All this is correct, and nevertheless one is obliged to admit that St. Augustine was in error and that consequently it sometimes happens that error is so like truth that it cannot even enter anyone's mind to imagine that it is error.

What to do? Descartes repeated stubbornly that God does not wish and is not able to lie. But if error is so like truth that, despite all our desire never to be deceived in anything, we nevertheless fall into error, whose fault is it? I raise this question not to reproach God. If God deceives men, this does not mean that God does wrong. It is men who do wrong. And this not in letting themselves be deceived—could man outwit God, his Creator?— but in having limited their Creator by imposing laws on the manifestations of His will. If man is subject to certain limitations, it must then be, men think, that God is also subject to certain limitations. Notice, furthermore, that it is not always forbidden men to lie. On the first of April one not only may but even must deceive, even if only in jest. And on other days also lies are permitted, if they do not pursue an interested goal. Legal medicine raises lying to the rank of principle or method—in the case, for example, where it is necessary to outwit a malingerer. To God everything is permitted; He may also deceive. And God does deceive us constantly. The chief source of our errors lies precisely in the fact that God does not wish to reveal His secrets to us. Man is obviously not equal to knowing the truth. We must

* Whether faith is meritorious.

only be surprised that the logicians and theorists of knowledge have until now still not recognized this elementary truth.

So it is in our case also. St. Thomas is convinced that *fides meritoria est.** St. Augustine, the St. Augustine who fought so passionately against Pelagius, is also certain that God can create man without his consent but that He cannot save him against his will. He is convinced of this, and he convinced others of a thing that has nothing in common with truth even though it resembles truth as one drop of water resembles another. However, St. Augustine himself felt at moments that man could do as little for his own salvation as for his entry into the world. But he did not believe this truth. He believed an error, and the whole world repeats it after him: *fecit nescientem, justificat volentem.*† It requires a special experience—like that which Tolstoi, Dostoevsky, Nietzsche, Shakespeare, or Luther lived through—to rid oneself of the Augustinian "truth." Do you think that Luther or Nietzsche always saw the real truth? No, not always, far from it. Quite like St. Augustine, they often took the opposite of the truth for the truth itself. And do you think that I, who tell you all this, see the truth whenever I wish? I see it when *it* wishes, but this does not happen often. Ordinarily it is error that attracts me more, and that is why I think it was entirely in vain that Descartes tried so hard to limit the rights of the Creator. The Creator deceives us by offering us errors that it is impossible to distinguish from truths and, in so doing, He probably does what is necessary for us.

I recall at this moment the words of Cardinal Petrucci, which were naturally condemned by the Catholic Church in the person of Pope Innocent XI: *Il niente è exemplare dell' anima mistica. Come stava egli prima che Dio creasse il mondo? Pensava egli*

---

* Faith is meritorious.
† He made you without your knowledge, but he justifies you only if you wish it.

*a se stesso e aveva cura di se? Certo, che no.** Do you understand what this means? God created the world out of nothing and
He could obviously not ask "nothing" if it wished to become a
world. And He will raise man to a new existence which will perhaps be as far removed from that of today as the latter is from
non-existence, and He will do this without asking permission of
man. For what can man say to God? As little as the "nothing"
which never reflected on itself and could not do so. You do not
believe in the possibility of such a metamorphosis? Well, that is
no great misfortune! You share the conviction of St. Thomas that
fides meritoria est? No, *fides* possesses no merit, just as the consent or non-consent of "nothing" played no role when God
created the world out of it. If you wish to act, then act, but you
are not helping God, you are only spoiling things. Indeed, you
will be incapable of doing even this: how can one think of
mixing in the affairs of God? You cannot even change the direction of the wind, you cannot even force a river to change its
course, and you pretend to come to God's aid!

But my words had a completely different object. Plato in his
Gorgias relates that in the other world the souls present themselves before their judges completely naked, without bodies even,
in order that the judges, the children of Zeus, may judge by the
appearance of the souls, their conduct on earth. And only pure,
stainless souls are received into the Elysian Fields; the others are
plunged into Hell. Well, there is a large element of truth here,
but Plato concealed certain things or, more correctly, he did not
know everything. He believed that there are certain souls that
are covered with repugnant sores and others that are completely
pure. But it has become authentically known that there are no
completely pure souls, that all are marked with stains and sores.

---

* Nothingness is the exemplar of the mystic soul. How was it before God
created the world? Did it think about itself and did it have any care for
itself? Certainly not.

And it has also become known that no action, no matter how beautiful it may be, no *exercitia spiritualia*, no elixir can make the stains disappear. Worse yet—and this is the most terrible thing—man does not wish to efface them, and this not through obstinacy, pride, or the inveterate habit of evil. At the Last Judgment all this will disappear of itself: there man will judge himself, and with a severity and pitiless rigor of which one cannot form the least idea here on earth. And that is why man does not wish to efface his stains.

You do not believe this? You are wrong. Man cannot wish this, just as Petrucci's *il niente* could not give birth to being. If you continue not to believe, I shall not try to persuade you. Your time will come; you will know and understand. In the meantime, have faith in St. Augustine! We stand here before a problem which terrifies mankind, for it appears insoluble both to our intelligence and our conscience: can one save the soul which was created out of nothing and which, filled with horror at its own ugliness, has condemned itself to return to nothing? How God does this, I do not know. But I feel at times that He does.

The Tower of Babel

Men have always racked their brains about the "meaning of war," particularly the historians and philosophers. There have already been so many wars; all of history is an uninterrupted chain of wars. And it is necessary to explain all this so that it becomes understandable. Wars have indeed been explained, and the explanations were quite understandable. When I was still in school I already understood why Alexander of Macedon undertook the conquest of India, why Caesar massacred a million Gauls and led an equal number into captivity, why the barbarians invaded Europe, why Napoleon marched into Russia, etc. And today, likewise, the present war is being explained, even though it has still not ended. But the more it is explained and the more understandable the explanations are, the more disgusted one feels. This is especially so when it is a question of explanations that in the last analysis invoke the "interests of nations." Germany needed the Berlin-Bagdad Railroad; England, open seas; France, Alsace-Lorraine. And Greece, Rumania, Montenegro—all of them needed something and sought to obtain some advantage. The contemporary historians know very well why people are fighting, that is, for what understandable, tangible interests. But they foregt that no railroad, no sea, nor anything similar can pay for the fantastic expenditures that the war has cost Europe. I do not even speak of the millions of human lives sacrificed, of the crippled, the tortured, the impoverished. And then the ideals! How many people who protested that they cherished ideals above everything else in the world were obliged to throw their dearest hopes on the altar of the insatiable god of war!

If the superhuman efforts and the material means which this war has already cost had been employed for the real defense of "interests," by the end of the three years that the war has now lasted all of Europe would have been transformed into a veritable paradise, into a tremendous, flourishing garden, and no one would have had any need of railroads or seas, for everyone would have had everything in abundance. To become convinced of this it is enough to have eyes and to know how to add. But even though everyone has eyes and knows how to add, no one wishes to profit from this knowledge, but everyone instead goes on repeating as a refrain: interests, interests, interests, we understand, we understand, we understand. But all this is self-deception: it is not at all a question of interests, and those who imagine that to understand the war means to understand interests, understand nothing. It is necessary to say it straightforwardly: from the point of view of human interests the present war, whatever may be its end, makes no sense. It has sense perhaps only from the point of view of the Americans and Japanese who, without any risk, have pumped all the gold out of Europe. Some Japanese philosopher may think that the meaning of this war lies in the development of the might of the Empire of the Rising Sun, which is destined to bring about the rejuvenation of old Europe by inculcating in it the new Oriental wisdom. Or perhaps an American banker, who before the war was only a millionaire and hopes by the end of it to have become a billionaire, sees the meaning of the war in his millions and in his office implores the devil to make it last as long as possible. If such people exist—and why should they not?—they are quite as right as those Europeans who do not stop talking about open seas and the Bagdad railroad.

To understand the war, one must tell himself that it has absolutely no sense, that it is a crying absurdity. This statement is—to
employ solemn language—the beginning of wisdom: the use of
solemn language is, indeed, permissible not only for those who
love to cry and blow trumpets to proclaim banalities and commonplaces. If I say this, moreover, it is not because I have any
need of their throats and trumpet fanfares. I desire only that they
not think that where people cry the loudest, there is the truth. A
loud voice presupposes only strong vocal cords, powerful lungs,
and the desire to shout.

The war, then, is a complete absurdity: it has no interest in
view but, on the contrary, ruins all interests. If this be so, the
way is opened wide to suppositions that have at least the great
advantage over the customary reasonings, that if they do not
correspond to reality, no one can prove it, for it is impossible to
verify them. A famous Greek poet once said, "Those whom the
gods love die young." At certain periods there live multitudes of
young people on earth who are more lovable and necessary to the
gods than we. And then great wars break out, like the one we
are now undergoing. Death cuts down millions of young people
who leave us for the other world whose inhabitants know better
how to appreciate them than we here. In this lies the meaning of
the war, not in the fact that the United States will have more
gold and the Germans fewer colonies. You do not agree? That
is your affair, but you have in any case no answer to me. Will
you invoke interests again? But I am not the only one, I think,
to whom these interminable discussions have become loathsome.
They will end by driving everyone to extremity, and then people
will become convinced that the meaning of the war does not lie
in wealth, colonies, or commerce.

O divine Plato! You loved myths and knew how to use them so
skillfully! Permit us to say what comes to our minds and so redeem your great sin: for it was you who invented dialectic and
you who wished that the philosopher should manage the affairs

of state. Fortunately the latter wish was not fulfilled, but dialectic rules over men, and you have been punished as you deserved. Formerly banality was simply banality but today, following your example, it is demonstrated and called truth!

Metaphysical Consolation

May I hope that sooner or later the truth that I now express will be recognized as truth by all reasonable beings? I raise this question in view of the fact that many philosophers have openly declared that they would not be satisfied with less. But it is clear that one cannot count on this. Let us be more modest and ask: may I hope that all men will recognize my truth? No, people will certainly answer me, I cannot count on this either. Finally, can I at least be sure that I myself will never renounce my truths as long as I live? I am very much afraid of losing all authority in the eyes of my readers, but nevertheless I answer: no, I do not have this assurance. And when people will thereupon reproach me, as ordinarily happens, that I am depriving men of their best consolation, I shall break out into laughter in the face of my accusers. Poor, foolish, ridiculous men: they imagine that they have already understood everything! And they are afraid lest there still be something in the universe that they do not even suspect! They are always afraid, they are always trembling. They should follow the example of non-rational beings. Look at the moth that throws itself fearlessly into the flame without asking anyone whomsoever, without asking itself, what will happen to it and what awaits it. You also, sooner or later, will have to throw yourselves into the flame where all your eternal truths will be consumed in a trice like the wings of the moth.

PART II

The Labyrinth

By a strange whim of fate the first fragment of the writings of the ancient Greek philosophers that has come down to us reads as follows: The origin of all things is the boundless (ἄπειρον) "and this very thing that gives birth to them is necessarily also the cause of their destruction, for at an ordained time they must undergo punishment and retribution by each other for their impiety" (διδόναι γὰρ αὐτὰ δίκην καὶ τίσιν ἀλλήλοις τῆς ἀδικίας κατὰ τὴν τοῦ χρόνου τάξιν). Thus spoke Anaximander twenty-five hundred years ago; such is the thought that came to the mind of men at the dawn of the history of philosophy. And these, as I have said, are the only authentic words of the ancestors of European philosophy that time has preserved for us. Certainly Anaximander reflected on many other things, and some of his ideas have come down to us in the exposition of other philosophers. We even know certain things about the doctrine of his predecessor and teacher, Thales. But of all that he himself said and wrote, this fragment is the only original text we have. What is striking is the fact that the thought it contains has determined in large measure the character and direction of the searchings of all later philosophy, not only Greek but European. Apparently Providence, which decided to destroy all that Anaximander accomplished, did not believe it possible to hide from the tribunal of history the name of the man who first suggested to European man this audacious thought about the essence of things. Why did Providence not decide to wipe out his words? Did they not contain a certain ἀδικία, a certain impiety, which for twenty-five hundred years has awaited its δίκη and τίσις, its punishment and retribution? Anaximander's thought deeply permeated the philosophy of his successors. Neither Plato nor Aristotle nor the Stoics nor Plotinus could have conceived anything without it. If, then, the thought of Anaximander was impious, all philosophy has also been impious and, together with philosophy, the religion of European man and also perhaps of Asiatic man. And a new and terrible δίκη awaits all of us precisely for that for which we expect to receive a great and merited reward. The responsibility falls first of all on Anaximander. It is probably for this reason that Providence preserved for us the authentic text of his words: it wished the future judge to have the *corpus delicti* in order to avoid all possibility of dispute.

But what is the deeper meaning of that single thought of Anaximander's that Providence has preserved for us with such care for so many centuries? Anaximander believes that "things," by being born, i.e., by detaching themselves from the original "universal" and "divine" unity in order to attain their present particular being, have committed an act that is impious to the highest degree, an act for which they must in all justice undergo the supreme punishment—death and destruction. *Things* means all visible objects: stones, trees, animals, men. Neither the stone nor the camel, neither the eagle nor man, has any right to aspire to the freedom of individual existence. From the fragment that has been preserved for us we do not know under what form, according to Anaximander, the camel or man should have existed —whether under the form, for example, of Platonic ideas or in some other way. It may be that, according to Anaximander, the ideas also have no right to particular existence and that their independent being, perfectly permissible from Plato's point of

view, also seemed an audacious impiety to the forefather of
Greek wisdom. Perhaps he thought that the One alone rightfully
existed and that every being which affirmed its freedom, limited
as this may have been, which detached itself from the One and
manifested itself as existing independently, was already something that had a beginning and consequently carried in itself the
threat of a terrible punishment—destruction, death. If it is permissible in such cases to trust one's "instincts" and admit conjectures, I should say that I personally am inclined to the latter
conjecture. Plato who, in general, adopts Anaximander's point
of view nevertheless permits himself a certain deviation by manifesting an indulgence, which theoretically is not to be justified,
toward the ideas. But Plotinus no longer shared this weakness:
even though he paid proper tribute to his great teacher and to the
already solidly established tradition of Platonism, he hated every
manifestation of individual being with all his soul. The One, for
him, was origin as well as ideal and God. He was ashamed, it
seems, not only of his body, as Porphyry tells us, but also of his
soul. His life was entirely motivated by the idea, and the impatient expectation, of union with the One. In the transports of
ecstasy he tasted the beatitude of super-individual life. And in his
ordinary, normal state—in the state of a "free thing"—he experienced the unbearable bitterness of independent existence detached from the One, the feeling which perhaps found its
strongest expression in the famous phrase of Pascal: *Le moi est
haïssable.** It seems that Goethe was also inspired by Anaximander's thought when he put into the mouth of his Mephistoph-
eles these words that are as well known as Pascal's phrase:
Denn alles, was entsteht, ist wert, dass es zu Grunde geht.† All
human *wisdom*—I say *wisdom* expressly—has carried on since the
most ancient times an obdurate struggle, a struggle to the bitter

---

* The ego is hateful
† For it is appropriate that everything that comes into being should also
come to ruin.

end, against individual being. Outside this struggle against the hateful "I," the great teachers of humanity see no salvation and find no solution to the contradictions and horrors of existence. The history of philosophy, of art, of morality, and even of religion clearly reveals this to us. The story of the fall of the first man, as it is reported to us by the Bible, was explained by the Christian theologians in a sense that agrees with Anaximander's philosophic thought. Already the first Christian thinkers, when they reflected on the mystery of the Incarnation and the death of God on the cross, did not seek any other answer than that which Greek philosophy whispered to them, the Greek philosophy which had already arrived at its full maturity by this time.

Cur Deus homo? All the answers to this question—even the most primitive—finally came down to the idea that God had to become human in order that man should become godly. Let us take as an example the thoughts of Gregory the Great. The famous pope reasoned thus: when the first man disobeyed God, God drove him out of paradise and handed him over to the devil who subjected him to all the torments of terrestrial existence, up to and including death. But later God took pity on His creature and wished to deliver him from his bondage. How could He do this? He Himself, in a fit of rage, had handed man over to Satan and had done so forever. God may not break his word. So God had recourse to a trick. He commanded His Son to clothe Himself in human form. The devil saw in Christ a man but did not understand that He was God and, like a fish that sees the bait but does not notice the hook hidden under it, threw himself on Christ as on one of his ordinary victims and subjected him to outrage and death. And so it was that the devil found himself caught. He had the right to torture and kill men but could not attack God. It was the devil who violated the contract, and God was thus able not to execute His word. So the death of the Savior of men, which is so mysterious for the believer, "explains itself."

In order that men should not die it was necessary that God die. Adam transgressed the commandment of God and detached himself from the divine being; to return to divine life—the only worthwhile life, according to Gregory the Great—the expiatory sacrifice of the Son was necessary.

A vulgar reasoning that is repugnant to us. And especially so is the comparison which, according to its author, made his thought all the more convincing and clear: the human nature of Christ served as a bait and His divine nature was the hook on which the father of lies was caught. But if we disregard the form of this reasoning and take cognizance of the fact that Gregory the Great, who lived at the beginning of the Middle Ages, could and had to use the language of his time, it appears that his reasoning is quite in agreement with Anaximander's thought. The Biblical account of Adam's sin means, according to him, that in tasting the fruit of the tree of knowledge, man detached himself from God, no longer lived in a common life with God, and began to "be" by himself. This thought was expressed in various ways by all the Fathers of the Church who examined the question *Cur Deus homo?* St. Augustine also believed that the beginning of sin was pride: *initium peccati superbia*. *Humilitas* is, above everything else, the renunciation by man of his own will and independent being in order to return to that paradisiacal life of which the Bible speaks. *Superbia* in St. Augustine does not at all mean pride in the sense that the Psalmist uses the word, but rather the affirmation by man of his right to particular, independent existence. Evidently the Middle Ages fought so relentlessly against physical love because they considered it the expression of *superbia*, of *amor sui usque ad contemptum Dei,** in contrast to *amor Dei usque ad contemptum sui,†* to use the language of St. Augustine. It was also from this point of view that the Gospel was explained: a man's enemies are the members of his family;

* Self-love even to the contempt of God.
† Love of God even to contempt of self.

if anyone comes to me and does not hate his father and mother, etc. The asceticism of monks—and not only Christian but also Buddhist and Moslem—set for its goal the destruction in this life of the "hateful I" which had rashly escaped from the lap of universal, supreme being in order to reach the realm of incomprehensible, painful, terrible and, consequently, unacceptable freedom.

The struggle against the "I," against individual existence, can and must be considered one of the most remarkable and exciting episodes in the history of the human spirit. Like all that we observe in life, this struggle is filled with contradictions. The rigorous ascetic who devised refined tortures for himself and others often manifested such a powerful personality that it entirely excluded any assumption that his soul could ever be united with some supreme principle. The popes of the Middle Ages—Gregory VII, for example—pitiless toward themselves and toward others, despite "the gifts of tears" which heaven had bestowed upon them, appear to us finally as the most powerful personalities of their time. It is not for nothing that his contemporaries called Gregory VII "holy Satan." Men are so constituted that it very rarely happens that their ideals are the adequate expression of their spiritual aspirations. But this in no way changes the situation. The historical fact remains that for thousands of years men acknowledged Anaximander's idea that individual existence is an impiety, that every particular being offends God or nature and is therefore condemned to annihilation. Nature itself has established this law, and the best, the highest thing man can do is to help nature by obeying its commandments. These philosophers who wished to be "wise men," i.e., those who taught men how they should live, taught that the chief and essential task of man consisted in destroying in himself his individual "I." "Spiritual" goods, indeed, have always been mainly defined in negative terms. *Amor intellectualis Dei* was elaborated by Spinoza in the

same way as the ἀταραξία * of the ancients. It is not for nothing
that Schopenhauer expressed such enthusiasm for the small treatise that Spinoza never finished, *De intellectus emendatione.*
Furthermore, Schopenhauer valued in Christianity only its scorn
for worldly gifts, for the individual. To be sure, one could say
of Schopenhauer what has been said of the monks and the inquisitors: he who stormed against the individual was himself an
extremely prominent and strong individuality. Indeed, he was so
interesting and attractive a personality that I should not have
been surprised if nature, at the sight of Schopenhauer, had forgotten its first decision, declared itself prepared to yield and,
in order not to destroy him, agreed to make an exception and
not punish him for his sin of individual existence.

Here now arises a question of capital importance. If nature is
not at all as faithful to its eternal purposes as we think; if it can
repent and renounce decisions that it has already taken, like the
Biblical God who regretted having driven Adam out of paradise;
if it took pity on Schopenhauer, preserved him from death and,
in order not to reveal its secrets to us, only subjected him to the
common fate—for he lived and died like all men; if it was not
only for Schopenhauer that nature made an exception but if it
also somewhere in its immense domains preserves Alexander of
Macedon, Mozart and still others—one can then ask oneself
whether the people who follow Anaximander in their philosophy
are really right. Was not the Greek sage a little too hasty in his
conclusions when he conferred on the first principle that immutability which we on earth are accustomed to venerate?

As experience shows, all things on earth perish, all living beings
die; consequently, all things deserve destruction, all living things,
death. For a theoretical mind such a general law appears extremely alluring and seductive. But it is natural to express some
doubts on the matter. Are we not too much inclined to cultivate

* *Ataraxia:* tranquillity, imperturbability.

in ourselves the need for theorizing? Do we not sacrifice everything, and even the truth in whose name theory proclaims its
rights, for illusory goals? If we would speak of impiety, would
it not be more correct to suspect not all of human nature of impiety, but only one of its elements? We wish immediately and
definitively to understand and explain everything, and it is because of this that we always and everywhere theorize. And,
imagining that theory is identical with truth, we have so much
confidence in it that the suspicion never even arises in us that it
is precisely theory itself that has seized the right to judge what is
pious and impious, that it is theory, with its pretensions to judging, that shows itself impious.

Indeed, assume that my supposition is correct—that nature can
really modify its decisions and laws; that there are, to use the
language of the Scholastics, two powers, *potentia absoluta* and
potentia ordinata; that nature not only spared Alexander the
Great and Mozart but protected them and continues still to protect them, loving and admiring in them precisely their independence, their pride, their daring aspirations, and the faculty they
possessed of living and existing not in "the lap of nature" but in
freedom. How would we then evaluate Anaximander's maxim
and that European wisdom which for so many centuries has been
nourished on it?

Let us further admit—for it is no longer inadmissible—that philosophy is not limited to reasonings but that words are transformed into acts, that those who believed in Anaximander killed
in themselves their individuality and the power to be themselves
and, being henceforth only neutral things, atoms easily replace-
able by other atoms, showed themselves completely superfluous
in this life as well as in the other and were therefore condemned
to destruction. What will you then say of the centuries-old
human wisdom? It may, indeed, be that he who believed that *le
moi est haïssable* will end by making of his ego a thing so feeble,
pitiable and shabby that it will henceforth deserve nothing but

scorn and disgust. It is still only a half-evil if nature is inexhaustibly rich and fears no sacrifice; yet the contrary supposition would contain nothing incredible. But what if nature is poor in "the individual" and what if the very goal of its creative work consists in creating individualities—not those of which Byron speaks: "To feel me in the solitude of Kings / Without the power that makes them bear a crown"—but those who, like eagles, do not fear but love solitude, for they have the power necessary to support the burden of the crown, i.e., exist independently and not in others? It may then be that we have committed a terrible crime in following the teaching of Anaximander, Plato, the Stoics, Plotinus and the Christian philosophers, and in trying to overcome our individuality, to kill our ego. Nature is silent and does not reveal its mysteries to mortals. Why? I do not know. Perhaps it does not wish to do so, perhaps it cannot do so. If it cannot do so, what must be its despair, what must be its hatred for the professors of wisdom who, in teaching that *le moi est haïssable*, kill in the germ all its efforts to attain independent and self-active being? They paralyze its loftiest, noblest and holiest attempts. It tries to make man a substance, *causa sui*, independent of anything whatsoever, even of itself that created him. But man, like a crayfish, crawls back into the bosom of nature from which he went forth. And this is what people call wisdom! Our teachers inculcate in us a struggle against nature; they have set as their aim to prevent by every means our mother nature from realizing her grand designs.

And why? Exclusively for theoretical goals! Man can understand the universe only if he assumes that everything which has a beginning has an end, only if he derives multiplicity from unity.

Now it seems to me that the Biblical story of the fall of man has a quite different meaning than that which the theologians, educated on Greek thought, confer on it. It is clearly said in the Bible that it was forbidden man to taste of the fruit of the tree of the knowledge of good and of evil while no ban was placed on all the other trees. But the theologians in their reasonings proceed from exactly the opposite assumption, as if God had permitted man to taste only the fruits of the tree of knowledge and forbidden him to touch all the other trees.

Recall the classic arguments of Anselm of Canterbury on this very subject, *cur Deus homo?* and you will become convinced to what a degree he was certain that the goal of man is not to live and, by living, escape from nothingness, but to reason and, by reasoning, arrive at the "understanding" of being. Later, of course, the reasonings of Anselm of Canterbury appeared as little acceptable as those of Gregory the Great. But both attained by means of their reasonings a certain goal which they called knowledge or understanding and which gave them the highest satisfaction. To put it differently, they fed on the fruits of the forbidden tree and, with the Greek philosophers, venerated only these by setting them as "spiritual goods" over against the other fruits which they forever branded by calling them material goods. How did it happen that those who saw in the Bible a revelation could, through courtesy to their pagan teachers, deform so greatly the clear and simple story of this remarkable book? Or was it the fault of the tempter, of the ancient serpent, the father of all lies?

I certainly do not know who the tempter was and how the great philosophers were led into temptation, and it would be vain to express conjectures on the matter. I know only one thing: There have always been on earth men who did not succumb to temptations and who, if not always, at least from time to time, felt disgust for the fruits of the tree of knowledge and were not afraid openly to express their feelings. Tertullian, for example, in the fragment of his reflections *de Carne Christi* that is generally cited as an example of the absurdities into which one who claims to renounce the compass of rational ideas in his earthly wanderings can fall, was such a man. I have already quoted this fragment several times, but I think that the more we recall it to others and to ourselves the more quickly we shall succeed in attaining our most essential and dearest goals. Mankind, which is haunted by the *idée fixe* of rational comprehension, on rising every morning should repeat the words of Tertullian: *Crucifixus est Dei filius; non pudet, quia pudendum est. Et mortuus est Dei filius; prorsus credibile est, quia ineptum est. Et sepultus ressurexit; certum est quia impossibile est.**

Tertullian wishes to know, and that is why he does not wish to understand, feeling clearly at that moment (but at that moment only) that understanding is hostile to knowledge and that this hostility will never end; that it is enough to "understand," i.e., to pluck the fruit of the tree of knowledge and taste it, immediately to lose all possibility of access to the other marvelous trees which grew so abundantly in the garden of Eden. The knowledge of good and evil has no positive value, as we have always been taught, but rather a negative one. And it is not eternal but temporary and transitory, not divine but human, all too human. God forbade plucking the fruits of this tree not out of fear that man would obtain more than what had been granted to him and not out of jealousy. The accursed serpent deceived Eve, deceived Adam, deceived Anaximander, and blinds all of us to this day. The tree of knowledge does not increase our powers but, on the contrary, diminishes them. We must choose between the tree of the knowledge of good and evil and the tree of life. But we believe that light comes to us from the first and that the second plunges us into darkness. And we boast of our perceptiveness, of our profundity, and of many other things besides.

I should like to quote a fragment of a work of the last of the great Scholastics, William of Occam, again on the same subject, *cur Deus homo?* Occam, like Tertullian, does not wish to understand why God became man, as if he felt that there is a certain

* The Son of God was crucified; it does not cause shame because it must shame us. And the Son of God died; again, it is credible because it is absurd. And having been buried, he rose again; it is certain because it is impossible.

limit beyond which we must cease to understand if we wish to go further. The attempts of Anselm and the other theologians to explain God or even His works appear to Occam impious. Understandable and reasonable are the works of men and everything that is limited, near, close at hand. Occam accepts everything the Church teaches about the incarnation of Christ, but he flees from explanations. He says: *Est articulus fidei quod Deus assumpsit naturam humanam. Non includit contradictionem, Deum assumere naturam asininam; pari ratione potest assumere lapidem vel lignum.**

If one recalls the customary reasonings of the theologians on this matter, if one recalls that Occam lived a short time after St. Thomas Aquinas who became the normative theologian of Catholicism, his audacity—which would have been astonishing even on the part of a modern mind alien to the Church—appears stupendous. To be sure, Occam's predecessor, Duns Scotus, was the first to establish the doctrine that God is not subject to any law, that absolute arbitrariness is the very essence of the divine will. Duns Scotus said: *Sicut omne aliud a Deo ideo est bonum, quia a Deo volitum, non e converso; sic meritum illud* (the voluntary sacrifice of Christ) *tantum bonum erat, pro quanto acceptabatur et ideo meritum, quia acceptatum, non autem e converso, quia meritum est et bonum, ideo acceptatum.*† But it was in Occam alone that this thought led to the audacious and challenging declaration that the principle of the divine essence is an arbitrariness which nothing limits and which is, consequently, unexplainable and cannot be deduced from anything whatsoever. *Deus assumpsit naturam asininam; pari ratione*

---

* It is an article of faith that God assumed human nature. It does not include any contradiction that God should assume the nature of a donkey; with equal reason he can assume the nature of stone or of wood.

† Thus every other thing apart from God is good because it is willed by God, but not contrariwise; thus that meritorious act (the voluntary sacrifice of Christ) was good insofar as it was accepted and therefore meritorious because it was accepted—not, however, on the contrary, because it is meritorious and good and, therefore, accepted.

*potest assumere lapidem aut lignum.** Occam's *non includit contradictionem* and *pari ratione* are the same as Tertullian's *quia*
which defies all our rational usages. For, translated into ordinary
language, the expressions "it does not include any contradiction"
and "on the same grounds" mean that contradictions exist only
for us who everywhere seek "reasons" and who without reason
not only cannot think but cannot even live. As far as God is
concerned, however, contradiction is a word devoid of all content, and "reasons" have simply no connection with God. He is
beyond contradiction and reasons as He is beyond good and
evil, to express it in modern language, to which Duns Scotus was
already very close. "For God everything is good insofar as it
corresponds to his will and not vice versa; that is why the sacrifice of Christ was good insofar as it was accepted by God and
meritorious insofar as God recognized it." If Duns Scotus was
not afraid to say that God is "beyond good and evil," Occam's
audacity went even further. He felt that God was beyond truth
—that truth which Aristotle, the *praecursor Christi in naturalibus*,
and his followers up to the normative theologian, St. Thomas
Aquinas, and the normative philosophers of our time, have considered above perfect as well as imperfect being. We now repeat
calmly *Deus assumpsit naturam asininam.* But, no, not calmly. I
quote this phrase in a language that is strange, dead and abstract;
I do not dare to translate it into my mother tongue. But Occam,
a monk of the Middle Ages, dared to pronounce it in a language
that was close to him, closer even perhaps than his mother tongue.
It sometimes happens that "reason," "light," and all those things
by which we let ourselves be seduced to such a degree that we
can represent God Himself only as reasonable and luminous—it
sometimes happens, I say, that all this appears unbearably banal
and empty. I shall not employ stronger expressions only out of
a sense of literary propriety. And just as ordinarily man aspires

* God assumed the nature of a donkey; with equal reason he can assume
the nature of stone or of wood.

from the depths of darkness to "light," in certain extraordinary moments he feels himself invincibly drawn away from "light." The history of philosophy tells us at length how wise men— following Plato, Aristotle, and their common inspirer Anaximander—fled transitory and changing reality to the immutable, the eternal, that which is always equal to itself. The opposite also sometimes happened, but the history of philosophy is silent about this. It happens that a man, with all the power of which he is capable only in moments of great despair or passion, overthrows the millennial walls of philosophic and other prejudices and flies toward that divine freedom where the last of the Scholastics were not afraid to discover the arbitrariness that is so shameful to all. Man is sometimes ready joyously to exchange all the eternal truths and all the eternal essences for the temporary and the transitory, for the "thing" that no one values and no one needs, for that "thing" which in its audacious impiety dared "to be" even though it ought not "to be." It is this "thing" that man wishes to obtain, and—who knows?—perhaps those who know how not to surrender and to "will" in their way are powerful enough to preserve "their own," even though universal reason condemned every "their own," everything that has a beginning, to death and destruction.

The great saints—St. Theresa, for example, or her disciple, St. John of the Cross—have told us at length of their immense despair and terror at the thought that they were the vilest and most worthless of all persons who had ever lived on earth. Why the vilest? Put this question to a man of common sense and he will tell you without hesitation that neither St. Theresa nor St. John was at all the vilest of persons and that there have been many at least as vile as they. But how does it happen that ordinary people know this simple truth while from the saints it was hidden? Or were the saints right and is it common-sense minds that are in error? Were St. Theresa and St. John really the vilest of all beings? And was Don Quixote's Dulcinea, contrary to all the evidences, a princess and not a keeper of swine? And the fool who first saw that he alone existed in the world and that the entire universe was only his "representation"—did he see what was, did he discover in his solipsism a great truth? Is self-evidence not "beyond time," and are there epochs when self-evidence no longer is? When *non pudet quia pudendum,* when *certum est quia impossibile,* when God decides *assumere naturam asininam, lignum aut lapidem?* When the whole universe begins to laugh aloud at human reason and its immutability? When we find ourselves beyond not only good and evil but also beyond truth and error?

We shall be told that truth is a limit that it is impossible to surpass. In antiquity people were persuaded that entry into the kingdom of shades was forbidden to living men. But the infinite longing of Orpheus and his marvelous song conquered invincible Hades and led him to Eurydice. When Orpheus began to sing, says the poet who relates the ancient myth, everything in hell was immobilized: Tantalus ceased to pursue the water that escaped him, the wheel of Ixion stopped, the Danaides forgot their bottomless casks, and Sisyphus himself sat down on his rock. Through his great love and his inspiration Orpheus succeeded in overcoming the laws of hell. Like St. Theresa, surely he imagined that he was the most miserable of men, that he alone was miserable, and that in general there was nothing in the world other than his Eurydice and his love. Obviously he was wrong: Anaximander would have seen it clearly, and Aristotle could have demonstrated it to him with a self-evidence that would have left nothing to be desired. But the gods decided otherwise. By their supreme will, by the will of that *potentia absoluta* which differs in virtually nothing from arbitrariness, they transformed his error into truth, into a great truth which did not exist before, which did not exist anywhere, neither in heaven nor on earth, and which could never have been born. Truths also have a beginning. The eternal truths have a beginning and perhaps have no end. What is the way that leads to them? If you follow Don Quixote, St. Theresa, or even Orpheus, you will never arrive anywhere; or if you do arrive somewhere, it will not be where your guides are found. When you lose the road, when the road loses you, then . . .

But I began by speaking of the labyrinth. Yet what can one say of the labyrinth except that it is a labyrinth? *Deus non est bonus, non est melior, non est optimus. Ita male dico quamdumque voco Deum bonum, ac sic ego album vocarem nigrum.** This was said by a man who had seen and heard much in his life. But then, where is the truth? To whom shall one listen? Whom believe? Anaximander and Plato, or Tertullian and Occam? Did Greek philosophy, in the person of its Adam, enter upon the right way? Or did this Adam, like the Adam of the Bible, allow himself to be seduced by the brilliant aspect of the tree of knowledge of good and of evil? And did mankind in following his example and feeding on the fruits of this tree, not approach its dearest goal but, on the contrary, remove itself from it? Or, what is still worse—for this introduces a still greater confusion into a question that is already sufficiently confused: are piety and impiety perhaps not such "general," forever unchanging concepts as our "intellectual" vision supposes? It may be that what appeared and was really impious in the eyes of Anaximander appeared and also truly was for Tertullian and Occam eminently pious; so that in general the question who is right does not allow itself to be raised. Still another possibility: it may be that impiety is simply an invention of a man who tasted the fruits of the tree of knowledge and thereby became limited and at the same time sure of himself in his limitation. Nature—before the fall of man—knew nothing either of good or of evil.

And yet each of us is obliged to choose his way. Some follow Anaximander and Plato, others enter on a different direction,

---

* God is not good, is not better, is not best. Thus I speak erroneously whenever I call God good, for thus I might call white black.

and the third, the fourth, travel on still different levels, so that their roads never come together and never cross. Who will resolve this great enigma? And how resolve it? What solution will not be fictitious? Does not the very essence of mystery impose upon us the renunciation of every solution? Who will answer these questions? Who will feel a desire to think about them?

Responsibility

Both Dostoevsky and Tolstoi meditated frequently and painfully on Napoleon. They always tried to understand how Napoleon could take upon himself the responsibility for all the sufferings and miseries he brought into the world. Their reasoning was something like this: if we happen to sin against someone or do him some injury, we can no longer sleep peacefully; how then could Napoleon, who almost every day destroyed thousands of people and at every moment risked the existence of his own nation as well as that of other nations, sleep in peace? They believed that all men are constructed in the same way, that if their consciences tormented them, Napoleon ought to suffer much more still.

Now men are not at all constructed in the same way, and moral conscience does not exist among all and everywhere. In the final analysis, even the conscience of Dostoevsky very little resembled that of Tolstoi; it differed from it quite as much as their lives differed from each other. For Napoleon the question of responsibility did not arise at all; he acted and lived "according to nature," as the Stoics demanded.

Do you recall the story Pushkin puts into the mouth of Pougachev? The eagle lives thirty years and the raven three hundred. The raven feeds on carrion, the eagle devours living prey. And the eagle cannot understand the raven, just as the raven cannot understand the eagle. Darwin taught us to believe that species change and transform themselves one into another. And Darwin had proofs, crushing proofs! Nevertheless, he was wrong, and even more wrong were the Darwinists who generalized his thought and wished to bring all living beings under a single concept. Not only will the raven and the eagle never be reconciled, but it is only rarely that two men even mutually understand each other. The Biblical story about the confusion of tongues is not a fairy tale or myth, as learned people in their arrogance imagine. Even when men pronounce the same words, they each mean and see different things. Two orthodox Moslems swear in the name of two different Allahs. And I would say more: every Moslem today worships a completely other Allah than the one for whom he risked his life yesterday. The principle of identity applies only in logic. And to one who thinks that responsibility is the consciousness of a moral principle that lives in the heart of each of us, it is not given to "understand" Napoleon; the latter, even though he knew the word "responsibility," did not understand it, or he understood it in such a way that in the mind, let us say of Dostoevsky, it would have been expressed by a completely different term, by "irresponsibility," for example.

The majority of men of action, if not all, have been irresponsible; for one who takes upon himself responsibility, if he be not God but a man, paralyzes in himself the nerve of action and condemns himself to idleness and reflection. All men ought to remember this, and especially those who think, that is, philosophic minds. For philosophers are also at times men of action and even very important. It is not only the soldier's truncheon that leaves traces in history; the word also acts. But the philosophers, insofar as they act, are likewise irresponsible; that is, they never know and cannot know what will come of their deeds, even in empirical reality. And in super-empirical reality? There the word is more effective than anything else, there the word creates and destroys worlds. If the philosophers who speak so much of responsibility knew what consequences their expressed and even unexpressed thoughts could have in the noumenal world, they would certainly take a vow of silence and forbid themselves even to think. But even this would not help them. "There" the vow of silence also leaves certain traces, and it may be—who knows—that silence, a word that has not been spoken, a thought that has not been fully developed, acquire a special significance there, where things are evaluated by a completely different standard than here.

So then . . . But here precisely is the end of all "so then." To obtain "so then" it is necessary to go to quite other places and, thank heaven, there are enough of these on our earth.

Pro Domo Mea

People take it amiss when I express two contradictory judgments at the same time. They demand that I renounce one of them or that, at least for propriety's sake, I do not express them at the same moment. But between these people and myself there is only this difference—that I speak of my contradictions openly while they prefer to hide them from themselves, and when others perceive their faults and point them out they pretend to see nothing. Contradictions seem to them the *pudenda* of the human mind, just as certain organs are the *pudenda* of the body. Thus, the demands of logic finally have for their source simply a deep-rooted human prejudice.

Furthermore, people feel very offended by the fact that when I express some judgment I do not say that I shall never renounce it. As if they themselves never renounced any of their judgments, and as if the judgments of a poor mortal could and should be immortal! Why do men think this? Why do they accept the idea that Plato, Aristotle, or Spinoza became victims of death but feel themselves seized with horror at the thought that the same fate threatens the doctrines of these great men? I should think that what ought to plunge us into horror is that death has taken away from us the divine Plato and not his ideas! But even the disciples of Plato observed without anguish the head of their venerated master becoming white, and they accepted the necessity of interring or burning his dead body, while they could not bear the thought that his ideas about the best republic or about rearing human beings could one day become false or tiresome. But if men are condemned to grow old and lose their beauty and charm, how much more fitting is this fate for the ideas created by these same men!

Heroes of the Spirit

Philosophers have always spoken eagerly and at length of the instability of human goods. And no one has ever reproached them for this; on the contrary, it has always been considered a great merit on their part. Why then do people become irritated when I speak of the instability of human convictions? The question is an interesting one and it seems to me that it would be worthwhile to consider it a bit.

To be perfectly frank, human convictions are very similar to all other human goods, such as riches and honors. It is forbidden man to aspire to riches and honors. This is considered vanity. But is not to aspire to the possession of human truth also vanity? Riches and honors have no value—so, at least, say the philosophers —because there is no way of preserving them. Today you may be rich, but tomorrow some misfortune may come upon you and you will then be a miserable beggar. When Napoleon approached Moscow he was omnipotent, but several months later he had to flee like a thief in the night. Many more such examples might be cited. Open the works of Cicero or Seneca. How long-windedly and eloquently they discuss this theme! But if I had their talent (and if to write as they do were not so boring) I could say much about how the Napoleons and Croesuses of thought lost their "spiritual" goods. To be sure, they sometimes managed to get them back, but how often did they leave this world as poor and miserable as they entered it! However, it is easier for one who is spiritually bankrupt to hide his poverty from the eyes of others. That is why all know and speak so much about Napoleon at St. Helena and Croesus in captivity, but few suspect the catastrophes that occur in the souls of heroes of the spirit.

It will perhaps be said that it is not necessary to know everything. It is not for nothing that it is said in the reflections of the wisest of mortals, who was imprudent enough at the end of his life to give men the results of his thinking: "My son, be admonished, of making many books there is no end, and much study is weariness of the flesh" (Eccl. 12:12). The warning is useful—that cannot be disputed. But it is known that it is not given men to stop in time.

Sursum Corda

When Adam and Eve walked in the garden of Eden, could it
have occurred to them to ask themselves what meaning life has?
And if Adam asked Eve—before the sin, naturally—what the
meaning of life is, would not his question have appeared absurd
to her? And Hamlet's question, which men have raised so often
before and after Shakespeare, would also obviously have been
ridiculous in paradise. How can man entertain any doubt about
whether to be or not to be? To experience "the best," it is at
least necessary somehow to be. For "non-being" there can finally
be no qualification, no definition even. But if the habit of reflecting, as Hamlet did, is so strong that these considerations
appear insufficient, I shall present you still another. Can you
imagine God Himself putting this question, to be or not to be,
to Himself? I am prepared to formulate this question once more
thus: Is it possible that God should suddenly prefer non-being
to being and by His omnipotent word plunge the whole universe
and Himself into non-being? If it were possible that non-being
appeared to Him preferable to being, everything would have returned to non-being long ago. I should not be putting these
questions to you, and you who are listening to me would not
exist. God, then, does not once raise this question, but man does.
Why? Does he wish to be wiser than God? No, it seems that it

is not a question of that. Human reason is not at all as proud as the books say. We shall perhaps become convinced of this if we recall the circumstances under which Hamlet raised the question. As long as his father ruled in peace and his mother followed the path of virtue, it did not even occur to Hamlet to ask himself "to be or not to be." Notice the continuation of the monologue: "Whether 'tis nobler in the mind to suffer the slings and arrows of outrageous fortune, or to take arms against a sea of troubles and, by opposing, end them."

Hamlet suddenly lowers his voice an octave. What concerns him is not the general question: "Which is better—to be or not to be?" Had the crime of his uncle and mother not taken place, that crime which shattered Hamlet quite as much as the appearance of his father's ghost, the fatal question would perhaps not even have arisen in his mind. I shall risk going even further. Today on earth, where death rules beside life and where it seems that death has even more rights than life, the question of Hamlet is perfectly possible. Certainly "to be" means for Hamlet to live, not to be to die. But imagine that this happens not on earth but on Olympus, among the gods who were, to be sure, pagan but nevertheless immortal. Could such a question have come to the mind of Jupiter, Apollo, or Mars? Even though they were omniscient, how could they have guessed that "being" has as its correlate "non-being"? Their being is by its very nature such that it does not at all presuppose non-being and cannot be transformed into non-being. Men also, whatever their intellectual capacities may be, could never have arrived by way of logic at the idea of non-being. But if Hamlet and all of us with him, philosophers or not, reflect on non-being, we do this only because empirical reality, which may perhaps be falsifying, shows us the possibility of non-being, which *an und für sich* * may be impossible.

And our so presumptuous reason fell this time, as it had already

* In and of itself.

done hundreds and thousands of times before, into a trap. It took an illusion of the senses that it always despises for its own ideas, and indeed the purest ideas. But do not think that I wish to present to you new proofs for the immortality of the soul. There is no need, I think, of new ones; the old ones suffice. They are even already too much. If it were in my power, I would perhaps forbid speaking of them for the reason, among others, that the habit we have of considering true only what is demonstrated is the most detestable and pernicious of habits. When one searches for proofs in the empirical sciences, this is still very well. In this domain everyone proceeds at least with a *reservatio mentalis:* * since it is proven only empirically it is only a conditioned and relative truth which may be replaced by another relative truth.

Experience teaches us, for example, that the seeds of beets produce beets and that the seeds of cucumbers produce cucumbers. We know this because it has always happened so. One sows beet seeds and beets grow; one sows cucumber seeds and obtains cucumbers. But if everything changed so that from beet seeds suddenly came oranges, bananas, pineapples, calves, or even rhinoceroses, we should at first be very astonished, for this would be contrary to our expectations, but we would have nothing to say against it and would only find ourselves under obligation to note the new order of things, which we would formulate thus: the seeds of beets sometimes produce pineapples, sometimes calves, and sometimes also rhinoceroses. Our descendants in ten or twenty generations, having become accustomed to the new order of things and having adapted themselves to it, will understand it as well as we understand the present order and will even explain it through the influence of climate, soil, the presence of radium, etc. For the fact that a small grain produces an enormous beet is as incomprehensible, despite all the explanations of the botanists, as the birth of a rhinoceros from the same grain. Is it not so?

* Mental reservation.

Here is another example—I am forever concerned with making myself clear. We know that light rays follow a straight line. Consequently, if we place between a source of light and a screen some object that intercepts the rays, a shadow must appear on the screen. But what if light rays become tired of following straight lines and begin to describe curves? We could do nothing but register our new experiences. Why, finally, must light rays always follow a straight line? Why not assume that they are afraid of certain objects and carefully curve around them? It may actually be that light cannot stand "witches" and that in the Middle Ages, when witches still existed, it was easy to recognize them by the sign that they did not cast any shadow.

In general, it must be admitted that the constancy of the phenomenon of nature is a fact that is enigmatic and mysterious to the highest degree. I am even prepared to say that it presents an almost anti-natural character. What great efforts we must expend before bringing any living being to even relative constancy. But light rays are constant, stones and metals are also, and they are so to such a degree and follow with such regularity the way on which they have once set out, that no mathematician could demand more. Whence comes this puzzling constancy? Why for millions of years has no light ray ever traced a curve, no stone floated on water, and no beet seed produced pineapples? Say what you will, I find this strange and monstrous, and only the inertia of our stupid and cocksure reason has found for this order of things the epithet "natural."

But this is still not all. You know, of course, what the theory of probability, the laws of great numbers, and statistics are. And you know also that in social phenomena a certain regularity and constancy of order has been established. Not only is the number of male births in each country always a little above the number of female births, but human absent-mindedness is even subject to a certain rule: the statisticians have established that the number of unaddressed letters deposited in post-boxes does not vary significantly from one year to another. Absent-mindedness, how-ever, assumes many forms. One can forget one's cane or umbrella, take someone else's hat, forget to write an address on an envelope. And if it be said that poor human beings must have a determinate index of absent-mindedness, one should at least allow us a certain liberty in the choice of the diverse manifestations of this absent-mindedness. But, no! Someone watches carefully that the number of envelopes without address, umbrellas lost and overcoats put on by mistake, etc., not pass the limits of the established norm. But there is yet more! Try to throw a coin into the air. As long as you repeat this act only a small number of times, complete free-dom is given you. The coin will sometimes fall heads, sometimes tails, as usually happens; but reproduce this act on a large scale and then there is an end to your freedom. It is as if someone begins to push your arm and, whether you wish it or not, the number of falls on heads or tails become almost equal. "Proud" reason felt very offended that regimentation was pushed to such details and, following its habit, immediately found a "natural" explanation. This must be so because, if there are no special grounds for the coin's falling on one side rather than the other, the number of falls on heads and on tails must almost balance. But is this an explanation? There is no ground for the number of falls to be equal! The correct conclusion would be the follow-ing: since there is no reason that the number of falls, heads or tails, should be equal, nor that one should be larger or smaller than the other, the results can be different each time: in one case the coin will fall heads more often, in another case tails will predominate, and in a third they will perhaps be balanced. And that this deduction is correct, that is, that the law of large num-bers does not at all dissipate the strangeness of the phenomena in question and does not explain anything, is indirectly proven by the fact that many logicians have tested the matter experimentally by throwing a coin into the air up to 10,000 times. And they be-came convinced experimentally that there was nothing to be done here: someone limits the freedom of the coin's fall and brings it about that a certain norm is realized. The experimental demonstration is obviously irrefutable, all the more so as it has been repeated many times under the most varied circumstances. But the explanation is worth nothing, or rather, it is not an explanation, just as there is no explanation for the fact that beet seeds never produce pineapples and that light rays never follow curved lines.

I insist that the customary explanations are unacceptable not through caprice and not even through conscientiousness, though, to tell the truth, these motives are not to be rejected as not answering the circumstances. On the contrary, in such cases we should encourage caprice and even—*horribile dictu*—conscientiousness, the most taboo virtue of our day. What matter that conscientiousness is not clothed in the latest fashion and does not know how to make much of itself. It also, despite its respectable age, wishes still to live.

But it is only in passing that I wished to take under my protection the caprice which would play at being a young man and that poor old grandmother, conscientiousness. In reality, I have completely other concerns. It is much more important to me at this moment to show in what nets modern thought struggles and how easily it accepts as indubitable truth the first absurdity that is offered to it—and this even though all the philosophers, following the example of Descartes, begin by trying to drive from their heads all the dust that thousand-year-old prejudices and superstition had deposited there. We are convinced that philosophy is a science and even an explanatory science. And we even imagine that "the metaphysical need" is the need to "understand" life. This prejudice is even older than the virtue of honesty and at least a thousand times more tenacious of life than all the virtues taken together.

I think that Thales, Anaximander and, in general, those Greek sages who first formulated this prejudice did not invent it themselves but found it already at hand. The monotonous centuries have passed and this prejudice is still living, and not only living but as young and fresh as if it were born yesterday, so that it appears incapable of growing old. Men willingly accept every explanation, even the most absurd, provided that the universe no longer have a mysterious aspect. They wish to "understand" life, to discover its meaning. But in reality if there is anything that needs to be explained it is "meaning" and not life. If we must explain something it is rather meaning in terms of life and not life in terms of meaning. They wish to explain nature "naturally," and with an obstinacy worthy of a better fate they have been training themselves to think for generations now that the "natural" is a principle to which everything that exists may be reduced. When it is impossible to do otherwise, they maim their logic, which is already sufficiently miserable, in order, by means of its feeble exorcisms, to drive out of life everything that is most charming and most attractive in it, devising the theory of large numbers, etc. Why all this? Why does mankind have such great confidence in what is limited? And to what will this lead us?

And yet, dear readers, *sursum corda*! I can console you very well. Whatever be the praises which human beings sing to the glory of the "natural," whatever be their struggles against the unnatural, their efforts will lead to nothing. The Demiurge of whom they do not wish to take account does his work all the more calmly. We have seen that light rays obey him and that even the coin a man holds between his fingers follows the way he indicates. Therefore, one can also omit reflecting on the meaning of life.

On the Sources
of Knowledge

Parmenides already said: τὸ γὰρ αὐτὸ νοεῖν ἐστί τε καὶ εἶναι. And Plotinus repeats after him: ὀρθῶς ἄρα "τὸ γὰρ αὐτὸ νοεῖν ἐστί τε καὶ εἶναι," that is, "it is rightly said that to think and to be is the same thing."

Plotinus, like most of the philosophers and metaphysicians, wishes to place rational knowledge above sensible knowledge. Here νοεῖν means something other than Descartes' *cogitare*. Descartes explained that *cogitationis nomine intelligo illa omnia, quae nobis consciis, in nobis sunt, quatenus eorum in nobis conscientia est: atque ita non modo intelligere, velle, imaginari, sed etiam sentire idem est hoc quod cogitare.** In Plotinus the intelligible world is opposed to the sensible world as reality is opposed to what is not real, as what truly exists is opposed to the non-existent. He argues chiefly by appealing to the unstable and transitory character of sensible phenomena and the eternity of the intelligible world. His proofs are nothing other finally than a kind of *exercitia spiritualia* which have as their goal to accustom man little by little to despise the sensible world and to adore the

---

* By the term cogitation or thinking, I understand all those things which are in us and conscious to us insofar as a consciousness of them is in us; and therefore not only knowing, wishing, imagining, but even sensing is the same thing as thinking.

intelligible world. Whole pages, chapters, entire books even, of his remarkable works are devoted to promoting this goal. Plotinus, like Plato, rises to the heights of true pathos when he speaks of the beauty of the intelligible world and of the defects of the sensible world.

A question: how did the philosophers themselves arrive at such a valuation of the two worlds? Were they first obliged to undergo those same *exercitia spiritualia* that they now make their readers undergo, or did they follow a different order: did they first feel—one knows not why—a disgust for the sensible world and then, when they failed to arouse the same sentiments in others, think up their argumentations? This is, for several reasons, a very important question. First, if their love for the intelligible world and their disgust for the sensible world is a fact, this would remain unchanged even if it should be found that their argumentation is insufficiently proven. Then, if we leave the argumentation aside, the fact itself will reveal to our eyes a completely different meaning. Plato and Plotinus prefer the intelligible world to the sensible world. They aspire only to pure ideas. And they say that there, in the world of pure ideas, everything is wondrously beautiful. One can give them no reply, and if one will trust the tone of their discussions, there is also no need for this: one feels that they speak of things they have seen.

But there are other people who have spoken just as well and with just as much passion about the sensible world. The painters in their works have glorified the world of colors no less than that of lines. The musicians will never renounce sounds: Colors, it is true, pale and sounds vanish as soon as they are uttered. But the painters and musicians know this, and it does not trouble them in the least. They continue to do their work and to love it. And I think that one can establish an identity between "thinking" and "being" only on condition of a certain *reservatio mentalis.* If one renounces it, he will be obliged to speak respectfully, to "interpret" Plato and Plotinus considerably, or, to speak freely and simply, to propose to them that they limit their pretensions. The intelligible world may be entirely surrendered to them: let them live there in that sublime joy of which they sing so enthusiastically. (Plotinus, in my opinion, speaks at times of the intelligible world quite as well as Plato himself.) But it would be better if they completely renounced arguments and proofs. Everything seems to indicate, indeed, that they loved their intelligible world before they found arguments proving its superiority to the sensible world. And, really, there is nothing bad in this; it is even very good, for we must say that, as far as arguments and proofs are concerned, the situation is much less favorable than people ordinarily think. I shall say even more: as far as arguments are concerned, it is very bad. Everyone can convince himself of this if he will read carefully any solid manual on the history of philosophy, so that it is not necessary for me to be concerned with justifying my statement.

Neither Plato nor Plotinus succeeded in demonstrating in absolutely convincing fashion that the world they preferred is actually the only real and the best of all possible worlds. But they succeeded, and that very well, in demonstrating that they loved their world and that this world was worthy of love. Is this too little? Is it absolutely necessary that all men and all reasonable beings be obliged to admit that salvation lies only in the intelligible world and that outside it there can be no life? Plotinus himself who, following Plato, glorifies pure reason and looks down contemptuously on the other sources of knowledge, could not prevent himself from having recourse to charming "conviction" and even once compares "pure reason" with its necessary deductions to brute mechanical force. When, then, was Plotinus right? When, following the general example, he glorified pure reason, or when he welcomed charming "conviction"? You will tell me that you do not understand this question, that "pure reason" cannot be compared to capricious "conviction," no matter how charming the latter may be, and that Plotinus, like Plato, always venerated pure reason and if he speaks of "conviction" it is only out of consideration for his readers. It may be so, but it may also be otherwise. It may be that the exclusive love Plotinus (and Plato) expressed for "pure reason" testifies precisely to an all too human weakness. Plotinus loves the intelligible world but is afraid—and this is very human—that his love may prove to be "forbidden," "illegal," and that someone may place a hand on it and tear it away from him. And he continues to be afraid until he succeeds in protecting it against every attack by the high walls of so-called proofs or in forcibly gathering together, at least in imagination, all men, all reasonable beings, in one place and wresting from them the solemn promise that they will never attack the object of his love. You see, he feels a very human fear. I shall go further: it is the fear of the bandit who has stolen and wishes to preserve the fruits of his theft, to defend them by force if necessary. Do not take amiss the crudeness of my expression: I love and respect Plotinus no less than you. This crudeness is not aimed at Plotinus but at the way in which he is read and understood. Certainly it is not we who invented this way. It has existed since the most ancient times. Men have always believed only in physical force and, following their ideals and beliefs, have created the image of "the truth girded with the sword." Without "necessity" no one would agree to subject himself, and people wish the λόγος to have the same power of coercion as the stone or club which, if one knows how to handle them, are alone capable of guaranteeing to man a peaceful and comfortable existence in this world. Obviously, if necessity is an intelligible essence, *primum movens immobile*, the supreme principle of the universe, then there is nothing to do. We must obey, just as we should have had to obey if the "force and matter" of the materialists were the final elements of being. But there is no occasion for rejoicing here. It would be good to love the intelligible world if it offered itself freely to our love, relying on charming "conviction" (πειθώ) and not on the brutal λόγος, alias mechanical force

($\beta i \alpha$). But then it would not need to arm itself with a sword or club. Then it would not need to be the only true world and to fight other worlds, disputing their right to the predicate "being." Beauty is neither jealous nor fearful: it has confidence in itself and calmly exists in proximity with another beauty. Only mortal man, who has still not left the period of struggle for existence, is jealous by nature. He must raise walls to protect himself against his neighbors or bury in the ground the riches he has acquired in the struggle for existence; otherwise they may be taken away from him.

Let us, then, render the homage due the wisdom of Plotinus and Plato. Let us accept their intelligible world, even though it does not appear to us as the only real world or, rather, precisely because it does not appear to us as the only real world. It is beautiful, but there are many other beautiful things on earth— where nothing is known of the struggle for existence, where there is no fear and therefore no λόγος, where men sing and do not demonstrate, where they cannot even understand why proofs were invented.

A Question

Today sensible goods are accessible to all. The crudest man, even the savage, sees the sun and the sky, hears the song of the nightingale, breathes the odor of lilac and lily of the valley, etc. Spiritual goods, on the contrary, are the lot only of the elect. But what if the opposite were the case: what if spiritual goods were accessible to all, what if everyone could assimilate geometry, logic, and the lofty ideals of morality, while sight, hearing, sense of smell were the portion of some only? How then would we establish our hierarchy? Would we continue, as before, to consider spiritual goods beautiful and sublime and declare sensible goods vile and base? Or would the *arbiter elegantium* (you know, of course, who he is and where he is to be sought) be obliged to proceed to a transmutation of values?

De Profundis

What must a man do to penetrate into the mysterious domain of philosophy? Schelling says: *Der erste Schritt zur Philosophie und die Bedingung, ohne welche man auch nicht einmal in sie hineinkommen kann, ist die Einsicht: dass das absolut Ideale auch das absolut Reale sei.** That is, as long as a man will not understand that the absolutely ideal is also the absolutely real, he will not be able even to approach philosophy. On the same subject Hegel writes: *Wenn man anfängt zu philosophieren, muss die Seele zuerst such in diesem Aether der Einen Substanz baden, in der Alles, wass man für wahr gehalten hat, untergegangen ist; diese Negation alles Besondern, zu der die Philosophie gekommen sein muss, ist die Befreiung des Geistes und seine absolute Grundlage.*† That is to say, for Hegel the beginning of philosophy consists in the soul's plunging into the ether of the unique substance; it is in this that the deliverance of the soul and its absolute principle consists.

* The first step to philosophy and the condition without which one could not arrive at it at all is this insight: that the absolutely ideal is also the absolutely real.
† When one begins to philosophize, the soul must first of all bathe itself in the ether of the one substance in which everything that one has taken to be true has been dissolved; this negation of everything particular to which philosophy must come is the liberation of the spirit and its absolute foundation.

We could certainly find among the ancients statements that are very close to those of Schelling and Hegel. But in Plato and Aristotle we also find statements of a quite different character. Plato says: μάλα γὰρ φιλοσόφου τοῦτο τὸ πάθος, τὸ θαυμάζειν. οὐ γὰρ ἄλλη ἀρχὴ φιλοσοφίας ἢ αὕτη, which means, "The faculty of being astonished is particularly appropriate to the philosopher, and outside this faculty there is no other origin for philosophy" (*Th. 155D*). Aristotle shares the same opinion: διὰ τό θαυμάζειν οἱ ἄνθρωποι καὶ τὸ νῦν καὶ τὸ πρῶτον ἤρξαντο φιλοσοφεῖν, that is, "both now and formerly men always began to philosophize through wonder or astonishment."

As for Schopenhauer, he is certain that a man becomes a philosopher only and for as long as he feels that the world "is his representation." He who has not become aware of this truth cannot be and will never become a philosopher. Schopenhauer believed, furthermore, that he had found this peculiar conception of philosophy in the works of Kant. From everything that Kant wrote, Schopenhauer took only this idea, which is not really to be found in Kant. At present philosophy is extremely ill-disposed to Kant and his phenomenalism. The slogan of modern philosophy is ontology. But one need examine modern ontology only a little more closely to become convinced that it is not so distant from Kant as it imagines, that it is even very close to him and continues to follow the same rut into which Kant fell without wishing it. The problem remains always the same: to justify, by all possible means, reason and its sovereign rights. The strange thing is that the phenomenalist Schopenhauer seeks to attain through the visible world the invisible essences much more passionately than the ontologists who are so sure of themselves. It is obvious that our oppositions finally do not express much: the difference between theoretical ontologism and theoretical phenomenalism is no greater than between St. Augustine's *amor Dei usque ad contemptum sui* and *amor sui usque ad contemptum Dei*. It may be that it is not possible and not necessary to break all the relationships between ontologism and phenomenalism: both come from God. And *amor Dei* certainly does not necessarily presuppose *contemptum sui*, just as *amor sui* does not demand *contemptum Dei*. Love for one's family and for one's country often imposes upon man, under the conditions of our actual existence, scorn and hatred for the family of others and for the neighboring country. For men are always obliged to distribute, and it is necessary to choose between one's own family and that of others. But with God it is not a question of sharing: one can love Him without this love demanding the renunciation of self, in the ordinary sense of the word. Moreover, love of God is incompatible with contempt for self. One can also love the invisible world without rejecting the visible world.

But in the philosophy which lives on concepts and seeks its ideals in pure concepts, in the philosophy which is constructed on the model of mathematics, contradictions are inevitable. The squaring of the circle is impossible. The circle loves itself *usque ad contemptum* of the square, and the square loves itself *usque ad contemptum* of the circle. And as long as philosophy holds its gaze fixed on the world of ideal essences and on mathematics as the science of ideal essences κατ ἐξοχὴν,* philosophy will be a science and assume that *verum index est sui et falsi* † and that *verum* and *falsum* are irreconcilables to such a degree that if one does not flee the false, one will never arrive at the true. Here is why, in opposition to the rationalist philosophers, it must be said that philosophy does not begin when man finds an indubitable criterion of truth. On the contrary, philosophy will begin only when man has lost all criteria of truth, when he feels that he cannot have any criteria and that there is even no need of any.

Likewise a sleeper will awake not when he has become convinced that his sleep-consciousness is the unity of all that exists or the identity of thought and being (for sleep also has its logic;

---

* Pre-eminently.
† The truth is the index of itself and of what is false.

in sleep men also aspire to "unity" and to the identification of thought and reality: it is necessary to keep this well in mind), but only when he will become convinced that he sleeps and that his dreams are not all of reality but merely a small part separated from the rest, or even only the presentiment of reality. In the state of waking we are obviously less bound than in sleep. But we are also far from free when we are awake. And as long as man does not feel this directly, as long as he is convinced that the state of waking is absolutely contrary to that of sleep, that only when he is awake is he free, and that his freedom is expressed in the creative work of that best part of his being which is called reason—he is still not a philosopher.

One must not stupefy his mind through "explanations," even metaphysical explanations, of the enigmas of being but, on the contrary, try to remain awake. Now, to awaken it is necessary that man become painfully aware of the chains that sleep imposes upon him. It is necessary that he recognize that it is precisely reason, which we are accustomed to consider as a liberating force and one capable of awakening us, which keeps us in the state of torpor. It may be that asceticism and the enigmatic tortures it imposes are the expression of that unconscious *élan* toward awakening which lives in the heart of man, while rational philosophy is born out of man's need not to pass beyond the limits of a partial awakening in this life. But another supposition may also be admitted. It may be that the irreconcilable hostility that exists between the rationalistic philosophers and the μισόλογοι (to use Platonic language) comes from a still deeper source. It may be that men are pushed toward this or that philosophy by their metaphysical predestination. We must not have too much confidence in the methods of ordinary reflection that operates through general ideas. It is very risky to consider ὁ ἄνθρωπος and τὶς ἄνθρωπος—that is to say, man in general and this particular man, exclusively from the point of view of their logical relationship, the first containing in himself the second. *Non includit contradictionem*, as the Scholastics liked to express themselves, that some τὶς ἄνθρωπος possesses a predicate which excludes all possibility of being brought into the species ὁ ἄνθρωπος. Certainly if some concrete individual is found to have only one arm or one leg, while man in general must have two, or if he is blind, deaf or mute, this will not at all prevent us from including him in the species man. But if someone were born with wings or with two heads, would we still be able to call him "man"? Or if someone possessed the faculty of transforming himself into some animal at will or of contemplating the past and future as clearly as we see the present? I shall be told that this has never happened and never can happen. I answer that not only have you no right to affirm that it cannot happen but you do not even know if it never has happened. You have never seen it—that is all. But there are many things that you have never seen. We do not see, and that very often even, what happens under our very eyes. We do not wish to see it because it is not fitting or because our soul does not presently accept it. At times, however, it would be well to see not only what is but also what is not and what has never been. If we wish to develop our faculty of perceiving the world we must give full freedom to our fantasy. We must "think" of beings with two or three heads or even without any head at all, of clairvoyant beings, etc. We must go even further: we know that the empirical destinies of men are very different. Some are born Alexanders and Platos, others, idiots and devoid of all talent. Why are we so sure that inequality is possible only in the empirical world? It is very probable that the metaphysical destinies of men are also extremely different. To one person it is given to live only once; he appeared for the first and last time by being born into this world; he has neither past nor future. He must make haste to eat his fill of days during his short existence on this earth between birth and death. His motto is *carpe diem;* he is always in a hurry. That is why he is a positivist and immanentist. Nothing exists and nothing can exist for him outside what he has here at hand. He wishes to see even God here (the

men of the Middle Ages called this *fruitio Dei*), for he feels that
if he does not see God here, he will never see Him anywhere.
It is, indeed, not only atheists who are positivists; believers are
no less inclined to positivism at times, as the history of Catholicism and many other histories show.
Positivism is certainly right as far as it goes. It is wrong only
when it generalizes its statements by declaring that they apply to
ὁ ἄνθρωπος and not to τὶς ἄνθρωπος. But there is perhaps a man or
men who have already existed more than once, who are called
to exist again after their death. The soul which Lermontov's
angel carried in his arms and which before appearing in this
world had already heard celestial melodies is also an ἄνθρωπος,
like the soul which was conceived naturally, developed in its
mother's womb and heard, at birth, not the singing of angels but
its own plaintive cry. It is completely impossible to unite in
one and the same species two "objects" so different from each
other. The fact that the two souls have similar bodies, that they
both live on earth, pay taxes, learn grammar, and earn their bread
by the sweat of their brow, does not suffice to justify treating
them equally. The whale, for example, appears to be a fish. It
lives in the sea, it has the tail of a fish, in short it has everything
a fish has, and yet only ignorant and uneducated people call it a
fish. Well, I think that when we speak of ὁ ἄνθρωπος, man, it is as
if we forced into the concept of fish not only the whale but also
lions, tigers, and royal eagles.

What to do? How manage to avoid errors that are shameful
and fatal in their consequences? I think we must begin by not
taking mathematics as the model of philosophic knowledge. I
know this is difficult, but it is just as difficult if we do take
mathematics for a model. Spinoza himself who, indeed, constructed his philosophy *more geometrico*,* ends his *Ethics* with
these words: *sed omnia praeclara tam difficilia, quam rara sunt.*†
But in the same Spinoza, philosophy resembles mathematics only

---

* In the geometric fashion.
† But all things excellent are as difficult as they are rare.

externally. In reality it is philosophy, which means that almost everything in it that needs be demonstrated remains undemonstrated, and, on the other hand, only what can be admitted without demonstration is demonstrated.

But this is still only the beginning. The further one goes, the greater the difficulties become. But why calculate them here? If it were I who had thought out the difficulties, I would have to justify myself and bargain. But I am to be left out of the question here, just as are you, my reader. If you wish to blame anyone, address yourself to Him who created this life that is so fantastic, so peculiar, so unnatural, that does not permit itself to be enclosed either in the formulas of mathematics or in general concepts.

Furthermore, it must be noted that the term "difficult" is very relative. It is difficult for a small child to smoke and drink alcohol, but many an adult would give up eating if only he had a pipe and a good bottle. And now, let me be allowed to quote a very famous philosopher, Plotinus. Ἡ δὲ ἀνδρεία ἀφοβία θανάτου. ὁ δ' ἐστι χωρὶς εἶναι τὴν ψυχὴν _οι σώματος. οὐ φοβεῖται δὲ τοῦτο, ὃς ἀγαπᾷ μόνος γένεσθαι. So speaks Plotinus, and I think that if one does not interpret them according to the ordinary methods of our "understanding," the meaning of his words cannot be in doubt. "Courage consists in not fearing death. Death is the separation of the soul from the body.* He will not dread this separation who loves to be alone." †

People will tell me—or they will not tell me, it is I who will tell myself—that Potinus was a decadent in philosophy. So? A decadent—then no longer a fish but a whale? Such a τὶς ἄνθρωπος that it is impossible to force him into the concept of ὁ ἄνθρωπος? You do not agree? You say that he was nevertheless only an ἄνθρωπος who was mistaken? You must necessarily say this in

* This is the customary definition of death in Plato. Cf. *Phaedo* 64E and *Gorgias* 254B.
† *Enneads* I, VI, 6. My translation is not literal. But it conforms, I believe, to the spirit of the Plotinian philosophy.

order to preserve the traditional philosophy. And I even helped you by suggesting to you that Plotinus was a decadent. But, then, he must be separated from the tradition of philosophy and examined apart. But even if you wish to reject him, you will perhaps nevertheless not refuse to listen to how the whale converses with fishes?

Why, then, does he only who "loves" to be alone not fear death? Precisely "loves"; he not only dares but wishes it. This means precisely that τὶς ἄνθρωπος escapes from ὁ ἄνθρωπος, just as a butterfly leaves the chrysalis, and will not for anything in the world go back into the prison of the general idea. He was a man like all others who easily found a place in the universals that had been determined for him. But suddenly some mysterious, unknown force drives him out of his customary domicile without even telling him where it proposes to lead him.

A strange thing! The decadents of all times, including our contemporary Nietzsche, tried to fight against destiny, against the fate determined for them. Nietzsche, like Plotinus, made desperate efforts to recover his place in ὁ ἄνθρωπος. But *fata volentem ducunt, nolentem trahunt.** There is no choice for man. Once he has fallen out of his "species" he cannot return to it.

And now listen to the testimony of some of these τὶς ἄνθρωπος. Nietzsche speaks to us of the Eternal Return: he has already been on earth an infinite number of times and will return to it an infinite number of times. Plotinus also had always existed in the One, and he announces in inspired words that soon, after his death, he will return to the kingdom where he was before his birth. It is clear that both of them speak the truth (though their statements, from our point of view, are mutually exclusive), that their metaphysical destinies were different. And it is clear also that the metamorphoses which await them are so different that it is absolutely impossible to reduce both of them to the same type, the same kind of being, without destroying the fundamental

* The Fates lead the willing man, the unwilling they drag.

rules of classification or, rather, without deliberately violating them. And certainly one cannot in any case reduce them to the type ἄνθρωπος, if we include in it, for example, Haeckel, who knows definitely that he is descended from an ape and who is so certain of it that, without the least hesitation, he considers Nietzsche's and Plotinus' statements absurdities.

These examples, it seems to me, reveal with sufficient clarity the fundamental defect of rationalistic thought, that thought which is *de facto* considered the only possible one by the representatives of all philosophical systems, whatever their differences in all other respects may be.

Let us listen to what Spinoza says in one of his letters (LXXIV): *Ego non praesumo, me optimam invenisse philosophiam, sed veram me intelligere scio. Quomodo autem id sciam, si roges, respondebo, eodem modo ac tu scis trea angulos trianguli aequales esse duobus rectis; et hoc sufficire negabit nemo, cui sanum est cerebrum.* And every philosopher must repeat after Spinoza: "I do not suppose that I have found the best philosophy, but I know that I have recognized the true philosophy. And if you ask me how I know this, I shall answer, in the same way that you know that the sum of the angles of a triangle is equal to two right angles. And that this is sufficient, no one who has a healthy mind will deny." Spinoza is simply more daring, frank, and consistent than the other philosophers. It was also he who said: *Ea enim omnia, quae clare et distincte intellegimus, Dei idea (ut modo indicavimus) et natura nobis dictat, non quidem verbis, sed modo longe excellentiore et qui cum natura mentis optime convenit, ut unusquisque, qui certitudinem intellectus gustavit, apud se sine dubio expertus est (Tract. Theol. Polit., I, 5).* And finally: *Qui veram habet ideam,*

* Now all the things which we understand clearly and distinctly, the idea of God (as we have just now indicated) and nature dictate to us, not indeed by words, but in a way far more excellent and one which agrees best with the nature of the mind, as every one who has tasted the certitude of the intellect has doubtless experienced within himself.

simul scit se veram habere ideam, nec de rei veritate potest dubitare (Eth. II, XLIII).*

I repeat and emphasize expressly: these statements of Spinoza are the true postulates of the thought of all those who believe that every τὶς ἄνθρωπος finds a place in ὁ ἄνθρωπος. And since I have never as yet met any philosopher who did not base himself on this postulate as on a self-evident truth, all the philosophers appear to be Spinozists. All of them, and the theologians also—for example, St. Augustine. The only exception—but only for a moment—is offered us by Tertullian in his well-known statement that shocks even the Catholic theologians but is worthy of being recalled as often as possible: *Crucifixus est Dei filius; non pudet quia pudendum est. Et mortuus est Dei filius; prorsus credibile est quia ineptum est. Et sepultus ressurexit; certum est quia impossibile est (De Carne Christi, V).†*

Apart from Tertullian I do not know of anyone in the philosophic literature who experienced, even if only for a moment, a similar illumination, permitting him to rid himself of the "commandments of reason." All wish, on general principles, *gustare certitudinem intellectus;* ‡ everyone who has a *vera idea, simul scit se veram habere ideam,*§ and knows it for the same reason that he knows that the sum of the angles of a triangle is equal to two right angles. Here is something to think about. If I have a true idea about something, I know at the same time that I have a true idea and can no longer doubt it. This is certainly not a simple tautology; Spinoza's formulas are extremely cautious and consistent. Spinoza wished to express in his theorem the same thought that is found in the *Tractatus Theologico-Politicus:*

---

* He who has a true idea at the same time knows that he has a true idea, nor can he doubt the truth of the thing.
† The Son of God was crucified; it does not cause shame because it must shame us. And the Son of God died; again, it is credible because it is absurd. And having been buried, he arose again; it is certain because it is impossible.
‡ To taste the certitude of the intellect.
§ A true idea at the same time knows that he has a true idea.

there is a certain state of mind, *certitudo*, which is born in man in connection with the appearance in him of a true idea and which, insofar as it puts an end to all doubts, is the proof and result of the discovery of the truth for all alike. It is clear that every philosopher who seeks the one truth for all must share Spinoza's thought. Otherwise, that seeker is not a philosopher.

But let us pass from general rules to particular cases. Let us ask, in other words, how Spinoza's theorem was applied in practice. The best method is to examine the truths found by Spinoza himself. Already in his *Cogitata Metaphysica*, in the paragraph entitled *Dari voluntatem*, Spinoza stops at the famous question of Buridan's ass. What would happen to a starving ass if it found itself at an equal distance between two bales of hay? And what would a man do if he found himself in a situation analogous to that of Buridan's ass? Spinoza answers without hesitation: *si enim hominem loco asinae ponamus in tali aequilibrio positum, homo non pro re cogitante, sed pro turpissimo asino erit habendus, si fame et siti pereat (Cogit. Met.*, II, XII).* Several years later Spinoza in his *Ethics* again finds himself before this question and gives it an exactly opposite answer: *Dico, me omnino concedere, quod homo in talio aequilibrio positus (nempe qui nihil aliud percipit, quam sitim et famem, talem cibum et talem potum, qui aeque ab eo distant) fame et siti peribit (Eth.*, II, XLIX, Scholium).† This means, brushing aside metaphors, that Spinoza in the first case affirmed the truth that the will is free and in the second case that it is not free. And in both cases he made his affirmation with perfect certainty, feeling undoubtedly the sentiment of which he said, *unusquisque, qui certitudinem gustavit, apud se sino dubio expertus est.*

---

* For if we should put a man in the same place as the ass and in a similar equilibrium, the man must be considered not a thinking being but a very stupid ass if he would perish of hunger and thirst.
† I say, I wholly admit that a man placed in such an equilibrium (namely, as perceiving nothing but hunger and thirst, a certain food and a certain drink, each equally distant from him) would perish of hunger and thirst.

What is involved here? If the same man, though at different moments (I say at different moments but the question may be posed in a wider fashion), sees the predicates of truth as such in judgments that are mutually exclusive, can these predicates be considered as belonging properly to truth, i.e., as distinguishing it from error? Either the will of man is free or it is not free. Nevertheless Spinoza *gustavit certitudinem,* both when he adopted the positive answer and when he accepted the negative answer to this question. And I assume that *unusquisque apud se sine dubio expertus est,* that everyone has more than once experienced the same thing as Spinoza.

It follows with complete clarity from this example that *gustamus certitudinem* not necessarily in direct connection with the knowledge of truth, that the feeling of certitude is autonomous and satisfies itself, that it comes and goes independently of whether we have found truth or error, and that it has nothing to do with the question whether in general there is any possibility of discovering any truth whatsoever. Spinoza, like every rationalist, i.e., every man who wishes under all circumstances at any price to understand everything that exists by his own powers, had recourse to a generalization that is completely unnecessary and impermissible. Certainly everyone knows through his own experience that the statement, the sum of the angles of a triangle is equal to two right angles, is accompanied by *certitudo.* But there is no reason to conclude from this that every *certitudo* is conditioned by the discovery of a truth. Our old whale again protests and is unwilling to be found in the company of the fish. There is *certitudo* and *certitudo.* There are, indeed, certitudes that are born from the grasping of truth, but there are others that derive from quite different parentage. One can even very well admit *generatio aequivoca,* spontaneous generation. And there is no reason to deny the possibility of certitude as a gracious gift of heaven, as *gratia* and precisely *gratia gratis data,* awarded not in recompense for our merits but through the great mercy of God and also (and this, to my mind, is most correct) in punishment for our sins.

Look at the uneducated people who are sure that the earth does not move, that the sun circles the earth, and that the moon moves through the clouds—as sure as we are of our truths. Whence comes their *certitudo*, when it is assuredly known that they are in error? And even we educated people—do we not admire the blue canopy of the heavens, having understood long ago that there is no canopy? The rationalist does not take account of this. He wishes to be proud and will accept nothing freely, or pretends in any case not to do so: if he possesses any certainty, he has obtained it himself. This is why Descartes repeated so obstinately that God could not deceive men. It seemed to him that if God could deceive men, everything was lost. But, first, he was factually wrong. God does deceive men. The Bible speaks of it often, and we can convince ourselves of it with our own eyes at every step. Recall the examples quoted above about the earth, the sun, the clouds. If God had organized our sight differently, we should not have had to wait thousands of years for the appearance of Copernicus to renounce the illusion of the geocentric system. But God, it seems, wished that we admire the sun and the skies and was not at all afraid to veil the truth through beauty. Man may not lie but God may, for to Him everything is permitted. The rationalists are unwilling to admit a deceiving God, for they do not trust God Himself very much. They wish to make their own reason divine and omnipotent. And, furthermore, it is not even this. In reality they are much more honest. It is perfectly sufficient for them to think that their reason is divine. That is why they never feel troubled by the fact that there are so many divine reasons. They simply ignore this. Each repeats with assurance: "I am right, I have the truth," as if he were deaf from birth and never heard his neighbor cry shrilly the same words, "I am right, I have the truth," even though his truth be a completely different one. It is clear that no one here is concerned with truth, that it is a question of completely other goods, that now as always man remains the same crude egotist that he was in prehistoric times, in the Stone and Bronze Ages.

Contrary, then, to what Hegel and Schelling said, it must be said that man begins to philosophize not when he understands that the absolutely ideal is the absolutely real or that everything is one but, on the contrary, when he drives such ideas beyond the threshold of his consciousness. Plato and Aristotle were much closer to the truth with their διὰ τὸ θαυμάζειν, and Schopenhauer was closer still when he affirmed that the world was his idea. It is only when we feel—διὰ τὸ θαυμάζειν—that the world we know is only our idea, that *certitudo* is possible only in sleep and that the more solid the *certitudo* the more heavy and deep is our sleep, that we can have any hope of awakening. As long as we "know," as long as we "understand," we sleep—and all the more strongly as our judgments are more "clear and distinct," more apodictic. Men must grasp this if they are destined to awaken on earth. But it seems that such is not their destiny. Very few of them, in any case, are so destined, and even these will only half awaken. The great majority die sleeping, just as they have lived sleeping.

So, then, the beginning of philosophy is θαῦμα, wonder, but a θαῦμα which never leads to ἀθαυμασία, the philosophic ideal of Democritus.

Music and Phantoms

Dostoevsky began with terror, reporting in his *Notes from the Underground* his torments and humiliations, and ended with *The Brothers Karamazov* and the prophecies of *The Diary of a Writer*. Tolstoi, on the other hand, began with *Childhood and Adolescence* and *War and Peace* and ended with "The Death of Ivan Ilitch," "Master and Servant," "Father Serge," etc. *Habent sua fata libelli* *—yes, not only *libelli* but *homines* also.

What is the object of philosophy: is it to examine the significance of everything and to seek at all costs to construct a finished theodicy on the model of Leibniz's and of other famous sages? or to explore to the end the destinies of individual men—in other words, to raise questions which exclude in advance the possibility of any intelligible answer whatsoever?

Many remarkable minds have thought—and who can wish to think otherwise?—that the supreme goal of man's earthly life consists in attaining a state such that he can sing a loud hosanna to the entire universe. So that Dostoevsky, if one takes his last "ideas" literally, has already obtained his recompense here on earth. But Tolstoi did not receive it.

Is it thus that the dispute between these two great writers ends? Or was there perhaps no dispute between them?

* Books have their own destinies.

It is only in our limited vision that there is a war of all against all—*bellum omnium contra omnes,* and not only for material rights but also for spiritual rights. Here is a problem that philosophy—one knows not why—carefully avoids, but it is with this problem that we ought to begin and also end. Why did Tolstoi not arrive at the hosanna while Dostoevsky did? The most natural answer is that something prevented him. In other words, Dostoevsky must have had some mysterious source which Tolstoi lacked. Dostoevsky obtained his reward. Is this certain, or do people only imagine that he received it while in fact he did not receive anything at all? And, furthermore, why do some obtain their reward while others receive nothing?

The most important and best works of Dostoevsky—*The Adolescent, The Idiot, The Possessed, The Brothers Karamazov* —were written in the course of the last ten or twelve years of his life, when he had already passed his fiftieth year. Tolstoi, after he was fifty, wrote only one important work. *War and Peace* and *Anna Karenina* appeared when Tolstoi was approaching the half-century mark.

In the last thirty years of his life, it is true, Tolstoi wrote some remarkable works—but all of restricted dimension, except *Resurrection,* which appears to me only an accidental anachronism, a kind of lingering echo of the first period of his literary activity. After *Anna Karenina,* in which Tolstoi still tries to appear as one who has already obtained his reward here on earth, comes a series of works which show us precisely that he had not received any reward and that he did not deserve any. Why, then, was Dostoevsky in such haste to sing hosanna while Tolstoi was incapable of it?

But wherefore could not I pronounce "Amen"?
I had most need of blessing, and "Amen"
Stuck in my throat.

So in Shakespeare speaks the criminal, the regicide Macbeth. When one reads the last works of Tolstoi, one involuntarily hears the words of Macbeth. Ivan Ilitch, Pozdnychev, Brekhounov—all are terrified that the amen dies on their lips. And Father Serge, who could be proud that Europe, skeptical Europe, knew and respected him, felt also what is felt by the soul that dies without penitence, without having received absolution for its sins. Dostoevsky, on the contrary, who produced one novel after another, sang his hosanna ever more loudly, and solemnly and cruelly crushed underfoot all who could not repeat his hymns.

I have here mentioned Tolstoi and Dostoevsky. I can also cite another pair if you wish—Schiller and Shakespeare. Schiller was a great master of solemn speech. It has been said that it was precisely from Schiller that Dostoevsky learned this art. And this, in part, is true. Though Dostoevsky had the greatest admiration for Pushkin, Pushkin lacked what is needed for the office of the teacher, the professor. And to attain the prophetic pathos without which he would not have been able to write much of what he wrote, Dostoevsky had to turn to Schiller.

And so I raise for the third time my question: why is it given to some to proclaim hosanna, while among others the supreme and solemn words die on their lips?

I proceed from the assumption that Schiller and Dostoevsky not only pronounced the words but also felt the sentiments that the hosanna arouses. I make this assumption without having the slightest ground for it. The soul of others is nothing but darkness. It may very well be that the man who shouts words of inspiration is only repeating what he had heard from others, as the contrary may also be: many a time a man takes on a sorrowful air, though every one of his gestures and even his face allow one to guess a more or less well-hidden joy or even triumph.

Look at Schopenhauer, for example. One cannot find, it would seem, in all of philosophic literature another writer who demonstrated with more perseverance and obstinacy the absurdity and purposelessness of our existence; but, on the other hand, it would be difficult to mention a philosopher who could more alluringly lead men into temptation through the mysterious charm of the accessible and inaccessible worlds he described. In this respect few writers, I believe, surpass him. Similarly his disciple who later became his adversary, Nietzsche, proclaimed himself officially an optimist. But in his writings lie so much bitterness, suffering, and horror that if men were capable of reading between the printed lines what the author lived through, it would probably be necessary to ban his books under threat of the worst punishments.

But at this moment it is not this purely psychological question that concerns me. I am not disposed to impart to my readers my reflections on the meaning and significance of this or that philosophic or literary work. Whether Schopenhauer glorifies the world and Nietzsche curses it, or whether the opposite is the case, there is no doubt of the fact that to one man it is given to understand and bless life here on earth, while to another this is not given. One could speak thus not only of writers or, in general, of well-known people. I cite famous names only because everyone knows them. And yet, among those of whom no one has ever heard, who were neither the first nor the second either in Rome or in the village, there are those who sing hosanna freely and easily and there are others whose lips open only to complain that it is impossible for them to pronounce the word. And I believe that these two categories of individuals, who often differ only slightly from each other in their external aspect and even in their earthly destinies and who therefore seem to the non-initiates artificially separated, must not under any circumstances be confused. The artificiality of this division is only apparent. In reality, the divisions that are generally admitted and customary have much less meaning.

Everyone understands, for example, that one can divide individuals into certain categories according to their nationality, religion, social class, etc. It is assumed that these empirical, tangible, and therefore easily realizable divisions apply to what is essential in the individual, and they are readily given even superempirical meaning. For example, when it is a question of nationalities—the French, the English, the Spanish, etc.—it is believed the French are destined to associate with each other and to be together not only here on earth but also in the intelligible world (I detest this stupid word, but for various reasons I do not wish to employ another). The metaphysicians also judge it possible to speak of the "soul" of France, of Italy, etc. And those who speak thus are entirely convinced that they are deepening human knowledge, that with a flap of their wings they can fly from the positive realm into the metaphysical. But can there be anything more superficial than this view?

The idea of the soul of a nation is the purest and most vulgar kind of positivism. Of course every people on earth constitutes a certain unity, bound together by a community of interests, a common past, language, etc. But on earth a herd of cows or horses is also bound together by a community of interests, a common life, and various other commonalities. I hope, however, that we shall not find a metaphysician so poor—even among our contemporaries who are so remarkable for their poverty—who holds it necessary to spur on his poor imagination to the point of "seeing" the soul of a herd of cows or horses. It is true that certain people would be rather inclined to see a soul in a herd of cows or horses—so incapable is everyone today of seeing anything outside of what has earlier been shown. However, the esthetic sentiment forbids it. "The soul of a herd" does not resound solemnly enough in the ears of the metaphysician. It must at least be the soul of Spain! But, actually, the soul of Spain is the same empiricism as the soul of a herd of cows or even of a herd of pigs. The essential thing in this matter is not that Spain is a beautiful country with a great history, while horses are only horses and pigs only pigs. The essential thing is that metaphysics is a more singular, more capricious, more fantastic thing than contemporary intelligence would wish—the intelligence which only seems to have escaped from the chains of positivism to which it has become accustomed and which are so dear to it. Metaphysics cannot in any way be adapted to visible reality. Among us on earth the Frenchman does indeed feel close to the Frenchman, the Englishman to the Englishman. They speak the same language, fight in the ranks of the same army, are protected by the same tariffs, gain and lose together, etc. But in the other world there are neither customs barriers, nor armies, nor expensive and cheap merchandise; there the "community of interests" which we are accustomed to consider the very foundation of being, something eternal and fixed, is only a combination of words devoid of all meaning. There, language itself, the "word," is to all appearance superfluous. There souls walk about not only without garments but also without bodies and do not require any words to communicate among themselves; they need only look at each other in order immediately to understand. So the Frenchman sees the very depths of the soul not only of the Frenchman but also of the Englishman, the Chinese, and even the savage living on some unknown island, if there still is such a thing on earth. I imagine, for instance, that Mozart and Beethoven do not now in the other world converse with their compatriots, Bismarck and Moltke, who ought to be constituents of the soul of Germany with them.

If I could imagine a war of souls in heaven it would be quite clear to me that Mozart and Beethoven together would fire invisible shells at Bismarck and Moltke and would be helped in their work by Musset, Chenier, Baudelaire, and Verlaine, while Napoleon and his marshals would fight with the ranks of Bismarck. In any case, Mozart would never agree to make common cause not only with Bismarck but even, it seems to me, with Kant; it would appear to him too dull, too boring.

Do not imagine, however, that I am here raising objections

against medieval realism or against the idea of the substantial unity of the universe, which is so often spoken of today. If I have ever made any objections against them, these were directed only against the definitions that contemporary philosophy, which wishes to be a rigorous science, gives us of these ideas. Either universalism or individualism, either realism or nominalism. And if it be realism, then it is a realism already completely prepared, conforming to general ideas already constituted; and if it be universalism, it is also a universalism completely prepared, conforming to social groups historically constituted.

All this is absurd, the invention of our poor and sluggish fantasy. Universalism is not at all hostile to individualism, and realism gets along perfectly well with nominalism. But, above all, men may not imagine that they will so easily succeed in untying the Gordian knot of reality. It is not so simple to pass from the visible empirical world to metaphysical realities. There is a Spain and a Denmark, therefore there is a soul of Spain and of Denmark; there are lions, consequently the idea of the lion must exist. You are quite wrong. Granted that collective souls exist, it is not so easy to see them. There is the soul of the musician, the drunkard, the maiden, the monk, the drug addict, etc. But we must not think that the metaphysical soul has taken into itself all the empirical souls whose characteristics correspond to it. It may be that Bernard of Clairvaux and Phidias have entered into the musician's soul, while Caesar Borgia and Nero find themselves included in the monk's soul, and that in the soul of the alcoholic or drug addict live people who never drank a drop of alcohol and did not even know the name of morphine or in any case never used it—Dostoevsky, for example, or Horace who sang of the *aurea mediocritas*. In passing from individual being to collective being, the soul undergoes metamorphoses such as would have astonished Ovid himself. We must always remember this and not allow ourselves to be led astray by the false hope that everything happens in the metaphysical universe as simply as those men who are accustomed to simplifying, through scientific methods, even our empirical reality wish.

But if the metaphysicians should become tired of reflections on the intelligible world, we can recall to them certain things concerning the terrestrial world, things better known and more "natural." In the Middle Ages different peoples, just as today, spoke different languages. But educated people used Latin and at that time even thought in Latin when it was a question of lofty things. Then the obstacles and the frontiers which exist today appeared less insurmountable and were in fact less so. And the books that were then read and from which men drew wisdom and inspiration were the same for all the people of Europe. To be sure, at that time also men argued and fought with each other, but while peoples were differentiated by the same signs that serve to distinguish them today, the souls of learned people, one could say, soared above the nations to which they belonged according to their earthly origins. The French as well as the English and the Italians were divided into Thomists and Scotists. Nominalists and realists wandered all across Europe. The fact that a man belonged to such or such a monastic order was considered a more important characteristic than his nationality. It seems that if one admitted a collective metaphysical soul, it would then have to be the Franciscan or Dominican soul rather than the French or English soul. This means that the substantial unity of men did not depend on the accident of birth but on the commonality of their aspirations and goals. I think, furthermore, that if the metaphysicians were not so afraid to lose all connection with the visible and tangible values of this world, they would also reject the Thomist, Scotist, Franciscan, and Dominican souls. From all this nomenclature emanates an odor—*sit venia verbo*—not only of the earth but of earthly cooking, of the fumes of the kitchen, and of repugnant human sweat. The metaphysicians should be more daring, much more daring, and try to live at their own risk and peril by renouncing values

and categories already made and elaborated by common sense
and history. To encourage them I would quote a famous ancient
philosopher.

I have in mind Plotinus, who today is praised and quoted so
readily by the very people who do not take a single line of his
writings seriously. "Yet among human things is there anything
so great as not to be scorned by him who has risen to a principle
that is above everything and no longer depends on lower things?"
(*Enn.*, I, IV, 7.) For the present this, as you see, is only one of
those statements that are so frequently encountered among philosophers. Who, indeed, has not spoken of the vanity of terrestrial things? What is interesting and striking is not this general
formula which, like every general formula, is irresponsible: it is
spoken, and one passes on. In reality, the whole question is to
know what is to be understood by the terms "supreme good"
and "terrestrial goods." There is nothing easier than to replace
in a formula, according to circumstances, one magnitude with
another. If one wishes, even wealth and power may be called
supreme goods, for it is known that wealth and power can be
used "disinterestedly"—and not only the wealth and power of
one's country or people but even one's own. Napoleon believed
himself a servant of a great idea, and even Brekhounov in Tolstoi's "Master and Servant" respected what he considered his
mission. The originality and audacity of Plotinus does not consist in this general formula, which is finally empty, but in the
content he introduced into it. "Such a man," Plotinus continued,
"will see nothing great in the ordinary favors of fortune, whatever they may be, such as kingdoms, ruling over states and
peoples, founding and building cities, even if it were himself
who had this glory, and he will attach no importance to the loss
of his power or even to the ruin of his fatherland." You see that
it is a question here of something completely different. I should
not be astonished if even a great admirer of Plotinus cried out,
in connection with this passage, that from such nobility to the

most vulgar cowardice is only a step. I think that at the moment
when the fatherland of the philosopher would have actually been
threatened by danger, such sublime speeches would not have
been tolerated; it would not have been noticed that he who pronounced them was destined to immortality.

This, then, is the difference between general ideas and their
realization. But Plotinus speaks with impassivity and assurance,
like a man who possesses the truth, the one eternal truth that is
obligatory for all reasonable beings. "If he regards all this as a
great evil, or even only as an evil, he will make himself ridiculous; he will no longer be a virtuous man for, by Jupiter, he
will regard as great things wood and stones and the death of
mortal beings, whereas he ought to know the indisputable truth
that death is better than corporeal life." Do not think that you
can succeed in frightening Plotinus with threats. Can threats act
upon one who is convinced that death is better than corporeal
life? Not only will he persist in his convictions, but he will
continue to declare them despite all threats, whatever may be
the dangers that lie in wait for him.

"But it is more beautiful not to surrender to what the vulgar
ordinarily regard as evils. To struggle against the blows of fortune it is necessary to act not as an ignorant man but as a skillful fighter who knows that the dangers he braves are dreaded
by certain natures but that a nature such as his own endures
them easily; they do not appear to him terrible but capable only
of frightening children." So the philosopher argues. He does
not wish to take any account of "real needs," of what are considered "real needs" among men. He despises even the holy
things and makes reckless attacks on the temples. He expresses
his own thought and, for him, what is, does not exist; for him
there exists only what for ordinary minds is not. If he rejects
what appears to men dearest, do you think he will stop before
the customary categories of thought? If for him the final truth
is "death is better than corporeal life," what then can resist the

destructive impulse of his soul? It may be that, among all the questions that have ever been posed to the philosophers, this is the most troubling and also the most capable of leading us into temptation. We return to that of which we spoke at the beginning: when is it given a philosopher to stop and sing hosanna? Or perhaps we must ask thus: what happens to the philosopher at the moment when he intones his hosanna? And can one be certain that, having proclaimed hosanna once, he will then die with chants of glory on his lips?

I would propose that you listen once more to Plotinus. He was the last of the great Greek philosophers and it was more difficult for him to live in the world than for all his predecessors. In his time the days of the pagan gods were numbered, and men were obliged, whether they wished it or not, to get along without them and be content with human powers. Men had to revive with their weak, mortal hands the very things that had been the source of all life. To whom shall one sing hosanna, when it is clear that the gods themselves grow old and live, to be sure, longer than men but not much better? Ἀναβατέον οὖν πάλιν ἐπὶ τὸ ἀγαθόν, οὗ ὀρέγεται πᾶσα ψυχή. εἴ τις οὖν εἶδεν αὐτό, οἶδεν ὃ λέγω, ὅπως καλόν. So solemnly and powerfully does the great philosopher, who had with his own eyes seen the gods growing old and dying and had not wished to submit and lose his faith even before so terrible a spectacle, begin his discourse.

> We wish now to return to the Good for which every soul yearns. Whoever has seen it knows what I mean, knows what the beauty of the Good is. . . . What transports of love must one feel who sees it, with what ardor must he desire to be united with it, with what ravishment must he be transported! He who has still not seen it must desire it as for all his good; he who has seen it must love it as the very beauty. He is stricken at the same time with amazement and pleasure, feels a terror that has nothing of the painful in it. Animated with true love, with unequaled ardor, he laughs at other loves and disdains things that he had previously called beautiful. This is what happens to those to whom

the forms of the gods and the demons have appeared; they no longer look at the beauty of other bodies. What then must he feel who has seen Absolute Beauty itself in all its purity, without flesh or body, beyond earth and heaven? All these things, indeed, are contingent and composite; they are not original, they derive from it. If one can come to see that which gives all beings their perfection while at the same time remaining itself immovable, without receiving anything—if one rests in the contemplation and enjoyment of it, becoming like it, what beauty will he still desire to see? It is the supreme Beauty, the original Beauty, which renders all who love it beautiful and worthy of love. Here is the great and supreme goal of souls, the goal which summons all their efforts if they would not be disinherited from that sublime contemplation whose enjoyment renders one happy and whose deprivation is the greatest misfortune. For the miserable is not he who does not possess beautiful colors or beautiful bodies or power or domination or royalty; it is he only who sees himself excluded from the possession of Beauty, a possession for which he should disdain Kingdoms, domination, the whole world, the sea, the heavens even, if he can, abandoning himself and scorning all these in order to contemplate Beauty face to face (*Enn.* I, VI, 7).

So speaks, no, rather sings, the great sage of the dying Hellenistic world. In all of world literature you will find few pages that are so exalted, with inspiration so sincere and powerful. The divine Plato himself only rarely attained such pathos (Cf. Plato's *Symposium,* 211 D ff.), and it is only in the Psalms that you will find similar moods. I believe there are few who, in response to these wonderful words, will not cry: "Hosanna, blessed be he who cometh in the name of the Lord!"

But it is here precisely that the greatest difficulty begins, and we must look it squarely in the face.

I ask: what relationship to philosophy has all this that Plotinus tells us? Is this still philosophy or has Plotinus, without realizing it, flown on the wings of ecstasy beyond the domain of one kind of knowledge to penetrate the domain of another kind of knowledge that has nothing in common with the first? What is philosophy? Ask any contemporary scholar. He replies—I take the first one who comes along but, fortunately, he is a Platonist—philosophy is the science of true principles, of origins, of ῥιζώματα πάντων.* Does what Plotinus tells us resemble science in any way? Plotinus himself does not at all consider it necessary to define philosophy as a science: τί οὖν ἡ φιλοσοφία; τὸ τιμιώτατον.† "What is philosophy? That which is most valuable." Who is right: the Platonist Husserl or the Platonist Plotinus? If Plotinus is right, philosophy is indeed the most valuable, and if what we have just read of Plotinus is philosophy (but to take this away from Plotinus would be equivalent to taking his soul away from him), by what right shall we drive out of the domain of philosophy Mozart and Beethoven, Pushkin and Lermontov? By what right did Plato exclude the poets from his republic? And would not Plato himself have had to be the first one banished from this republic which denied civic rights to poets?

And since I have said this much I shall go further: I shall now quote a fragment of Lermontov's "Demon," which is a kind of counterpart to Plotinus' song and which it is particularly appropriate to recall when it is a question of philosophy as τὸ τιμιώτατον:

From the moment I saw you
I felt suddenly a secret hatred
For my immortality and my power.
Then I saw with envy, robbed of peace,
The incomplete joy of earth,
For terrible it is to be far from you
And torment to live not as you.

I think it is not necessary to quote other fragments of the speeches of Lermontov's "Demon." It would be better if one

---

* Edmund Husserl, *Philosophie als strenge Wissenschaft*, Logos (1910–11), 340.
† *Enn.*, I, III, 5.

could express in words the music of Mozart and Beethoven.
Those who know it have only to remember it. The chief thing
for the moment is that the immortal spirit, the demon of whom
Plotinus also speaks so often, suddenly envied *involuntarily* the
incomplete joy of earth, and that precisely this incomplete joy
of earth becomes for him the most valuable, τιμιώτατον. It is to
this that he, the son of clouds and sky, turning away from the
plenitude of being that is offered him, dedicates hymns as passionate and beautiful as those Plotinus had dedicated to his One.
And I ask again: what is it that justifies Plotinus? Why does he
affirm with such assurance that his Beauty is the only thing
worthy of adoration? For it he is prepared to give up kingdoms,
crowns, seas, and skies! The demon does not remain behind him:
he also gives away crowns, kingdom, and a power such as no
mortal on earth ever possessed. He does not even regret his
immortality; he will add it to all the goods that the Greek sage
throws with such audacity into the balance.

But here doubtless you remember Husserl's definition, "philosophy is a science." Consequently, you will say, the power
of Plotinus consists not in his pathos but in the arguments that
he has found in support of his thesis and that are developed in
other parts of his writings. Well! Science is—science. Let us lower
our tone and examine his proofs: do they contribute anything
to the force and justification of his statements? Is not rather the
contrary true, and are not his proofs themselves nourished on
that divine beverage which the great philosopher so generously
offers us?

In order to observe a certain order, let us listen first to what
Plotinus himself tells us about proofs. On this as on many other
questions, we cannot establish in him a unity of view; his opinions vary. As is known, men of genius have the privilege of
not hiding their contradictions and even of exposing them with
impunity to the gaze of others. So Plotinus declares in one place
of his *Enneads:* δεῖ δὲ πειθὼ ἐπάγειν τῷ λόγῳ μὴ μένοντας ἐπὶ τῆς βίας,

that is to say, proofs must be followed by persuasion, for one should not limit oneself to methods of mechanical constraint. Proofs are likened to mechanical force, and the final resort turns out to be charming "persuasion." But, on the other side, Plotinus shows himself obviously unhappy with the tendency of man to accord too great importance to persuasion: καὶ γὰρ ἡ μὲν ἀνάγκη ἐν νῷ, ἡ δὲ πειθὼ ἐν ψυχῇ. ζητοῦεν δή, ὡς ἔοικεν, ἡμεῖς πειοθῆναι μᾶλλον ἢ νῷ καθαρῷ θεᾶσθαι τὸ ἀληθές (*Enn.*, V, 3, 6). This means: "In reason—necessity, in the soul—persuasion; apparently we are more inclined to be persuaded than to contemplate truth by pure reason." The second statement does not agree with the first. The second glorifies the "necessity" that was so loved by the Greeks, without which neither their reason nor their λόγος could or would have existed. Plotinus, as a faithful disciple of Plato, could not believe that it was given him to contemplate truth by pure reason.

Plato taught that thought is a conversation of the soul with itself: Οὐκοῦν διάνοια μὲν καὶ λόγος ταὐτόν. πλὴν ὁ μὲν ἐντὸς τῆς ψυχῆς πρὸς αὐτὴν διάλογος ἄνευ φωνῆς γιγνόμενος τοῦτ᾽ αὐτὸ ἡμῖν ἐπωνομάσθη διάνοια, "Are not thought and speech the same thing—only that we have given the name thought to the dialogue that the soul conducts with itself inwardly without sounds?" Plato and, after him, Plotinus wished that thinking be a conversation of the soul with itself and not differ in any way from the conversation carried on between two men except that it proceed in silence and within the soul. Thinking must proceed by means of words, just like conversation, but by silent words. If there are words, then there will also be ἀνάγκη, and that saving dialectic that is alone capable of helping men in their search for the eternal and immutable truth.

Following Plato, all the other philosophers have accustomed themselves to believe that dialectic must be considered the source of wisdom, and formally Husserl is justified in calling the definition of philosophy he proposes Platonist and in considering himself a Platonist. This however cannot prevent us from posing and examining our own question: what is the source of philosophy—charming πειθὼ or the λόγος, the brother of ἀνάγκη and even of brutal βία? To avoid all misunderstanding, I shall say in advance that in raising this question I do not at all believe that the philosopher is necessarily obliged to choose between one or the other of these solutions. I am far from denying the importance of the λόγος, ἀνάγκη, and even of βία and of the dialectic produced by them. It is obvious to me that it is impossible to get along without them, and if Plato and Plotinus valued them so highly they had very serious grounds for doing so. But this is not the essential thing. In ordinary life, not only in philosophy, men are obliged to use language, to accommodate themselves to necessity; Apollo himself was one day forced to abandon the lyre and take his staff in hand. But why have the ancient and after them the modern philosophers decided that wisdom must be based on the very same thing as common sense is based?

Why have they seized the legal rights of common sense? Plato, in my opinion, should not in any way have used the method of reasoning by means of which he triumphed over his adversaries. As is known, he always began his argumentation with the examination of the most ordinary things, those that are most common and accessible to the senses. He spoke of the art of carpenters, cooks, doctors, etc., and, setting out from the definition of these arts, passed to the examination of purely philosophic problems. But, as I have said, Plato should have forbidden himself such a procedure. Perhaps he is right, surely he is right, that the doctor is distinguished from the cook in that he knows what is useful for the body and therefore gives advice that is useful for health, while the cook knows only what is pleasant to the body and can therefore injure the body's health. This reasoning is based on common sense, and no one will object to it. But to conclude from it that philosophy must be concerned with making itself useful to the soul, as the doctor is concerned with being useful to the body, is absolutely impossible, for the needs of the body have nothing in common with the needs of the soul. It may be that flattery of the body, κολακεία, is indeed hurtful for the body, while flattery of the soul preserves the soul. It may also be that flattery has no effect on the soul. In any case, questions concerning the soul must be examined in complete independence and cannot be resolved through analogy with the problems of medicine or of the culinary art.

If Plato, following Socrates, commits so important a methodological error, this is explained, it seems, by the fact that he feels for the human soul the same fears that the doctor feels for the human body. He was relentlessly pursued by this thought: may it not be that bad treatment of the soul has the same consequences as bad treatment of the body? A medicine for the soul must be discovered.

The further one goes into the forest the thicker become the trees. If one admits that dangers and even death threaten the soul just as they do the body, it is justified to suppose that the hygiene of the soul is a way of protecting the soul against deformities, just as the hygiene of the body is a way of protecting the body against premature decomposition. And then one comes to the following conclusion, quite as correct as the preceding from a formal point of view, but quite as obviously essentially faulty: if the principle of bodily hygiene is moderation in everything, the soul also must above everything else fear to pass beyond certain limits—μηδὲν ἄγαν, "nothing too much." We shall say nothing of further conclusions; the preceding is quite sufficient.

Let us compare them with the statement of Plotinus: "death is better than corporeal life." We recall that this statement did not escape him by chance but that it runs through all his writings as a kind of leitmotif (see *Enn.*, III, II, 15). And we recall also that this same thought likewise inspired Plato, who says in the *Phaedo* that the goal of philosophy is ἀποθνήσκειν τε καὶ τεθνάναι, "preparation for dying and death" (*Ph.* 64 A); or in the *Theatatus:* πειρᾶσθαι χρὴ ἐνθένδε ἐκεῖσε φεύγειν ὅτι τάχιστα, that is, "one must try to flee from here to there as quickly as possible." But if this is so (and one cannot imagine Plato and Plotinus without these ideas), how can Plato declare that medicine and its principles must serve as the model of philosophy? It is clear as day that medicine is the worst enemy of philosophy. It protects and strengthens the body, that body the destruction of which and the escape from which is the dearest goal of the soul!

If, then, one wishes to pay attention to medicine and study it, this should be only in order to realize to what a degree it can injure the soul and prevent it from realizing its purposes. And the natural ally of the philosopher will then not be the doctor but the cook, not medicine but the art of cookery with its κολακεία that Plato so detested.

I have dwelt on these arguments of Plato's concerning the κολακεία only because their invisible presence is always felt in Plotinus' argumentation. It appears to me that if we succeeded in attaining what in philosophy is known under the name of ῥιζώματα πάντων, we would discover in the final analysis, in almost every philosopher, this opposition between the doctor and the cook. Such is the influence of Plato—or is it not a question of Plato here? I hope I shall have occasion to treat this question again in detail. But now let us pass on to the argumentation which belongs properly to Plotinus himself. Naturally I cannot here deal exhaustively with all his "proofs," but this is not necessary. What is important for the moment is to establish why the soul aspires to that Beauty of which Plotinus speaks to us so inspiringly.

> Pure intelligence and being itself constitute the true and primary world, which has no extension, is weakened by no division, has no defect even in its parts (for no part is separated from the whole). This world is the universal life and the universal in-

telligence; it is the living and intelligent unity, for the part here reproduces the whole and there rules in their agreement a perfect harmony, for nothing is here separated, independent, and isolated from others; therefore no thing commits any injustice toward, or finds itself in contradiction to, any other thing. Being everywhere one and perfect, this intelligible world is permanent and immutable (*Enn.* III, II, 1).

This statement is undoubtedly already a "proof"; Plotinus aspires to νῷ καθαρῷ θεᾶσθαι τὸ ἀληθές. But do we discover here that necessity on whose power of constraint all proof rests? Is it true that in order for there to be in the world no discord and injustice, the world must be one? Cannot injustice be avoided some other way? And as for discord would it be such a great misfortune if it remained? In any case, is not to transform the world in order to avoid discord too heroic a means and even a bit ridiculous in its radicalism? In brushing discord aside we shall brush aside at the same time many things that are worth far more than any harmony or concord. It appears, furthermore, that in Plotinus, as in most philosophers, the source of wisdom, eternal and immutable wisdom, is the perhaps transitory need to drive out of life those elements that are particularly painful and therefore unacceptable to us. This need is certainly understandable and perfectly legitimate. What is not understandable is only why he uses such means of combat. Is it that he had already tried all others, I shall ask once more, and did he begin to transform the world only after becoming convinced that these means were useless? No, he was far from having tried all other methods, and not only he. If we gathered together the works of all the philosophers of the world, we would see how far we are from being justified in our assumption that men have already experienced everything that it is possible to experience. And truly, we have no reason to believe that we have already experienced everything: that is why every "last word" appears to us more unjust than all the injustices because of which Plotinus fled from the sensible world into the intelligible world.

Plotinus continues: "It is from that true and one world that the sensible world which is not at all one draws its existence; it is multiple and divided into a plurality of parts which are separated from and alien to each other. It is no longer friendship that rules in it but rather hatred produced by the separation of things whose state of imperfection makes them enemies of each other. For each part does not suffice for itself, but is preserved by another thing and is no less inimical to that thing that preserves it. The sensible world was created not because of a judgment establishing its desirability but because it was necessary that there be a nature inferior to the intelligible world which being perfect, could not be the last degree of existence" (*Enn.*, III, II, 2).

I do not wish to praise or justify our world: it has its imperfections, and they are many. The struggle of all against all is mostly a spectacle that is far from consoling. But not all discord is necessarily hateful. The struggle of ideas, for example: this even has a special charm, and if I were to construct an intelligible world I should prefer to keep in it the struggle of ideas and still other kinds of struggle. In any case, neither discord nor the other imperfections of our visible world should frighten us to such a degree that, out of the desire to forget the horrors of reality, we renounce all new searching.

Inspiration is a great thing and a great power. But it may act on its own responsibility, at its own risk and peril. Why must it hide behind the λόγος, ἀνάγκη, or, as the modern philosophers do, behind rigorous science? Do you wish to save men from despair? Do you fear catastrophe? But despair is an immense, colossal power, which is not less but perhaps greater than any ecstatic eruption.

Plotinus, like Dostoevsky, wished to teach men wisdom, and that is why he tried to proclaim as an indisputable truth: οὐ γὰρ πρὸς τὸ ἑκάστῳ καταθύμιον, ἀλλὰ πρὸς τὸ πᾶν δεῖ βλέπειν—"We must consider what happens not in relationship to the needs of a particular being but in relationship to the whole" (*Enn.*, II, IX, 9). This is the favorite commonplace of philosophy: the entire theodicy of Leibniz derived from this. I would quote another maxim of Plotinus which could also occupy an honorable place in any theodicy and which is worth just as much as the first. To those who ask why there is so much evil in the world Plotinus replies: "This is to demand for the sensible world too great a perfection and to confuse it with the intelligible world of which it is only the image" (*Enn.*, II, IX, 4). And corresponding to this is morality: "The virtuous man is therefore always serene, calm, content; if he is truly virtuous, his state cannot be troubled by any of the things which we call evil. If one seeks another kind of joy in the virtuous life, one seeks something other than the virtuous life" (*Enn.*, I, IV, 12).

This is certainly an ideal, a true human ideal—to be always serene, calm, and content. But I am glad to point out that this ideal does not express Plotinus, just as Father Zossima or Alyosha Karamazov does not express Dostoevsky. Why must a virtuous man always be serene and content? And does the value of his virtue reside in this virtue itself or in his serenity and contentment? Needless to say, serenity and contentment are very attractive. It may be that if Dostoevsky had not spoken so much of the always serene and joyful Father Zossima and of his final, definitive truth, no one would have recognized him, and those who today venerate him would have had to seek some other idol. Nevertheless, Zossima is not Dostoevsky, and the strength of Plotinus' genius lies neither in his proofs nor in his morality. Proofs, morality, moving and venerable images of holy personages—all this gilded tinsel without which obviously neither art nor philosophy can exist—will pass away. There will remain only . . . But let us rather give the word to Tolstoi, and not to the prophet Tolstoi—are the prophets alone able to give us what we need?

But first of all, a bit of information, for the purpose of comparison. When Goethe was eighty years old he received many letters of congratulation, among others from his noble protector, the Grand Duke of Weimar. Looking back over the eighty years that had passed, the old man, crowned with laurels, cried out, *Der feierlichste Tag!* So Goethe. And Tolstoi? Tolstoi fled from his house the day after his anniversary; he fled posthaste without looking back, abandoning glory, protectors, admirers, memories. Eighty years of unheard-of glory, wisdom, and virtue—what more could a man want? But it seems that Tolstoi, like Lermontov's Demon, unwillingly envied the incomplete joy of men. Toward the end of the last century, long before his flight, Tolstoi admitted,

I often imagine the hero of a story that I would like to write. As a young man he is a member of a circle of revolutionaries. He is first a revolutionary, then a socialist, then orthodox. A monk on Mount Athos, then an atheist, then father of a family, then a Quaker; he begins everything but leaves everything without achieving anything. People laugh at him. He has accomplished nothing and dies unknown in some hospital. And dying, he thinks he has wasted his life. And yet he is—a saint.

So, at the end of the last century, spoke Tolstoi. And the day when, after the celebration of his anniversary, he secretly left his house, he would probably not have deemed it necessary to add the last phrase. If the hero of this entire story did not himself know that he was a saint, must we absolutely know it? Would it not be better if we, like the martyred hero, did not know why this heroism and why these sufferings?

And if we must have an epitaph on the tomb of a man, let it not be composed by men. I believe that if in our time the nymphs were interested (as they once were) in the destinies of mortals, they would have dedicated to the memory of Tolstoi's hero and to Tolstoi himself—these words with which, according to Ovid, they immortalized the daring youth Phaeton:

Hic situs est Phaeton, currus auriga paterni,
Quem si non tenuit, magnis tamen excidit ausis. *

* This is the place of Phaeton, the driver of his father's chariot; and if he did not steer it well, still he fell engaged in a bold venture.

Socrates
and Saint Augustine

Τὴν πεπρωμένην μοίρην ἀδυνάτά ἐστιν ἀποφυγέειν καὶ θεῷ—"Even to the gods it is not given to escape fate." So men already thought at the dawn of their conscious life. Did they thereby correctly guess the final mystery of creation? Are the gods really subject to an eternal and immutable law? It would perhaps not be useless to raise another question: what did he who first "grasped" the idea of fate and its iron laws wish? Did he wish to have over himself a God whom nothing bound, or was such a free God bound by nothing more terrible for him than all iron laws?

This question must be raised, for men, as each of us has had opportunities to observe, are inclined to see not what is, but what they wish would be. One can express oneself even more strongly: in those cases where man can see what he wishes should be, he never sees what is in reality. And it seems that all or most men would not for anything in the world accept a God who was not, together with and like themselves, subject to the power of eternal laws. No matter how often they repeat "Thy will be done," in the secret places of their souls there is always hidden a *reservatio mentalis:* * the will of God is nonetheless subject to certain determinate laws and must take account of

* A mental reservation.

these. Precisely determinate, that is, well known laws, and known not by some Supreme Being but by us men. Saint Augustine repeats in all kinds of tones: *da, quod jubes et jube, quod vis.** But he says this only because he succeeded in persuading himself that God would not command him to do what according to his, Augustine's, conception is blameworthy. It is not for nothing that he said that before believing one must know *cui est credendum*, who is to be believed. And it is certain that he also, before believing, knew whom he had to believe. That is why he wrote without hesitation, *Firmissime creditur, Deum justum et bonum impossibilia non potuisse praecipere*, "we believe firmly that God, a good and just God, will not demand of man anything impossible." Whence did Saint Augustine know this?

It is not difficult to guess whence he knew it. This knowledge comes from where all the other self-evident human truths come. If Socrates had posed to Saint Augustine the question he proposed to Eutyphro—is the good good because the gods love it, or do the gods love it because it is the good?—Saint Augustine would certainly have answered without hesitation that the gods too must love the good, otherwise they would not be gods. The prophets, it is true, taught that the ways of God are inscrutable, but those who accepted these words of the prophets found ways of binding God through the methods of the ancient Greeks and especially of Socrates. The Hellenization of Christianity of which so much has been said in recent times is nothing other than the grafting of "rational" principles, i.e., principles acceptable to human reason, on to the revelation deriving from the Orient.

The Greco-Roman world expected and demanded a new doctrine. The rulers of the world had lost the ground under their feet and they demanded before everything else of the new religion that it re-establish the shaken foundations. The ancient mythology had grown old and lost all influence over minds; it

* Give what you command and command what you wish.

seemed childish and empty. As for philosophy, it left men too much freedom and independence. Always to think, always to seek, thereby running the risk of not arriving at any final goal and not finding anything—this was too difficult a burden for mankind. Was not Plato a great philosopher? But after Plato there appeared another great philosopher, his disciple, who pitilessly smashed all the sublime conceptions of his master. It was necessary to arrange things in such a way that for a very long time or, according to human terminology, "forever" ("a very long time" in the eyes of men is like eternity), the Platos and Aristotles be deprived of the possibility of shaking the foundations of life.

The problem, as you see, was already old: from its birth Greek philosophy directed its efforts only to putting an end to the painful doubts of men. But all its efforts ended in nothing. It counted in its ranks many great philosophers whose like we do not find in later philosophy, but the truth, that truth which could oblige all men to worship it, was always lacking.

And then something unheard of, something which had never yet happened and which did not repeat itself later in history, came about: the Greco-Roman world, so powerful and so cultivated, turned toward a small, weak, and ignorant people of the Orient with a request for truth. Give us the truth you have found by means other than those we use to attain it; the most important thing for us is that the truth be found by processes different from those we use to discover our truths. It is necessary for us that the ways that lead to the truth should be closed to us forever, for the experience of our thousand-year, relentless, and continuous searchings have convinced us that if these ways remain open we can never be sure of the immutability of the truth. Give us the truth and we, by means of our philosophy, this ancient weapon forged by our best minds, will know how to defend it. And the Greco-Roman world brilliantly accomplished its work in creating Catholicism.

I have said above that men willingly agree to call a more or less lengthy period of time eternity. No less willingly do they call a more or less extended space the universe. Catholicism very quickly felt itself eternal and universal: *quod semper, ubique et ab omnibus creditum est*—this was its formula. Certainly what Catholicism taught and teaches was not at all recognized everywhere, always, and by everyone, but rather for a long time, in many places, and by many people. And if the Catholics wished to know and spread the truth, it is thus that they should have spoken. They should have admitted that their doctrine can pretend neither to eternity nor to universality. But Catholicism ran up against the demands of Greek philosophy and the Roman state. Rome extended its authority over all the *orbis terrarum;* Greek philosophy was accustomed to consider itself the mistress of souls.

Look, for example, at Socrates. Despite his external modesty, despite his apparent lack of pretentiousness—he conversed with artisans, slaves, and children, lived in poverty, dressed poorly, ate whatever came along, bore patiently the complaints and insults of his wife Xanthippe—he defended with all the power of his genius his right to call himself the wisest of men. He yielded to others wealth, honors, and even the handsome Alcibiades, but he would not yield to anyone else his truth: he who wishes to be just, must follow Socrates. And, furthermore, could Socrates renounce his right to this? He renounced, as I have already said, everything for which men live, all sensible goods. He declared without hesitation that it is preferable to suffer injustice than to do injustice oneself. And in his mouth this was not an empty phrase. All the ancient writers confirm that Socrates' words conformed to his deeds, and not metaphorically but in the literal sense of the word. When he had to, he accepted injustice, even crying injustice, but he did not permit himself to do injustice even to one who had hurt him. And since in life one who does

not wish to hurt others is obliged constantly to suffer the injustices done by others, Socrates' life was very difficult and painful. This is demonstrated clearly to us by his last trial. It sufficed
for two insignificant creatures, Anytus and Meletus, to wish it,
and Socrates was poisoned as a mad dog is poisoned.

How then could Socrates, who had given away everything he
possessed, live? He created his own spiritual nourishment. Man
lives not by bread, nor honors, nor other human sensual pleasures,
but by virtue of the consciousness that he has of being just, of
being right. Man can so live as to feel himself always in the
right, and when he feels that he is in the right he does not need
anything else. This thought of Socrates, this act of Socrates,
constitutes the foundation of all Greek philosophy. It is also at
the foundation of all the millennial wisdom of men. Socrates
taught that philosophy was nothing other than κάθαρσις, purification, that man here on earth can purify himself so completely
that he will be able to present himself even before the gods snow-
white, without a single stain, and that there, in the other life, the
pure will be allowed to pass directly into paradise, where no one
will ever be able to hurt them any more. As for those who
are not purified on earth, it will be too late for them to dream in
heaven of salvation, since the fate of man, his eternal life, depends
on the way he has conducted his earthly existence. In Plato's
Apology Socrates spoke to his judges, but above their heads he
addressed himself directly to the gods. He proclaimed his virtue
and his rights proudly and assuredly, and not before men—he
knew that men would not be willing to listen; he knew that one
can and must scorn men—but before the immortal inhabitants of
Olympus. The chief meaning of "spiritual good" as Socrates
understood it, and as all of Greek philosophy after Socrates
understood it, is that it nourishes men and gods alike. Nectar and
ambrosia may be found not only on Olympus but also in our
poor valleys. To obtain them it is necessary only to understand,

and one obtains them not by the methods by which we acquire ordinary "earthly goods" but by exactly opposite methods. You must do not that toward which you feel yourself directly drawn but rather kill in yourself every natural impulse, and the result will be the eternal good.

After Socrates, European mankind until the present has not been able to free itself from this thought. I do not even know if one can call "thought" that which constituted the very essence of Socrates' philosophy. When Socrates tried to express himself, he certainly gave to his words the form of judgments. He argued with everyone and tried always to convince people that they could live on that on which he himself lived and as he himself lived. He declared that those who lived otherwise than himself were in ignorance and error. Comparing himself to others, he felt in himself a kind of immeasurable superiority which gave him the right to consider others as much weaker beings, as beings not yet completely formed. He, Socrates, already knows everything; he has already attained that degree of perfection which a reasonable being in general can attain—not only a man but a reasonable being—while others must still develop to this point.

I call the reader's attention precisely to this circumstance, for it has played, I believe, an extraordinary role in the fate of Greek philosophy and consequently in the fate of all mankind. Socrates saw that there was an enormous difference between him, on the one side; and Pericles, Alcibiades, Anytus, and Meletus, on the other side: he and they, one might say, were created out of different substances. It is not enough to say that they were on a lower level of development and had to rise several degrees to arrive where Socrates was. No, it was necessary for them to be reborn, to be transformed. And Socrates himself—must and could he rise still higher? In other words, is there still in the whole universe a reasonable being who is as superior to Socrates as Socrates is superior to Anytus and Meletus? And then, further, above this being is there another still higher? Socrates himself did not raise such a question and in Plato and all his disciples we do not encounter it either, as far as I know. The important thing is that they could not raise it. All of them thought, all of them had to think, that they had discovered a truth such that after it there could no longer be anything unforeseen and completely unexpected. The adult contemplates with a feeling of condescension the suckling child who cries when he is taken from his mother's breast. He knows that the child cries because of his limited knowledge, that he will stop crying and be consoled, and that he will himself later be astonished at having been so ardently attached to a good such as mother's milk and having considered it the good *par excellence*. Cannot a similar transformation occur in an adult? Socrates, the wisest of all men, was attached to virtue, to the spiritual good that he had discovered: may it not be that he later discovered, like the infant, that his good is not at all the good *an und für sich* and that that he feels for it the same disgust that the adult feels for mother's milk?

Socrates, as we know, admitted that men could change: Alcibiades and Pericles were capable, according to him, of becoming quite other than they were. Socrates compared his art, dialectic, to the art of his mother, who was a midwife: he helped men give birth spiritually. But if a second birth is possible, why not admit also the possibility of a third birth, the possibility of Socrates himself being born anew—that is, renouncing the good as he had renounced mother's milk to acquire a thirst for something else? Socrates, I repeat, did not admit such a possibility. He considered himself definitively born. It was in him that the truth which gave him the right to judge not only men, but also the gods, had ripened. For the gods themselves, the Greeks taught, are not absolutely free but are subject to the sovereign laws of fate. Or, as Socrates himself taught, the gods are not free to choose the object of their love; like mortals, they are obliged to love the good and to hate the evil. The good is not good because the gods love it but, on the contrary, the gods love the good because it is the good. And Socrates knows in advance what is beloved of the gods and what is disapproved by them, for he knows what the good is. He also could say, as the Catholics say today, "the good is that which *semper ubique et ab omnibus creditum est.*" His truth was in his eyes universal, ecumenical, and consequently definitive. If someone had tried to take away from Socrates' truth the predicate of universality, nothing would have stopped him from defending it—not even the threat of death, as he many times proved.

Could Socrates admit that several centuries later a small, barbaric people would forge for itself a new truth, in no way resembling his truth, and that his own Greek world would wrest from his truth the predicate of universality to transfer it to the truth of the Jews, whose name no one even knew at the time the oracle proclaimed Socrates the wisest of all men? Could he admit that those who had been instructed by the writings of his own disciples would declare with assurance that *virtutes gentium splendida vitia sunt?* Saint Augustine, it is true, did not utter this sentence: it was attributed to him by error, as has recently been established, but such is finally the meaning of all his teachings. The virtues of the pagans are only brilliant vices, and Socrates is a pagan like all other pagans. The best and sincerest pages of Augustine's *De Civitate Dei* are devoted to his polemic against the Stoics on the question whether virtue can replace for man all that is valuable in life. And yet, a very strange thing! Saint Augustine polemicized in all kinds of ways against the pagans. In disputing with them he made use mainly of the customary methods, i.e., he denounced their prejudices, their foolishness, their immorality, being concerned—as is always the case —much more with presenting his adversaries in an unfavorable light than discovering their real errors. In this respect, *De Civitate Dei* strongly recalls Tolstoi's *Critique of Dogmatic Theology.* Saint Augustine's work is, in effect, a kind of critique of the dogmatic theology of the pagans. But the most powerful and extraordinary pages of the book, those that make us think most, are not those where Saint Augustine accuses the pagans of foolishness and immorality but where he rises against the rationality and the nobility of paganism. "No matter how intelligent and noble you may be"—such is the meaning of his remarkable objections to the Stoics—"neither your reason nor your boundless devotion to high principles will save you from eternal destruction." I think Socrates would have read the terrible philippics of Saint Augustine against the immorality of paganism with a smile, for he would have immediately understood their true value, that is, that they contained little truth and much exaggeration, that they were only *argumenta ad hominem*, and especially *ad hominem* whose opinion could very well be ignored and which Saint Augustine himself did not share. But to accuse Socrates of being reasonable and moral—this is something else! No one in this case could reproach Saint Augustine for being dishonest or even exaggerating. It is true: Socrates was a reasonable and moral man. So said the oracle, so said Socrates of himself. Only neither the oracle, nor Socrates, nor anyone in the world could ever have imagined that to be reasonable and moral is shameful and sinful, and that reasonable and virtuous men would on another level, on a superhuman and divine level, be condemned. But it is precisely on this that Saint Augustine most insists. The virtue of the Stoics provokes his indignation. To be sure, he did not accuse them, any more than did Socrates, of hypocrisy and dissimulation. He knew that they were really virtuous and that they sincerely scorned or at least disdained terrestrial goods. But it was precisely this sincerity that revolted him most. One must not love virtue *an sich*, one must not see in it the final goal and find in the virtuous life complete satisfaction. "If you declare," he says, addressing himself to the Stoics, "that the consciousness of virtue makes even the most painful human existence happy, why do you permit suicide? Why, in certain particularly difficult circumstances, do you leave life and save yourself from your happiness in non-being? You do not then always find consolation in your virtue!"

This argument appeared to Saint Augustine absolutely irrefutable. And he used it pitilessly like an experienced warrior who leans his knees on his fallen opponent's chest and seizes him by the throat. He must overthrow the opponent and break his resistance in order to wrest from him the precious talisman for which the struggle broke out. Socrates and his disciples laid claim to virtue, to the right, and had succeeded in convincing the whole world that they knew the secret of virtue, were in possession of it, and that the secret is transmitted from one generation to another only to initiates, only to philosophers. There is no salvation for him who has not accepted from Socrates' hands the sacred talisman, or, to speak more simply, who has not followed the way pointed out by Socrates.

In engaging in his struggle against Greek philosophy, Saint Augustine certainly did not look down on his opponents, as we look down, for example, on weaklings and children. He saw in Socrates an enemy whom he had absolutely to overcome in order to seize the talisman called right. According to his convictions, which he had drawn entirely from Greek philosophy, there was only one talisman capable of rendering man happy, and if this talisman was in Socrates' hand Saint Augustine could not have it. But whence does he know that there is only one talisman? Saint Augustine did not even ask this. It was, in his eyes, a self-evident truth. Neither did he ask from what source the miraculous power of the talisman came. Socrates was not only a midwife, as he called himself, but also a siren. He had sung with such charm of the divine qualities of his wisdom that the whole world finally believed him. And the Christian Saint Augustine threw himself into the struggle for the possession of the incomparable treasure with the same passion that Hannibal once displayed in his wars against the Romans for power and riches!

Dialectic, eloquence, physical force—all means are equally good to attain victory. That is why it seems strange to recall that the same Saint Augustine also undertook that relentless struggle against Pelagius which made his name so famous. Saint Augustine was not afraid to proclaim, following Isaiah and Saint Paul, the doctrine of predestination and of salvation through faith. God saves not those who deserve to be saved but those whom He has chosen out of the multitude of human beings by the act of His free will. That is why man does not obtain salvation by his own works. It is not even given man to accomplish good works by his own powers; he accomplishes them by the grace that is given him without any merit on his part: *gratia gratis data*. So taught the great prophet, so taught the great apostle. And it is this doctrine, as unacceptable to our conscience as to our reason, that Saint Augustine dared to proclaim *urbi et orbi*.

I have already said, and I consider it necessary to say again, that this doctrine, if one does not modify it by explaining it through skillful sophisms, takes away from man the principles on which his existence is founded. Beginning with the moment he admits that God does not take any account of what we consider just and rational, he absolutely no longer knows what he should do for his own salvation and even, in general, if he must do anything for his salvation. The limits between the rational and the absurd, the good and the evil, disappear; all that Socrates and Greek philosophy taught us vanishes without a trace, and we enter a realm of eternal and hopeless darkness. But we recall that Saint Augustine was not willing to entrust his fate even to God without inquiring first about the God who must be believed: *cui est credendum?* In reality Saint Augustine was not faithless to the Hellenic tradition. Cicero says: *Socrates autem primus philosophiam devocavit e coelo et in urbibus collacavit, et in* *domos etiam introduxit et coegit de vita, de moribus, rebusque bonis et malis quaerere* (Cicero, *Tusc.*, V, 4).* At first blush this statement is surprising. It was the opposite, it seems, that happened: Socrates transferred philosophy from earth to heaven. Cicero, however, is right: Socrates wished to bind heaven, to restrain it; he wished to make the whole universe rational. And this doctrine was carefully preserved not only by his disciples and successors but also by the Catholicism of the Middle Ages. The defeat of Pelagius did not save Catholicism from the yoke of Greek philosophy. The medieval theologians, like the Greeks, exercised all their powers to obtain the exclusive possession of the miraculous talisman which gave him who held it the possibility of entering freely into a better world. Saint Augustine taught that pride is the beginning of sin, *superbia initium peccati.* He demonstrated with all the power of his genius and tried to inculcate in the minds of men the great Biblical idea of original sin, which was strange to the pagan world whose ideas had nourished him. But the same Saint Augustine could not, or rather was not willing to, renounce pride and the dream of final justification. He demanded the condemnation of Pelagius and succeeded in having him condemned.

Saint Augustine could not bear pride in others; the pretensions of man to holiness and righteousness appeared sacrilegious to him. But, just like Socrates, he could not live without being certain of his own righteousness. Others could and did in fact fall into error: this is natural, for it is human to err. But he, Augustine, could not live in falsehood; therefore he knows the truth, and indeed that truth which will necessarily procure him salvation. The distinction between Socrates and Saint Augustine was only apparent, only a verbal distinction. Socrates affirmed that he drew his truth from his own reason, while Saint Augus-

---

* Socrates, however, called philosophy down from heaven and placed it in the midst of our cities, even introduced it into our homes, and forced it to ask questions about our life, morals, and the good and bad in things.

tine said that he had received his from the holy Catholic church: *ego vero evangelio non crederem, nisi me catholicae (ecclesiae) commoveret auctoritas.**

If you turn even to the Catholic historians of the Western church, you will be able to become convinced that Saint Augustine had already created a theory which justifies conversions by violence and the right of the spiritual authority to persecute by all means those who have departed from its doctrine and dogmas (relying on the Gospel according to St. Luke 14: 23: *compelle intrare*). What interests us especially, however, is not so much the doctrine of Saint Augustine as the source of his ideas on constraint understood as the fundamental and inseparable predicate of truth, logical as well as metaphysical.

In his *Confessions* he never stops expressing variations on his basic theme: "My heart is restless and will not be at rest until it has found Thee." This theme is as old as the world. The hearts of the pagan philosophers also well knew the terrible and fateful torments of the lost human soul. From Socrates and even from Thales to Plotinus, a whole series of remarkable men reported to the world their insuperable anxieties and also, naturally, the means they had employed to overcome their doubts. But if the anxiety of Saint Augustine was not new to the Greco-Roman world, the solution he indicated was not new to it either. He also taught—as did Socrates, Plato, and Aristotle—that the solution consisted in putting an end to anxieties and overcoming them, and that one could put an end to them only by discovering the final truth—that is, a truth after which one would no longer have to search, to torment oneself, to doubt. What is extraordinary is that many hundred of years later, Catholicism, while accepting Saint Augustine, succeeded in preserving in its depths, probably as a kind of indispensable ferment, both doubt and anxiety. This is not the place to inquire how these could coexist

* I should truly not believe in the Gospel unless the authority of the Catholic Church would move me to do so.

with faith and the idea of the infallibility of the Catholic Church. It is certain that the Protestants are right when they speak of Catholicism as a *complexio oppositorum*. Beside the immutable dogmas there always lived in Catholicism an anxiety which nothing could appease and which raised continuous storms in the souls of its sons, even the faithful. If then it is correct to say that the Catholic dogmatic was determined entirely by the goals that Greek thought had set for itself, it is no less true that Holy Scripture provoked, through its profound disagreement with the spirit of Greek philosophy, the most surprising reactions among those who were destined to experience the supreme anxieties of human existence. Aristotle ruled over the minds of medieval Catholics. And following Aristotle, all the sons of the Church sought to define in clear and indisputable terms the essence of the doctrine they confessed. They wished that this doctrine not offend either their reason or their conscience. But, in reality, if the efforts of Philo to reconcile the Bible with the demands of the philosophically cultivated mind were condemned in advance to failure, it was the same with all the attempts of the first apologists. Whatever may have been the depth and beauty of their philosophical-religious conceptions, they always testified to the absolute impossibility of reconciling Judaism with Hellenism. This appeared already with particular sharpness and clarity in the polemic that Pelagius provoked. The Pelagians declared through the mouth of Julian: *Sanctas quidem apostoli esse paginas confitemur, non ob aliud, nisi quia rationi, pietati, fidei congruentes erudiunt nos.** And Saint Augustine thought the same. It is impossible to "think" otherwise. Saint Augustine declared that a good and just God could not demand the impossible. But to demand of men that they confess a doctrine contrary to reason and conscience—is this not equivalent to demanding the impos-

---

* Indeed we confess that the pages of the apostle are holy, but not for any other cause than this—that they instruct us, while agreeing with reason, piety and faith.

sible of them? Catholicism never admitted that the dogmas of the church are not reconcilable with reason. On the contrary, the Catholicism that condemned Pelagius anathematized those who declared that faith and reason are irreconcilable. Pelagius was conquered, but the conquered prescribed laws to the conqueror. And still today Saint Thomas Aquinas is considered the normative theologian of the Church.

Socrates and Hellenism triumphed. Does this mean that it will continue to be so, that it will alwaye be so? This is very possible, and even probable. And if all that is real is rational and speaks to us of what is eternal, the phiolsophers could calmly fold their hands. But it is not only the real that is rational, and it is certain that what is rational is not always real and that what is not rational is not always unreal. So then, if Socrates is destined to remain forever the conqueror on earth (and I repeat that he has all the chances of doing so), this does not mean anything as far as the "quality" of his truth is concerned. For I hope that there is no need to demonstrate that truths can be of different qualities. Whence do we know that triumph on earth is guaranteed to truth, or even that such triumph is necessary to it?

History teaches us many things; but when the historian imagines that the future reveals the "meaning" of the present, or when he justifies some idea, as often happens, by saying that "it had the future on its side" and brushes another away under the pretext that it did not have the future on its side, he certainly introduces order and harmony into his science or even transforms history, i.e., a simple account, into a science, but he does not at all approach the truth. The truth is not constituted by the material out of which ideas are formed. It is living, it has its own demands and its own tastes, and even fears above all else, for example, what in our language is called incarnation.

It is afraid of it as all that is living is afraid of death. That is why only he can see it who seeks for himself and not for others, who has made the solemn vow not to transform his visions into judgments obligatory for all and never to render the truth tangible. As for him who wishes to seize the truth, to grasp it in his crude human hands, to "incarnate" it in order to be able later to show it everywhere and to all—he is condemned to eternal deceptions or even to live in illusions: all incarnated truths were never anything but incarnated illusions.

Perhaps, I shall be told, mankind has only gained thereby, but it is not a question of this. Must truth also be useful? Was not pragmatism dead the day after it was born?

PART III

On the Roots of Things

I

A commonplace of philosophy: "Only that possesses true reality which does not know change, which has no beginning and is not subject to destruction."

Even if one grants that this is correct (but one cannot grant it), the opposite statement, that everything that is not subject to change or destruction possesses true reality, cannot be at all considered correct, if only for the reason, in any case, that it is absolutely impossible for us to know that which is not subject to change and destruction; we know only things that are not subject to more or less rapid change or destruction. It seems even that it is only thanks to a misconception that the existence of the ideal is considered eternal and immutable. A general idea—the lion, the mosquito, the ichthyosaur, for example—remains while living lions, mosquitos, and ichthyosaurs disappear, one knows not where. And the concept "man" continues to exist to the present day, even though there remains only a memory of Socrates, of Caesar, and of Alexander the Great, a memory which will also one day sink into Lethe. But where is true being—in the vanished Socrates who, though only for a short time, nevertheless was alive, or in the concept "man" that has been preserved to this day but was never alive? For Hegel such a question did not even exist. But there is certainly a question here, and one of cardinal importance. For, after all, though the concept "man" is more long-lived than Socrates, it is nevertheless not eternal, and many general ideas have already perished so completely that not even the memory of them has been preserved.

"He who knows what true philosophy is," says Hegel, "is not troubled by Plato's mythology; he understands his theory of ideas as the theory of general concepts." But here also a question arises: who knows what true philosophy is, and wherein is it distinguished from that which is not true? More exactly: Who has the sovereign right to give the final and definitive answer to this question, and by whom has this right been granted? As is known, every philosopher pretends to this right. It is true that the great majority of philosophers since distant times have been persuaded, as I have already said, that only the eternal and the immutable may be the object of their researches. In this respect, Hegel is not at all distinguished from the majority, one could even say the great mass, of the philosophers, if one did not disdain certain very effective polemical methods currently in use among the scientists.

It is true that the eternal presents many very seductive external advantages over the temporal, such that one can admit that weak human nature has manifested itself in the philosophers in this case also: the eternal and the immutable has seduced them not only because it is superior by its "nature" to the transitory and the changeable, but also, among other things, because it lets itself more easily be fixed and therefore studied. Heraclitus teased reason: one cannot, he said, bathe twice in the same river. In reality, however, one cannot even bathe once in one and the same river. The river flows ceaselessly; at every moment it becomes something else; one cannot stop or fix it, even if only for the brief moment that is required to plunge into the water. And it is not only the river that flows—everything flows, everything changes, everything becomes something else. General ideas, however, remain. And it is only through general ideas that it is possbile to stop the crazy dance of being.

General ideas appear to the philosophers, so to speak, like a rainbow above a waterfall: the rainbow remains immobile and immutable, while the water gushes, crashes, and evaporates into a cloud. Where then must the essence of things be sought—in these splashes and these drops that are born and disappear, or in the rainbow? To what must our thought be applied? So men put the question, losing sight of the fact that the rainbow also passes, that it ceases to exist when the sun sets, while the drops of water remain, though they disappear much earlier from our field of vision. The drops which appear and disappear so quickly are finally more "eternal" than the rainbow; even though they follow one another and disappear, they do not perish but only change their place. So then, if what is essential is what endures, it is evident that it is not the rainbow that is the essence but the drops of water. But this is still not the most important thing. The imporant thing is that philosophical realism (I here take the term realism in its medieval, not in its modern sense), which has always been so proud of its nobility and which arrogantly despised materialism as a non-philosophical theory, is so close to materialism in its fundamental character that one can only be astonished at the relentless war that has always been carried on between these doctrines. This must be said especially of the philosophy of Hegel.

I have said above that Hegel did not take Plato's mythology seriously. Nor did he like the way in which Plato wrote. He even speaks in one place of the "babbling" of the divine philosopher. It is true that, following custom and obedient to tradition, he begins by praising the beauty and nobility of Plato's style, but he could not and would not pass over his prolixity in silence. And this is not at all a matter of chance, so that there is room to regret that Hegel did not further develop the thought which he threw out in passing. Plato's "babbling" obviously stands in direct relation to the interest he manifested in mythology.

From the point of view of the philosophy which Hegel represents, all mythology is finally nothing but babbling. The philosopher must think in conceptual terms, and he who does not know this does not know what philosophy is. Neither Hegel nor his predecessors could ever demonstrate this statement, and it can never be demonstrated, for every demonstration presupposes it.

The problem of philosophy for every realistic philosopher (I recall once more that I have always in mind realism in the medieval sense of the term, i.e., what is today called idealism) is the statics and dynamics of the ideals. Concepts are in motion and are transformed into one another according to their own laws which are immanent in them. The task of philosophy is to grasp the inner logic and necessity of this movement. Hegel is then consistent with himself when he transforms logic into ontology. He remains likewise faithful to himself when he rises against the critique made by Kant of the ontological proof for the existence of God. It is known that Kant declared that the idea of "a hundred thalers" does not presuppose the existence of the hundred thalers. Hegel considers such argumentation dull and vulgar. Certainly, he says, for the individual person (that is, the common man), this difference exists: he wishes to have a hundred real thalers and not the idea of a hundred thalers. But he must rise to the philosophic state; then it will be completely indifferent whether he has or does not have a hundred thalers, even if they constituted his entire fortune. Hegel goes even further in his claims: for the philosopher, he says, it must be indifferent whether he himself exists or does not exist, at least— he adds—in this earthly, finite life. Hegel goes so far as to recall the famous verse of Horace:

Si fractus illabatur orbis
*Impavidum ferient ruinae,**

and he makes of it a fundamental philosophical law that is still more obligatory for the Christian philosopher than for the pagan philosopher.

But Hegel was wrong to limit his thought by demanding of man that he remain indifferent only to his own earthly, finite being. He was wrong, for there is an obvious and fatal error here. Infinite being is to such a degree separated from finite being that it is only through the customary confusion of our ideas that one can explain how Hegel brought these two concepts into one and the same genus. It would have been more correct to designate them by different and even directly opposite names, as Hegel, by the way, at times did. In other words, if we speak of the being of the finite, the particular, the individual, we must apply to the general the predicate of non-being, and vice versa. So then, for Hegel's judgment that I have just quoted to have been expressed in the exact sense of the terms, it would have been necessary to brush aside the limitation he introduced there and to say simply that for the philosopher who has risen above the everyday, the ordinary, whether the whole world exists or does not exist must be a matter of indifference. Particular being must be led back to being in general in all its proud and sublime abstraction—this is the first theoretical and practical demand presented to the philosopher. To know how to scorn the particular in favor of the general means to raise oneself philosophically.

Before proceeding to determine the value of this thesis of Hegel's, I would draw the reader's attention to the fact that it was not Hegel who invented this demand and not he who first

* If the earth, falling to pieces, were to slip away, still the crashing ruins will strike him unafraid.

formulated it. It dominates all of philosophy and, as I have already had occasion to say, was already expressed in that single fragment of Anaximander's writings that has come down to us. But Hegel repeats it with special insistence, as if he wished to emphasize that it is the *articulus stantis et cadentis philosophiae*.* And it is for this reason perhaps that no idealistic system is as closely related to materialism as Hegel's. His "thought," his "ideal," contain in themselves as little of life, of the animate, as the materialists' matter. And his God (Hegel mentions God more often than any other philosopher), his Absolute and Spirit—all these sublime ideas are not at all distinguished from matter. It is obvious that the first condition and postulate of scientific thought is the death of what is animated. Hegel, his predecessors and successors, idealists and materialists—all triumph when they succeed in establishing for all living beings γένεσις καὶ φθορὰ (birth and destruction). God Himself, if He is living, must be subjected to γένεσις καὶ φθορὰ, and God must then rise above Himself and be absorbed in the general idea which is the only object worthy of the philosopher's attention.

It is for this reason that it is absolutely impossible to deny that the pretensions of the extreme Hegelian Left Wing to the right to the *magister dixit* † are perfectly legitimate. The master said, really said, all that the school of economic materialism has deduced from his theses. History is a process, and materialism is not at all "individual." Materialism also rises above individual existence. Horace's verses are as sacred for it as for Hegel, and it is completely indifferent to individual beings. As far as the personal God is concerned, materialism is even more radical than Hegel and resolutely denies to Him the right to the predicate of being.

Only matter and order exist. For these are permanent and do not change. All the rest is only superstructure.

If you wish, the Hegelians of the Left Wing were wrong to

* Proposition on which philosophy stands or falls.
† The master has spoken.

call themselves materialists: their matter is just as ideal as their order, and in any case it does not contain a dram more of that criminal life against which, following Anaximander, all of Greek philosophy struggled and against which Hegel also warned. The fundamental demand of philosophical morality—philosophy also has its morality, morality forms the very essence of philosophy—is maintained with all the rigor to which the most scrupulous science can pretend. For the crime of individual or animated being consists in its arbitrariness. But in the kingdom of economic materialism there is no place for individual arbitrariness, for everything there is accomplished with "iron necessity," according to an order established once for all.

II

I am not in any way accusing Hegel of atheism. Today such an accusation would appear ridiculous: Hegel himself is no longer of this world, and even if he were still living, no one would persecute him for his atheism; on the contrary, he would perhaps be highly praised for it. But it is certain that the materialists who openly deny God express more correctly the final thought of Hegel's philosophy than Hegel himself. And the idealist Schopenhauer formulated the very essence of idealism more happily when he declared that religion is only for the mob, while philosophy— atheistic philosophy naturally—is only for the elect, for those to whom it is given to see and understand the truth. The mob are those *die das Allgemeine nicht erreichen,* who are not capable of raising themselves to the general. It is not I who have added "raising themselves"; these words are always found in Hegel when it is a question of the relationship between the individual and the general. According to Hegel, God too, like Kant's one hundred thalers, is much more sublime when He is transformed into an idea than when He remains alive in His individuality. That is why Hegel accepts the ontological argument for the existence of God and argues with Kant.

Let us for the moment leave the demands of morality aside. It may be that it is indeed more elevated to give preference to

the general over the individual; it may also be that it is not
exalted but on the contrary very low. I say: let us leave this
aside, for I do not at all know how one could decide this question and even whether it can be resolved in one sense or another.
To my mind, there is no solution and there cannot be any. Some
will say that the God who is only an idea is no more God than
the white bull of certain Oriental peoples or than the idol of
the savages, and that if God really has, as Hegel affirms, only
"being in truth," that is, a being like the concept of a hundred
thalers, this is equivalent to saying that God has no being at all.
The moralist can climb on his highest stilts and demonstrate,
following Horace, that *justum et tenacem propositi virum* *
must remain impassive, even if the celestial vault falls in on him;
this will not change the situation in any way. Morality is autonomous and prescribes its laws without taking any account,
naturally, of laws of any kind decreed by the other incorporeal
inhabitants of the empirical human soul. But since when did the
Epicurean Horace become an authority in moral questions? He
extols courage as an absolute virtue, and Hegel repeats this and
declares with assurance that the Christian must be even more
courageous than the pagan. Hegel speaks thus in his own name
and on his own responsibility; but here one can set opposite his
conviction a contrary conviction. It is certainly appropriate for
the pagan to push his courage to the limits of which Horace
speaks; for the pagan morality is in fact the supreme court of
appeal. For the pagan the "good" rules over the gods as over
men, and no power in the world can abrogate what the "good"
has prescribed. For the Epicurean as for the Stoic, *virtus*, courage, is the primary, fundamental, and supreme virtue. It is not
for nothing that the Romans designated by this term courage as
well as virtue in general. But the Christian also knows other
virtues; for the Christian, and in general for one who believes
in God, the fear of God is the beginning of wisdom. Even

* The just man tenacious of his purpose.

Schopenhauer, whose soul had preserved at most only weak re-membrances of his erstwhile faith, knew that courage is only an empirical virtue of the subaltern officer. In this respect, certain animals surpass man: do we not say, fearless as a lion?

In fact, courage is a conventional virtue—I should say, an immanent virtue, and as such it plays a cardinal role in the doctrine of the Epicureans and the Stoics. *Nil admirari*—not to be astonished at anything and not to fear anything: for one who is persuaded that there is nothing beyond the limits of the visible world, it is natural to aspire only to understanding, and it is quite as natural for him to drive far away from himself sentiments such as astonishment, fear, hope. The most remarkable representative in modern philosophy of this attitude is obviously Spinoza, whose influence on Hegel cannot be exaggerated. The idea of the absolute spirit belongs entirely to Spinoza and it is in him also that, with a force one does not find in anyone else, everything individual and particular is transformed into a mode of the single, eternal substance. And repugnance not only for the Platonic but also for the Biblical mythology is expressed with still greater force in Spinoza than in Hegel; he believed in the spirit and only in the spirit. Doubts, hesitations of the soul, were for Spinoza only signs of weakness, and he scorned alike those who let themselves be led by fear and those who let themselves be enticed by hopes. For him, i.e., for the philosopher, there is only one duty: *intelligere*. Consequently his ideal is *amor Dei intellectualis*. The word *intellectualis* can, in my opinion, be applied as well to love as to God. We may then translate it thus: intellectual love for an intellectual God.

Horace was certainly right when he said in his *Ars Poetica*:

> *Pictoribus atque poetis*
> *Quodlibet audendi semper fuit aequa potestas.*

"The power of daring was always granted to painters and poets." The right to all imaginable audacities was always granted not only to poets and painters but also to philosophers, and I would not wish that what I say here about Schopenhauer, Spinoza, and Hegel be considered an "accusation" against these philosophers of "free thinking." On the contrary, if one asked my permission, I would be ready to grant all seekers, painters, poets, theologians, philosophers, or even simple pilgrims, the *potestas audendi* in whatever measure they desire: let them dare as much as they wish! My observations are intended only to defend the right of philosophers to all audacities, no matter how dangerous and measureless these may be. If I argue, it is quite simply because I am more and more convinced that the rationalist philosophy that comes from the Greeks has always had as its secret object to limit the *potestas audendi*. This purely Greek need is manifested even in Holy Scripture. The Fourth Gospel begins with the words ἐν ἀρχῇ ἦν ὁ λόγος—"In the beginning was the word." Just as did *virtus* among the Romans, so did λόγος among the Greeks have a twofold meaning: λόγος signifies both word and reason. And this is obviously not a matter of chance either. The Greeks supposed reason to be already contained *implicite* in the "word"; it is in the word that they sought it, particularly Socrates and the schools deriving from Socrates.

In the *Phaedo* Plato says that the worst misfortune that can come to a man is to become a μισόλογος, that is, a hater of reason, and that he must guard himself against this above all else. This thought persists throughout the history of all of Greek philosophy and, apparently through the intervention of Philo of Alexandria, passed into the New Testament and from there into Christian philosophy. Socrates always triumphed over his adversaries in debate in the same way: he proved to them that their life and their actions lacked that unity and that rigorous logic which he always succeeded in discovering in thoughts and words. And he certainly was right. There is in language, in the "word," more logic than in the life and soul of any man. It is finally only in the word and in logic that one finds a rigorous consistency.

If one could clarify the inner life of Alcibiades, of Pericles, or of Socrates himself, there is room to believe that it could not be compared in respect to logical rigor and consistency with the language of the Greeks, which was so carefully worked out and which in the hands of a master was a model of plasticity and precision. This comes from the fact that language operates chiefly if not exclusively through general ideas. Proper nouns themselves are general ideas: each proper noun indeed is the product of abstraction, for it presents such or such a concrete object not in a determinate place and time but always and everywhere. Caesar is Caesar, as a child, as an adolescent, as a mature man, in Rome, in Gaul, awake, asleep. When we have called a man or an object by name, we have immediately passed from the complex, enigmatic contingency, inexpressible in words, that belongs to everything real, i.e., "particular," into the domain of the general, with its simplicity, its clarity, its necessary laws and, consequently, its comprehensibility.

According to a widespread opinion, man as a rational being differs from the animals as irrational beings in that, through thinking, he is capable of passing, or as Hegel puts it, raising himself, from the particular to the general. I believe that a grave error, a very grave error, lies here. The faculty of distinguishing the geneal in objects does not at all belong exclusively to man: all the animals perceive the general, and the lower animals even more than the higher. For a wolf or a lion the lamb is only food, and in this respect all lambs are to them only lambs in general. It is the same with the eagle and the condor. Animals very rarely notice the "particular," generally only their own young, and that not always. It is known that birds are often incapable of distinguishing their own eggs, and thus it is that the owl hatches the egg the cuckoo has laid in its nest. I will not even speak of lower organisms for which, it seems, only the most general representations exist—what is edible and what is not edible.

So then, contrary to Hegel and those from whom he took his

fundamental principles, there is room to consider the faculty of passing from the particular to the general not as a rising but rather as a falling, provided naturally that it is admitted that in the scale of living beings man occupies a place above that of the animals. But if it be so, we must believe that the λόγος, the word, cannot contain all reason, just as all of virtue is not to be found in *virtus*. If you wish, in the beginning was the word; but this was only because in the beginning, in that beginning at any rate that man could distinguish with his myopic eyes, everything was still very elementary (in the beginning, I repeat, living beings sought only nourishment, any nourishment, whatever it might be—nourishment in general), and many things still did not exist. Later, when nourishment in general, and all that "general" which is the necessary condition of the existence of living organisms, was found, and especially when civilized man with his great reserves of the "general" appeared so that one no longer needed to concern himself with it, when therefore leisure was born and with leisure the possibility of interesting oneself not only in the necessary but in anything one wished—then only did the meaning of the particular and the individual manifest itself with all its power. In the beginning all men were equal and were distinguished among themselves only quantitatively: the one was physically stronger, the other weaker. In the beginning there was neither Socrates nor Meletus, neither Patrocles nor Thersites, but only man in general. Then Homer, Schiller, and the other poets would have had nothing to do, for then there was only a general of which all sang in the same words, we must assume, and in actions still more alike.

III

How did it happen that philosophy, and precisely that philosophy which pretended so stubbornly to sublimity and which indeed seems to have wished to be sublime, nothing but sublime, glorified the ideal of the caveman and even the invertebrate animals? Is this atavism, or is there some other mystery here? Why is it that Aristotle triumphed in history and not Plato? Why did Christianity itself allow itself to be led into temptation by the λόγος? Why could not modern thought free itself from the spell of Hegel's philosophy, and why could even those who have faith believe only in a "general" God, only in a God-concept, and why are they convinced that every other faith is reprehensible and even impossible for an educated man? Is it truly impossible to accept? Or have we the right finally to demand, as far as the heritage we have received from the Greeks is concerned, the *beneficium inventarii* * of which our fathers did not dream? But how and of whom demand it? Who will tell us with certainty if the first verse of the Fourth Gospel is a revelation or an interpolation dating from the time when Holy Scripture was no longer in the hands of the poor in spirit, for whom it had been destined, but in the hands of a Roman aristocracy instructed

* Benefit of a listing [i.e., the help of a catalogue].

by Greek masters? And who will help us to resolve this question: where must we seek the true Plato–in his mythology or in his theory of ideas scientifically developed by Aristotle?

European philosophy is today conducting, as is known, a bitter struggle against "psychologism." The problem is certainly not new. Psychologism has always existed, and idealistic philosophy has always struggled against it. In modern times, none among the philosophers was a more relentless and irreconcilable enemy of psychologism than Hegel: this follows clearly from what I have already said of him. In Hegel himself, however, we find the following argumentation: "Every man says without hesitation: 'It is obvious that the objects I see exist.' But it is not true that he believes in their reality. He assumes rather the contrary, for he eats and drinks them; that is, he is persuaded that these things do not exist in themselves, that their being has no stability, no essence. The ordinary intelligence is better in its acts than it thinks, for its acting being is the complete spirit."

Let us leave Hegel's explanation aside for, like every explanation, it is debatable. But one fact is indisputable: the man who believes that things exist knows at the same time that they do not exist; and this knowledge is expressed not in words but quite otherwise, in action, but in such a way that others–Hegel, for example, and following him, his readers–can become acquainted with it.

Let us take now another fact of the same order, relating no longer to the ordinary man but to the philosophers. All the philosophers have always considered the psychological point of view false, and particularly Hegel. Just as ordinary men believe that the things they see exist, the philosophers assume that the truths they think also exist, and all therefore declare themselves antipsychologists. But read Husserl's *Logische Untersuchungen* and his other works, and you will become convinced that if the philosophers openly pronounced against psychologism and did not keep silent, their acts did not at all agree with their words:

just like ordinary men, they ate and drank the very truths they proclaimed eternal. What then should be our attitude toward the philosophers: must we consider that they had the "truth" when they "acted," that is, impose on them the same demands as on the man in the street, or must we accord them the privilege, in view of their high station, of not being subject to general laws?

This is all the more important in that Hegel himself, according to Husserl, did not avoid the common fate; he also said certain things but did, in his philosophy and through his philosophy, others. But if one accepts my testimony, it appears that Husserl finds himself in the same situation as Hegel. He also eats and drinks his eternal truths, and he eats and drinks them in even greater measure than any other philosopher. One could say that in him the destruction of the truths is directly proportional to his conviction of their indestructibility. And so I raise the question: Of what must we take account—the words of the philosophers or their acts? Their words tell us that their truths are eternal, but their acts show us that their truths are quite as transitory as the sensible things which appear existent to ordinary men but which for "reason" are only pure phantoms that vanish at the first contact with logic. To put it differently: should we be instructed by the philosophers through studying the theories they have invented, or through observing their lives in all their manifestations, that is, not only their words but also their acts, their attitudes, etc.?

It may be assumed, however, that one would probably not succeed in giving this question a single, complete answer that is valid for every case, as the reader, and particularly the specialist in philosophy who loves the general and appreciates only the unchanging, would wish. For the complete spirit (*der ganze Geist*), to employ Hegel's terminology, sometimes manifests itself in acts and sometimes also in words. At times it produces such a *complexio oppositorum* that the contradiction between words and acts cannot be avoided by the poor two-legged animal. So, for example, the ordinary man is obliged to affirm that bread and water exist, and at the same time to eat bread and drink water for, as experience has proved to him, he cannot eat or drink what does not exist (even though, if he could, he would often prefer the non-existent to the existent). Thus the question appears extremely complex, and we can neither avoid it nor simplify it. Furthermore, in general, the desire to simplify what is complex never leads to anything good. We can introduce into our heads a certain harmony and apparent order, but reality remains what it was and does not conform either to idealist or materialist conceptions. Whatever be the systems of thought that we build, the ordinary man will not find there sufficient place to bring in all that seeks a refuge.

I repeat, materialism is finally not at all distinguished from idealism even though, to judge from their external aspect, these two conceptions differ completely from each other. In both cases one tries, and with equally small success, to force life under a roof, into a cellar, into a subterranean room. But life leaps over the thickest walls, the most solid vaults. Sooner or later philosophy becomes philosophy *en plein air,* whatever minds attached to traditions and old ideas may do. Men will finally understand that in the "word," in the general idea, one can shut up tired human souls for the night so that they may sleep and rest but that, when day comes, their freedom must be returned to them: God did not create the sun and the heaven, the sea and the mountains, that man should turn his gaze away from them. The fathers of the Vatican Council were right: *Si quis mundum ad Dei gloriam conditum esse negaverit, anathema sit.** And it is the Platonic mythology which Hegel under various pretexts

---

* If anyone denies that the universe has been founded for the glory of God, let him be anathema.

drove with such relentlessness from philosophy—and not only Hegel but almost all his predecessors and successors—that tells us that the world was created for the glory of God. And if we do not permit the philosopher to speak of this, what will remain of philosophy?

IV

But the materialist philosophy, just like the idealist, has always tried to rise above God. And finally theology itself which, as I have already indicated, was even in the Middle Ages, at the time of its highest flowering and triumph, the servant of philosophy (*ancilla philosophiae*), wished absolutely to be above God and beyond God. The entire *potestas audendi* of the philosophers and theologians expressed itself chiefly in the endeavor to subordinate God to man. So that it seems today, at this moment, after the relentless struggle that reason has waged for twenty-five hundred years against God, that it would be extreme audacity to speak of the true God, of that God who is called, in the Holy Bible and in the creed that millions of men repeat, the creator of heaven and earth. There once was a time when it seemed that one had to be a madman to deny the existence of God: "The fool saith in his heart, 'there is no God.'" (Psalm 14:1). Nowadays the existence of God is proved and people wish to restore the ontological argument for His existence. And this is so not only in Hegel but even in Descartes. The presupposition of the proof is the μετάβασις εἰς ἄλλο γένος ("passage into another realm"), the favorite method of speculative philosophy, the surest means it possesses to reach its goals. I repeat that the God of Hegel is not distinguished in any way from the materialist principle. And if the examples already quoted do not suffice, I would indicate another which, in certain respects, is still more interesting and more instructive. This is Hegel's reflection on the fate of Socrates, a reflection so significant that it is worth the trouble to quote it *in extenso*.

It is said of Socrates that, since he was condemned to death without being guilty, his fate was tragic. But such a misfortune happening to an innocent man would only be sad and not at all tragic, for it is not a rational misfortune. Misfortune is rational only when it is provoked by the will of the subject, who ought to be infinitely moral and just, like the forces against which he rises. It is for this reason that these cannot be simple forces of nature or a despotic will, for it is only in the former case that man is himself guilty of his death, while natural death is an absolute right, a right that nature realizes in relation to man. In the truly tragic, therefore, two forces equally just and moral must run into conflict; and such was indeed the fate of Socrates. And it was not only his personal, individual, romantic destiny; in it is manifested a general morally tragic destiny, the tragedy of Athens, the tragedy of Greece. Two opposed rights enter into combat and mutually destroy each other; both are conquered, and each of them is right in relation to the other, and neither is wrong. One of the forces is the divine right, the established custom whose laws are identified with the will that lives in it as in its own being, freely and nobly. And we, expressing it abstractly, can call it objective freedom. The other principle is the right, just as divine, of freedom, the right of consciousness or the right of subjective freedom. *This is the fruit of the tree of the knowledge of good and of evil, that is, reason drawing out of itself the general principle of philosophy for all time to come.* These are the two principles that entered into conflict in the life and philosophy of Socrates.

I have taken this fragment from Hegel's *Lectures on the History of Philosophy*, but what concerns us is obviously the philosophy of history as the greatest and perhaps most consistent of the rationalists understood it. The principle of philosophy for all time to come is found to be reason which draws it out of itself. This is true; there is nothing to reply to this. Post-Socratic philosophy—I would rather say, and it would be very close to the truth, post-Platonic philosophy—was entirely and exclusively determined by this principle. After Plato the philosophers have deliberately scorned every other source of knowledge, and in this respect the empiricists and positivists are very little distinguished from the metaphysicians. Plato himself, however, always wavers. He uses myth, and even very gladly. He believes in revelation but, while believing in it, he pushes it away, as the following fragment of the *Timeaus* testifies: "The best proof that God has given the faculty of prophecy precisely to human folly is the fact that no man in possession of his reason attains divine and true prophecy, but only those whose sleep binds their power of reason or those who in a state of illness or ecstasy are beside themselves."

It is obvious that Plato despises prophetic gifts of every kind, holds them in suspicion, refuses to consider them pure sources of knowledge. He who prophesies is not in possession of himself: his reason is enchained by sleep, sickness, or ecstasy. Would it not perhaps be more correct to say "unchained"? And then Plato forgets one very remarkable case, which he knew very well, wherein the gift of prophecy was not at all conditioned by the slumber of reason. Socrates' demon revealed the future to him not in dreams but while he was quite awake, with his body and his mind in their normal state. Plato wishes in one way or another to consider reason the only source of the knowledge of truth, and it is only by an inconsistency proper to human nature that he turns to myth. We have seen, however, through the example of the man who eats and drinks what exists, that inconsistency is sometimes more fruitful than the most rigorous logic.

But here is something still more striking: even Plotinus, the mystical philosopher, lived exclusively in the intelligible world, but his ecstatic states not only did not remove him from reason but, on the contrary, brought him closer to it. It may be said that Plotinus needed these ecstasies only to deliver himself from what the philosophers call the hold of sensible reality. Or, to employ the language of the Bible, which was at times not strange even to Hegel, in the state of ecstasy Plotinus renewed the sin of Adam: in a state of voluntary irresponsibility he tasted the fruit of the tree of knowledge of good and of evil in order to transform his human essence into a purely rational essence. Of all the gifts of God, the philosopher accepts only reason.

This is the meaning of the words "reason which draws out of itself"; this is the content of the "general principle" which, according to Hegel, determines philosophy for all time to come. Obviously if reason can, must, and wishes to draw everything out of itself, and if philosophy and that alone is what reason can draw out of itself, the philosophy of history and in particular the history of the philosophy of history must be constructed *more geometrico*. That is to say, we must establish the inner relations of pure concepts and show how one concept is transformed into another dialectically, i.e., through natural necessity. Socrates lived, taught the good, and died. He died not of his own free will, as—from the human point of view—should have happened to so great a man, but was condemned and executed as a criminal by his fellow citizens. Plato wrote his famous dialogue *Phaedo* on this subject. And then what did reason, which draws everything out of itself, do? The first rule is: reason never loses its head, being always certain of finding in itself the required explanation. Socrates was poisoned; consequently, he had to be poisoned. He had to be. If he did not have to be, he could still have been poisoned, but this would no longer have been anything but accidental—sad, it is true, but nevertheless only a matter of chance. To become a tragedy the misfortune had to be "rational," and

Hegel strives to demonstrate that the death of Socrates was precisely a rational misfortune and is therefore worthy of being the object of historical-philosophical reflections. Objective freedom had to make place for subjective freedom: the process was accomplished, and Socrates was poisoned.

But, first of all, the historical process could very well have been accomplished without Socrates being poisoned. If Socrates had died at sixty-nine years of typhus or some other sickness, the process of passing from objective freedom to subjective freedom would in no way have been delayed. And, then, why does Hegel speak of a sad accident, a misfortune, a tragedy? What is sad or tragic in the death of an aged Greek? From the point of view, naturally, of reason which draws everything out of itself? That Socrates should have died or not died, or that his death should have been the consequence of a conflict of two opposed principles or of a collision with a speeding chariot—what difference would there be? And how did reason draw out of itself expressions such as "sad misfortune," "tragedy"? Plato could weep for his friend and master. But pure reason does not know and does not wish to know tears: for it sadness and joy are only manifestations of individual perception. If one seeks pure knowledge he must renounce all "possessions" and, follow Spinoza's heritage, treat the human passions as he treats triangles and perpendiculars. Everything must be reduced to "understanding," that is, to mechanical explanations. Objective freedom is transformed into subjective freedom: it is in this that the content of history consists. The capitalist regime is replaced by the socialist—this is again a content of history. All this is certainly very well thought out, and it is difficult to refute Hegel or the materialists while remaining on their ground.

But if it be permitted to raise objections of a psychological character, I would recall what Hegel said about the naïve man who imagines that bread and water exist. For Hegel does not always dwell on the "heights" of pure speculation and, no matter how high he rises in the domain of the general and the metaphysical, he remains nevertheless always clothed, so to speak, in the "particular" and "empirical." He eats and drinks without distinguishing the real from the illusory, and his own acts refute him much better than his most relentless adversaries could. It is not for nothing that he speaks of the *Festigkeit der Allgemeinheit:* he wishes to condense, I would say to *materialize,* the general. And he attains his goal: his "general" is almost *tangible,* and it is this, I think, that constitutes the secret of his immense success.

On the one hand, he detached himself from the individual that philosophy is not suited to manage; on the other, there remain to him the "matter" and "motion" that have always seduced those who aspire to a philosophy with a beginning and an end. These are guaranteed only to a philosophy that recognizes a single source of truth. This philosophy "raises itself" above the particular and the contingent; it overcomes all the difficulties and insoluble contradictions of life. It "understands" life; death itself does not frighten it, for *der naturliche Tod nur ein absolutes Recht ist, was die Natur am Menschen ausübt.** If the very heavens collasped on its head, it would not fear anything. And God? Him it would fear even less. For God is an idea, certainly the purest idea, the idea most free of every individual element. It cannot give anything to or take anything away from men. "In history, certainly, the idea manifests itself as an absolute power: in other words, God rules over the world. But history is an idea that is *naturally* and not consciously fulfilled." It is quite evident that the essence of Hegel's rational philosophy is *die Idee, die auf natürliche Weise vollbracht wird.*† And further, I do not believe that I am mistaken in saying that the term "naturally" exhausts the essence of materialism.

* Natural death is only an absolute right which nature exercises over man.
† The idea that is naturally fulfilled.

I do not know who first introduced the use of the term "naturally." I know only that it has existed for a very long time, probably since philosophy has existed. I know also that it requires today immense daring to rid oneself of the power of this word. Try to renounce it—see what will then remain of philosophy. It seems that without it, it is impossible not only to philosophize but even to speak. It is for this reason that the philosophers have always been so drawn to the scientific method of thinking.

Res nullo alio modo vel ordine a Deo produci potuerunt quam productae sunt, * says Spinoza. In these few words he expressed, in a way that could not be improved upon, philosophy's historic goals and methods of research. In creating things, in creating the world, God only obeys His own nature with the same necessity that geometrical theorems are deduced from axioms and definitions. The sum of the two sides of a triangle is more than, and their difference less than, the third side. The side of a regular hexagon inscribed in a circle is equal to the radius of the circle, etc. To the last theorem, everything flows necessarily from the fundamental principles. And just as the geometer cannot inscribe a rhombus in a circle, God could not go so far as to create winged men or lions endowed with speech. And just as the geometer sees that the side of a regular hexagon inscribed in a circle must be equal to the radius of the circle, the philosopher will feel satisfied only when he will be convinced that man must be wingless, that Epictetus could not not have been a slave, and that Socrates had to die the death of a criminal. To understand is the final goal of philosophy. When Hegel "understood" that the death of Socrates was a "rational" misfortune or a tragedy, when he ate or drank "this" truth, he was satisfied and appeased. It then seemed to him that all those who read his writings would be equally satisfied and feel themselves content

---

* Things could have been made by God in no other way or order than the way in which they were made.

and that his *The Fate of Socrates* is therefore a more philosophic work than Plato's *Phaedo*, which is not an answer but a question, and a question to which no one, it seems, will ever be able to give a satisfactory or reassuring answer.

V

Spinoza goes even further than Hegel. In his asceticism, in any case, he is more daring, more resolute, more free. We know the puzzling and provocative statement of the father of Cynicism, Antisthenes: "I would rather lose my reason than experience pleasure." It is related that Diogenes called Antisthenes a powerful trumpet which did not hear itself. But it is not known just why the disciple spoke thus about his master. It is probable that it is precisely this statement that furnished Diogenes the occasion for his "psychologistic" criticism. The philosopher, according to Diogenes, must not speak but act. And I believe that among modern philosophers it is Spinoza who would have best satisfied Diogenes' demands. He truly "acted" according to his philosophy, lived it, and carefully pruned away from his "being" all "sensible" elements, so that he succeeded better than anyone else in transforming his soul into a general idea. He ceased to be Spinoza *hic et nunc;* he became *philosophus,* that is, a being not only bodiless but "without senses," like the God whom he worshiped. I think that it is precisely because of this that he provoked in his contemporaries so superstitious a repugnance, and that it is because of this also that he later captivated the hearts of his distant followers who discovered him anew, or, rather, disinterred him after long years of oblivion.

The biography of Spinoza tells us that among the living beings of the seventeenth century there wandered for a long time a phantom, i.e., a being knowing how to think like men and even interesting itself in its way in earthly life, but deprived of all the sensible qualities that permit us to distinguish living beings from apparitions. A phantom is intermediate between the living and the dead. It is not dead, for it enters into relationships with men; but it is not living either, for what exists does not exist for it. And men have different attitudes toward phantoms: some fear them, some worship them.

But how was so strange a metamorphosis produced in Spinoza? Why from man did he become a phantom? A question all the more interesting in that, though according to Spinoza's teaching *res nullo alio modo vel ordine a Deo produci potuerunt quam productae sunt*, we have every reason to believe that this *res* which in its time existed under the name of Benedict Spinoza became what is was—that is, an object of fear and astonishment—not by virtue of "necessity" and not even by virtue of the necessity of its inner nature. God Himself had nothing to do here. To this *res* a truly extraordinary thing happened: it escaped outside the bounds which attached it to other objects, outside the milieu where its destiny had placed it, and became not what it had to be by virtue of necessity but what it wished to be according to its own individual caprice. And if it be true that God creates things, we must believe that in this case He stopped midway. He began to create Spinoza according to His ordinary fashion, but when He perceived that the matter that had fallen into His hand was extremely special, He abandoned it to itself and permitted it to complete itself as it wished. And certainly the Spinoza we know was not created by God by virtue of necessity but created himself by an arbitrary act, in the realization of that freedom, perhaps, of which Dostoevsky speaks to us through the mouth of his Kirilov. I would say more. According to Spinoza, if the stone were endowed with consciousness, it would imagine not that it falls to the ground in obedience to the law of gravity but that it flies freely in space at its own whim. Ah well, a conscious stone would perhaps not guess that it does not fly but only falls, but even an unconscious stone must understand that Spinoza became Spinoza not by virtue of necessity but by a free decision of his will.

Now we would see how he was transformed into a phantom or into what men took for a phantom. The answer to this question is not to be found in any of his chief writings, neither in the *Ethics* nor in the *Tractatus Theologico-Politicus*, nor even in his letters. He appears to us there already as an accomplished *philosophus*, a man who has overcome all doubts, who has rooted out everything of the human in himself, in short, man as a concept, a pure intellect, with this fundamental principle: *de natura rationis non est res ut contingentes, sed ut necessarias contemplari.** But in the *Tractatus de intellectus emendatione* we are able at least in part to follow the process by which "this man," that is, the living man, transforms himself into man in general. It is true that Spinoza shows himself here also very reserved and niggardly as far as confessions that one expects of him are concerned—as if these teachings should be given only to initiates by allusion, an allusion from which it may be concluded that behind the exoteric philosophy there is hidden an esoteric one. It is known that the admission of such a duality profoundly revolted Hegel. But it seems to me in this case Hegel was not sufficiently clear-sighted, perhaps *ex officio*. It is indubitable that every man has two philosophies: the one open, expressed, accessible to all; the other secret, not only inaccessible to all, but even at moments inconceivable to himself who has created it and carried it in his soul. It almost never succeeds in finding a form capable of expressing itself. Fragmentary phrases that the author lets escape, one might say, involuntarily, some words, an intonation, an

* The nature of reason is not to contemplate things as contingent but as necessary.

exclamation—it is only through these that this invisible, secret, but perhaps most important part of the human soul's life manifests itself. Even Hegel to whom, by the nature of his aspirations, such confessions were so alien could not fail to note, at least in passing, with disdain or scorn, the fact of the existence of a "musical" consciousness. But, as we know, Hegel tried to materialize even general ideas, sought *die Festigkeit der Allgemeinheit,* and feared above all the "animated," in which he discovered quite rightly that contingency and arbitrariness to which he was so deeply hostile. And that is why one feels such a difference between Hegel and Spinoza, despite the resemblance of their pantheistic ideas.

Hegel is more heedless, more self-confident than Spinoza, like a man for whom his predecessors have prepared the ground, accomplishing the hardest part of the work. He received as a heritage his power to bind and to unbind, his *potestas clavium;* this power was handed over to him through a long series of generations, and he believed that it came from God. Spinoza had acquired it himself and well knows, like every man who has himself conquered power, what it cost him. It is for this reason that we find in Hegel answers to all questions, while Spinoza has only his *Ethics,* in other words, the science that shows us that the man who is prepared to undertake the supreme renunciation and to accomplish *exercitia spiritualia* of the most difficult kind can become a metaphysical being. Such a man can transform himself into pure thought, which is as independent of the hazards of earthly existence as of the changeability of individual fate.

Spinoza was certainly not the first to set himself such a task, and he was not the first to fulfill it. But the question of priority in this case is of no importance. In *such* cases the experience of predecessors is of no help. One must himself accomplish from beginning to end everything that the metamorphosis of a living man into an idea or concept demands. In ancient times men often set themselves such tasks. Indeed they were not alien even to the pre-Socratic philosophy. But our information concerning the ancients is too meagre for us to be able to risk seeking among them an ultra-esoteric philosophy. We do not know very much even of the Cynics and the Stoics. In modern times, in any case, the most striking example of such a philosophy is offered us by Spinoza.

In his *Tractatus de intellectus emendatione,* he reports to us briefly what happened to him. In his youth it seemed to him, as to all men, that the best things in life were *divitiae, honores, et libidines.* But he soon became convinced that all these are acquired only at the price of great difficulties, that those who attain these goods are very rare, and furthermore that they are vain. Moreover, by their very nature they are incapable of procuring for us true satisfaction. The rich man wishes to be still richer, honors provoke the desire for still greater honors, and pleasures leave after them only a feeling of emptiness. What to do then? Like a man attacked by a mortal sickness, Spinoza felt himself condemned to a desperate remedy: renunciation. The medicine itself could kill him. But there was no other solution. He renounced the world and found that *amor erga rem aeternam* which alone could heal the human soul and grant to it the supreme good, obviously an intellectual good, of which the miserable descendants of Adam have been dreaming ever since the day their ancestors were driven out of paradise.

VI

I know perfectly well that Spinoza, even more than Hegel, was the enemy of all mythology, and that in his eyes the Biblical mythology did not present any advantage over the mythology of the pagans. And, nevertheless, it has been impossible for me not to remember Adam and the original sin.

Spinoza concluded his *Ethics* with these words: *Omnia praeclara tam difficilia, quam rara sunt.** What is this if not the free transcription of the terrible words addressed by God to Adam and Eve when He drove them out of Paradise: "In the sweat of your brow shall you gain your bread," etc. . . . ? Why must everything beautiful be rare and difficult? It ought to be just the opposite, one would think: man ought to gain his daily bread easily and joyously and woman ought to bring children into the world without pain. For all that is "natural," assuming the word "natural" has any meaning whatsoever, ought to correspond to the will and aspirations as well as the physical organization of man. Work ought to be a need for us, and childbirth not only painless but even pleasant. Death itself, as a natural end, ought to be something welcomed, not an object of horror.

But Spinoza, like all the great philosophers, felt that in philosophy one should follow not the line of least but of greatest

* All beautiful and excellent things are as difficult as they are rare.

resistance. If it is true that πόλεμος πατὴρ πάντων, "war is the father of all," philosophy must be essentially πόλεμος. It is for this reason probably that the eudemonistic, hedonistic, and even utilitarian theories have never survived long here on earth. The philosopher seeks what is difficult; he seeks struggle. His true element is the problematic, the eternally problematic. He knows that Paradise has been lost and wishes to regain the lost Paradise. If it is impossible to regain it immediately or in a more or less near future, he is ready to wait years, decades, to the end of life, and if it be necessary, to postpone the task to the time after death, even if he should for this reason have to live in an extreme tension at all moments and to feel perpetually only the pains of an unending childbirth.

In Spinoza, despite his external calm which is so strange and dominates everything, this interior tension attains an unheard-of degree. What is perhaps most remarkable in his philosophy is that he knew how to speak of the most difficult and greatest events of his internal life in simple and even meagre words. His famous sentence, *non ridere, non lugere, neque detestari, sed intelligere,** does not at all mean that he did not laugh or weep or curse. I am even ready to translate it by those words of Pascal which, at first blush, seem directly opposed to it: *Je n'approuve que ceux qui cherchent en gémissant.*† When, like a monk who takes vows of chastity, poverty, and obedience, Spinoza renounces *divitiae, honores, et libidines,*‡ it seems that the tragedy of the expulsion of Adam and Eve from paradise is repeated anew. For what are *divitiae, honores, libidines?* Three little words, it seems, and words that, furthermore, never contained anything very attractive for philosophy. But behind them, finally, lies the entire universe of God. And even, if you wish, paradise. For, as the Bible tells us, in paradise there was an im-

---

* Not to laugh, not to weep, not to curse, but to understand.
† I approve only those who seek with lamentation.
‡ Riches, honors, and pleasures.

mense abundance of riches, and joys were not forbidden there; there man was honored, and all passions except one, the passion to know, were there not only permitted but even encouraged. Now before all these things stands an angel with a fiery sword, and it is only to the tree of knowledge, to the *intelligere*, that we have free access.

Obviously the angel and the fiery sword are only symbols; I do not wish to trouble the mind of the modern, educated reader by demanding of him that he believe in the supernatural. And, in general, I do not impose any demands. But such is reality. Whether you wish it or not, Spinoza is right: *divitiae, honores, et libidines*—my God, how miserable and empty they are here on earth! If the laconic reflections of Spinoza on this matter do not satisfy you, reread Schopenhauer: he will speak to you of these things with the *éclat* and verve which are his own. And he will add that all this is already contained *implicite* in Spinoza's little treatise.

VII

But I shall perhaps be asked: what have the angel and the fiery sword to do here? Both exist, only they are found not outside of man but in him, just like that apple which Adam ate. They are manifest in our desire *intelligere*, in our art of creating general ideas. It suffices for a man (as Spinoza, following the suggestions of his predecessors, did) to employ the language of concepts for Paradise immediately to transform itself into Hell. Where beautiful gardens were, where birds sang, where young lion cubs played perpetually, where people rejoiced, loved, where a free life ruled triumphantly, there suddenly arose *divitiae, honores, et libidines*—as concepts which, whether one translates them into Latin or into another language, mean only one thing: death, death, and death! And the philosophy of Spinoza, which bears at its proud summit *Amor Dei intellectualis*, is also death. Man carries in himself an angel armed with a burning sword which forbids him access to Paradise.

The ancient curse continues to weigh upon us. We also are guilty and we are our own willing executioners. *Res nullo alio modo vel ordine a Deo produci potuerunt quam productae sunt (Eth.* I, prop. XXXIII), or, as Hegel put it, *vernünftiges Unglück*! How is it that man could come to find supreme satisfaction in the knowledge that misfortune is rational and that God could not create things otherwise than He did create them? And yet, it is at this that we are asked to stop; it is in this that one sees the supreme wisdom, the highest good that life can give us. Even the sweet singer Horace assures us that the most enviable fate on earth is that of the wise man:

Sapiens uno minor est Jove, dives,
*Liber, honoratus, pulcher, rex denique regum.**

Who speaks thus? The ancient serpent who took on the form of a poet and began anew to lead men astray by praising them the beauty of the fruits of the tree of knowledge. If it were a question of Horace only, one could refuse to listen to him: πολλὰ ψεύδονται οἱ ἀοιδοί (the poets lie a great deal). But Horace only repeated what the philosophers constantly proclaim, the philosophers who know perfectly well that there is not a grain of truth in these statements. The wise man is not at all beautiful or free and he is not the king of kings. He is enchained, ugly, the least of slaves, and stands in all things not only behind Jupiter but behind the most miserable of mortals.

The "exoteric" philosophy must obviously be silent about this. I think that even the initiates do not speak of these things among themselves. It is only among the saints that you will find confessions of this kind, but the saints expressed themselves in such a way that no one ever believed them. And, in general, this is one of those great mysteries of life that remain hidden, even when one speaks of them loudly in all public places. The philosophers, like the saints, need *sancta superbia*. And Spinoza, finally, lived only thanks to *sancta superbia*, of which he tells us nothing in his writings, for it is impossible to treat of it as one treats of perpendiculars and triangles. One must sing of it as the food of the gods, as nectar and ambrosia. Spinoza's *Ethics* in its

* The wise man is only a little less than Jove, rich, free, honored, handsome, and, lastly, king of kings.

entirety is precisely a triumphal, but not a triumphant, hymn to the glory of *sancta superbia*.

It is said that intuition is the only means of grasping the supreme truth. Intuition comes from the word *intueri*, "to see." Men have very great trust in their vision, and for this they certainly have sufficient reason. Yet it is necessary to know not only how to see but also how to hear. The philosophers should have found a substantive from the word *audire* and granted to it all the rights of intuition. And even more rights still. For the most important, the most necessary thing cannot be seen; it can only be heard. The mysteries of being are whispered silently only to him who knows how, at the right time, to be all ears. At these moments one discovers that everything in life is not "rational" and particularly so "misfortune"; that God is not a general idea and that not only does He not act "according to the laws" of His nature but that He is Himself the source of all laws and of all natures; that things are such as they were created by God but could have been created quite otherwise; that the philosopher, who is obliged to know the universe by means of general ideas, is not *rex regum* but *servus servorum*, the least of all men, as the famous saints, St. Theresa or her disciple St. John of the Cross, and still others, were. But it is impossible to see all these things: we can only hear them.

In recent times, Husserl has defined philosophy as the science of the roots of things, ῥιζώματα πάντων. This definition, in which one cannot fail to notice a remembrance of Empedocles' verse, τέσσαρα γὰρ πάντων ῥιζώματα πρῶτον ἄκουε (before all else, learn the four roots of all things), is extremely seductive and, in its way, expresses exactly the object which philosophy, in the person of its most remarkable representatives, always set itself. Nevertheless, one cannot characterize it as exhaustive. Man obviously tries to know the roots and sources of everything that exists. But Plotinus was also right when, to the question "What is philosophy?" he replied, τὸ τιμιώτατον, "the most important, the most valuable." Man seeks the roots not because he is pushed by an unsatisfied curiosity. Rightly or wrongly he believes that where the roots and origins are is also what is most important, most valuable, most necessary for him. If it turned out, for example, that vulgar materialism contained the "final truth," philosophy would obviously no longer be entitled to call itself the science of sciences. If everything arose from dust and will return to dust, is it worth the trouble to be interested in roots and origins? So then, in seeking the ῥιζώματα πάντων philosophy aspires to τὸ τιμώτατον, that is, it wishes to find the sources of life-bringing and death-bringing elixirs.

Even the monk Spinoza, who had made a vow of renunciation, tells us (*Eth.* I, prop. XI): *Posse non existere impotentia est, et contra posse existere potentia est . . . Ergo, ens absolute infinitum, hoc est Deus, necessario existit.** Complete monk that he is, he nevertheless aspires to *potentia*. And yet *potentia* is the same as *divitiae, honores,* and if you wish, *libidines,* but freed to a certain extent from those contingencies and conditions that are the property of earthly existence.

A rich and honored man is above all a powerful man and consequently a free and proud man. But Spinoza himself rejected wealth and honors only because man is incapable of preserving by his own powers the *divitiae et honores* that he has conquered or inherited. But when he called them *potentia* it seemed to him that things had changed completely, for *potentia,* at least the *potentia* of which he dreamt, had been defined by him in terms and predicates that did not admit the idea of destruction. But the whole argumentation here is obviously false. To begin with, *posse non existere* can be considered a power as well as a weakness. It may be that the choice between existence and non-existence must be left to the supreme being. But then, even if

---

* The potentiality of non-existence is a negation of power and, contrariwise, the potentiality of existence is a power . . . Therefore, a being absolutely infinite—in other words, God—necessarily exists.

one admits with Spinoza that *posse non existere, impotentia est,* who can then oblige us to accord the preference to power over weakness? Or, more exactly, is the desire for power not *libido,* one of those passions which Spinoza vowed to renounce? Is there any place in geometry for *potentia,* and especially the desire for *potentia?* If one reasons mathematically, *potentia* is a certain curve, that is, the geometric locus of points having a certain determinate character; *impotentia* is another curve, that is, likewise the geometric locus of points having a certain determinate character. Let us say that the first is a circle and the second an ellipse. It is completely evident that there is no reason to accord preference to the circle over the ellipse. God can have as a predicate *posse existere* as well as *posse non existere,* if the question of his existence is treated *more geometrico.* I mean that the "proof" contains a *petitio principii,* and that it cannot be otherwise. It is clear that, before establishing his argumentation, Spinoza, in a certain process which does not express itself in his works (probably deliberately) decides the question not only of God's existence but also of all His predicates, and he remembered geometry only when he had to address men. He remembered it because he was afraid that his thoughts, deprived of their proofs, would be received with scorn and with shrugging of the shoulders. But, his philosophy was for him τὸ τιμιώτατον, the most valuable. And he had to protect it by all the means, whatever they might be, that were in his power. If Spinoza had been a king or a pope he would have had recourse to pyres and tortures. But he was poor, weak, unknown. He possessed only his reason. So he wrote his *Ethica more geometrico demonstrata.* And it turned out that by this method it was possible to preserve many things for a long time and even better than by means of pyres and tortures. But not forever. If the philosophy of Spinoza should not find other means of defending itself, his God will not have the power, any more than the God of the inquisitors, to withstand time. And then it is obvious also that the question must be posed differently, as the men who were still free of our self-sufficiency and of our prejudices posed it: it is not man who "defends" God but God who defends man. To put it another way: it is not necessary to defend God but to seek Him and, consequently, if philosophy wishes, following the thought of Plotinus, to be τὸ τιμώτατον, reason must renounce its pretensions to sovereignty. It is not given to it "to draw everything out of itself"; it is not reason that was "in the beginning." The sources and roots of life lie beyond the boundaries of reason.

VIII

But it is most difficult for us to reconcile ourselves to this thought. And the philosophy of Schopenhauer furnishes us the best proof of this. Nietzsche says somewhere that morality was always the Circe of the philosophers. That is true. But it is still more true that reason also knew how to enchant the philosophers. It is known that Schopenhauer was not at all inclined to rationalism, not only on theoretical grounds but by the very nature of his mind. For him, reason is a parasite, almost a prostitute, as it is for Luther. And no one among the philosophers knew as well as Schopenhauer how to recognize and underscore so cleverly the weak sides of reason. He alone among the pupils and disciples of Kant accepted entirely the transcendental esthetic and logic of his master. Reason does not and can not give us true knowledge. Its function is to create an illusory world, the world of Maya, through the forms of sensibility, space and time, and the categories, chiefly the category of causality. Hence our knowledge does not extend to reality, which reason by its very nature is incapable of grasping, but only to "phenomena" which do not "reveal" but rather hide true reality. It would seem that in these conditions—after Kant had divined that reason is the source not of truth but of error and falsehood—that the whole task of philosophy should have reduced itself to delivering men from the deceptive truths imposed by the parasite and liar, reason. The essence of the world is will and its voice, its decisions, should be for us the only source of true knowledge. But the force and power of Circe-like reason are such that it succeeds in subjecting the finest and most daring minds, and there still has not been found any wise Ulysses capable of discovering the miraculous flower and breaking the magic of the sorceress.

All the philosophers have sung and glorified reason, and Schopenhauer could not avoid the common fate. What once happened to the Biblical Balaam happened to him: he wished to curse reason but in reality blessed it. His philosophy reduces itself to a kind of debate between will and reason, a debate in which it is almost always reason that triumphs. As soon as the "will," that is, the true metaphysical essence of being, tries to raise its voice, reason begins to rattle its arguments and drowns the voice of the will. The will of man aspires to life and joy; reason "demonstrates" that joys are ephemeral and life poor and empty. The will aspires to love, but reason delivers a brilliant, witty, and long discourse on the theme of the metaphysics of sexual love, from which it follows that love is only falsehood and illusion. The will of man aspires to eternal life; reason, relying on Aristotle (reason cannot do without Aristotle), proves, as if it were $2 \times 2 = 4$, that everything that is born must necessarily die and that consequently man must die, that our fear of death and our repugnance before the end is only a prejudice which is not justified by anything and which pales and vanishes like the flame of a candle under the immortal sun of understanding.

However, according to the doctrine even of Schopenhauer, reason does not know anything and cannot know anything; reason is a servant, a slave, whose role consists only in executing the orders of the will. By what right, then, does it permit itself this arrogant tone in arguing with its mistress? It ought to obey without murmuring but, being a rebellious slave, it dares to command and dominate. Schopenhauer himself remarks that reason in him betrayed its role, "emancipated itself," and began to function on its own account. He notices this but does not disturb himself on its account and even rejoices in it. He rejoices that the magician whom he had succeeded in chaining for a moment has again escaped and taken up its criminal activity! Why does he rejoice in it? For the reason, probably, that otherwise philosophy would be impossible, at least philosophy as "rigorous science." But philosophy does not wish to be only "rigorous science"; it seeks also the most important, it wishes to discover ῥιζώματα πάντων, to arrive at the roots of life. And thus the dilemma: if you obey reason, you will obtain "rigorous science" but you will find yourself infinitely removed from the ῥιζώματα πάντων; if, however, you aspire to the ῥιζώματα πάντων, in other words, if you admit that the most important, τὸ τιμιώτατον, is found where these deep roots are hidden, you must renounce reason and the hope of ever obtaining the certitude that what you consider as the roots of things are indeed roots. For if reason has always seduced man, it is because it gave him assurance, *certitudo*, of which Spinoza, who was ordinarily so reserved and so chary of words, speaks in inspired tones.

Reason is the sister of morality, and it has always known how to act by irrational means, by what are called in logic *argumenta ad hominem*. To be sure, reason will never admit this and even gets angry when it is suspected of such disloyalty. It pretends to absolute impartiality and supreme objectivity. Yet I believe that if, in place of his "epiphilosophy," Schopenhauer had written a special chapter on "The Metaphysics of Objective Reason," following the programme of his article on "The Metaphysics of Sexual Love," his philosophy would have gained much by it. For if it be true that the will is the metaphysical principle of life, it is hardly right that reason be delivered and emancipated from its subaltern role. In all probability, among the other illusions that reason has created at the order, and following the indications, of the will, its dream of freedom is likewise only pure illusion, an illusion created by the needs of the will. The will required that reason believe itself autonomous and in possession of all its rights. Therefore it inspired in some the idea that ἐν ἀρχῇ ἦν ὁ λόγος, "in the beginning was the λογοε," and in Schopenhauer that, though the λόγος was not in the beginning, it was given to it to free itself from the metaphysical principle of life. Schopenhauer, who mocked human illusions with so much spirit, allowed himself to be tricked by his own reason and ended by believing in the fundamental lie of life, thus sharing the fate of all men.

There are here more than enough contradictions and complications, but I do not believe that the object of philosophy consists in unraveling or at least in cutting, at any cost, the Gordian knots of existence. If life is filled with complications, philosophy can not and must not aspire at any cost to "clarity and distinctness." If there are contradictions in life, philosophy must live from these contradictions. I think that the very abundance of contradictions and complications constitutes the merit of Schopenhauer. It is true that he let himself be seduced by "reason," but we must also do him justice: the "will" in him speaks sometimes with such force and so loudly that the considerations of reason completely cease to exist. It is not for nothing that he so insisted on the metaphysical significance of music. In his philosophy there is much music, which did not take any account of the "word," neither at the beginning nor at the end. To be sure, the essence of every philosophy, even that of Aristotle, consists entirely in music. In other words, philosophy not only sees but hears, and the source of philosophy is not only "spiritual" vision but also "spiritual" hearing, and perhaps even—who knows?— "spiritual" feeling (as in Plotinus), smelling, tasting.

One cannot even be sure that there do not exist certain "sensible faculties" still not discovered by psychology which will be found to be, and always to have been, the source of highest metaphysical revelations. It is clear, in any case, that Schopenhauer under no circumstances should have forgotten the will for the sake of reason, even if it appeared that the will, i.e., the supreme metaphysical principle, could not furnish scientific knowledge. One could have concluded from this only that scientific knowledge is not the final and most perfect form of knowledge and cannot lead us to the ῥιζώματα πάντων, the roots of things. And, further, that there is a certain knowledge whose "logical structure" does not at all resemble the logical structure of scientific knowledge. The philosopher not only has no right to scorn it, but his duty, or rather, his royal privilege, is to seek this knowledge. But Schopenhauer, bewitched by his Circe, wrote: *Die Philosophie hat ihren Wert und ihre Würde darin, dass sie alle nicht zu begründenden Annahmen verschmäht und in ihre Data nur das aufnimmt, was sich in der anschaulich gegebenen Aussenwelt, in der unseren Intellekt konstituirenden Formen zur Auffassung derselben und in dem allen gemeinsamen Bewusstein des eigenen Selbst sicher nachweisen lässt* (W.a.W.u.V.,II 720 Recl.).

These words contain all the commonplaces and all the prejudices of traditional philosophy. So could speak only the reason which imagines that it has been delivered finally and once and for all from its subaltern role and has become its own master. Just as in the popular Russian fable of the fisherman and the goldfish, reason suddenly wishes that life itself be at its service. It disdains everything that cannot be proven, admits only the consciousness common to all, and values only sure knowledge. It does not accept any "gifts," it takes only what belongs to it, and it "draws everything from itself." All this is certainly only a conventional lie, and the best refutation of the lie is offered us by the very works of Schopenhauer himself where we find at every turn statements which are based on nothing and which have no right to pretend to prove anything whatsoever. And if one eliminated from his writings all the passages which do not conform to the demands imposed by him on philosophy, there would remain to us only a few dozen pages of general dissertations having no relationship to philosophy—that is, a broken vessel, as in the fable in question: this is all that remains of the philosophies which have conscientiously observed the tradition of scientific rigor.

But Schopenhauer himself is different: without any embarrassment, he sometimes glorifies and sometimes insults reason. When he needs to, he recalls the "primacy" of the will and rails against those who believe in pure reason. Turn the page following the phrase I have just quoted above and you will see Schopenhauer in the company of people in whose midst he would be embarrassed even to speak of reason, and much more so of rigorous science. He converses with Angelus Silesius, admires Meister Eckhardt and the *Theologia deutsch*, praises enthusiastically the famous quietist Molinos, and, as if he had not just spoken of the scientific rigor of philosophy, says: "Every philosophy which is obliged to reject such a way of thinking . . . must necessarily be false" (*Ibid.*, 724).

Then several pages further, in order to enable everyone to establish clearly that paradoxes are dearer to him than "well-founded" truths, he quotes the words of Saint Augustine: *Novi quosdam, qui murmurent: quid si inquiunt, omnes velint ab omni concubitu abstinere, unde subsistet genus humanum? Utinam omnes hoc vellent! Dumtaxat in caritate, de corde puro, ex conscientia bona, ex fide non ficta: multo citius Dei civitas compleretur, ut acceleraretur terminus mundi.* (I know those who murmur: if everyone wished to abstain from intercourse with women, what would happen to the human species? O that everyone might wish it! With love, with a pure heart and a good conscience, with an unsimulated faith, the city of God would arrive much more quickly and the end of the world be hastened.)

Now let someone try to be clever and understand what this means: through theses based on reason, the only theses that have the right to be quoted in philosophy, or arbitrary statements coming from a mysterious source: *sic volo, sic jubeo, stat pro ratione voluntas.**

I do not wish to quote other fragments, even though they be very interesting, of the same chapter or of other writings of Schopenhauer to render still more evident his perfect indifference toward the principles that he himself had raised. It is quite clear that it is not "pure reason" nor the "consciousness common to all" that is the source of his philosophic aspirations. He sees, hears, touches, and has much more confidence in his impressions than in "proofs."

Schopenhauer could become what he was only because he was not afraid to scorn, when he needed to, *ratio* of every kind and to give full freedom to his own *voluntas*. To his own *voluntas* and not to *voluntas* in general, i.e., to that "personal," creative, living will which, contrary to all "eternal" laws, escaped from the bosom of the general and the immutable in order to realize its perhaps temporary and changing but independent existence. And if, nevertheless, reason appears in Schopenhauer *de jure* as the supreme tribunal of the living and the dead, this only indicates, it seems to me, how solid and deeply rooted are human prejudices or, if you wish, how immutable are the decrees of God.

For "reason" is the fiery sword by means of which the angel placed by God at the gates of Paradise drives men away. How strange: Schopenhauer did not like the Old Testament. But in the legend of the original sin he sees a profound meaning and a great mystery. Yet he could not or would not see that what constituted the horror of the original sin, which is transmitted from generation to generation, is that the man who has tasted the fruit of knowledge cannot do other than think by means of general ideas and forever seek "proofs." To listen to Molinos, Schopenhauer must first test his sayings by those of Angelus Silesius or of Meister Eckhardt. It was only when he became

---

* Thus I will, thus I command, my will is reason enough.

convinced that "all" say the same thing that he was willing to believe them and invited others to believe them. That is, he recognized as the supreme judge of truth and of error the "consciousness common to all." But even if the testimony of all those whom Schopenhauer invoked were found to be in agreement and if it were proven, as Schopenhauer supposes, that they could not have influenced each other directly or indirectly, this would not at all guarantee the truth of their teaching. They could all have been victims of the same falsehood and the same illusion. Were not the inhabitants of the New World as certain as the inhabitants of the Old World, from which they were separated by oceans, that the sky is a solid vault and that the truth is immovable? They were all similarly mistaken.

So, then, Molinos and Angelus Silesius and Madame Guyon could all be mistaken in the same way, and the method of "reason" on which Schopenhauer counts so greatly gives us only the appearance of certitude. Also the philosophy which hopes to find the truth by the help of general ideas lives an illusion.

What happened to Molinos, what he saw and understood, existed only for him, and beyond the limits of all "general." Angelus Silesius lived something else, and St. Theresa something still different. To verify or test Silesius by Eckhardt and vice versa is equivalent to renouncing the experience of both. And what is still worse is to conclude from the experience of two or three men, or even of a great number of human beings, what happens in general and what can happen.

By this method the logical "eye" creates for itself the illusion of solid, transparent concepts, just as the physical eye creates for itself the illusion of a crystal vault above our heads. The general and the necessary are non-being *par excellence*. And only when it recognizes this will philosophy redeem the sin of Adam and arrive at the ῥιζώματα πάντων, the roots of life, at that τιμιώτατον, that "most important," of which men have dreamt for so many thousands of years.

PART IV

Memento Mori

(On Edmund Husserl's Theory of Knowledge)

What is philosophy? That which is most important.

—Plotinus

Evidenz ist in der Tat nicht irgendein Bewusstseinsindex, der, an ein Urtell angeheftet, uns wie eine mystische Stimme aus einer bessern Welt zuruft: Hier ist die Wahrheit!, als ob solch eine Stimme uns freien Geistern etwas zu sagen und ihren Rechtstitel nicht auszuweisen hätte.

—E. Husserl,
Ideen zu einer reinen Phänomenologie *

* Evidence is in fact not any index of consciousness which, attached to a judgment, calls to us like a mystical voice from a better world saying: "Here is the truth!"—as if such a voice had anything to say to us free spirits and did not need to present its credentials.

—E. Husserl,
Ideas Toward a Pure Phenomenology

I

The question is often raised what distinguishes philosophy from
the other sciences, but it seems that the most essential of these
distinctions, that precisely thanks to which philosophy is what
it is, i.e., a science totally different from other sciences, is always
deliberately brushed aside. I say *deliberately* for it seems to me
that everyone recognizes the difference but at the same time
obstinately seeks to efface it, to make it non-existent. This has
happened since the most ancient times. The Greeks had already
observed that philosophy is constituted otherwise than the other
sciences; nevertheless, they tried to demonstrate by all possible
means that it did not in any way differ from them. Even more:
they tried to convince themselves that philosophy is the science
of sciences and that it is particularly qualified to resolve all problems by its special method. The other sciences possess only
opinions, Parmenides already said, while philosophy reveals to
us the truth: "It is necessary that you learn to recognize everything, both the unshakable heart of the well-rounded truth and
the opinions of mortals in which there resides only true belief."

It is quite evident, however, that neither "roundness," whether
good or bad, and still less the "unshakable heart" belongs properly to the truth, but that these virtues qualify precisely the
opinions of mortals. All mortals know that night follows day,

that stones sink in water, that drought kills plants, etc.; human beings possess a large number of opinions of this kind that are firm and unshakable. As for the truths, they flicker only for a moment and are immediately extinguished; they always tremble and shake, like the leaves of the aspen. When Parmenides proclaims his truth, "being and knowing are one and the same," he needs all the passion and ardor of his great soul to pronounce these words with that firm tranquility with which the ordinary man expresses his opinions, even those whose error will appear the very next day.

For error is one of the accidental predicates of opinion, while it appears to be mysteriously bound to the very essence of truth. When I am of the opinion that Caesar killed Brutus or that Alexander was the father of Philip of Macedon, my error is easily correctable: it suffices for me to be taught by a better instructed person or to open a manual of history for me to be delivered from my erroneous opinion. In brief, the opinions of men in what concerns daily life are false only temporarily. Often we are too quick to reach a conclusion or we do not possess sufficient data to answer the question that has been raised, but we know well that when we shall have examined things more carefully, when we shall have obtained the necessary data, we shall arrive at solid and true opinions. Let us take an example: Are there living beings on the planet Mars? Some believe in their existence, others do not. But a time will come when people will cease to believe, for they will become convinced, either that Mars is inhabited or that it is not.

The situation is quite different when it is a question of purely philosophical problems. Parmenides believes that thought and being are identical. I believe that it is not so at all. Some will agree with Parmenides; others will join me. But none of us has the right to declare that his judgment contains the whole truth. The supreme, authentically certain truth, on which men will sooner or later reach agreement, is that in the metaphysical domain there are no certain truths. One can argue about the laws of chemistry and physics, and these arguments are fruitful in the sense that they lead the opponents little by little to common convictions that are solid and certain. When Archimedes investigated the laws of the lever, he established the same relationships that we can confirm today. And he who presented objections to Archimedes and fought him wished finally the same thing as Archimedes. One can say the same of the disciples of Ptolemy and Copernicus. All of them wished to know the truth about the movements of the sun and the earth and when, at a certain moment, this truth appeared clearly, arguments ceased of themselves, having become useless.

In philosophy, on the other hand, it seems that arguments do not come from the unclarity of the object: uncertainty and contradiction are here inherent in the very nature of the problem. Heraclitus and Parmenides will be incapable of agreeing not only in this world, but in the other also, if they should meet there. The truth that they served on earth and in the other world not only exists but still lives. And like every living thing, it is not always equal to itself and not always similar to itself. I think that it is necessary to admit this. I think that it is impossible to accept blindly the conviction transmitted to us by the Greeks that philosophy, by its logical structure, is a science like other sciences. Precisely because the ancients, under the hypnosis under which we continue to the present day to live and think, tried to make philosophy the science *par excellence*, we are obliged to doubt these statements.

However, philosophy today as in the past avoids posing the problem in this form. The works of our time dealing with the theory of knowledge, like those of ancient times, pursue a quite different object. They wish at all costs to justify our science as the only possible one, and to demonstrate that philosophy also must be a science. We are convinced that our knowledge is perfect; the difficulty consists only in explaining on what this conviction is based. In the course of the entire nineteenth century the representatives of scientific philosophy always tried with extreme obstinacy to overcome this difficulty. And the twentieth century, in this respect, does not wish to remain behind. We too encounter not a few attempts at new theories of knowledge which continue to strive for the realization of the ancient object.

I think I shall not be in error to say that among these works the most remarkable are those of Edmund Husserl. And I think it would be extremely useful to test the results of his investigations. It is obviously impossible for me here to study in detail everything that Husserl has written. Furthermore, it is not necessary. Husserl published in the first number of the review *Logos* an article entitled "Philosophy as Rigorous Science" (*Philosophie als strenge Wissenschaft*). In this extremely well-developed article Husserl sums up the results of his long meditations. It is chiefly to this study that I shall here refer, touching on Husserl's other works only, so to speak, in passing, in the measure that they explain his thoughts to us.

The very article of Husserl's article, "Philosophy as Rigorous Science," already clarifies for us to a certain degree the orientation of the author's ideas by emphasizing that the problem Husserl raises is quite in the historic tradition. Husserl, it is true, complains that the philosophers who preceded him, obeying the necessities of the moment, often agreed to compromises, abandoned the direct object of their searches and aspired not to philosophy but to "wisdom" or even a "general conception of the universe," and thus, so to speak, betrayed their mission. But he declares, nevertheless, that philosophy always wished to be a science; it did not always succeed, however, in confining itself within limits and often manifested a criminal impatience in its haste to attain its supreme goal, thus itself hampering the accomplishment of its work. The most important epochs in the history of philosophy were the Socratic-Platonic period in antiquity and the Cartesian in modern times. The last representatives of scientific philosophy were Kant and, to a certain degree, Fichte. According to Husserl's terminology, Schelling and Hegel among the moderns and Plotinus and the Stoics among the ancients were not philosophers but "wise men"—that is, not representatives of rigorous science but brilliant and profound improvisors who choose the first and last problems of being as their theme.

This opposing of philosophy and science, on the one hand, and wisdom and profundity of thought, on the other hand, is extremely original and curious. As far as I know, it was first expressed in this formulation by Husserl. Before him it had always been admitted that wisdom and profundity of thought, which were everywhere driven out, could find asylum only in the bosom of philosophy, where also, as is known, virtue, which is forever hunted down, finds rest. But Husserl energetically refuses to let philosophy be the refuge of wisdom and virtue. He is prepared to accord to the latter all marks of respect (perhaps sincerely and perhaps also merely to conform to tradition), but wisdom and virtue must seek their means of existence elsewhere, even though they be reduced to applying to public or even private charity.

I am not disposed to take on the role of defender of oppressed virtues—for reasons, however, quite different from Husserl's. I also am of the opinion that wisdom has too long occupied a throne that does not belong to it. Wisdom, i.e., a long white beard, a large forehead, eyes deeply sunken under tufted eyebrows, and crowning it all, the blessing gesture—everything in this image of ancient piety breathes the falsehood of carefully masked impotence. And, like every falsehood, this image irritates and disgusts us. One can venerate wise men and pity them. Pushkin venerated and loved the metropolitan Philarete and dedicated some wonderful verses to him. But no great perceptiveness is required to guess that Pushkin would not have agreed for anything in the world to become himself a wise man with silver hair, the object of veneration and even adoration. And the gods spared their favorite by dispatching to him in good time his murderer d'Anthes who, with the greatest calmness, as if aware of the high mission with which he was charged, accomplished his role as executioner of fate. And Lermontov and Nietzsche were also spared. As for Tolstoi, toward whom Providence was less indulgent, he did not finally have the power to bear the torture of his unwanted glory and himself hastened the denouement: is not his flight several days before his death the brusque, violent deed of a man completely beside himself? The makeup of wisdom—the white hair, the solemn mask, the halo of the genius and benefactor of humanity—all this was for him a veritable martyrdom and, with impatient hand, he tore away this tinsel which disgusted him. Venerable old age and the glory of the wise man are certainly much heavier to bear than the royal crown, and much less attractive!

But Husserl rises against wisdom for reasons quite different from those that drove Tolstoi out of Yasnaïa Poliana. Husserl is a positive and sober mind. He rejects wisdom not because it presents itself as exaggeratedly clever but because it appears to him insufficiently solid and rational. It is not its heavy respectability and the rigid attitude that tradition confers upon it that are repugnant to him. On the contrary wisdom and depth of thought appear to him as a sign of youth and an indication of a lack of maturity; they recall to him the time when men still believed in astrology and alchemy. Now mankind is older and more mature; it possesses astronomy and chemistry, which are exact sciences. It is time that philosophy finally arrive at maturity and be transformed, in its turn, into a rigorous science.

Edmund Husserl thus formulates the problem: we need neither wisdom nor depth of thought; we need rigorous science.

Once the problem is posed in this form, the theory of knowledge naturally passes to the first rank. In other words, the question is: can philosophy be a science, and is there any truth outside of science? And Husserl's problem immediately appears less new and original than at first sight. Let us recall Kant: what Husserl calls "wisdom" Kant called "metaphysics." Kant also admitted as indisputable the existence of positive sciences that furnish us certain unshakable truths and, setting out from the analysis of the possibility of these sciences, he concluded the impossibility of metaphysics, i.e., in Husserl's language, the impossibility of wisdom and profundity of thought. What brings the two thinkers still closer, despite the century and a half that separates them, is that both of them are convinced that true knowledge, i.e., science, can only be *a priori*. Kant formulates his questions and conducts his arguments otherwise than Husserl, but this difference does not interest us for the moment. What is important for us is only to clarify the reasons why the problem of knowledge acquires such great significance for these two philosophers. If we lend an attentive ear to their argumentation, we shall also establish that the theory of knowledge has constituted the fundamental problem of philosophy since the most ancient times. The Greeks already—and not only Socrates, Plato, and Aristotle but those who are called the fathers of Greek thought —conferred on questions of the theory of knowledge a capital significance. The inconstancy of human opinions troubled them and, as Parmenides' example shows us, they tried by every possible means to escape from this inconstancy and to find repose in the bosom of the truth that is always equal to itself. The well-known struggle between Socrates and his famous disciples, on the one hand, and the heirs of the thought of Heraclitus, the Sophists, on the other, was in very large part a struggle about the theory of knowledge. Plato and Aristotle, following Socrates, tried to kill in germ the anxiety that the skeptical reasonings of their adversaries aroused. "To every statement one can oppose a contrary statement," "man is the measure of things,"—such theses appeared to Socrates and his disciples not only false but even sacrilegious. And that is why they were not content with opposing arguments to them but even tried to persuade their hearers that the partisans of such ideas were immoral men. Such a method of argument, very inappropriate in general, appears particularly superfluous in cases where one possesses a complete theoretical argument against the skeptics. But this theoretical demonstration the successors of Socrates had in hand, as many passages from Plato and Aristotle testify.

I shall quote a short fragment of Aristotle's *Metaphysics*, directed against the statements of the extreme skeptics:

> Therefore all such views are also exposed to the often expressed objection that they destroy themselves. For he who says that everything is true makes even the statement contrary to his own true, and therefore his own not true (for the contrary statement denies that it is true), while he who says everything is false makes himself also false.—And if the former person excepts the contrary statement, saying it alone is not true, while the latter excepts his own as being not false, none the less they are driven to postulate the truth or falsity of an infinite number of statements; for that which says the true statement is true, is true, and this process will go on to infinity (*Met.*, I, 8, 1012b).

From this refutation, truly classic in its brevity and clarity, of skepticism, it follows that the skeptical position is devoid of all foundation. One would then think that there was no need to crush the skeptics under arguments of a moral order: one does not strike an enemy who is already conquered. Nevertheless, the theoretical arguments appeared insufficient and the opponents of the Sophists gave them the reputation of being greedy and immoral people, even though we still do not know precisely what ruined the Sophists' work, whether their bad philosophy or their bad reputation. The latter, it is known, often exercises the decisive weight in the balances of history's scale.

II

Let us now raise the question: What is philosophy? It must be a science, Husserl answers us. Those who, according to Husserl, replaced philosophy with wisdom said the same thing. But this is only one of philosophy's characteristics. And, then, a new question: What is science? Before listening to Husserl's answer, let us hear again once more what the ancients tell us. Let us listen first to the word of Plotinus who gives us a definition of philosophy that is extremely brief and simple but very remarkable in its kind. Τι οὖν ἡ φιλοσοφία; τὸ τιμιώτατον, "What is philosophy? It is the most important." As you see, Plotinus does not even think it necessary to tell us whether philosophy is a science or not. It is the most important, the most necessary. It is a matter of indifference to him whether it be a science, an art, or something as different from art as from science. Let us listen now to Aristotle: "For the most divine science is also the most honorable; and this science alone must be, in two ways, most divine. For the science which it would be most meet for God to have is a divine science, and so is any science that deals with divine objects; and this science alone has both these qualities; for (1) God is thought to be among the causes of all things and to be a first principle, and (2) such a science either God alone can have, or God above all others. All the sciences, indeed, are more necessary than this, but none is better" (*Met.*, A. 2, 982b).

So spoke the great thinkers of antiquity. Husserl ought certainly to have accepted the definitions of Plotinus and Aristotle. However, he probably would have rejected certain of the latter's expressions; I do not think he would have agreed to repeat after the Stagyrite that philosophy is the divine among the sciences, that it is most proper to God, and that it has God for its object. No, Husserl would not agree to make these words his own. The word "God" would have recalled to him wisdom, which he considers, as we know, the enemy of philosophy and drives out of his domain, as Plato drove out the poets. Nevertheless, one would not be mistaken in saying that Aristotle's words express entirely Husserl's attitude toward philosophy, with the difference that where Aristotle, following the custom of the ancients, speaks of God and the divine, Husserl employs expressions to which modern ears educated by science are more accustomed. To this question, What is philosophy? Husserl replies, "A science of true principles, of sources, of origins, of ῥιζώματα πάντων (the roots of all things)." But Aristotle also says: "Clearly, then, Wisdom is knowledge about certain principles and causes" (*Met.*, A. 1, 982a).

When a modern scientist speaks of principles, of the roots of things, it is obviously God that he has in mind, but a God whose existence he places outside of every theological or even metaphysical system. The fear of reducing philosophy to the role of *ancilla theologiae* has still not completely disappeared in us, and we prefer to express our thoughts in our own way. This is perfectly understandable and even commendable; it is more than probable that if Aristotle had lived in our time he would have wished to avoid every approach to dogmatic theology. If one assumes that the words "God" and "divine" were used by Aristotle in the character of the superlative, the most beautiful, the most powerful that may be, one can say that Husserl has no reason to argue with him. This, furthermore, is what his article "Philosophy as a Rigorous Science" proves, an article which not only applies itself to determining the object and methods of philosophy but also sings to the glory of philosophy a veritable hymn in an inspired, prophetic tone.

Husserl says: "In all of contemporary life there is probably no idea that is more powerful, more irresistible, more triumphant, than that of science. Nothing can stop its victorious march. It seems that its legitimate goals embrace absolutely everything. If one thinks of it in its ideal achievement, it appears as reason itself, which does not admit any other authority beside or above itself" (*Logos*, I).

So, then, in Husserl's eyes philosophy is the supreme achievement of mankind, and its dominion will finally extend over all domains of human activity. For Husserl, just as for Aristotle, philosophy is divine and its object is God. Not, naturally, the God of Catholic or Mohammedan theology, but such a God appears necessary only from the point of view of practical goals. Aristotle says, "It is right to call philosophy the science which seeks truth, for the goal of theory is truth and the goal of practice is action," and Husserl would have subscribed to this sentence.

Husserl is not content with simple declarations of principle, but tries to demonstrate that the pretensions of science are well-grounded. "General statements do not mean much if one does not prove them, and the hopes that are founded on science have no importance if one does not point out the ways which lead to the realization of the goal" (*Logos*, p. 296).

That is correct. If one is content with inspired declarations and prophetic promises, one falls back into that very wisdom we have so solemnly renounced. But how shall we discover these ways? How shall we justify the pretensions of science to becoming that supreme court where all questions that trouble mankind will find their solution?

Let us recall that science does not recognize any other authority outside itself. *This is the fundamental and dearest idea of Husserl.* He declares categorically: "Science has spoken; from that moment on, wisdom is obliged to conform to it" (*Ibid.*, p. 334). In other words: *Roma locuta, causa finita.** Philosophy proclaims the infallibility of scientific judgment in the same terms (apparently intentionally) and according to the same formula as those that Catholicism used in the Middle Ages to affirm the infallibility and supreme authority of the papal throne. The rights of the pope were based on the revelation given to men by Holy Scripture, but on what does modern philosophy base the rights of reason?

We shall proceed to this question in a moment, but first let us observe once more the immense importance that the theory of knowledge has and must have in philosophy. The theory of knowledge is not at all an abstract, harmless reflection on the methods of our thought; it determines in advance the sources whence our knowledge flows. It waters the ῥιζώματα πάντων out of which our life grows. Just as Catholicism needed the idea of the infallibility of the Church in order to obtain the right to point out to mankind the ways to salvation and life eternal, so philosophy, to attain the goals that it has set for itself, cannot and does not wish to admit any limitation to its power. When reason speaks *ex cathedra*, it cannot be mistaken. And so long as the theory of knowledge will not have led thinking man to this conviction, what sense can there be in raising any questions? For what is important to us is not simply to raise questions but to be able to answer them and to answer them "scientifically," i.e., in such a way that the answer will be obligatory on every rational man.

Husserl's task was bequeathed to him by Greek philosophy. It would be erroneous to think that, in affirming the infallibility of reason, modern philosophy is inspired by the theology of the Middle Ages. On the contrary, Catholicism derived the idea of

---

* Rome has spoken, the case is finished.

infallibility entirely from the ancient Greeks. But realizing well the fragile foundations on which the pretensions of reason rested, Catholicism tried to base its own pretensions on other principles. Husserl's problems then, are quite in the ancient tradition. He himself declares: "What characterizes the Socratic-Platonic revolution in philosophy, as well as the scientific reaction against Scholasticism at the beginning of modern times and especially the Cartesian revolution, is such a fully conscious will to rigorous science. Its impulse carries over to the great philosophers of the seventeenth and eighteenth century, is radically renewed in Kant's critique of reason and still dominates Fichte's philosophy. Ever anew the searchings have for their goal the true principles, the decisive formulas, the exact methods" (*Logos*, p. 292).

These words contain briefly the entire genealogy of Husserl's thought: from Socrates and Plato through Descartes to Kant and Fichte. But this genealogy is correct in part only; we must not forget that, in denying metaphysics, in manifesting a kind of repugnance for it, Husserl separates himself from Plato, Descartes, Spinoza, and Leibniz. Differing in this respect from Kant also, he even abstains from openly raising the question, Is metaphysics possible? He assumes that for all his readers, as for himself, this question can be answered only in the negative. Metaphysics is wisdom—in other words, a hasty, prescientific attempt to resolve certain problems of the universe whose solution is most important to us. Metaphysics thus finds its justification, to a certain degree, in considerations of a practical order. It is good to console suffering mankind by telling it that there is a God, that the soul is immortal, that the wicked will be punished in another world, etc. And if this teaching is given by men of great talent, one can raise no objection to it. But it would be truly criminal to forget that all teachings of this kind answer only to temporary, passing needs: "We must remember our responsibility toward mankind. We must not sacrifice eternity for time; we must not, in order to satisfy to a certain degree our needs, bequeath to future generations our accrued and insurmountable difficulties. *Weltanschauungen,* different forms of wisdom, can argue: science alone can decide, and its decisions bear the stamp of eternity" (*Logos,* p. 337).

I believe it necessary once again to draw the reader's attention to the character of the expressions employed by Husserl to clarify the object and claims of science. It is clearly seen from these quotations that Husserl's vocabulary could be perfectly well replaced by that of Aristotle, or even of the Catholic apologists; for Husserl, just as for Aristotle, philosophy is something divine, for its object is God. But the God of Husserl, quite like Aristotle's God, can be found only by following the way of scientific research. We must then consider "the theory of knowledge as a discipline preceding metaphysics." In other words, Husserl is willing to admit only a God to whom reason can testify for, as we know, there is no authority other than reason. But in modern as in ancient times, God was found by ways other than those of reason. Because of this and only because of this Husserl avoids the Aristotelian definitions of philosophy.

Husserl is mistaken, I think, only on one point: men, and Husserl himself, have never been able, have never even wished, to admit a God to whom reason refused to bear witness. In this respect all religions, at least all the so-called positive religions, do not differ at all from secular wisdom and from rationalist philosophy. They also try to attain a "scientific" knowledge of truth, that is, a knowledge which can impose itself on every rational man. They have not been able to attain this result, but this does not mean anything. Philosophy also, as Husserl himself declares, has, in the person of its most illustrious representatives, made desperate efforts to conceive the truth in rational terms. Despite this, "there have not yet been established even the foundations of a scientific doctrine; the historically transmitted philosophy as well as the living philosophy which replaces it is at most only a scientific semi-fabrication, or a confused and undifferentiated mixture of general conceptions (*Weltanschauung-en*) and theoretical knowledge" (*Ibid.*, p. 335).

These words are hardly flattering to philosophy. Astrology and alchemy themselves would be justified in claiming more indulgence, not to speak of Catholic theology! It is not that astrology, alchemy, and Catholic theology have scorned reason. If the results of their efforts were, according to Husserl, so piti-ful, the cause of this must be sought elsewhere. And quite naturally one then asks himself: is it not the contrary of that which Husserl assumes happened here? It may be that the results obtained by astrology, theology, and philosophy were so poor precisely because men did not agree to renounce reason where, "according to the very nature of things," reason must be silent and efface itself! In his theory of knowledge, which must pre-cede metaphysics, Husserl does not even suspect that the problem of the theory of knowledge consists perhaps in determining the moment when he must deprive reason of its directing role or limit its rights. Husserl is convinced in advance that if there were failures, these derived from the fact that the sovereign power of reason was limited by someone. That is why his theory of knowl-edge, like those of his predecessors, applies itself to justifying reason and to re-establishing its rights by all possible means.

III

We arrive here at the very source of Husserl's philosophy. The first volume of his *Logische Untersuchungen*, entitled "Prolegomena to Pure Logic," was devoted almost exclusively to this question, formulated, it is true, differently than I have done. Husserl does not once say that the theory of knowledge must test by every means at our disposal whether reason truly possesses the rights to which it pretends. Posed in this form, the question, from his point of view, already contains a contradiction and therefore cannot be admitted. He begins his investigations by refuting what in modern philosophical language is called psychologism. He quite correctly sees psychologism in all the representatives, without exception, of modern philosophical thought: Mill, Bain, Wundt, Sigwart, Erdmann, Lipps—all are psychologists. Psychologism for Husserl is relativism, but relativism contains a contradiction which renders it absurd and, consequently, totally unacceptable to reason.

We know that the contradiction inherent in all relativism was already formulated by the ancients. Relativistic theories destroy themselves, says Aristotle, speaking in this case not in his own name, not as if he had discovered a new principle, but as if he were expressing a commonplace of philosophy. This principle

for Husserl is an *articulus stantis et cadentis ecclesiae*.* Furthermore, for his opponents also, the English psychologists and the
German theorists of knowledge, the attitude of Protagoras and
his maxim—"man is the measure of things"—are completely unacceptable. But Husserl declares that their thoughts conceal this
contradiction unconsciously and implicitly, and that they do not
realize it for the reason only that they are not absolute relativists, but, according to his expression, "specific" relativists.
That is, they see the absurdity of the statement that each man
possesses his own particular truth, but they do not notice that
those who affirm that the human species possesses its own truth,
its human truth, necessarily fall into the same contradiction.
Such a specific, i.e., "species" relativism does not have any advantage over individual relativism. For he who declares that
men possess their own purely human truth thinks that the contrary truth is absolutely false. His statement is absolutely true
and, therefore, contradicts itself.

This reasoning is simple and comprehensible and also well-
known. What distinguishes Husserl's position is that he pitilessly
uncovers the traces of relativism in all philosophical systems without exception and shows in his researches a rigor and obstinacy
that are often almost provoking. But this is precisely what constitutes, to my mind, the greatness of the service he renders and
the significance of his work. Husserl reproached his contemporaries for not having confidence in the demonstration deduced
from the consequences of a thesis. He himself has full confidence
in this kind of demonstration. That is, having set up a certain
statement, he boldly accepts all the consequences that flow from
it. Having dethroned specific relativism, he declares openly:
"What is true is true absolutely, in itself; the truth is one,
identical with itself, whatever may be the beings who perceive
it—men, monsters, angels or gods" (*Logische Untersuchungen*
I, p. 117). This is said very daringly. Other theorists of know-

* Proposition on which the church stands or falls.

ledge, even such as Sigwart, never dared express such statements. Sigwart, for example, writes:

> The possibility of establishing criteria and rules of progress in thought, progress that is necessary and has general value, rests on the faculty of distinguishing objectively necessary thought from thought that is not necessary, and this faculty is manifested in the immediate consciousness of evidence that accompanies the necessary thought. The experience of this consciousness and the faith in its certainty are a postulate that one cannot deny. When we ask ourselves if and how it is possible to solve the problem in the sense that we have posed it . . . we can answer only by referring to the subjectively experienced necessity, to the *inward feeling of evidence* that accompanies a part of our thought, to the consciousness that, given the suppositions, we could not think any other way than we do. *The faith in the legitimate character of this feeling and in its trustworthiness is the final basis of all certainty in general;* for one who does not recognize it there is no science but only accidental opinion (*Logik,* I, p. 15 f. Italics mine.–L.S.).

Where Sigwart, then, sets up a postulate, in other words, an indemonstrable statement, Husserl sets up an axiom. And if Husserl is right, if the argumentation deduced from consequences is everywhere and unconditionally admissible, Sigwart's words are absurd, for they are tainted with specific relativism, i.e., they contradict themselves.

How could it happen that a thinker as rigorous and severe toward himself as Sigwart could have admitted such an obvious error and one that completely ruins his theory of knowledge? This contradiction had, furthermore, already been indicated even before Husserl by Wundt. But Sigwart maintained his point of view. Even more: the very same Wundt who accused Sigwart of founding knowledge on a deceptive feeling did not escape the same accusations: his theory of knowledge is also tainted, according to Husserl, with relativism. Who, then, is here mistaken, consciously or unconsciously? Who is blind? I am certain that

Sigwart would not have been willing for anything in the world to renounce the traditional attitude of philosophy toward skepticism. And I think, likewise, that Sigwart had no need of Husserl to see that specific relativism contains the same contradiction as individual relativism. And Sigwart would certainly have been very happy to be able solemnly to proclaim that our truths are absolute truths which impose themselves on all beings —angels, demons, and gods. But the old scholar who had dedicated his entire existence to searching for the foundations of truth was obliged toward the end of his life to declare that our truth is based in the final analysis only on a postulate and that trust in the feeling of self-evidence is the cornerstone of our scientific certainty. I think that one cannot pass indifferently over such an admission and believe himself justified in setting it aside for the reason only that it contains a contradiction. If it were a question of Mill, this would not have been so serious. One can indeed admit that, in the heat of his polemics, Mill was capable at times of expressing extreme judgments in which he himself did not fully believe. Even here, however, suspicion would be a bad counsellor. But as far as Sigwart is concerned, one can say with certainty that relativism was for him a very heavy cross to bear and that only his intellectual honesty as a scholar and scientist obliged him to this painful admission.

Sigwart, it is true, could not resolve to develop explicitly the idea contained in his admission. To say what he said amounts finally to saying that beyond certain limits the competence of reason comes to an end and a new power then imposes its rights upon us—a power that has nothing in common with reason and whose effects we men feel here in our empirical world. Sigwart, however, did not conclude thus, no more than did Lotze, who admits that we are condemned to move constantly in the same enchanted circle; and no more than did Kant, who found himself in the same situation as Sigwart and Lotze. According to Kant our most indisputable judgments, synthetic *a priori* judgments, are also the most false, for they flow not from the power that reason possesses of seizing the very essence of things, but from a necessity that is imposed upon it externally and that it represents as its prerogative to create its own ideas, valid for it alone— in other words, illusions and fictions. Kant's conclusion that metaphysics cannot be a science since it does not have any special source for its synthetic, *a priori* judgments (a conclusion generally considered as a refutation of metaphysics), argues rather in its favor. Mathematics and the natural sciences are rigorous disciplines and obligatory upon all because they have agreed to submit blindly to blind masters. Metaphysics, however, is still free, and therefore can not and does not wish to be a science and pretends to independent knowledge. Kant did not dare take up the defense of metaphysics in this way. The empiricists of the school of Hume and Locke did not dare to do so either (perhaps also because metaphysics did not interest them), nor did the idealists of Sigwart's type. To do so it would have been necessary, indeed, to question the rights of reason—something that none of the philosophers could accept. They would have been obliged to admit a metaphysics that is fantastic, arbitrary, alien to science. Who would have dared this? Philosophy preferred to remain in the middle way. It did not pretend to absolute truth, but it did not renounce the sovereign rights of reason. The latter were brilliantly proven by the rapid blossoming of the positive sciences. In the domain of logic, however, one never went beyond admissions of the type made by Sigwart and Lotze.

In order to justify such a self-limitation men thought to establish a rigorous distinction between the point of view of the theory of knowledge and the psychological point of view. The task of the theory of knowledge is not to establish the origin of our knowledge. Its task is to show its structure, the inner relationship of the laws by means of which man's thought leads to the knowledge of truth. But the question whence these laws came is in the province of psychology and of no interest to the theory of knowledge; the problems of the theory of knowledge must not be confused with psychological problems.

Let us examine this argument. It is extremely important for us, since Husserl uses it in the same way as the Neo-Kantians of the end of the last century. But we must first of all emphasize that Husserl does not agree to admit relativism, either implicitly or explicitly, under any form whatsoever. Specific relativism is for him as absurd as individual relativism. This decisiveness constitutes, in my opinion, the great merit of Husserl. It is time at last to lay all the cards on the table and to raise questions as radically as Husserl did: either reason can express absolute truths that angels and gods, as well as men, must accept, or we must renounce the philosophic heritage of the Greeks and re-establish the rights of Protagoras of which he was robbed by history.

Let us recall that in his critique of the ancient theories of knowledge Husserl uses the classical argument: every theory that contains statements contradicting it is absurd. To establish his own theory of knowledge, however, he makes use of a different argument. In order to avoid the attacks of psychologism he tries, quite like the Neo-Kantians, rigorously to distinguish the psychological point of view from the point of view of the theory of knowledge. But to justify reason he develops his own theroy of ideas, which is close to that of Plato and the realism of the Middle Ages.

But can one separate the point of view of the theory of knowledge from that of psychology? And why do theories of knowledge, or rather apologists of the theory of knowledge, avoid so carefully all demands for genealogical information? Both in the first and in the second volume of his *Logische Untersuchungen* Husserl repeats dozens of times that genetic questions are of no concern to him. He admits that logical concepts have a psychological source but rejects the psychological conclusions that are drawn from this fact. Why? Because for his discipline the psychological question of the birth of abstract ideas does not present any interest. In other words, whatever may be the origin of truth, it is a fact that truth exists and that it rules our judgments. It is for us therefore to determine, by means of a rigorous analysis, how, by what methods, and by the action of what laws truth realizes its sovereign rights.

The theorists of knowledge are willing to compare, for more clarity, truth with morality. The goal of the moralists, they say, is not to explain the origins of the "good." The moralists, quite like the theorists of knowledge, are persuaded that the good in itself (*an sich*) has no origin. One can speak of origins only in connection with real objects which are born and disappear. But ideas are outside of time: they exist, they have always existed, they will always exist, they would have existed even if the universe had never existed, or if, having existed, it returned to the nothingness whence it arose.

What is true—is true. We must admit that if one renounces the search for origins, the tasks of the theorists of knowledge and the moralists, who aspire to absolute truth and absolute good, appear much simpler and easier. Pretenders to the throne are generally fearful of genealogical researches. Try to "explain" morality, as utilitarianism and economic materialism did, and its rights will immediately appear quite illusory. Plato understood this perfectly well and in his reasonings always took the good as his point of departure. In analyzing human actions, he discovered that they were completely determined by an independent principle, one which could not in any way be deduced from the experiences of daily life and reduced to pleasure or usefulness or anything else. If I kill a man, I can feel a certain satisfaction: if I am rid of a rival, for example, I can draw profit from this by seizing the wealth of the deceased or even his throne; nevertheless, my action was, is, and always will be evil—and not because of the wrong that I have done to the deceased. It may be that the soul of my victim has immediately flown from this vale of tears to the Elysian Fields and gained by the change. Despite this,

I have done evil and no power in the world can take away from my action the stamp of evil. And, on the other hand, if I have suffered for the cause of truth, if I have been despoiled of my goods, if I have been imprisoned and condemned to death, I have acted well, and neither men nor angels nor gods have the power to transform my good action into an evil one. The good is sovereign and does not admit any power above itself. Plotinus himself, who was not as rigorously consistent as Plato, speaks of the ἀρετὴ ἀδέσποτος,* which in modern philosophic language is equivalent to the autonomy or independence of morality.

In despotic states court jurists developed similar theories about the origins of royal power. These jurists never admitted, indeed could not admit, any reflections on the historical development of the autocratic idea. The monarch, from their point of view, is the source whence all powers and all rights flow; consequently his rights cannot come to him from any source. They are beyond and above time, they are the ῥιζώματα πάντων. Or, if one will allow theological phraseology, their source is in the heavens. The monarch is the autocrat through the grace of God; he is the anointed of God. Only explanations of this kind, or the complete absence of all explanation, can guarantee absolute ideas the rights which they claim. Under our very eyes, as it were, a miraculous transformation occurred: after having tried to "explain" morality, Nietzsche arrived at the formula "beyond good and evil." Or, more exactly, when the good had lost its power over Nietzsche, he discovered for it a genealogy such that it could only take away from us all desire to worship morality.

Such, in brief, are the reasons for the obstinacy with which the theorists of knowledge refuse to confront the psychological and logical problems of the theory of knowledge. They cannot, however, completely renounce genetic questions, for then they would be obliged to allow metaphysical and theological assumptions that are completely discredited by contemporary positivist

* Virtue that is not a tyrant.

thought. Indeed, neither Husserl nor Sigwart nor Erdmann could seriously develop the Platonic theory of ἀνάμνησις, or rely on the Ten Commandments that Moses brought down from Mount Sinai directly from God's hands. Husserl even rises against Plato's desire to hypostatize the ideas. Postulates and metaphysical theories are as inadmissible for Husserl as for the Neo-Kantians. They try to base philosophy exclusively on the *lumen naturale;* hence they are obliged to endow the *lumen naturale* with absolute rights. The negative method that Husserl employs in this task is the same as that of the Neo-Kantians: he forbids himself to test the pretensions of reason through investigations about its origin. But this still does not suffice for him: he proposes to us his theory of ideas which ought, once and for all, to justify the absolute confidence that we place in reason. Let us look, then, somewhat more closely at this theory.

IV

Husserl takes upon himself the defense of the rights of universals (ideal objects) as equal to those of individuals (real objects). "This is the point where relativist and empiricist psychologism separates itself from the idealism which represents the *only possibility* of a theory of knowledge that is in agreement (i.e., that conceals no inner contradiction within itself) with itself" (*Logische Untersuchungen*, II, p. 107. Italics mine–L.S.). And he adds immediately, in order to avoid all equivocation, that his idealism does not presuppose any metaphysical doctrine: "Naturally, in speaking here of idealism, I do not have in view any metaphysical doctrine but the form of the theory of knowledge which recognizes the ideal as the condition of the possibility of objective knowledge in general without giving this term any psychologistic interpretation." These two statements are of major importance for the philosophy of Husserl. He seeks to attain objective knowledge and admits the existence of an ideal world but is convinced that he has no need to betake himself to metaphysics. The father and creator of the theory of ideas was not afraid of metaphysics. Even more: for Plato the theory of ideas had meaning only because it opened to him the way to metaphysical revelations and, conversely, it appeared to him true and eternal insofar as it expressed certain metaphysical visions.

It was the same for Descartes, whose argumentation and point of departure did not remain without influence on Husserl; metaphysical principles were the *conditio sine qua non* of his thought. Husserl declares that one cannot relativize thought without relativizing being and, arguing with Erdmann, who defended relativism, he says: "There would perhaps be beings of a special kind, *logical supermen so to speak, for whom our principles are not valid* but who have other principles such that what is truth for us is error for them. For them it could be true that they do not experience the psychic phenomena which they sometimes experience. That we and they exist would be true for us but false for them, etc. Certainly our own judgment, that of ordinary logical men, would be the following: these beings have lost reason, they speak of truth and abolish its laws, they affirm that they have their own laws of thought and they deny those to which the possibility of laws in general is bound" (*Logische Untersuchungen*, I, 151).

When we hear these reasonings we recall quite naturally the reflections of Descartes that led him to his *cogito ergo sum*. Descartes, it will be remembered, had pushed his doubt to the farthest limits. He had come to the point of admitting that God had set himself the task of deceiving men in all things. But there is one thing about which God cannot deceive us: our own existence. For to be deceived, we must be. Husserl makes in short the same reply to the relativists: deny and relativize all you wish, but your existence and the truth of your existence cannot be denied. You are not, then, relativists but "absolutists" just as I am.

This argumentation appears irresistible: the heritage of Plato (for Descartes also reasons according to Plato) is a great help to us in difficult cases.

But a very interesting question then arises. I have already indicated that these reasonings appeared to Plato perfectly correct but nevertheless insufficient, whereupon he went to seek the roots of things in another world, different from our own. Des-

cartes did the same. It might seem that having demonstrated that
God could not deceive us about everything, Descartes should
have glorified the human reason which is triumphant over all the
higher and lower powers of the world that had conspired against
it. And, indeed, he appears for a moment quite disposed to chant
a song of victory. But turn the page and you will find that the
lumen naturale, such as we understand it now, is insufficient.
The very Descartes who has just demonstrated to us that God
could not deceive us, feels himself once again invaded by a feeling of anxiety and, quite like Plato, throws himself toward an
asylum metaphysicum which is, according to our ideas, only
an *asylum ignorantiae* or, to use Husserl's language, a flight to
wisdom. It is not enough that God cannot deceive us—that is,
that God, even if He wished it, found it impossible to outwit
man. Descartes affirmed that God does not even wish to deceive
us, for falsehood is not worthy of the Supreme Being. And it is
on this conviction finally that the philosopher bases his confidence in reason. There is obviously here a true *testimonium pau-*
*pertatis.** Descartes well saw that man could not overcome God
by means of natural reason and that he must finally, whether he
wishes it or not, bend his knees before the Creator of the universe
and not demand of Him truth but obtain it from His mercy
through supplication. As Luther said: *Oportet ergo hominem*
suis operibus diffidere et velut paralyticum remissis manibus et
pedibus gratiam operum artificem implorare.†

And again, that same question that I previously raised and
because of which we are continually obliged to return to the
theory of knowledge: who is right? The ancient philosophers
who sought truth only in the metaphysical domain where they
found a refuge against all relativism? Or the modern philosophers
who, having renounced metaphysics, are obliged to admit rela-

---

* Testimony of poverty.
† Man should therefore distrust his works and like a cripple, with slack arms
and legs, beg the artificial grace of works.

tivism under the form that is least offensive for the human reason? Or, finally, Husserl, who demonstrates with all the conviction and ardor of fanaticism that one can, without addressing himself to metaphysics, escape relativism, and that men know few things but what they do know, they know truly, for neither angels nor demons nor gods can deny their human truths? Here is the problem, the only problem that the theory of knowledge tries to solve. And on the solution of this question depends the philosophy of the thinker. Or, rather, his philosophy—if this word also designates a certain disposition of the mind—will lead him toward such or such a theory of knowledge. Such a person who has felt with the totality of his being that life goes beyond the truths that can be expressed by means of judgments obligatory for all and that can be developed by the traditional methodological procedures will not be satisfied either with the specific relativism of Sigwart and Erdmann or with the extreme rationalism of Husserl. He will here clearly discern the desire not to escape outside the limits of positivism—a desire dependent not on metaphysical considerations but on the profoundly inculcated habit of living and thinking in certain conditions of existence already well known and comfortable, a desire determined also at times (though this may appear paradoxical) by an obscure metaphysical need which incites the individual "reason" to take refuge and withdraw into itself and into its own shell. He will then be prepared to allow Husserl's argument in its entire compass to pass as valid.

No, specific relativism is not in any way distinguished from individual relativism. The one as well as the other transforms the world of our truths into a world of visions and dreams. All the guarantees of solidity and certainty that logic and the theory of knowledge furnished us collapse: we are then obliged to live in constant anxiety and ignorance and to be prepared for everything. Postulates in this case not only do not calm us but, on the contrary, even intensify our unrest. But philosophy since Parmenides has promised us a solid truth and an unshakable heart. And if Husserl has succeeded not only in making us see the relativism of traditional theories of knowledge but also in overcoming the relativism in his own thought, and has made us a gift of that tranquility of mind to which humanity has aspired for thousands of years, was he not fully justified in setting the theory of knowledge before everything else? The expansion of our knowledge becomes almost a question of time, one could say, once it is demonstrated that the truth we perceive imposes itself on gods as well as on men. The postulate of Descartes that God does not wish to deceive us, a postulate as problematic as Sigwart's, now becomes quite superfluous. We also no longer have any need of Plato's ἀνάμνησις, in which we do not have any great confidence: who today would seriously maintain that our souls existed in another world before their birth and still recall in this earthly existence truths previously seen? Even if the human soul is born at the same time as the body, even if God is a liar and an immoral Being, our science and our knowledge would have nothing to fear. Reason will not leave us in the lurch. It possesses all authority.

How does Husserl overcome relativism?

The answer to this question is bound to the question of what the object of knowledge is. This is obviously a fundamental question. Plato and Aristotle already affirmed that the object of knowledge is not the individual but the general. The realism of the Middle Ages adopted the same thesis. It is only in modern times that scientific thought has seen the impossibility of speaking of the general as an "object." And it was on the ground of Kant's and Fichte's philosophy that the theory of Rickert, who teaches that the object of knowledge is "that which should be" (*das Seinsollende*) was born. The philosopher of Freiburg imagined that he succeeded through *das Seinsollende* in delivering poor human thought from the chains in which it has struggled for centuries. Like Husserl, Rickert tries to escape from the claws of relativism which tear the conscience of the thinker. But Rickert's joy was of short duration. It soon appeared that *das Seinsollende* is only a weak remedy for doubt; it is at most an anesthetic whose action does not last. As for Husserl, he re-solved the difficulty quite differently by re-establishing—under a new form, it is true—the Platonic theory of ideas or Scholastic realism.

Husserl begins by opposing the act of the individual's true judgments to the truth. I say that $2 \times 2 = 4$. My judgment is a psychological act and as such can be the object of psychological study. But whatever the psychologist may do to clarify the laws of thought, he could not in any way deduce from these laws the distinction between truth and error. On the contrary, all his argumentations already presuppose that he has a criterion through which he distinguishes truth from falsehood. The theo-rist of knowledge is not at all interested in the individual judg-ments of John or Peter according to which $2 \times 2 = 4$. What concerns him is the truth of the judgment, $2 \times 2 = 4$. Judg-ments carrying such a truth are reckoned by the thousands, but the truth is one.

"When a natural scientist deduces from the laws of the lever, the law of weight, etc., the way a machine acts, he certainly feels in himself all kinds of subjective acts . . . In this case, to the associations of the subjective thoughts there corresponds an objective unity of meaning which is what it is, whether or not it be actualized by anyone in thought" (*Logische Untersuch-ungen*, II, 94). The same point of view is still more clearly ex-pressed in the first volume of the *Logische Untersuchungen*: "If all the masses subject to gravitation disappeared, the law of gravitation would not be destroyed but would simply remain without any possible application. The law, indeed, says nothing about the existence of gravitational masses but about what is inherent in these masses as such" (*Ibid.*, I, 149).

In both cases Husserl emphasizes that the theorist of knowledge is not at all concerned with the resemblance established between the different psychological acts of a single or several individuals. What is important is not that you, I, and millions of individuals experience the same thing and express it in the same way by establishing the laws of the lever or of gravitation. To understand Husserl rightly we must never lose sight of this. He returns constantly to this point both in the first and in the second volume of his *Logische Untersuchungen*, where this thought resounds as a kind of leitmotif. I quote again this important passage:

For example, the meaning of the statement, "π is a transcendent quantity": what we understand by reading it or think by speaking it is not an individual characteristic but is always individually different, while the meaning of the statement must be identical. If we or other persons repeat the same proposition with the same intention, each of these persons has his own phenomena, words, and moments of understanding. But despite this limitless multiplicity of individual experience, what is expressed in them is everywhere something identical, *the same* in the strictest sense of the word. The meaning of the proposition is not multiplied with the number of persons and acts; the judgment, in the ideal and logical sense, remains one. The fact that we here maintain the strict identity of the meaning by distinguishing the latter from the constant psychic character of the interpretation does not come from any subjective inclination for subtle distinctions but from a firm theoretical conviction that it is only in this way that one can arrive at a true appreciation of the situation that is fundamental for the understanding of logic. Likewise, it is not a question here of a simple hypothesis which must be justified by its explanatory usefulness; but we consider this as a truth apprehensible immediately, obeying in this the supreme authority for all questions concerning knowledge, i.e., evidence. I perceive that in repeated acts of representation and judgment, I certainly think the same thing, the same concept, i.e., the same proposition, and that I cannot think otherwise; I perceive that, for example, where it is a question of the proposition or truth, "π is a transcendent quantity," I do not think of anything less than of an individual experience or of a moment in the experience of any person. I perceive that this reflected statement has really for its object what constitutes the meaning of this simple statement. Finally, I perceive that what I mean in the proposition in question or what I grasp as its meaning when I hear it is identically what it is, independently of the fact that I think and exist or that, in general, thinking persons and acts exist or do not exist. . . . This true identity that we affirm here is none other than the identity of the species (*Identitat der Spezies*). It is in this way, but only in this way, that it can embrace in an ideal unity, ξυμβάλλειν εἰς ἕν, the scattered multiplicity of individual particularities (*Logische Untersuchungen*, II, 99).

And further, "Ideal objects exist truly . . . which does not prevent the meaning of this existence and, with it, the meaning of the predicate from being here completely, specifically the same as that, for example, in cases where to a real subject a real predicate is attributed or denied. In other words, we do not deny it but rely rather on the fact that inside the conceptual unity of what exists (or, what is the same thing, of the object in general) there exists a fundamental categorical difference of which we take account through the distinction between ideal being and real being, being as species and being as individual. But this difference does not abolish the supreme unity in the concept of the object" (*Ibid.*, 124).

V

Here are the three principal theses on which Husserl bases his rationalism. First of all, every theory which admits statements destroying the possibility of any theories whatsoever is absurd. This thesis, which was transmitted to Husserl by the ancient tradition and which all the theorists of knowledge consider indisputable, serves him to refute the present theories of knowledge.

The second principle is not new either: a rigorous distinction between the points of view of psychology and theory of knowledge. As I have already said, this principle was proclaimed by the neo-Kantians to justify Kant's doctrine that reason dictates its laws to nature. What pertains here especially to Husserl is the rigor and boldness with which he develops and applies this principle, a rigor and boldness that distinguish all the works of this remarkable figure. Even though he gave to the second volume of his *Logische Untersuchungen* the title "Untersuchungen zur Phänomenologie und Theorie der Erkenntnis," he proposes finally to rid himself of all theory in the strict sense of the word. In a note on the expression "theory of abstraction," which he had himself used, he declares: "the word theory does not fit completely here, for what follows in the text does not give any place to theoretical construction, i.e., to explanation." One could then perhaps say that his theory of knowledge tries to put an end to every theory of knowledge. His success would have been the supreme triumph of rationalism, for it would then have appeared that reason has no need of being justified but, on the contrary, can itself justify everything. Husserl saw correctly; it is precisely thus that the problem of the theory of knowledge must be posed. It is because of this that he defends his first principle with such ardor and applies it so boldly.

It is for the same reason also that he insists on the reality of ideal objects, a reality which appears evident in direct intuition, and introduces these objects into the same category as real objects, for both have being and exist. If his "arguments" are really irrefutable, Husserl can consider his work finished. Psychologism will forever have to abandon the domain of philosophy where, henceforth, absolute truths will reign. Science could then go forward in all tranquility without fear of an attack from the flank. All its judgments will be definitive and unalterable. No other court will be able to set itself above it. Everything will be according to its decisions: *Roma locuta, causa finita.*

I repeat, we must do justice to Husserl. No other theory of knowledge poses the problem with such rigor, clarity, and frankness. Husserl will accept no compromise: all or nothing. Either evidence is the final goal to which human thought tends when it seeks the truth and this evidence can be obtained by human methods, or the reign of chaos and madness will be established on earth and it will be permitted to anyone who has the whim to seize the rights of reason, its scepter and its crown. And then "truth" will no longer have anything in common with the unshakable deductions which the exact sciences have sought and obtained until now. Then it would perhaps be necessary to recall with a certain gratitude the immature "wisdom" that Husserl had set aside, perhaps even alchemy and astrology. These were not sciences, of course, but constructions of a more or less scientific appearance which relied on argumentation. One would perhaps even come to the point of thinking back longingly about Catholic theology: Saint Thomas Aquinas, whatever else he was, was a faithful disciple of Aristotle.

Let us, however, examine a little more closely Husserl's "argumentation."

I have put the word "argumentation" in quotation marks because Husserl, who pretends to rely only on intuition and self-evidence, tries to pose the problem in such a way that every demonstration becomes superfluous. He leaves to other sciences the concern for *Erklärungen*, but the task of phenomenology is beyond all demonstrations. His concern is not *das Erklären*, but *das Aufklären* (*Logische Untersuchungen*, II, p. 120). Such is the axiom: every theory which denies the possibilities of any theory whatsoever is absurd and, therefore, unacceptable. As Aristotle says, such theories refute themselves.

Setting out from this, Husserl, as we recall, overthrows the specific relativism he had discovered in the theories of knowledge of Sigwart, Erdmann, Mill, etc. But is this thesis really indisputable? If we admit that our truth is only a human truth, do we really introduce into our reasonings an element which ruins them and takes away all their meaning?

At first blush, this seems indisputably so. It is not for nothing that Greek thought has dominated men's minds for centuries. And then there is the evidence on which Husserl relies: we establish directly that a statement which conceals its own negation is absurd.

But from another side an extremely strange fact solicits our attention. Despite all the efforts that have been made to expel that unfortunate relativism, it continues to live in philosophy, and its power of action and contagion after thousands of years of continuously vagabond and hunted existence not only has not weakened but, on the contrary, grown stronger. Husserl himself establishes that the most conscientious and penetrating thinkers, without taking account of the *aquae et ignis interdictio* * which threatens it, not only maintain constant relationships with this inveterate sinner but even render homage to it and honor it. How explain this mystery? Why have the frightening curses of reason not been effective? Why does Husserl see himself again obliged to raise his voice and to hurl his anathema at the philosophical community in the person of its most remarkable and most loyal representatives? Husserl does not raise this question and, moreover, cannot raise it. The very nature of his philosophical tendencies forbids him to take reality and history into consideration and treat them as independent factors. For one who admits the primacy of autonomous reason, reality always recedes into the background. He is persuaded in advance that every fact must necessarily find its place marked out in the thought which possesses all the purity of the *a priori*. *Wir werden uns nicht zu der Überzeugung entschliessen, es sei psychologisch möglich, was logisch und geometrisch widersinnig ist (Ibid.,* II, p. 215).†

One cannot fight against Husserl if one remains on his ground. You will hardly have opened your mouth to answer him before he immediately stops you: if you admit a thesis that denies the possibility of all theses, you speak words devoid of meaning and must withdraw your word.

But let us make an experiment. In a general way Husserl avoids metaphysics, that is, he does not like it and is not interested in it. But he is prepared to examine carefully any metaphysical ideas whatsoever on the condition that they are presented to him not as "rigorous scientific truths" but as hypothetical suppositions and on the condition also that they do not contain any inner contradiction.

Let us then make one of those suppositions which came to

---

* Banishment.

† We will not commit ourselves to the proposition that that which is logically and geometrically absurd is psychologically possible.

Descartes' mind and which, though inadmissible for certain other metaphysical considerations, are nevertheless possible. Let us assume that God can deceive men and that He does in fact deceive them. As Descartes has demonstrated to us, we see clearly that in order to be able to deceive us, God must somehow bring it about that we exist and that we even know the truth of our existence. But then after having granted to us, even if against His will, this unique truth—for otherwise it would have been impossible to deceive us—God can perfectly well deceive us about everything else and make us believe that our other truths are as indisputable as the truth of our existence. Descartes is perhaps right in rejecting with indignation the idea that God, who is perfection Himself and the supreme good, is capable of duping men. But it may also be that Descartes is wrong. Despite his great genius, the father of modern rationalism could have been insufficiently informed about the designs of Providence. And then, in any case, in supposing that God is truthful, Descartes makes a purely metaphysical assumption on which Husserl's theory, which is purely *a priori* and relies on evidence, has no right to lean. It is possible, then, that God deceives us about everything except about our own existence. It may then be that other beings exist—angels or gods—whom no one deceives and who see the real truth. What then? From the point of view of these beings, the human truth will be a specific truth—useful and necessary (perhaps, on the contrary, hurtful and bad) for men but inapplicable in other worlds. It is said that we cannot imagine any consciousness other than our own, but this is not true at all.

As if it were not enough for nature to deceive us, but as if it wished expressly also to make us sadly suspect the deception, nature itself plunges us from time to time into states whose "evidence" is very different from that which serves as the basis for Husserl's theory of knowledge. Let us recall the state of drunkenness, the action of morphine and opium; let us recall ecstasy and finally the so-called "normal" state of sleeping which alternates regularly with the state of waking. Compared to the man who is awake, the man who is asleep can be considered as a being from another world. The sleeper has his own reality which is quite different from daily reality. He even has—and this is particularly important for us—his own logic and his own *a priori*, a logic and *a priori* which have nothing in common with the relative truths accepted by relativists like Sigwart and Mill. And this logic also rests on evidence. If a man dreams that he is the Emperor of China and that in this character he is engraving monograms on the surface of a sphere with one dimension only (dreams constantly offer examples of reality of this kind), the dreamer does not at all experience the contradictoriness of the elements out of which his representations and judgments are composed. On the contrary—and this happens constantly in dreams, as everyone knows from his own experience—when suddenly the sleeper begins to doubt that one can engrave monograms on a surface with one dimension, or that a man born in Russia or England and not knowing a word of Chinese can be Emperor of China, when, in a word, the memory of a "truth" strange to the universe of the dreamer tries to disturb the "natural" and "normal" march of the thoughts immanent in the latter, the *logic* of dreams immediately intervenes. It imposes its rights upon us and with indisputable *evidence* leads us to the conviction that all these memories are only the effect of an inveterate relativism, for, as appears clearly to the dreamer, the Emperor of China can never be a Chinese and monograms must necessarily be engraved on the surface of a one-dimensional sphere. In short, the "evidence" which conquers doubts, the "evidence" which pretends to be the supreme court and leads the thought of the dreamer according to its desires, plays the same role in dreams as in the state of waking.* And, then, it often happens that in dreaming we

---

* Cf. the end of Tolstoi's *Confession:* "And then, as often happens in dreaming, the mechanism by which I maintain myself seems natural, understandable and indisputable, though in the waking state it is absurd."

begin suddenly to feel that the events which unroll before us are false, that they are only the product of our imagination, that we are sleeping, and that to deliver ourselves from this network of falsehoods and of absurd *a priori* which ensnare us, we must awake. In other words, in the state of dreaming, among the truths which are true only for the *species Homo dormiens* there suddenly emerge two truths that are no longer specific but absolute. If we reason in the dream state as Husserl and the Greeks reason, we shall have to reject precisely these two truths as containing an inner contradiction. If we say that we are sleeping and that our evidence is the evidence of a sleeper, i.e., a deceptive evidence, the statement that we are sleeping is also false. *Homo dormiens*, in relativizing the truth of his dream, relativizes being, etc. But this conviction which has arisen in us that we are sleeping and that we must awake in order to obtain the truth, these judgments that relativize the truth of our dreams, *are the only ones that are true*, and this is even too little to say, for *they are the only ones that permit us to rid ourselves of the absurd and outrageous falsehoods of the state of dreaming.*

VI

I am not at all thinking of identifying our existence with the dream state and of pushing the parallel further. And, moreover, there is no necessity for this. It was important for me to establish that Husserl's first argument, his fundamental argument, is not at all as strong as he imagined. We are not *always* right to argue according to consequences, and it is not *always* necessary to be afraid of contradictory judgments. There is a certain limit beyond which it is necessary to guide oneself not according to the general rules of logic but according to something else which still does not, and probably never will, have any name in the language of men. Therefore, we must not have too much confidence in our *a priori* truths; we must sometimes renounce them, contrary to all philosophical traditions. If, then, one separates the point of view of the theory of knowledge from the psychological point of view, it would perhaps be better to follow the example of Sigwart and Erdmann who, in their theories of knowledge, brush relativism aside and leave it outside their theoretical reasonings. So, at least, the first condition which every theory of knowledge must satisfy is fulfilled: the postulates are formulated sharply and clearly. One can then remain a positivist and restrict himself to the immanent. But the situation of

Husserl, who like Ibsen's Brand, does not admit compromises and at the same time fears or scorns metaphysics, appears completely insoluble, even though he does not even suspect it. He sees clearly the absurd conclusions to which one who decides to relativize the truth is led, but he does not notice that the danger is no smaller if one pretends to attain absolute truth without leaving the domain of the immanent. Let us examine this in more detail.

Husserl's doctrine about the object of knowledge (a doctrine which is related to that of Leibniz about the *vérités de raison* and the *vérités de fait*) affirms, as we remember, the existence of the ideal, an existence which belongs to the same category as that to which the existence of the real belongs: these are two species of the same genus. The *vérités de raison*, however, have an existence completely independent of the real; I would say that they "are" *par excellence*. Even if there were not one living being, if all real objects without exception disappeared, the general laws, the truths, and the concepts would continue to exist.

If the real world had never been born, the existence of the ideal world would not have suffered any harm. The ideal world would then occupy entirely the category which actually includes, besides the ideal world, the real world. "$2 \times 2 = 4$" would have remained the same even if no being had ever thought this statement. And the laws of gravitation would remain what they are even if all masses should disappear, and these laws already existed before any masses came into existence.

But what, then, is the relationship between the truths of reason, or the ideal truths, and the world of the real? Autonomous reason decrees its laws without concerning itself with reality, as if the latter did not exist. Indeed, since ideas exist, since they have their own being, why should they concern themselves with other kinds of existence? Have we, who proclaim the doctrine of sovereign reason, the right to say anything whatsoever about the real world before asking permission from the supreme master, the λόγος ἀδέσποτος? * We know that there is no authority other than reason. And reason is not something real, something psychological, a certain *hic et nunc*. Reason is also ideal, something in the genus of "consciousness in general" or of "the subject of the theory of knowledge" of the older German schools. And as this reason will decide, so shall it be.

But it suffices to put to reason the question of the existence of real objects immediately to obtain a perfectly clear and *categorical* response: real being does not exist and cannot exist; the existence of the real is a kind of *contradictio in adjecto*,† much worse even than that psychologism toward which the myopic philosophers turn continually despite the interdictions of reason (Cf. *L. U.* II, pp. 21–22, where Husserl says: *nicht die mindeste Behauptung über reales Dasein* ‡ and *ob es überhaupt so etwas wie Menschen und eine Natur gibt*). Indeed, if reason is autonomous, how will you oblige it to recognize the individual reality over which it has no power? In general, how will you constrain reason to anything whatsoever—that reason which has the power of constraining us and which, by its very nature, does not bear even the shadow of constraint? It will never accept any such limitation of its rights, for it knows well what this means. But that individual reality is the irreconcilable enemy of reason— this, I think, is a truth as evident (i.e., a truth about which reason does not admit any debate) as the truth of the principle of contradiction. All that is real, all that exists *hic et nunc*, as Husserl expresses it, is in the eyes of reason *pure absurdity*, which nothing can justify. We can still admit the *idea* of reality, the idea of space and time in which the real exists, but cannot, that is to say, our reason cannot, admit the real itself without abdicating. So, then, if reality had need, in order to be, of the recognition of reason, it would still not have come out of nothingness

* Reason which is not a tyrant.
† Contradiction in addition.
‡ Not the least affirmation about real being.

to the present day. We discover, then, between the ideal and the real or, to use Husserl's terminology, between reason and reality, an irreducible antagonism, a cruel struggle for the right to exist. In the measure that reason triumphs, there remains less and less place for the real, and the complete victory of the ideal principle would mean the disappearance of the universe and of life. Contrary, then, to what Husserl thinks, I would say: to affirm the absolute existence of the ideal is to relativize and even destroy all reality. Husserl's efforts to reconcile the ideal and the real, the rational and the individual, by bringing them into the same category, that of being, where each has equal rights, lead not to a solution of the problem but to its obscuring; for thus is created the possibility of a μετάβασις εἰς ἄλλο γένος—a leap into another realm, which is, so to speak, legal and in which this very relativism that is constantly hunted down, a relativism that no matter how many times killed—like the phoenix—is always born anew from its ashes, takes refuge. Both species of being belong to the same genus; what then can be more tempting and natural than to substitute the ideal for the real, or vice versa?

When Husserl declares that a mathematical law would continue to exist even if there would not be a single real consciousness to conceive it, he commits this μετάβασις which would have been completely impossible if he had not admitted the existence of ideal beings. He would also not have been able to say that the law of gravitation would be preserved even if all gravitating masses disappeared. If this statement is not a tautology empty of all meaning (and one cannot suspect Husserl of this), it is certainly false, for not only would the law cease to exist with the disappearance of masses, but even if masses continued to exist the law of gravitation could very well lapse. One can perfectly well admit the supposition of Mill that somewhere, in other planetary spheres (or, perhaps much closer to us), masses are not subject to the law of gravitation but come closer or move away from each other freely, without their movements being subject to any established plan. One can, one even must, admit this possibility, if one does not admit Kant's doctrine that reason dictates laws to nature. Our ideas of the regularity of phenomena, of rational relationships, of "unchangeable meanings," as Husserl says—all these ideas have an empirical origin. Husserl himself also understands this, it seems, but he assumes that he must forget it in order not to fall under the anathema already hurled by the Greek fathers of the Church of Science against all those who do not submit to the commands of reason. But no, on the contrary, we must not forget it. It will then appear that even the old "$2 \times 2 = 4$" would not have been able to exist without the human intelligence capable of discovering one, two, and four and that law of multiplication according to which the product arises out of the multiplicand as the multiplicator is composed of unity. If one bears this in mind he will see that the ideal entities that exist outside of time, and therefore appear eternal, are essentially temporary and perishable.

So it is in a chess game. Husserl himself will tell you that in chess the king, the queen—in short, every piece—is an ideal entity which does not undergo any change from the fact of its real incarnations. Whether the king be of gold, of ivory, or of paste; whether it be in the figure of a cow or a sparrow; whether its head bear a crown or a tiara, will not in any way change its ideal being, which would no more have changed even if no chess figure had ever been incarnated. One can say the same of all other pieces. Consequently the idea of the king remains always equal to itself and identical, in the strictest sense of the term, whatever way the individual empirical consciousness may grasp it. One can even solemnly declare that monsters as well as angels and gods will have to see in it what men see in it, and to conclude from this that it is outside of time and eternal, and that the ideas of chess will continue to exist even if the entire universe disappeared. But whatever may be Husserl's daring, it does not occur

to him to speak of eternal ideas in connection with chess pieces,
though he once mentions the game of chess.

It is evident that the word "eternal" contains an equivocation
that Husserl did not avoid, even though he constantly warns us
against the dangers of the ambiguous use of terms and words. But
it follows clearly from the example quoted that "eternal" and
"atemporal" are not at all synonymous. On the contrary, the
meaning of the word "atemporal" is much closer to that of the
word "transitory." Ideal beings are just transitory things, and no
proofs or argumentations of reason will be able to save them
from inevitable death. They have triumphed for centuries and
thousands of years, and their triumph will perhaps be of still
longer duration. I am even inclined to believe that the power of
the ideas will not fall for some time to come and perhaps will
always persist on our earth. The arguments of reason exercise
an irresistible power over the human mind, just as do the charms
of morality. When it is necessary to choose between the rational
and the real, man will always incline toward the rational. What
Husserl expresses philosophically is finally only the free and bold
expression of the state of mind of the immense majority of men:
let the world perish, provided justice is saved; let life disappear,
but let us not sacrifice reason! So men have thought, so men
will think, and one can predict for rationalism a long, peaceful,
almost "atemporal" existence.

But it requires only a moment for all this to change.

Indeed there are moments in the life of man when the impera-
tives of pure reason and the seductive chants of the siren called
morality suddenly lose all their power. Man then perceives that
reason and good are only the work of his own hands. It seems
to me that all the philosophers have known such *lucida intervalla;*
but they considered them the sign of a spiritual weakness, or they
were unwilling or could not express them completely in their
works. I think that the father of the theory of ideas himself, the

divine Plato, knew such moments, and that his theory of ideas arose in him precisely in such lucid moments. This seems to be indicated by a passage of Aristotle's *Metaphysics* where it is said that Plato and his disciples obtained their ideas by setting before concrete words the term τὸ αὐτό—προστιθέντες τοῖς αἰσθητοῖς τὸ ῥῆμα τὸ αὐτό.* They thus obtained such expressions as αὐτοάνθρωπος,† αὐτόιππος,‡ etc. This remark is very subtle and exact but it does not attain the goal Aristotle set himself: it does not at all discredit Plato's ideas but permits us, it seems, to penetrate further to their most inward esoteric essence and confers upon them the new charm of an intuition that is infinitely profound and inexpressible.

Plotinus, likewise, speaks openly not only of the idea of man but also of the idea of Socrates without fear of irreconcilable contradictions, as is appropriate to great philosophers. Once he writes that the ideas relate, in general, not to Socrates but to the species man (V. 9, 12). But another time he declares in the same categorical tone: "If there is a Socrates and if the soul of Socrates exists, there is also a Socrates in himself, inasmuch as the individual souls exists there (in the spiritual or noumenal universe)" (V. 7, I, beginning). Plotinus had apparently taken pity on Socrates and did not agree to submerge him in the general idea "man." Plotinus suddenly felt for a moment that τὸ τιμώτατον § is precisely Socrates, the Socrates *hic et nunc* who was the teacher of Plato and whom the Athenians poisoned at the accusations of Anytus and Meletus. He understood that philosophy could not get along without the living Socrates and that it was better for once to disobey reason than to refuse Socrates a place in the intelligible world.

In Plato the love of the individual shines through still more

---

* Placing in front of all objects of sense perception the word *to auto* [itself].
† Man himself.
‡ Horse itself.
§ The most important.

clearly than in Plotinus. For Plato the general ideas are only a kind of outer vestment, a breastplate under which he hid from strangers and from the mob that which was dearest in life to him. The elect have the gift of catching a glimpse in very rare moments with their own eyes of what is best, and they see this, no matter what theories may be constructed. But for the mob it is necessary to show the "general" which can be distinguished by common sight and demonstrated to all, i.e., the ideas. Καὶ τὰ μὲν δὰ ὁρᾶσθαί φαμεν, νοεῖσθαι δ'οὔ τὰς δ'αὖ ἰδεας νοεῖσθαι μέν, ὁρᾶσθαί δ'οὔ (Rep. 507b).*

One perceives, by means of the reason that is common to all, only the general, the neutral. As for sight, one must have one's own. Such is the meaning of the myth of the cave at the beginning of the Seventh Book of the Republic. Real objects, the things that surround us, are only the pale reflection of true realities. We see Socrates and admire him, but this is not yet the true Socrates, him whom our soul saw in its prior existence, him whom it will see in its future existence. And, likewise, lions, horses, cypress trees that we admire on earth, are infinitely paler and poorer than those that exist in true reality and that it is given man at times to glimpse in brief moments of extraordinary exaltation.

In short, the "theory" of ideas such as the young Plato discovered in a particularly happy moment of inspiration meant that the idea is the quintessence of reality, the being κατ' ἐξοχὴν † of which the images of daily reality present only a weak copy. It was only later when, under the pressure of an external necessity, he had to transform the ideas into a permanent and immutable good common to all, when he was obliged to defend them before the opinion of the mob and to demonstrate to every-

* Further, the many things, we say, can be seen but are not objects of rational thought, whereas the forms are objects of thought but invisible.
† Par excellence.

one who came along what is by its very nature undemonstrable —it was then, in a word, when he had to make a "science" out of philosophy, that Plato saw himself under obligation to sacrifice reality and to place on the first level that which could be "evident" to all. And the last stage was the theory of the ideas of numbers, for one can hardly imagine anything more evident than mathematics. If, then, at the beginning Plato had the right to claim that real objects are only the shadows of ideas, the contrary resulted later: his ideas became no more than the reflection of real objects, shadows with sharply delimited contours which, by this very fact, could be the object of that ἐπιστήμη (knowledge) for which men have so much respect. And it is under this aspect that the ideas pass into modern science. The prototype of ideas, of Husserl's and Leibniz' *vérités de raison* is offered to us by mathematics. The science created after the pattern of mathematics claims supreme authority to decide all the doubts of mankind. And indeed, if the first quality of the judge must be perfect knowledge of everything in his province, science must take for its object the ideas in the sense that Husserl uses the term, i.e., that which does not and cannot contain any reality, like everything that is the work of man. The real arose one knows not whence; it is surrounded by a deep mystery infinitely rich with the unforeseen. And it is precisely this mysterious variability, this inconstancy, of the real that confers upon life its meaning, its charm, its beauty. But no science, as Husserl himself admits, is capable of plumbing the depths of this capricious and changing reality. Science finds in the real only what it has itself introduced into it; only the immutable is subject to it (ideal, *also starr*, as Husserl expresses himself); it feels itself master only in the domain which belongs to it, in the domain whose creator is a creature—man. Spinoza, it is true, teaches us and, we must believe, rightly that *ille effectus perfectissimus est, qui a Dei immediate producitur, et quo aliquid pluribus causis intermediis indiget, ut producatur, eo imper-*

fectius est * (*Eth.*, I, XXXVI, Append. Cf. Plotinus, *Enneads*, V, I. 7). But in this domain, at least, reason can autocratically command and make itself obeyed, for there are absent from it living beings, those intractable beings to whom the whim of showing their own free will can occur. As for animating the ideas, this is not given to man; even if this power had been granted to him, he would not have dared so risky an enterprise. Therefore, in order to place the ideas on the level of things created by nature while at the same time maintaining them in obedience, Husserl confers upon them the predicate of being but categorically refuses to them the predicate of reality.

* That effect is most perfect which is produced immediately by God, and insofar as something has need of many intermediate causes in order that it be produced, so much the more imperfect is it.

VII

Let us return to our principal theme, the sovereignty of reason. Reason affirms that our truths are not only human but absolute truths, and demands that we recognize that the contrary thesis is inadmissible because obviously absurd. Reason affirms that reality is not and cannot be, for the existence of the real is a defiance of the existence of reason. Reason demands furthermore that we admit all the consequences of the given principles and brand as a crime against mankind every deviation from this demand. But, while admitting evidence and, consequently, the logical legality of the pretensions of reason, we feel with all our being that in certain cases self-evidence and logic do not guarantee the chief thing, τὸ τιμώτατον—*the truth of our judgments.* Just as it often happens that the sleeper protests in his dream state already against that "unity" of consciousness which penetrates and organizes all the particular perceptions of his dream and, without even realizing what he is doing, tries no longer to maintain but to overthrow the conviction imposed upon him from the outside that the unity of consciousness guarantees the truth of his perception; so also the philosopher sees arising before him this question: where is the truth to be sought? To whom, to what, confide my destiny? Must I submit to the demands of reason, or at the risk of becoming the laughingstock of all and of appearing ridiculous in my own eyes, refuse obedience to reason and consider it no longer a legitimate master but a usurper who has exceeded his powers?

The evidence that supports reason enters into a struggle with an obscure sentiment which does not succeed in finding any justification. Husserl complains that demonstration deduced from consequence does not have sufficient influence over men. But this is a calumny against fate, men, and history. On the contrary: we should stand astonished at the power of this kind of argumentation. The best weapon in intellectual struggles is *reductio ad absurdum,* an even more efficacious weapon than the accusation of immorality. Husserl himself uses it constantly, and with what success! All who admit specific relativism, even thinkers as eminent as Sigwart and Erdmann, are, according to him, mad. This "argumentation" acts on minds in irresistible fashion. Sigwart was still living when the first edition of *Logische Untersuchungen* appeared; he was extremely troubled and felt himself almost crushed by Husserl's attacks. In a note to the fourth edition of Volume I of his *Logik* he tries to respond to his triumphant adversary. But assurance and energy are lacking in his voice. One feels that he is not at all certain that his response can push back Husserl's attack. And it could not be otherwise. Sigwart knew well that his own attempts to find an immanent basis for the absolute pretensions of reason always failed against an insurmountable obstacle. But how rid oneself of the argumentation deduced from consequences? If one rejects it, does he not risk being shut up in an insane asylum? Furthermore, Sigwart himself, like Rickert and Erdmann, constantly made use of this kind of argumentation, had complete confidence in it, and could not take exception to it. Sigwart was already an old and sick man when Husserl's book appeared; he died before the publication of the edition of his *Logik* where his answer to Husserl appears. We must then believe that he carried his last doubts to the grave.

Before the philosopher who left this world for another a truly tragic question arose. All his life he had believed that he was living in peace with reason, but here, at the brink almost of his death, Husserl comes to him to pour the poison of doubt into his soul. Sigwart died without having put his conscience at rest. Can we be certain that Husserl will preserve his faith to the end of his days? Will there not come to him also the fearful hour when he will find himself obliged to ask himself if reason is truly the heir of Saint Peter, the representative of God on earth, the supreme authority which alone possesses the right to speak in the name of Him who sent it and consecrated it king? And if he doubts—at the risk of being shut up in an insane asylum where the οἱ πολλοί send the daring—will he not imagine that this star invisible to all, which shines in him, is perhaps precisely that star of Bethlehem which leads man toward the supreme truth that is completely different from ordinary human truths? If you turn to the right you will lose your horse, if you turn to the left you will lose your life—as the Russian fable says. Remain on the middle way, the way of positivism and of well-ordered family existence. But it is not appropriate to the philosopher to even think of this! *Ein verheirateter Philosoph gehört in die Komödie,** according to Nietzsche.

Husserl will perhaps take me at my word: I speak of the star of Bethlehem, of that absolute truth which he also tries to discover by means of his phenomenological method. He will tell me that I admit that the criterion of truth is one. But if I admit this, he will oblige me to accept all the consequences of this statement and will thus lead me again to swear fidelity to reason, the only legitimate master. But I do not believe that this objection is correct, even if one places himself at Husserl's point of view. I recall once again what I have said about different states of the soul, states whose "evidences" bring us testimonies so opposed that if one confronted them they would devour each other rather than come to agreement.

* A married philosopher belongs in comedy.

The invisible star which is under discussion here does not at all resemble that to which the rationalists aspire. If one flees reason, this does not mean that one sets himself necessarily in such or such a determined direction. On a surface one can trace passing through a given point only one line perpendicular to a determinate straight line, but in a space of three dimensions one can trace an infinite number of these perpendiculars. One who is accustomed to planimetry can conceive only with great difficulty the laws of stereometry: until he becomes accustomed to conceiving the third dimension, he will obstinately repeat that, given a point and a straight line, one can construct only a single perpendicular, and he will be persuaded that he is right. This example will, I believe, render my thought clearer, insofar as analogies that are so distant can be of some use.

The rationalist will perhaps answer that planimetry and stereometry do not destroy the unity of consciousness. But I wished to present here only a vague analogy, being obliged to use the same terms by means of which "common truths" are expressed. One can also tell me that, in debating with Husserl, I presume to put in the place of his binding truths my own truths that are just as binding. And this has already often been said to me by people who consider this "psychological" objection very serious. But I think it is not even worth the trouble to pause over this anecdotal argument.

But there is still another thing which is much more important and cannot be passed over in silence. Husserl says, "The process of development of the rigorous sciences consists essentially in the transformation of the guesses of wisdom into rational formulas that are perfectly clear. The exact sciences have also had their long period of wisdom. And as in the course of the struggles of the Renaissance the sicences raised themselves from wisdom to scientific clarity, so philosophy, I dare hope, will also attain, in the course of the struggles we are now traversing, this scientific rigor" (*Logos*, p. 339). We already know on what Husserl bases his hopes: he believes that phenomenology will lead humanity to the realization of this "great goal." And he is right to a certain degree, inasmuch as it is true that "wisdom" never succeeded in long fixing on itself the attention and interests of men. Almost everyone will readily agree with Husserl's words: "Wisdom, depth of thought, is a sign of that chaos which science tries to transform into a cosmos, into a simple and perfectly clear order." Man is a ζῷον πολιτικόν, a social animal, and aspires to cosmos, a simple and clear order, for no social life is possible in chaos; this, I trust, does not require demonstration. Not only the naturalists but every man, among our contemporaries as well as among the ancients, considers and will for a long time still consider that it would be a "sin against science" (Husserl was not afraid to use a Biblical term, and I think that this is not a matter of simple chance; positivism also has its source in certain hopes that are not at all positive and that it is not advisable to examine) "to imagine a free conception of nature" (*Logos*, p. 335). This is true as long as centripetal forces dominate the soul, as long as man wishes to know what has meaning and is valid for all, as long as all his interests are bound to the empirical world and truth appears to him based in the final analysis on evidence which renders it convincing for each of us. For him "it is clear that the abstract or nomological sciences are the truly fundamental sciences, and that from their theoretical content the concrete sciences must draw everything that makes them sciences, namely, theory" (*L.U.*, I, 235).

But Plato speaks to us of a deep mystery that only the initiates know. This mystery consists in the fact that philosophers have only one purpose, which is to prepare themselves for death and to die. Husserl had certainly read the *Phaedo* and knew the passage of which I speak, but he does not take it into consideration, perhaps because in his judgment this is the domain of wisdom, of depth of thought. But if he thinks thus, then he does not see what is involved here. It is an incontestable fact that besides the centripetal forces visible to all, there are in the human soul centrifugal forces. These are less constant; they are distinguished only with difficulty and people so rarely notice them that when they manifest themselves and disturb or even alter the order established by men and which they believe is a cosmos instituted by nature itself, they are amazed as if at some supernatural event. But indignation and the protestations of reason are useless: the fact remains a fact.

Plato is right. Men are not concerned only with living and with organizing their lives but also die and prepare themselves for death. And when the breath of death touches them, they no longer aspire to attach themselves more strongly to the center which binds men to each other but rather strain all their powers to escape beyond the limits of that periphery which even yesterday seemed to them eternal. And they then try above all else to destroy the illusion of the unity of consciousness as well as the evidences that nourish this illusion.

Then they must, to speak in modern language, pass "beyond" human truth and error, beyond the truth and the error which are deduced from the fact of the existence of the positive sciences and of the most perfect of these, mathematics.

Philosophy then no longer wishes and no longer can be a rigorous science which amasses truths that by virtue of their evidence must impose themselves sooner or later on all men. Philosophy then aspires, as to its τιμιώτατον (what is most important), to the truths which do not wish to be "truths common and good for all." And in the light of this search, it is the transformation of the "vague hopes of wisdom" into clear and simple "rational forms" which then appears as the philosophic sin, to speak Husserl's language. The truths convincing for all are treasures that rust, that moths destroy, and that have no value "in heaven." Even if they should be, as Husserl holds, outside time and space, they would not for all this become eternal. There are in "concrete" reality many more elements of eternity than in all the ideas discovered and remaining still to be discovered by phenomenology. If we still need a witness for the character of the goal that philosophy sets, I would recall these words of Nietzsche: "A philosopher, this is a man who constantly lives, sees, hears, doubts, hopes, dreams extraordinary things; who is struck by his own thoughts as if they came from outside, from above or below, as events or as claps of thunder; a fateful man around whom it always thunders and rumbles and everything happens in sinister fashion. A philosopher, alas, is a being who often flees from himself, who often is afraid of himself, but who is too curious not to 'return to himself always.' "

One can, it is true, discern in these words certain nuances which could leave the way open to those who would like to find rational truths in them. Nietzsche, it will be said, also pretends to reach a truth that is obligatory for all. But we must not take everything literally and make a great thing of the least word. If we wish to understand a writer, we must know how to forgive him for what is inadequate in his works. We are all children of Adam, and even those among the philosophers who prepared themselves to die and saw the meaning of life in death continued to live and better arrange their existence.

VIII

Husserl stops at nothing in his attempt to make of philosophy the science of absolute truths. His theory of knowledge extends its rights not only to the natural sciences and mathematics but also claims to impose its directives on history and, consequently, to rule all the manifestations of the human spirit. Husserl does not wish to listen to the teachings of history; it is history, on the contrary, that must accept his teaching. One really cannot deny him rigor of thought and a spirit of consistency, nor can one deny him a noble audacity and an ardor which are very rarely found in our time among "academic" philosophers.

His dispute with Dilthey is particularly significant in this respect. Husserl has the greatest respect for Dilthey. Despite this, he sends him to the insane asylum along with Sigwart and Erdmann, though using expressions—it is true—that are less rude. But a madhouse is always a madhouse, whatever words we use to designate it. Here is what provoked the pitiless judgment of Husserl. I shall quote only a few lines but they will suffice to make clear for us what Husserl considers a scientific sin.

Dilthey writes: "For him whose vision embraces the world and all its history, the absolute truth of any form of religion, philosophy, or practical organization completely disappears. And thus the elaboration of the historical consciousness destroys, in a more radical way than the examination of the struggle of systems, belief in the absolute validity of any of the philosophies which try to formulate in constraining fashion the universal relationships of being by means of a relationship of concepts." To this Husserl replies:

> It is easily seen that historicism, rigorously developed, leads to skeptical subjectivism. Ideas, theories, truths, sciences would then, like all ideas, lose their absolute validity. That an idea is valid would then mean simply that it is a spiritual form, a fact to which a meaning is granted and which, as such, determines thought. In that case there no longer exists validity as such or *an sich*, which is what it is even if no one can realize it and no historic mankind has ever realized it. This is true as well of the principle of contradiction and of all of logic which, already without this, is now in total flux. Then one is finally obliged to admit that the logical principles of noncontradiction will transform themselves into their opposites. Then all the statements that we now make, all the possibilities that we examine and take into consideration, can find themselves deprived of all meaning and validity, etc. There is no need to continue this discussion and to repeat here what has already been said elsewhere (*Logos*, pp. 324–25).

"Elsewhere" means, as Husserl explains in a footnote, in the first volume of his *Logische Untersuchungen.*

We already know what was said on this subject in the first volume of *Logische Untersuchungen.* The last word of this discussion is the insane asylum, where all those who accept relativism, even specific relativism, belong. I do not know how the aged Dilthey reacted to this severe judgment (he was seventy-six years old when Husserl's article appeared). Did he, under the pressure of his adversary's arguments, grant the right of reason to judge history, or did he persist in believing that history judges reason and everything that reason imagines?

This case is more complex than that of Sigwart; and Husserl's pretensions here appear infinitely vaster, for now Husserl's ideas demand that they be granted not only the predicate of being but of real being. There then appears that μετάβασις εἰς ἄλλο γένος (change to another genus) because of which alone it appeared to Husserl necessary to place real objects and ideas in the same category. Husserl continues thus:

> History, the empirical science of the spirit, is incapable by its own means of deciding either in a positive or negative sense whether there is room to distinguish religion as a particular form of culture from religion as an idea, i.e., as valid religion, art as a form of culture from art possessing true meaning and validity, historical right from valid right, and finally historical philosophy from valid philosophy. Neither can history tell us whether the relationship between each of these two terms is or is not that which exists between the idea, to speak Platonic language, and its obscured, phenomenal image (*Logos*, p. 325). Only philosophical understanding must unveil for us "the riddle of the world and of life" (*Logos*, p. 336).

Rationalism here blooms magnificently with a splendor such that, to speak frankly, I am not even completely convinced that Husserl truly "dared hope" that some day human reason, even after having passed through the school of phenomenology and after having fully accepted the phenomenological method, "must unveil for us the riddle of the world and of life." Husserl said this, but he does not, it seems to me, think it; or rather, I believe that he has not yet thought truly either about the riddle of the universe or the mystery of life, postponing these "questions" to some future day, as do the majority of very busy people. Husserl confined himself always to the middle zone of being and has still not arrived at the extreme regions. He speaks of these regions with so much assurance because he sets out from the supposition that, thanks to the "unity" of being, the knowledge of the middle zone permits us by way of deduction to judge concerning the farthest regions. The meaning and attractive power of rationalism come from this postulate, and I think that it is the source of the saddest misunderstandings in the domain of philosophy and that it is here precisely that we find the original sin of which Husserl has a presentiment but does not succeed in discovering. We must have the courage to say it firmly: the middle zones of human and universal life do not at all resemble the polar and equatorial zones. The difference is so great that if one concludes from what one sees in the middle zone and applies it to what exists in the extreme zones, not only does he not approach the truth but he flees from it. The constant error of rationalism derives from its faith in the limitless power of reason, *der Schrankenlosigkeit der objektiven Vernunft* (*Logische Untersuchungen*, II, p. 80). Reason has done much, therefore it can do everything. But "much" does not mean "everything"; "much" is separated from "everything" *toto coelo;* "much and "everything" belong to two different, irreconcilable categories.

That is the first point. The second is: to answer Dilthey, Husserl was obliged to commit a real μετάβασις εἰς ἄλλο γένος (change to another genus) and to make use of Plato's language about the relation between the idea and its darkened image. Plato had the right to speak thus: the idea was for him the reality κατ' ἐξοχην, *par excellence*, and the reality that we perceive appeared to him an obscured form of the primary reality. But, according to Husserl, the idea is not real; Husserl's idea possesses only a certain "meaning," only a being that is *an und für sich* and cannot "manifest itself" in reality under any form whatsoever, pure or cloudy. Husserl obviously had no other way out. If philosophy pretends to unveil the mystery of the universe and of life, it must have ideas richer in content and more alive than those with which one can combat Sigwart's logic. And Husserl hopes that his ideas will give him the possibility of answering all questions, that they will serve him not only to describe religion and art as "forms of culture" but to decide which of the religions has validity in itself—in other words, in which religion the voice of God is heard and in which the divine voice, revelation, is replaced by a human voice, and whether, in general, there is a God on earth. Such was certainly the meaning of his statement that the theory of knowledge precedes metaphysics.

Husserl, to our great regret, has still not written a phenomenology of religion; I daresay he will never write it. We must believe that he will not judge himself entitled to put to his reason, outside of which there is not and cannot be any authority, the question of the "validity" of religions. And he will not, furthermore, take it upon himself to answer the question which of the existing religions has "validity in itself" and where the final truth is to be found—in the Old and New Testament, in the Koran, in the Vedas, or even in *Also sprach Zarathustra*. Nevertheless, he pretends that only his phenomenology is capable of resolving our doubts about the final truth!

I have already said more than once that theory of knowledge is the soul of philosophy. One could express oneself with still greater force: tell me what your theory of knowledge is and I will tell you what your philosophy is. And this is understandable: in accordance with what he wishes to know, man invents his method of knowledge and his definition of "truth." Rationalism fears and detests the extreme zones; it holds itself firmly in the middle zone, in the center, around which are disposed all the points of the surface that it studies and with which it is concerned. And it admits the phenomena that it encounters on its way only insofar as they can be utilized for the needs and necessities of the center. Religion itself—I do not even speak of art, of morality, of law—acquires importance and meaning only in the measure that it is in agreement with the conditions of existence at the center. The rationalist wishes at all costs to bring it about that religion have "validity" in itself—in other words, that it bear the seal with which the functionaries of reason mark all merchandise carried to the spiritual marketplace. And it does not even occur to it that religion does not tolerate any control or mark, and that at the merest touch or brushing by the hand of official registrars it transforms itself immediately into its contrary. It is enough to recognize any religion whatsoever as true for it immediately to cease to exist.

Husserl's idea about the "validity" of religion was certainly not invented by him. Following his custom, he only expresses in an open, sharp, almost brutal manner the goal of the aspirations of the "positive religions," even of those which imagined that they lived in the most elevated regions of fantastic mysticism. All of them wish before everything else that their "truths" should have objective validity, persuaded that "the rest will come." And all of them would cease to love and respect their God the moment they saw themselves obliged to renounce the objective (i.e., admitted by reason) validity of religion, not even suspecting that the thirst for objectivity comes from the devil, from the prince of this world, and that it is the indisputable sign of indifference to other worlds. The most difficult thing for man is to renounce the idea that his truth is and must be true for all! And yet he must separate himself from this "truth." It is possible that "validity in itself, a validity which is what it is even if no one can realize it and no historic mankind will ever realize it" exists, but it is not and will never be in the "public domain," for "by its very nature" it does not admit the conditions and laws that the public domain always imposes. So long as logic rules, the way to metaphysics is barred. At times man feels that so long as he does not awaken from the sleep where the evidences rule, the truth will not disclose itself to him. But, as we know, this feeling, according to Husserl, is the worst and most serious of sins.

It is because of this presentiment, expressed very modestly by Sigwart, Erdmann, and Dilthey, that Husserl launched so violent an attack on modern philosophy. But the arguments through which he wishes to force Dilthey to renounce psychologism, on the contrary, only support psychologism. For if man has still not expressed "validity in itself" and will never express it, how could reason not rise up in wrath against itself? Or if reason is too fearful or has too much self-love and decides not to accuse itself, is it really true that there will not be found in the human soul forces capable of rebelling against the centuries-old slavery? And is not psychologism, which, despite all attacks, continues to live, the expression of this rebellion? Is it not precisely that *momento mori* which always lives in the souls of men, that supreme mystery of philosophy that Plato had revealed in his ἀποθνῄσκειν καὶ τεθνάναι * and that he himself forgot when he had to make of philosophy a science capable of imposing itself always and upon all men? If one can reproach modern philosophy for anything, it is not that it disdains argumentation deduced from consequences but rather that it has not the courage to defend its rights and to deliver itself from the tyranny of reason. The ancient Greeks doubted whether men possess the powers necessary to attain truth. Among others, Aristotle bears witness to this. "One could say," he writes, "that the possession of truth is not proper to man. For it may be that man is by nature a slave; that, as Simonides says, the privilege [of freedom] is given only to God; and that it is appropriate for man to aspire only to that knowledge for which he is destined. If one accepts what the poets say, and if the gods really are jealous, this applies precisely to the case at hand and he who rises too high perishes" (*Met.*, 982b, 29 ff.). So thought the ancients. Aristotle himself, however, is of a different opinion. "It is absurd to assume that the gods are jealous. It is necessary rather to suppose that the proverb is right: the poets lie a great deal. Let us not think any science more important, more elevated than this."

"The poets lie a great deal." Husserl will certainly acquiesce in this judgment of Aristotle's and will gladly repeat with him πολλὰ ψεύδονται οἱ ἀοιδοί. In his eyes all that Sigwart and Erdmann bracket in their theories of knowledge, Dilthey's statement that history makes us doubt the absoluteness of human knowledge— all these are only inventions of the poet that reason cannot

* Dying and the state of death.

justify. "The gods are jealous" is a metaphysical statement and consequently completely arbitrary. Descartes' thesis that God *qui summe perfectus et verax est* * cannot lie is also a metaphysical statement, but it constitutes *de facto* the unexpressed postulate of all Dilthey's demonstrations. And are not the melancholy admissions of Sigwart and Dilthey finally the expression of that obscure feeling which the sleeper experiences when suddenly the reality of the dream begins to seem to him illusory, when the vague recollection of another reality to which he belonged in another life begins to destroy the "unity of consciousness" and despite all the evidence demands imperiously of the sleeper that he awaken?

* Who is wholly perfect and true.

IX

With his customary daring Husserl declares: "Our statement that every subjective statement allows itself to be replaced by an objective statement signifies basically nothing other than the *limitless character of objective reason* (*Schrankenlosigkeit der objektiven Vernunft* [author's italics] *Logische Untersuchungen*, II, 90).

What Husserl promises us here has always been the object of men's most ardent desires, as the promised land was for the Jews. Reason has so often deceived us that we really have all grounds for not trusting it any more than sense-impressions which, as daily experience demonstrates, are equally deceptive. The philosophical skepticism which for thousands of years has ruined the established truths was born and developed on the soil of observed errors. We have certain sensations, we also have subjective observations whose evidence appears indisputable to all, but where shall we find the supreme sanction—the guarantee that all of us, the human species as such, do not live in a world of phantoms and that the truth we distinguish is really the truth and not an error? Husserl gives to the questions so formulated a precise answer: "to the subjective association of thoughts there corresponds here an objective . . . unity of meaning, which is what it is whether it be actualized in thought or not" (*Ibid.*, 94). And he adds with still greater force: "the scientist knows also that he does not create the objective validity of thoughts and of associations of thoughts, of concepts and of truths, as if it were a question of accidents of his mind or of the human mind in general, but that he *intuits and discovers* them. He knows that their ideal being does not have the meaning of a 'psychic being in our mind' where, through the negation of a real objectivity of the truth and of the ideal in general, all real being, including objective being, would be abolished" (*Ibid.*, p. 94. Cf. *Logische Untersuchungen*, I, p. 129: "Truth and being are both, and in the same sense of the term, 'categories,' and obviously correlative. One cannot relativize truth and maintain the objectivity of being.")

And again in Volume I of *Logische Untersuchungen:*

> the experience of the agreement existing between thought and the real that is thought, between the actual meaning of the statement and the facts of the case is evidence, and the idea of this agreement is truth. But the ideality of the truth constitutes its objectivity. It is not an accidental fact that a proposition, in this place and at this moment, is in agreement with a given state of things. The relationship concerns rather the identical meaning of the proposition and the identical facts of the case. "Validity" and "objectivity" (or "nonvalidity" and "nonobjectivity") belong to the statement not insofar as the statement is temporal but to the statemen *in specie,* the (pure and identical) statement $2 \times 2 = 4$ (I, pp. 190–91).

The explanatory example given here is again drawn from arithmetic. And this is certainly not a matter of chance. All of Husserl's philosophy is constructed as if there were nothing in the world but mathematics. And if it had not pretended to discover for us the ῥιζώματα πάντων, the roots of all things, it would perhaps have conformed to its definition. As the theory of knowledge for mathematics and the mathematical sciences it could find its use and justification.

But it pretends to much more, and it is generally considered much more important. When Husserl, wishing to satisfy the "eternal" need of man, speaks of the limitless power of our reason besides which there is not and can not be any other authority, what is involved is no longer a question of the multiplication table. One then discerns the voice of Saint Thomas Aquinas who, when he asks *utrum fides meritoria est*, whether faith is praiseworthy, knows that there cannot be two answers to this question or, to speak Husserl's language, that the answer will have an objective value. One hears also the voice of Saint Thomas Aquinas' opponent Luther, who, even though he called reason a whore and vulgarly insulted Aristotle, cried out passionately: *Spiritus sanctus non est scepticus, nec dubia aut opiniones in cordibus nostris scripsit, sed assertiones, ipsa vita et omnia experientia certiores et firmiores.** Husserl's theory maintains and nourishes precisely this kind of assurance. "It is necessary," he says, "to consider theory of knowledge a discipline which precedes metaphysics" (*L.U.*, I, 195). This means that before tasting the infinite riches of life it is necessary to admit that reason is objective and limitless. It is necessary to believe that mathematics determines the character and possibilities of human understanding in this world as well as in all those that have already existed and those that will exist in the future and that, consequently, it may be that the solutions we propose to metaphysical problems will show themselves to be false but that in principle the fashion in which these questions are raised does not admit of any modification.

To put it differently, when Saint Thomas asks *utrum fides meritoria est*, it is necessary to answer him "yes" or "no," and this "yes" or "no" will be accepted both by Luther and by the *spiritus sanctus* in the name of which he speaks or, to use Huss-

* The Holy Spirit is not a skeptic, nor does it write doubts or opinions in our hearts, but rather assertions more certain and firm than life itself and all experience.

erl's language, by monsters, angels, and gods. Likewise when Luther speaks of his *sola fide* one must either agree or disagree with him. In the kingdom of truth, metaphysical as well as empirical, the supreme ideal is unshakable order. From this comes the religious and philosophical intolerance which, to flatter human weakness, has always been considered a proof of our love for God and the truth. In 1525, in connection with the Wars of the Peasants, Luther wrote: *Der Esel will Schläge haben und der Poebel will mit Gewalt regirt sein; das wusste Gott wohl, darum gab er der obrigkeyt nicht eynen Fuchsschwanz, sondern ein schwert yn die Hand.**

Who knows? It may be that the creators of rationalism were moved by the same considerations as those of which Luther speaks. Perhaps they also thought that it is necessary to beat the donkey and to keep a tight rein on the rabble and therefore they created their reason in the image of the sword. But he who takes up the sword will perish by the sword. Luther, Saint Thomas, and many other great men of this world, suffered from the autocratic power of the tyrant they had placed on the throne no less than the rabble whom they despised. For in the end the tyrant demands above all complete submission of those very ones who helped him ascend the throne.

It is deliberately, for the sake of greater clarity, that I have touched here on metaphysical questions, but I could have spoken also of the problems of the exact sciences. "Every theory in the experimental sciences is simply a hypothetical theory. It does not draw its explanations from fundamental laws that are obviously certain but only obviously probable. Thus the theories themselves possess only obvious probability; they are provisional and not definitive theories" (*L.U.*, I, p. 255). "If we could intuit clearly the exact laws of psychic processes they would show

---

* The donkey wishes to be whipped and the mob wishes to be ruled by force; God knew this well and therefore gave the government not a foxtail but a sword in its hand.

themselves as eternal and invariable as the fundamental laws of the natural theoretical science and would therefore be valid even if there were no psychic process" (*L.U.*, I, 149). One would, I think, have to be blind not to see clearly that Husserl does not keep, and does not wish to keep, within the limits of the "positivism" that he proclaims. Or rather, Husserl believes that he has the right to raise his positivism to the rank of metaphysics. Having begun by establishing the equality of the right to be of the ideal and the real, he ends by subordinating the latter to the former. The ideal world is the eternal order which determines and supports the real world. The real world was born yesterday and will disappear tomorrow; the ideal world was not born and will never pass away. This is the foundation of the limitless power of reason; it is because of this that we can transform every subjective statement into an objective truth. The *spiritus sanctus* of Saint Thomas Aquinas and of Luther, which was born of the Greek λόγος, has become the ideal cosmos of Husserl. And the *spiritus sanctus* gives men the power to perform miracles, or what they consider such. If Christ had said to Saint Thomas *bene de me scripsisti*,* this would mean—and this is precisely the essential thing—that what Saint Thomas had understood was not his subjective experience but objective truth. All of us, consequently, must think and write what Saint Thomas thought and wrote. Christ himself, as is said in Dostoevsky's "Grand Inquisitor," can add nothing or take anything away from the writings of Saint Thomas. And Luther, who was saved by faith, already "knows" not only that he himself was saved by faith but that *all men* can only be saved by faith. The Mohammedan, the Hindu, the scientist of Göttingen or of Marburg, who have subjectively experienced certain things, have transformed them into limitless, ideal, objective truths and are unshakably convinced that it is in this transformation that the supreme goal of mankind consists; and they do not even ask themselves *pro forma* if they

* You have written well of me.

are not betraying mankind by barring it, through such philo-sophic sorceries, from the way to salvation.

Naturally in our time, when the scientist cannot use the vo-cabulary of the church, the *spiritus sanctus* has been replaced by the theory of ideas, as formerly when men had lost confidence in reason they put the *spiritus sanctus* in the place of the λόγος. But the goal of every philosophy "which had a future" was always to give man the possibility of passing from the subjective to the objective and of thus transforming limited experience into absolute judgments. Men have already more or less arrived at this. Husserl has also succeeded in it. His ideas have found an echo among many contemporary philosophers. People have al-ready for a long time aspired to proclaim proudly, lifting their heads high, the absolute, unshakable truth. And when Husserl daringly began to develop his ideas hundreds of voices responded to his call. Who today does not possess the absolute truth, and who dares doubt that the absolute truth is now definitively the truly absolute truth and that philosophy has entered into a period of sure scientific discoveries? Men have again plunged into a peaceful rationalist slumber—for the moment, naturally. The printer's ink had not yet had time to dry on the pages written by Husserl when the world was shaken by events which could in no way have found a place in the "ideal" order per-ceived anew by the Göttingen professor. Will men awake, or are they destined to a heavy slumber to the end of time? There have always been events of immense importance, some of which entered into history while others—the most important—remained outside of history and left no testimony, but the need for a well-defined and peaceful existence was stronger than everything. And all *memento mori*, beginning with relativism and up to death itself, troubled—and this but for a moment—only a few rare spirits, without succeeding in overthrowing the order of the en-chanted kingdom in which we are destined to be born and to end our ephemeral existence.

But, despite everything, it is not given to rationalism, with all its "arguments deduced from consequences" and its threats of confinement in the madhouse, to choke in the heart of men the obscure feeling persisting there that the final truth, the truth which our ancestors sought unsuccessfully in Paradise, is found ἐπέκεινα νοῦ καὶ νοήσεως, beyond reason and what can be conceived by reason, and that it is impossible to discover it in the immobile and dead universe which is the only one over which rationalism can rule as sovereign.

What Is Truth?
On Ethics and Ontology*

οὐ γὰρ δεῖται ἱδρύσεως, ὥσπερ
αὐτὸ φέρειν οὐ δυνάμενον.
Plotinus, VI, ix, 6.

τότε δὲ χρὴ ἑωρακέναι πιστεύειν,
ὅταν ἡ ψυχὴ ἐξαίφνης φῶς λάβῃ.
Plotinus, V, iii, 17.

It does not need a support, as
though it could not carry itself.

But indeed we must believe that we have seen,
when light *suddenly* dawns on the soul.

I

Hering calls his essay *Sub specie aeternitatis*. These are words
of very great purport. In a certain sense they sum up the philosophic thought of Europe, if not of mankind. Eternity has ever

* This section is a reply to criticism made by Professor Albert Hering to
my essay *Memento Mori*. [Shestov's essay appeared in Russian in 1916 in
the Russian journal *Rouskaia Misl*. A French translation appeared in the
Revue Philosophique for January, 1925. Professor Hering's criticism, entitled *Sub Specie Aeternitatis*, can be found in the 1927 volume of
Philosophischer Anzeiger (Berne).]

been the object of philosophic thought, and all arguments conceived by the opponents of philosophy have always foundered on the firm rock of eternity. Nevertheless, those who know Husserl's work cannot evade one question: this idea is old and venerable, and even absolutely definite, but in any case not "scientific"; can the author of the *Logical Inquiries* shelter behind it?

Sub specie aeternitatis—this is surely the quintessence of that wisdom and profundity which Husserl attacks with such force and passion in his essay *Philosophy as Strict Science*. Hering, however, disregards this. He even resorts to the scriptures and appeals to the Gospel according to Saint Matthew 10:39. He writes: "Will Shestov's *Memento Mori* make any impression on the champions of scientific philosophy? Will not his warning to them not to lose their lives in seeking for the λόγος* be answered with reference to the words of the Logos-Messiah: 'He who finds his life shall lose it, and he who loses his life for my sake shall find it?' " I am ready to admit that my *Memento Mori* will make no impression on the champions of scientific philosophy. I cannot, however, allow them to appeal to the words of the Gospel. It is true that God is called λόγος in the Gospel, but can the λόγος of the Gospel be equated with that of the philosophers? And will Husserl's philosophy, which rejects profundity and wisdom, ever agree to admit that it cannot get along in its inquiries without the doubtful support of a young Jew who was condemned innocent to a felon's death two thousand years ago? Husserl's argument is based on self-evident truths; has it then a right to enlist the support of the Gospel commandments? Dostoevsky was able to take the passage in Saint John (13:25) as motto for his *Brothers Karamazov;* but Dostoevsky is hardly a fitting mate for Husserl. Husserl has never appealed to the authority of Scripture in anything which he has written hitherto, and I am

---

* I never gave this warning, but I will not enlarge on this point, in order not to diverge from the main issue.

convinced that he will not approve the method discovered by Hering of defending phenomenology.

After what Hering has said, it is comprehensible that he should think my account of Husserl's views incorrect. I tried to show that Husserl shuts himself off in the strictest fashion from both profundity and wisdom. Hering insists that I am exaggerating, that Husserl made no such clean break with profundity and wisdom, and even recognized that they can be of practical use. But I never denied this; I even said so in my essay. Why, then, does Hering insist on it? Read what he says: "Then philosophers have nothing left but the necessity of a decision. . . . But no one is forced to throw his spiritual salvation to the winds because his speciality, whether it be chemistry or scientific philosophy, says nothing about it." I did not, indeed, say this, but I shall permit myself to state that Husserl will not accept a word of what Hering writes. These thoughts were quite usual toward the end of the last century and the beginning of the present. Even today there are many philosophers who think thus. They have, however, nothing of Husserl in them and are as alien to him as the specific relativism with which, again, many did and still do content themselves. Hering says: "There is no necessity for a decision." How so? There is a necessity. Husserl's whole force, his enormous significance, is based precisely on the fact that he had sufficient acumen to see this necessity and sufficient boldness to take the decision. Before him philosophers clung patiently and even willingly to wisdom. Its rights had been hallowed through centuries, and no one dared doubt them. Every one would have thought it the most frightful blasphemy; but Husserl was not afraid to proclaim aloud what the others dared not confess even to themselves, what they dared not see. But Hering tries to justify Husserl, as though he were ashamed for him. I cannot repeat here the quotations which I adduced from Husserl's *Philosophy as Strict Science* and other works. Any reader interested can look

at my *Potestas Clavium.* If he reads the *Memento Mori* he
will easily be able to convince himself that this was precisely how
Husserl posed the question: there is no alternative, we must
decide between philosophy and profundity and wisdom, and
profundity and wisdom are as out of date as astrology and
alchemy.

Again: "because his speciality, whether it be chemistry or
scientific philosophy, says nothing about it." Hering thinks that
the questions which the wise have discussed hitherto are no concern of philosophers, as they are no concern of chemists, because they go beyond the limits of their speciality (in another
passage he even speaks of a "modest speciality"). And the same
opinion is ascribed to Husserl! But Husserl maintains the exact
opposite. He says that philosophy is the "science of the true
beginnings, of the origins, the ῥιζώματα πάντων (roots of all
things)." And again: "Science has spoken, now it is for wisdom
to learn." Once more, I cannot repeat the quotations which I
adduced in my essay, but surely the above shows very clearly
that Husserl will not be content with the modest role of a specialist which Hering assigns him (when, indeed, did a great philosopher ever display the virtue of modesty?) and is certainly
not inclined to leave profundity and wisdom in their old rights.
Many are shocked by Husserl's decision and challenging boldness. They think that a bad peace is better than a good war, and
try, as far as possible, to soften down Husserl's words or change
their meaning. He himself is not at all pacifically inclined. "Perhaps there is no more powerful, more irresistibly progressive
idea in modern life than that of science. Nothing can stop its
victorious advance. It is, indeed, all-embracing in its legitimate
ends. In its imaginary ideal completion it would be reason itself,
which can have no authority beside it and over it." Do these
words need any addition? And are Husserl's words such that
we should hold him for a "modest" specialist? Is Hering right

in saying that Husserl is ready to live in peace and good understanding with wisdom and that my account of the thought of
the creator of phenomenology is not sufficiently exact?

II

And yet in a certain sense Hering is right in calling his essay *Sub
specie aeternitatis*. He is even right in appealing to the Scriptures.
There is a certain connection between phenomenology and the
wisdom which it rejects. Somewhere, at the last end, phenomenology loses belief in itself and its self-evident truths and seeks
help and blessing from wisdom. In Husserl's works themselves
this relationship was not perceptible, but the moment his pupils
take up the word it becomes evident at once. Why do the pupils
deviate from their master and deny him? Why did the master
speak of "illimitability of reason" while the disciples only wished
to be modest specialists and to hide in the shadow of *sub specie
aeternitatis*?

I think that here we have reached the fundamental question,
and that insofar as we succeed in throwing light upon it, we
shall also find an answer to all the objections brought forward
by Hering. *Sub specie aeternitatis* is, of course, the basic theme
of Spinoza's philosophy. *De natura rationis est res sub quadam
aeternitatis specie percipere* ("It is in the essence of reason to
perceive things from the aspect of eternity") (*Ethics*, II, xliv,
Cor. 2). Further: *Quidquid mens, ducente ratione, concipit, id
omne sub eadem aeternitatis seu necessitatis specie concipit*
("Whatever the mind, guided by the reason, perceives, it perceives from the same aspect of eternity or necessity"). In other
passages, too, of this and his other works he has much to say on
this point. The close of the fifth part of the *Ethics* is simply a
symphony on the theme *sub specie aeternitatis: Mens nostra,
quatenus se et corpus sub aeternitatis specie cognoscit, eatenus*

Dei cognitionem necessario habet, scitque se in Deo esse et per Deum concipi ("Insofar as our understanding cognizes itself and the body from the aspect of eternity it necessarily has cognition of God and knows that it is in God and is conceived through God") (*Ethics*, V, Prop. xxx).

But at the same time Spinoza says in his Letter LXXVI, in which he is answering Burgh: *Ego non praesumo, me optimam invenisse philosophiam, sed veram me intelligere scio. Quomodo autem id sciam, si roges; respondebo, eodem modo ac tu scis tres angulos trianguli aequales esse duobus rectis; et hoc sufficere negabit nemo, cui sanum est cerebrum.* ("I do not assume that I have found the best philosophy, but I know that I have the true one. And if you ask how I know this, I reply: just as you know that the sum of the three angles of a triangle is equal to two right angles; and no one of sound understanding will deny that this suffices.")

At first sight these sentences seem to agree completely with one another and with the whole tendency of Spinoza's philosophy. In reality, however, they are so dissimilar that they must be considered as mutually exclusive. In his letter Spinoza maintains that his philosophy is by no means the best, but only the true. And he knows that it is the true for the same reason by which his correspondent knows that the sum of the angles of a triangle is equal to two right angles. According to this, the task of philosophy is to seek not the "best," but the "true." And philosophical truth shall be sought precisely where we seek the answer to the question of to what the sum of the angles of a triangle is equal. Any number of passages could be quoted from Spinoza's works in which the same thought is expressed with equal sharpness and clarity. He rejects with the utmost scorn any attempt to see in man and his claims anything greater than one among many natural phenomena. *Imo hominem in Natura veluti imperium in imperio concipere videntur* ("They seem to treat man in nature as a state within the state") (Part III, Beginning). He speaks of the *praejudicia de bono et malo, merito et peccato, laude et vituperio, ordine et confusione, pulchritudine et deformitate et de aliis hujus generis* ("prejudices concerning good and evil, merit and sin, praise and blame, order and confusion, beauty and ugliness, and other suchlike things") (Part I, Appendix). He also say that these prejudices would have necessarily hidden truth from man for all eternity, *nisi mathesis, quae non circa fines, sed tamen circa figurarum essentias et proprietates versatur, aliam veritatis normam hominibus ostendisset* ("had not mathematics, which deals not with ends, but with the nature and properties of figures, shown to man another norm of truth"). And he assures us that *de affectuum natura et viribus, ac mentis in eosdem potentia, eadem methodo agam, qua in praecendentibus de Deo et mente egi, et humanas actiones atque appetitus considerabo perinde, ac si questio de lineis, planis aut de corporibus esset* ("I shall treat of the nature and forces of the affections, and of the power of the spirit over them, using the same methods as I employed in the previous part of my work, when I treated of God and the soul, and shall treat of human actions and appetites as though dealing with lines, planes, and bodies").

How, now, is Spinoza's idea that the science of mathematics must serve philosophy as model to be harmonized with his passionate hymns to the theme *sub specie aeternitatis?* I will answer frankly: it cannot be harmonized at all. This is the basic and, if you will, the intentional and premeditated contradiction of Spinoza's system. When he speaks of his methods of investigation he assures us that living man with his ambitions, fears, and hopes does not concern him. But when he tries to show his ultimate truth, he forgets his mathematics, forgets his solemn vows, *non ridere, non lugere, neque detestari.* He wants to know *an aliquid daretur, quo invento et acquisito continua ac summa in aeterno fruerer laetitia* ("whether there is anything, the discovery and acquisition of which would give man lasting and supreme joy through all eternity"). Mathematics has, of course, nothing to do with human joys, whether eternal and sublime or transitory and debased. Similarly, the following words are meaningless for a mathematician: *Sed amor erga rem aeternam et infinitam sola laetitia pascit animum, ipsaque omnis tristitiae est expers; quod valde est desiderandum, totisque viribus quaerendum (De Intellectus Emendatione)* ("But the love of the eternal and endless feeds the soul with pure joy, and is itself free from all sorrow; which is greatly to be desired and to be sought after with all our force"). The mathematician recognizes that the sum of the angles of a triangle is equal to two right angles, or that the relation between the circumference and the diameter is a constant; that is the end of it. And if Spinoza has found a Something which enables him to lift himself into those spheres in which there is no mourning and no wailing but only joys without ceasing, this is certainly not because he found the *norma veritatis* in mathematics. And finally—and this is the main point—there is absolutely no doubt that a philosophy which affords man pure joy and frees him from sorrow is simply not able to say of itself that it is only *vera philosophia;* it is, in the most exact sense of the phrase, *optima philosophia.* It brings the *summum bonum, quod est valde desiderandum totisque viribus quaerendum.*

But here arises the difficult and even fatal question which philosophy cannot possibly evade. What is the relationship between *verum* and *optimum?* Has the *verum* to adapt itself to the *optimum,* or vice versa? And it is not one question that confronts us here, but a whole series. We must answer the following: (1) What is "truth"? (2) What is the "best"? (3) To whom is power given to determine the relationship between the "best" and the "true"?

Spinoza assures us that mathematics must be the model of philosophic thought, and gives us the *norma veritatis:* he who finds that the sum of the angles of a triangle is equal to two right angles has the answer to all questions that could stir in the breast of man. But is an assurance enough? It is clear that an assertion is not enough, in spite of the fact that it is neither necessary nor possible to interpret his words to Burgh as though he thought the methods of investigation applied by mathematicians to be the only correct ones and eternally applicable. When he says that success and failure fall equally to the just and the unjust, or that the good things for which the crowd yearns—*divitiae, honores, libidines*—are unstable and deceptive, he knows very well that to establish his assertions he need make no subtractions or multiplications, need draw no circles nor triangles. But when he says nevertheless that mathematics must give us the *norma veritatis*, this only means that there is no place in philosophy for free choice and arbitrariness, and that the truths of philosophy are as compelling and beyond repeal as those of mathematics. Thus the "best" has to adapt itself to the "true." But the "true" belongs exclusively to the domain of reason. In this respect the so-called empirical truths differ in no wise from the *a priori* truths. They, too, are imposed upon man with inexorable compulsion. Our knowledge is, of course, still at the lowest stage of evolution, and the *cognitio intuitiva, tertium genus cognitionis* (intuitive cognition, the third kind of cognition) is so far only the ideal of human achievement. But this does not in the least diminish or reduce the sovereign rights of scientific cognition. "In its ideal perfection it would be reason itself, which can have no other authority by its side or over it." These words are from Husserl, but are an almost word for word translation of the passage quoted by me from Spinoza's Letter LXXVI. And does this not mean that the "best" is entirely subjected to the rule and disposition of the "true"? Hering does not observe this. He asks, and obviously quite sincerely: "Then why not quietly admit that under certain circumstances even the scientific philosopher can find his necessary spiritual food in religious revelation, experience and tradition?" Why not admit that? Simply because it would mean evading a fundamental question. And I repeat once again that Husserl, the creater of phenomenology founded on self-evidence, will never agree to the compromise which Hering proposes; this would be for him tantamount to giving up the task which he had set himself. Not to make an unsupported statement, I will give another quotation from Husserl: "Self-evidence is not in fact a sort of index of consciousness attached to a judgment, calling to us, like a mystic voice from another world, 'here is the truth!', as though such a voice had something to say to us free spirits, and had not to prove its title." This is how Husserl answers any attempt at interference with judgments, with the verdict of reason. And if tradition, whether that of the church or another, personal "experience," or what is called revealed truth, tried to raise their voices, would he not ask from them what he calls their "titles"—what the Roman jurists called *justus titulus*? And is it not then quite clear that the cause of revelation must be regarded as hopelessly lost at the forum of reason? Perhaps it is rather less clear, but it is equally indubitable that Husserl's task, like Spinoza's, lies precisely in eradicating from human consciousness, root and branch, all remnants and remains, as though there could be any lawful sources of cognition at all outside reason. In this he sees the necessary presupposition of free inquiry ("for us free spirits"). This conviction is certainly not new. It was not Husserl who evolved it, and not Spinoza. Perhaps it has existed as long as there has been a philosophy, for philosophy has always wanted to be a rational philosophy, and rational inquiry has always passed for free inquiry. Revelation must justify itself before reason, otherwise no one would ever trouble about it. Even God Himself, insofar as He claims the predicate of existence, must apply to reason in respect, precisely, of that predicate. And reason may give it Him, or it may—and this is more likely—refuse.

III

If we admit, what no one will deny, that the essence of philosophy lies in finding how to put the question, then it becomes perfectly clear that Husserl's fundamental and enormous service lies in the fact that he was bold enough to contrast philosophy with wisdom. Philosophy must and can be strict science, which rejects wisdom as decisively as it does all kinds of relativism, disguised or open. To use Spinoza's words, philosophy wishes to be *vera*, but not *optima;* but there is absolutely no intrinsic connection between the "true" and the "best." Job says: If my grief and my calamity were laid in the balances, it would be heavier than the sands of the seas. He thinks that there is a balance in which human sorrow and the sand of the seas can be weighed, and that there are cases in which human sorrow would weigh more heavily than the sand of the seas. Husserl will, of course, not think of discussing Job's words; they are quite clearly "nonsensical." There is no such balance in which human experience could weigh heavier than the weight of physical bodies. What we hold for the *optimum,* for right and significant, cannot be measured with what is *verum.* Were one to heap ever so much human *optimum* in one scale, and in the other only a handful of sand, the latter would still be the heavier, and sink. This is the fundamental and most self-evident assertion of that philosophy which aims at being strict science. And if we were to ask a philosopher how he knows this, he would answer with Spinoza: *eodem modo ac tu scis, tres angulos trianguli aequales esse duobus rectis* ("Just as you know that the sum of the three angles of a triangle is equal to two right angles.") But Job, who has not ceased his lamentations, would interrupt curtly: *non ridere, non lugere, neque detestari.* And not to Job alone, but also to Him whom Hering calls the Logos-Messiah, who cries aloud: "My

God, my God, why hast Thou forsaken me?" the philosopher
could reply with certainty: *Intellectus et voluntas, qui Dei
essentiam constituerent, a nostro intellectu et voluntate toto caelo
differre deberent . . . non aliter scilicet, quam inter se conveniunt canis, signum caeleste, et canis animal latrans* ("The intellect and will which constitute the essence of God must differ
from our intellect and will as does heaven from earth . . . clearly
they agree in no other way [than that a common term denotes
them both], just as the single term *canis* signifies the heavenly
constellation of the Dog and the animal that barks.") As we see,
the answers are quite exhaustive. Both Job and the Logos-Messiah have been put in their places; they must bow before the truth
and be silent. But if they will not be silent, but continue to cry
aloud, the philosopher will examine their lamentations with the
same equanimity and the same tranquility with which he ex-
amines perpendiculars, planes, and circles. And so it must be. But
it has never been so, neither with Spinoza, who assured the world
that his philosophy was not the true, but the best, nor with the
other great representatives of human thought. Spinoza did not
discover his *sub specie aeternitatis* himself. All philosophers before and after him, even those who, like Husserl, have wanted
philosophy to be a strict science, have sought help and support
from wisdom; and wisdom at all times and by all philosophers
has been reduced, more or less to the formula which Spinoza
terms *sub specie aeternitatis*. It is no chance that Spinoza's main
work is called the *Ethics;* all his works might bear this title. The
meaning of his *sub specie aeternitatis* lies in the bridge which
it makes between the *vera philosophia* and the *philosophia
optima*. For him the *cognitio intuitiva vel tertium genus cognitionis* is nothing else than perfected *intelligere*. But *intelligere*
does not mean "understanding" but working out within oneself
such a relationship to the world and to life that it is possible to
attain the *acquiescentia animi* or the *summum bonum* of which
all philosophers have always dreamed.

Now, how does Spinoza attain his *summmum bonum?* in other words, how does the *vera philosophia* turn into an *optima philosophia?* That which is called *verum* cannot be altered by an effort of our will. Spinoza is unshakably convinced of this; this is the compelling truth dictated by reason. It is not possible to arrange for the sum of the angles of a triangle to be equal to three right angles, for good fortune to be granted to the just alone and ill fortune to the unjust, for things and men dear to us not to fall a prey to the passage of time. And Job in his tribulations cannot be helped, and we cannot arrange that the last, dreadful cry of the Logos-Messiah should not ring out into infinite space. All these are self-evident and irrefutable truths. So reason tells us, and reason allows no authority beside her equal to her own. But there wisdom comes to our help. It says to us: *Mens ducente Ratione sub eadem specie aeternitatis seu necessitatis concipit eademque certitudine afficitur* ("Whatsoever the mind conceives under the guidance of reason, it conceives under the form of eternity or necessity, and is therefore affected with the same certitude.") (*Ethics*, IV, lxii, Dem.); it is senseless to strive after the impossible. It is fruitless to fight against the truths determined by reason. But if we cannot fight, we must submit. We must realize that the individual being, whether Job or the Logos-Messiah, is destined in virtue of an unchangeable law which has existed from all eternity, destined from the beginning, to sorrow and destruction. Consequently man must renounce everything which has "self" existence, and first and foremost himself, and must direct his eyes toward that which knows neither origin nor beginning, and consequently neither end nor destruction. This is what is meant by comprehending life *sub specie aeternitatis vel necessitatis.* To love that which knows no beginning and has no end (*amor erga rem aeternam*) means to love God. This is man's highest end and his purpose. So wisdom speaks in Spinoza. In this way the *vera philosophia* turns in wondrous wise into a *philosophia optima.*

It teaches *quomodo circa res fortunae, sive quae in nostra potestate non sunt, hoc est circa res, quae ex nostra natura non sequuntur, nos gerere debeamus; nempe utramque fortunae faciem aequo animo expectare et ferre: nimirum quia omnia ab aeterno Dei decreto eadem necessitate sequuntur, ac ex essentia trianguli sequitur quod tres ejus anguli sunt aequales duobus rectis* ("how we are to behave with respect to things of fortune or things which lie outside our power, respect, that is, to things which do not follow from our nature; we have to bear either aspect of fortune with an equal mind, for without doubt all things follow from God's eternal decree with the same necessity as it follows from the essence of a triangle that the sum of its three angles is equal to two right angles") (*Ethics*, II). I do not know whether after all this it is necessary to expatiate further on the fact that Spinozism simply cannot be identified with naturalism, still less with pantheism. Although Spinoza speaks regularly of *Deus sive Natura*, yet his philosophy is the fruit of a purely ethical principle, which he equates, with full consciousness of what he is doing, with an ontological principle: *per realitatem et perfectionem idem intelligo* (*Ethics*, II, 6). Spinoza's main historical significance lies in the fact that after the long struggle, lasting more than a thousand years, which was carried on with such vehemence throughout the Middle Ages, he was the first to resolve to step forward openly in defense of the old wisdom which the world inherited from the Greeks. In mentioning his relationship with the Greeks I do not mean to attack either his originality, his profundity, or the direct inspiration of his philosophy. But the idea of equating perfection with reality, or rather, the interpolation of the idea of reality into that of perfection, was given to them, not by Spinoza, but by the Greeks. The Greeks already taught that we must consider the *res quae in nostra potestate non sunt* as ἀδιάφορα, as though they were non-existent. Socrates proclaimed in the most solemn of words: οὐ γὰρ οἴομαι θεμιτὸν εἶναι ἀμείνονι ἀνδρὶ ὑπὸ χείρονος βλάπτεσθαι

(*Ap.* 30 D). (I do not think that it is lawful for a better man to suffer harm from a worse.) The whole post-Socratic philosophy rests on this principle. This is also the source of the quite erroneous belief that ancient philosophy set itself practical rather than theoretical aims. These words of Socrates' which describe so exhaustively the fundamental ambition of Hellenic thought cannot possibly be understood or interpreted as Xenophon interpreted them. For Socrates, who was the first to express this thought, for Plato, who developed it so persistently in his Dialogues, for the Stoics and for Plotinus, who carried it out in their lives and their works, questions of practical character always took the second place. And indeed, can the "truth" that the worse man can do no harm to the better, be of any use in practical life? Or have we a right to think that the ancients did not see, as Spinoza saw, that good and ill fortune fall on the just and unjust alike? Neither Socrates nor Plato, nor even Epictetus or Marcus Aurelius, can be suspected of such naïveté. They knew, only too well, that good and ill fortune fall on the just and unjust alike, and they knew much else besides, and yet—or rather, precisely for that reason—they declare that the worse man can do no harm to the better. It is only when we keep this in mind that we can understand the relationship between Spinoza's *sub specie aeternitatis* and his assertion that *res quae in nostra potestate non sunt . . . ex nostra natura non sequuntur,* and understand also why and under what circumstances the wisdom which Husserl rejects could have been born among the Greeks. Wisdom is an illegitimate child of reason, but her true child for all that, flesh of her flesh, blood of her blood. When Anaximander, and after him Heraclitus and the Eleatics, led by reason, recognized the instability and impermanence of all existence, the soul of man was poisoned with an eternal sorrow and unrest never again to cease. Everything flows, everything is changeable, everything impermanent, nothing is stable—so wisdom teaches us to regard the world. So long as the Olympian gods lived, elementary and somewhat imperfect as they were, one could hope that they would help in some way. But the gods died a slow but sure death, and in Socrates' day they had to be protected from the criticism and even the scorn of enlightened men by the threat of heavy penalties. Socrates himself was called to account for despising the gods.

The gods died, for all that, and man had to take their tasks on himself. How was he to cope with this duty? The gods created the visible world, visible man, etc. It is not granted to man to create all that—that is *res quae in nostra potestate non sunt.* Now when man had taken the place of the gods, the visible world, which survived even after their death and submitted to no one, had in one way or another to be replaced by another world. Socrates' deepest and most secret thought was expressed by those men who are commonly called one-sided Socratics: the Stoics. Epictetus says (*Diatr.* II, 11): ἀρχὴ φιλοσοφίας συναίσθησις τῆς αὐτοῦ ἀσθενείας καὶ ἀδυναμίας περὶ τὰ ἀναγκαῖα. ("The beginning of philosophy is the realization of our own weakness and impotence with respect to the necessary things.") In no philosopher is so open an admission to be found; the beginning of philosophy is the recognition of human impotence and the impossibility of conquering necessity. But the same Epictetus says: "This is the wand of Mercury. All that thou touchest with it will become gold. Give me what thou wilt and I will turn it for thee into a Good (ὃ θέλεις φέρε, κᾀγὼ αὐτὸ ἀγαθὸν ποιήσω). Bring hither sickness and death, poverty and suffering, condemnation to death, through the magic wand all this shall be turned to profit" (*Diatr.* III, 20). How could so extraordinary a metamorphosis come about? Man felt his complete impotence, the absolute impossibility of fighting necessity—and suddenly it appears that he could turn anything you like, the most trivial and useless things into gold, the most dreadful and repulsive into a Good. Where did weak and wretched man find his magic wand? We find our answer if we ask Epictetus how he performs his miracles. He does not conceal it from us, he will tell us all; the Stoics had no mysteries. Ἐν τοῖς ἐφ' ἡμῖν ἡ οὐσία τοῦ ἀγαθοῦ . . . Μία δὲ ὁδὸς πρὸς τοῦτο, καταφρόνησις τῶν οὐκ ἐφ' ἡμῖν (*Ench.* XIX). ("The essence of the Good lies in that which is in our power. . . . But there is one road to it, to despise what is not in our power.") If we would use Mercury's wand, we must learn to despise everything that does not lie within man's power, for the essence of the good is that which lies within man's power. That which does not depend upon us is of the ἀδιάφορα, the indifferent, even (as the less honest but still bolder Platonists said) the non-existent.

I think that it is now clear what reason and the "wisdom" born of it effected. Reason saw that necessity is invincible, and that it is not given to reason to rule over the world created by the old, dead gods. Wisdom, which has never dared dispute with reason, which it holds to be the beginning of all things (even Plotinus repeated—ἀρχὴ οὖν λόγος), accepted everything which reason regarded as self-evident. And then it had nothing left to do but to declare that the Good, and reality itself, is only that which is within the power of reason, and that all that which is not within reason's power is to be rejected as evil or unreal. In this way ethics usurped the place of ontology in ancient philosophy. And so it has remained to this day. This is the meaning of Spinoza's *sub specie aeternitatis*, which leads men away from what he calls *res fortunae, sive quae in potestate nostra non sunt*. This is also the meaning of Hegel's *was wirklich ist, ist vernünftig* ("what is real is rational").

IV

I cannot, of course, sketch here in any detail the history of how the conviction grew among the Greeks that life must be regarded *sub specie aeternitatis*, and that accordingly only that is to be regarded as true and real which depends on us—ἐφ' ἡμῖν—and not that which does not so depend—τὸ οὐκ ἐφ' ἡμῖν. I will only repeat once again that even Anaximander was convinced that this was the meaning hidden in Heraclitus' "everything flows, nothing persists" (πάντα ῥεῖ οὐδὲν μένει); that Parmenides is speaking of the same thing in his "Being and thinking are one and the same" (αὐτό ἐστι τὸ εἶναι καὶ τὸ νοεῖν), and that consequently the ἀρχή (the beginning) of Greek philosophy was indeed the συναίσθησις τῆς αὐτοῦ ἀσθενείας καὶ ἀδυναμίας περὶ τὰ ἀναγκαῖα—the realization of our own weakness and impotence with respect to the necessary things. The ancient philosophers disputed about every subject in the world, but of one thing they were unshakably convinced: there is in the world an invincible necessity which lays down to man the bounds of the possible and impossible, and which was revealed as the supreme and final principle of the universe after the disappearance of the gods. This seemed to reason so self-evident and indubitable that there could be no two opinions about it. More than this: it seemed that the very possibility of thought itself was founded on this self-evident truth. For if there is no immutable order, how are we to think? How ask, answer, prove, convince? Even the deepest and boldest philosophers among the Greeks, even as among ourselves, still remained naïve realists in their methodological processes and proceeded from the presupposition that truth is an *adaequatio rei et intellectus*—an equation of object and intellect. Aristotle's famous definition (*Met.* 1011, b 15), "A false statement is the statement that that which is, is not, or that that which is not, is, and a true statement is a statement that that which is, is, and that which is not, is not"—this definition lived in the souls of the ancients, as it lives on in our souls today, although many times proved untenable by the theory of knowledge. It is, however, completely sufficient for the needs of common sense and for those of scientific investigation. Heat expands a body, cold contracts it; the smith putting on a new wheel and the learned physicist deducing the most difficult theory of calorics equally admit the truth of this assertion, as framed by Aristotle. It retains its force even in the most complicated scientific arguments, as in those between Copernicus and Ptolemy, Einstein and Newton, Lobatchevsky and Euclid. However much the sages dispute, they will never think of raising the question of what is truth. They are all convinced that they know already what truth is, and that all, Ptolemy and Copernicus, Einstein and Newton, the smith and the joiner, insofar as they seek the truth, are seeking one and the same thing, so that in this respect the sage is no different from the ordinary, common-sense man. This principle has been accepted by science, common sense, and philosophy. Even philosophers argue and prove, and thus start from the supposition that our judgments have, as it were, a pre-existent model which they must resemble if they want to be truths. It is impossible for heat both to expand and contract bodies, for the specific gravity of mercury to be both greater and less than that of iron, for the velocity of light to be a maximum and for there to be velocities of over 180,000 miles a second. Everything is dominated by the law of contradiction for which, again, Aristotle found an excellent expression when he called it the βεβαιωτάτη τῶν ἀρχῶν, the most unshakable of principles.

But now an astonishing fact: Aristotle, who told us what truth is and placed this truth under the protection of the all-powerful law of contradiction, heard a rumor that one of the greatest philosophers of antiquity, Heraclitus, refused to recognize the law of contradiction. It appears that Aristotle, for all his assurance, was greatly perturbed by Heraclitus. He returns twice to the subject in his *Metaphysics*. The first time he contents himself with the mocking remark: "It is not necessary for a man to believe what he says" (οὐκ ἔστι γὰρ ἀναγκαῖον, ἅ τις λέγει, ταῦτα καὶ ὑπολαμβάνειν) (*Met.* 1005, b 25). The second time (1062, a 34) he repeats almost the same words: Heraclitus is talking without really realizing what he is saying: οὐ συνεὶς ἑαυτοῦ τί ποτε λέγει. But this still seems to him insufficient, and he adds another objection—an entirely unacceptable one, since it contains a *petitio principii;* it proceeds from the supposition that Heraclitus did not doubt the law of contradiction. So it comes down to this, that in either case Aristotle can only make one answer to Heraclitus: that what he says is not what he thinks.

Another example out of Aristotle's *Ethics.* He is speaking of those who said that the so-called external goods were not necessary for εὐδαιμονία (happiness); one can be happy even inside Phalaris' bull. Now Aristotle declares that anyone saying this is, intentionally or unintentionally, talking nonsense (ἢ ἑκόντες ἢ ἄκοντες οὐδὲν λέγουσιν) (*Ethics,* 1153, b 21). Many philosophers of antiquity, both before and after Aristotle, not only asserted that a man could be happy even inside Phalaris' bull, but actually made this assertion the foundation of their ethics. Epicurus himself, who is clearly not at all the man to make fun of human reason, did not hesitate before this paradox. Aristotle could give no answer either to Epicurus or to Heraclitus; he could only say: οὐδὲν λέγεις—you are talking nonsense.

Now comes the question: is Aristotle's a sufficient answer to Heraclitus and Epicurus? Incidentally, in another passage Epicurus produces an equally glaring paradox. He allowed it "to be possible" that the atoms in their motion—only once, indeed, very long ago, and only to an infinitesimal degree—deviated from their proper motion. What would Aristotle have said if this "possibility" had been laid before him for his approval? Here, again, no proof could be adduced. Nobody was there when, in the infinitely distant past, the atoms assumed the liberty of diverging on their own authority from the universal laws of motion. Aristotle would thus have had no choice but to resort again to οὐδὲν λέγουσιν, to anger and abuse. And yet he had to take to such an "argument" often enough. Even of Plato he wrote, more than once, κενολογεῖν ἐστι καὶ μεταφορὰς λέγειν ποιητικάς (*Met.* 991, a 21 ff.) ("Those are empty words and mere poetic metaphor"). Or if he is pressed too hard with objections, he declares (*Met.* 1006, a 6):

"It is simply lack of education (ἀπαιδευσία) when we cannot distinguish where proof is necessary and where not." I think that if Aristotle were deprived of the right to argue in this way, his philosophy would lose a great deal of its perfection and convincing force. If, for example, we assume that Phalaris' bull simply has to be faced in composing any system of ethics? Or that Heraclitus' doubt as to the sovereign rights of the law of contradiction simply cannot be set aside in constructing a theory of knowledge? Or that the idea of the mean, so carefully cherished by Aristotle, an idea with which he surrounded the universe as with a Chinese wall, is by no means so enticing and noble as to enchant all who look upon it?

Meanwhile, how are we to get away from Phalaris' bull and all the other obstacles which the philosopher encounters on his way, if we make up our minds to abstain from angry exclamations and not pour our moral indignation on everyone who reminds us too often of these things? Moral indignation is not enough; to "repress" such questions, or to answer them, we must take a decision which Socrates took, and after him all the ancient philosophers, Epicurus not excepted. We must make up our minds that morality offers the *summum bonum*, that it is the source of the elixir of life and death, that here and here alone can man find his last refuge. Socrates, as I said, did this, and here lies the meaning of his assertion that a bad man can do no harm to a good. He who enjoys the secrets of virtue to which wisdom holds the key need not fear Anytus and Meletus, with all the Athenians, nor the fury of the tyrant, be he never so powerful. No one is lord over virtue. And morality, from which all the virtues derive, has become by Socrates' will a creative principle. Through it the ancient philosophers attained to the *summum bonum* which they could not find in the world they inherited from the old, dead gods. In the world of the gods were good and ill, which fell to mortals variously and at haphazard. Man, when he attached significance to good and ill as they happened in the world of the gods, placed himself in complete dependence on chance. This seemed fearful even to an Epicurus; it was still more intolerable to a Socrates, a Plato, the Stoics, and after them the Neo-Platonists. "The Good" must not be made dependent on chance. It is autonomous, it takes nothing from anyone, creates everything itself and only gives. How, then, could Aristotle assert that a good life needed something more, which is not subject to the good? Or that the good man should fear Phalaris' bull? We see that Aristotle's judgment was too hasty; it is not possible to say of those who faced Phalaris' bull that οὐδὲν λέγουσιν. There was a deep, a very deep meaning in their words. Thus and only thus can the ethical problem be posed. There is no ethics so long as the good man must tremble before the dreadful face of existence or await the good things of life, like a beggar, from blind fortune. Ethics begins by teaching man to see the nothingness of everything on earth, both of that which is commonly looked upon as good and of that which is commonly looked on as ill. Royal crowns, Alexander's fame, Croesus' riches, a day in May, fragrant lilac, the rising sun, are just as insignificant and despicable as everything else *quae in nostra potestate non sunt*, τὰ οὐκ ἐφ᾽ ἡμῖν. On the other hand, ill fortune and oppressions, small or great, do not touch us. Sickness, poverty, ugliness, death, ruin of the fatherland cannot disquiet the wise man. The *summum bonum* is beyond good and ill. It is conditioned by the termini of good and evil, by a Something which is dependent neither on nature, nor on the gods (who do not exist), but only on man himself. Ancient philosophy created a dialectic which understood how to find in that which has a γένεσις (origin) and is condemned to φθορά (destruction), in that which appears and vanishes, a Something which never began and will therefore never end. It discovered also the κάθαρσις (purification)—the last word of Greek wisdom—spiritual exercises which transform, not the world, but man himself, by elevating him to the consciousness that it is the fundamental duty of the reasonable being to learn to renounce himself, his own ego, as directly cognized, and to transform himself into a simple entity, the ideal entity. Until this is done, until the living man has broken the bond with the visible world, reason does not become free from the intolerable feeling of impotence in the face of necessity, and neither the philosopher nor the ordinary man can grasp Mercury's desired wand.

Aristotle knew all this just as well as Plato and his Stoic followers. He knew that until ontology is transformed into ethics, philosophy, which had begun with consciousness of man's impotence in the face of necessity, can never come to consciousness of its strength. And if he still evaded Phalaris' bull and preferred altogether to shun the farthest reaches of existence, he had his reasons for it, or rather, he was guided by the just, unfailing practical instinct of a clever man. He naturally trusted reason and was certainly not one of the μισόλογοι. But he had besides another great gift, that of moderation. It was said of him that he was μέτριος εἰς ὑπερβολήν—moderate to excess. In his soul there is something always whispering to him—perhaps, who knows? he had his own demon, like Socrates—that too consistent and careful thought involved the greatest dangers. He, like his predecessors, loved spiritual goods; and he was convinced that there is a moral law above man; he always defended wisdom and praised it. But he never dared pursue reason and the wisdom born of reason to the end, and he was always mistrustful of Plato. The consequences showed that he was not wrong. We shall see this at once in the example of the last great philosopher of antiquity, Plotinus.

V

Not only is Plotinus chronologically the last great representative of ancient philosophy; in him ancient philosophy reached its *completion.* I have already said that with the Greeks reason gave birth to wisdom, and wisdom brought them the recognition and conviction that true reality must not be sought in the world inherited from the dead gods, but in the ideal world created by that reason which had become heir to the rights of the gods. Greek philosophy, the philosophy of reason, was bound in the end to set ethics on the throne of ontology. If there are no gods, the world is masterless. How can we live in such a world? In it everything is false, fortuitous, transitory. In it is neither truth nor justice. So the ancients taught; so the world revealed itself to them when they regarded it with eyes of reason. So, too, Plotinus saw the world. And thus he, like his predecessors, was faced with the necessity of finding for this world another which should answer the demands of reason. In this respect he treads paths which had been trodden before him. And he strives with all forces at his disposal to prove that the "visible" world is a false world, a world of shadows and non-existence, while the only real world is the moral world. He carries out this task with astonishing persistence and incomparable mastery. He makes use of all the achievements of the ancients; the Pythagoreans, Heraclitus, Parmenides, Socrates, Plato, Aristotle, the Stoics had prepared him sufficient material. He was able to blend everything which had been collected by the great Hellenic thinkers in the course of a thousand years into a single system, the magic of which not even the leaders of the rising force of Christianity could withstand.

Plotinus begins: Ἀρχὴ οὖν λόγος καὶ πάντα λόγος (III, ii, 15). (Reason is the beginning and everything is reason.) Reason is lawgiver and creator, it does all things, what it will and how it will. At the same time it is also the original source both of truth and of good. Dialectics, in which the working of reason is expressed, not only reveals truth to man, but also brings him the good. In this way the *vera philosophia* and *optima philosophia* blends into one. Οὐ τοίνυν τοῖς ἡδομένοις τὸ εὖ ζῆν ὑπάρξει, ἀλλὰ τὸ γινώσκειν δυναμένῳ, ὅτι ἡδονὴ τὸ ἀγαθόν. Αἴτιον δὲ τοῦ εὖ ζῆν οὐχ ἡδονὴ ἔσται, ἀλλὰ τὸ κρίνειν δυνάμενον, ὅτι ἡδονὴ ἀγαθόν. Καὶ τὸ μὲν κρῖνον βέλτιον ἢ κατὰ πάθος. Λόγος γὰρ ἢ νοῦς, ἡδονὴ δὲ πάθος· οὐδαμοῦ δὲ κρεῖττον ἀλόγον λόγου. Πῶς ἂν οὖν ὁ λόγος αὐτὸν ἀφεὶς ἄλλο θήσεται ἐν τῷ ἐναντίῳ γένει κείμενον κρεῖττον εἶναι ἑαυτοῦ; (I, iv, 2). (Thus the good life does not belong to those who enjoy, but to him who is able to know that pleasure is the good. And the cause of good living will not be pleasure, but the power of judging that pleasure is good. And judging is better than sensation. For the mind is λόγος and pleasure is sensation; and the irrational can in no wise be better than the rational. How, then, should the λόγος abandon iteslf and call something better than itself which is of opposite nature to itself?) These words epitomize Plotinus' whole "doctrine"; they are also the sum of what his predecessors taught him. Reason (it is not by chance that he speaks here of λόγος ἢ νοῦς) will not under any circumstances admit that there is something over it, which is not like itself, and will never renounce itself and its own sovereign rights. To it and to it alone is given to judge what is truth and what the good. Truth lies in the fact that the law of impermanence rules in the visible world, and good in the fact that man shall not seek for that which he desires but for that which reason prescribes as the best. And the highest good, *summum bonum*, that which appears the end of the εὖ ζῆν, is not ἡδονή, for ἡδονή is not subject to reason (and neither is that visible world with which all ἡδοναί are bound up) but the ability to *judge* that ἡδονὴ τὸ ἀγαθόν. To make it clearer what is the contrast between τὸ κρῖνον and κατὰ πάθος, I may quote another passage from Plotinus (I, vi, 4): "How lovely," he writes, "is the face of justice and self-control (σωφροσύνης), before whose beauty even the morning and the evening star grow pale!" He repeats the same thought in even stronger expressions at the end of VI, vi, 6. Reason decides on its own authority that justice and self-control are more beautiful than the morning and the evening star, and since, as Plotinus has just told us, it will not abdicate its rights to anyone, this will always remain so forever, and man must submit, even were he to find, κατὰ πάθος, that the morning and the evening star are far lovelier than such virtues as justice and self-control, which are, after all, only mortal. Man must submit. Or is it permissible, after all, to ask: Has not reason overstepped its bounds here? It has power over self-control and over justice, for it has created them. But it did not create the morning and the evening star. Has it a right to dispose and judge where it is unable to create? Ancient philosophy felt exceedingly strongly the whole importance and significance of this question—and Plotinus knew this better than anyone else. This is why he puts his assertion in so categorical a form. In such cases the positiveness of an assertion is a reliable index to the doubts which still cling about it. Aristotle would of course have preferred to evade this question, even as he preferred not to talk too much about Phalaris' bull. And in fact, reason's sovereign rights can only be thought to be guaranteed when all κατὰ πάθος is absolutely and unconditionally placed at its disposal. Κατὰ πάθος in Phalaris' bull is terrible; κατὰ πάθος a man, even one who lives a virtuous life, would perhaps be able to forget himself in contemplation of the morning star. But philosophy requires of him that before he fear or rejoice, he shall come to reason, ὅτι κρίνει, ἃ ἀνακρίνει, καὶ ὅτι τοῖς ἐν ἑαυτῷ κανόσιν, οὓς παρὰ τοῦ νοῦ ἔχει (V, iii, 4) (because he judges what he judges according to the canons within himself, which he has from the mind); and learn from reason whether what attracted him might be the good, and what repelled him, the evil. For only under these conditions can it promise him the Magna Charta of the poor earthly freedoms proclaimed by the old wisdom and confirmed again by Plotinus: ὀρθῶς λέγεται, οὐδὲν κακὸν τῷ ἀγαθῷ, οὐ δ' αὖ τῷ φαύλῳ ἀγαθόν (III, ii, 6). (It is rightly said that there can be no evil for the good man and no good for the bad man.) We know that this passed as quite unquestionable; men can only overcome the accursed chance which rules in this God-forsaken world, when everything which is κατὰ πάθος is overcome and the

last word left to the λόγος by whose decision anything you please
is turned into a good. We remember, too, that the beginning of
philosophy is the knowledge of impotence, and we remember
how Epictetus found his magic wand. The Stoics repeated tire-
lessly: *Si vis tibi omnia subjicere, te subjice rationi. Nihil acci-
dere bono viro mali potest . . . est enim omnibus externis
potentior* (Wouldst thou submit all things to thyself, then submit thyself to reason. No evil can befall a good man . . . for he
is mightier than anything that comes from without). Plotinus
adopted the Stoic wisdom complete, but lent it an indescribable
charm and a quite new profundity; here his inner kinship and
congeniality with Plato showed itself. While Epictetus and
Marcus Aurelius himself sometimes seem to us mere wooden
moralists and preachers, the inspired philosopher ever stirs in
Plotinus. He, too, says, in the imperative of course: γενέσθω δὴ
πρῶτον θεοειδὲς πᾶς, καὶ καλὸς πᾶς, εἰ μέλλει θεάσασθαι θεόν τε καὶ καλόν
(I, vi, 9) (therefore let him who would see God and the Beautiful
first become godlike and beautiful); but one gets an impression
as though this imperative of his were bound up by invisible
threads with the ultimate mystery of the universe. In reality
Plotinus is much nearer the Stoa than he seems. His verdicts that
the virtues are more beautiful than the stars of heaven, and the
passage quoted above, always contain the same fatal consciousness of impotence which haunted Socrates and which Epictetus
admitted openly. And this consciousness, which is suggested to
man by reason, the discoverer of γένεσις and φθορά in the world,
forces Plotinus to rank the moral world above the real world
and to oust ontology by ethics. He looks on κατὰ πάθος as the
original sin: ἀρχὴ μὲν οὖν αὐταῖς (ταῖς ψυχαῖς) τοῦ κακοῦ ἡ τόλμα, καὶ
ἡ γένεσις, καὶ ἡ πρώτη ἑτερότης, καὶ τὸ βουληθῆναι δὲ ἑαυτῶν εἶναι (V, i,
1). (The beginning of evil was for them [the souls] the audacity
and the birth and the first differentiation and the desire to exist
for themselves.) The κάθαρσις, the moral perfection, becomes
accordingly a method of seeking for truth, a road which leads

to truth. But the κάθαρσις consists in isolating one's soul, not allowing it to depend on other things, not letting it consider those things at length. Hence ἡ τῶν λεγομένων ἀγαθῶν τοῦ σώματος καταφρόνησις (I, iv, 4)—just like Epictetus's contempt of the so-called physical goods. Everything which does not lie within man's power is only shadowy, imagined being. "And here (in life) as in the theatre, it is not the inner man, but his shadow, the outer man, which laments and groans" (οἰμώζει καὶ ὀδύρεται; III, ii, 15).

As we see, wisdom goes hand in hand the whole time with reason. Reason, proceeding from the self-evident truths (νοῦς δίδωσιν ἐναργεῖς ἀρχάς; I, iii, 5), determines what it can do and what not, or, as it prefers to express itself, what is possible and what impossible. Wisdom, however, convinced that οὐδαμοῦ ἄλογον κρεῖττον τῷ λόγῳ, that the irrational can never be better than the rational, calls that which is possible for reason the good, and that which is impossible for it the evil, or stronger yet (in Plotinus; the Stoics were not so bold): that which is possible for reason it calls true reality, and that which is impossible, deception and illusion. The gods when they died took with them the secret of the world which they had created; reason is unable to decipher how the world was created, and cannot gain mastery over it, and wisdom declares this world non-existent. In the depths of men's souls, even after the death of the gods, an ineradicable love for their creations has survived; wisdom gathers all its forces and arms against ἡδονή and κατὰ πάθος, as it calls man's love of God's world. It demands that men should regard the world with the eyes of reason, not treasure what they desire, not hate what is repellent to them, not love or hate at all, but only "judge"—on the ground of the ready-made, universal rules which reason offers, and judge only with respect to what is good and what evil. Therefore it describes as the "outward man" that which laments and sighs (Spinoza says later: *non ridere, non lugere, neque detestari*). For this reason, too, it declares the individual, differentiated man not only illusory but an unlawful, sinful intruder into existence, and sees in his appearance a τόλμα, an impious act of audacity. Accordingly it considers it its task to expel this pushing intruder out of existence, to drive him back again into that general being whence he sprung. Here, and here alone, has the task of wisdom always lain: in taming recalcitrant man.

Thus it appears that wisdom is only another name for morality. Wisdom demands and orders, just as morality does. Wisdom is just as autonomous, as self-sufficient as morality. Its last wish is to transform and remold the world and man. But it never finishes with the world. It is, however, easier to finish with man. Man can be brought to obedience, can be convinced by threats and enticements that obedience is the supreme virtue, that all daring is impious, that independent existence is a sin and a crime, that man has not to think of himself but of the "Whole," not to love the morning and the evening star but to call moderation and reason divine, even when his sons are slain, his daughters violated, his fatherland ravaged—but this divine reason which boasted that it could do what it would, confines itself to discussions on the theme that here only the "outward man" suffers and only the "outward man" cries out: "My God, why hast Thou forsaken me?" And if reason, with the help of morality, really or only in imagination forces "the individual man" to be silent—only then does philosophy reach its last end: ontology, the doctrine of real existence, turns into ethics, and the wise man becomes unlimited ruler over the universe.

VI

Thanks to the extraordinary strength of his vast intellect and his irresistible gifts, Plotinus called into life for the last time the best and most significant of what the Hellenic spirit had created in the course of a thousand years. He did not evade the most difficult and torturing riddles of existence. If we read his *Enneads,* so quickly written, never reread, yet so full of glowing spirit, it seems to us that reason, in which the Greeks had put their trust, brilliantly justified all expectations; that a world does actually exist, created not by the dead gods, but by reason, which has always lived and still lives today; that philosophy, which had turned ontology into ethics, had solved all the secrets of being; and that *sub specie aeternitatis,* as it revealed itself to the Greeks, it was no loss that the gods died a natural death and men perished for the glory of wisdom. It seems as though in the last great philosopher of antiquity reason had once again shone with a new radiance and established its mastery in the universe in *saecula saeculorum,* and as though it would never give up its place. Reason rules; everything must submit. All disobedience to reason is an unjustified, impious, eternally damnable τόλμα.

So Plotinus taught himself and the rest. He taught how to think, to live, and, I might say, "to be," to be as reason with its self-evident principles would have one be. But while he taught, while he listened to himself, and the others, intoxicated by the nectar of his words, listened to him, somewhere in an invisible, secret corner of his own soul new feelings and premonitions were growing up, and they waxed and a mighty force ripened which was destined to cast down and break asunder the noble altar of wisdom which Plotinus had erected with such pains and diligence. The impious τόλμα, which Plotinus had, apparently, utterly destroyed, had eradicated not only from himself but also from the universe, showed unexpected vitality. And even the human ego, which by its forbidden and despised γένεσις had broken through into being, showed itself by no means so peaceable and gentle, even before the "self-evident principles." *Suddenly,* after steadily proclaiming the blessings and joys of the yoke of reason, Plotinus feels it to be simply intolerable. Formerly he, like Plato, had been convinced that to be a μισόλογος was the greatest of misfortunes. He repeated the saying of the

Stoics that the individual man should not and must not think of himself. We must look on the universal, not on the individual. For reason can only realize its high aims if all "individuals" fulfill the demands made on them dumbly and without contradiction, *ac cadaver*. At reason's command the individual will chant joyous songs if his daughters are violated, his sons murdered, his fatherland ravaged before his eyes. Sons, daughters, fatherland—all these have a beginning and thus, as reason knows positively, have also an end: τούτῳ τὸ φθείρεσθαι, ᾧ καὶ τὸ πάσχειν (III, vi, 8); *hujus perire est, cujus et pati*. At reason's command he must turn away from the morning and the evening star and bow his knee piously before the modest, hand-made virtues of moderation and justice. Reason, or, more accurately, the wisdom born of reason, sees in servility the essence and basis of being and can endure no "self-hood," much less any independence. Plotinus, who had inherited and imbibed the faith of the ancients that true life, true good, is only possible in the ideal atmosphere, in untroubled agreement and harmony, and who lived according to this faith, begins suddenly to feel as though he were stifling, that such life is no longer possible. One could and must submit oneself to reason so long as it limited its pretensions and did not attempt to transform itself into the ἀρχαί (principles) the πηγαί, ῥιζώματα πάντων (sources, roots of all things). Useful and necessary as a tool in man's hand, as lawgiver and mistress of the universe, it became a fearful menace to all that lives. But it was too late. The whole of Greek philosophy before Plotinus had exerted all its force uninterruptedly for a thousand years to ensure reason its sovereign rights. Reason sits firm in its place and will not under any circumstances move from it of free will. Least of all is it inclined to abdicate its rights to the hated human "soul." How to overthrow it? How to fight with it? By convictions, by proofs? It is clear from the first that all convictions, all proofs, are on reason's side. Plotinus himself collected with the utmost care all that his predecessors had accumulated in the defense of reason, and himself

contributed not a little to it. He knows well that if one begins
to strive with reason one is certainly defeated, and yet he proclaims: ἀγὼν μέγιστος καὶ ἔσχατος ταῖς ψυχαῖς πρόκειται (I, vi, 7). (A
supreme and final battle awaits the soul.) Not a "struggle," but
a "battle." We must not seek for proofs which do not exist, but
for new words of incantation, καινὴ ἐπῳδή (V, viii, 18), to awaken
from self-evidence, to break the spell woven by reason. He himself speaks thus on the subject: "Often when I awake to myself
from the slumber of the body (ἐγειρόμενος εἰς ἐμαυτόν) and issue
forth from the outer world to visit myself, I behold a wonderful
beauty: then I believe assuredly that I have been created for a
higher lot (τῆς κρείττονος μοίρας εἶναι), that noble life works
mightily in me and I am become one with Godhead and lifted up
above all that is rational" (IV, viii, 1). If Plotinus came with
these words before the forum of reason, reason would not merely
condemn, but crush, him. Here is every indication of a case of
lèse-majesté, and of that impious τόλμα to whose destruction
Greek philosophy had applied its best forces. How can a mortal
permit himself to dream of so lofty a destiny; to melt into God
and soar aloft above that which the νοῦς has created? And what
means this "awakening to oneself"? Does it not mean assigning
value to that which had a γένεσις and is condemned to φθορά, taking this doomed creature, against all traditions hallowed by
antiquity, and placing it under the shield and protection of Something which "in its nature is something quite different from
reason"? And finally the awakening, the ἐγρήγορσις: this word
contains something quite intolerable to reason, an inner contradiction. Thus the soul sleeps ever, and its whole rational activity passes as in sleep. And to participate in reality one must
first awake; then it must be that something happens with man
which *non sequitur ex natura sua* (does not follow by nature),
and is therefore clearly impossible. There can be no doubt that
Plotinus' words would be declared criminal before the forum of
reason, that Aristotle would have said of them οὐδὲν λέγουσιν, or

something of the sort; and it is equally indubitable that Plotinus
knows very well how Aristotle would have taken his words, but
cares for Aristotle's judgment only so long as he sleeps. But the
moment he awakes (which does not, indeed, happen often, but
very rarely, he tells us) there are no forums and no verdicts
which touch him. On the contrary, the highest possible delight
fills him at the thought that reason has been left somewhere far
below, and that neither its κρίνειν nor its κανόνες are at all valid.
Reason, indeed, does not yield at once, but makes desperate
efforts to recover its rights, to subject to itself the new reality
which revealed itself to Plotinus after his awakening. He continues to repeat that submission and humility are the lot of man,
the good is only that which man has in his power. But the hymns
which Plotinus used to sing to humility, now seem to him dull,
intolerably lukewarm, blasphemous. He has passed through the
strict school of humble obedience and carried away from it an
irreconcilable hatred against everything that he was taught. The
idea that man must content himself with what lies within his
power, and find in this contentment the meaning of life, seems to
him heavy and oppressive as a nightmare. We must awake, awake
at all costs, escape from the enchanted realm of the "Good" in
which the ancient wisdom thought to find the true reality. Precisely in the *res fortunae, sive quae in nostra potestate non sunt,*
in that which is οὐκ ἐφ' ἡμῖν, there where the morning and the
evening star are, there and only there dwells τὸ τιμιώτατον, the one
thing that we need, which alone holds true reality. And that is
why Plotinus fell into such a rage when he learned the doctrine
of the Gnostics, who, trusting reason and wisdom, had determined to leave forever the world not created by them. An almost
mystic horror seizes him when he thinks that he was within a
hair's breadth of treading their path. He, who is usually so quiet
and peaceable, is overcome with rage and says, nay, shouts: "A
man is not good simply because he despises the gods, the world,
and all beauty in it" (II, ix, 16)—as though he himself had not

preached with Epictetus τὴν τῶν λεγομένων ἀγαθῶν τοῦ σώματος καταφρόνησιν (contempt of the so-called physical goods) and that the human virtues were more lovely than the stars of heaven. Plotinus does not usually recall or contrast what he had taught with what was revealed to him later after his awakening. Had he done so he would have had to justify himself and bring proofs. But he has no proofs and does not know how to justify himself. Or rather, did not the most treasured privilege of his lofty destiny (κρείττονος μοίρας) lie precisely in the fact that he no longer needed to justify himself before anyone? Justifications and proofs are necessary in the realm of reason. But here in the world where Plotinus had now arrived, what "criteria of truth" could be applied? Plotinus does not raise this question. By virtue of the power which he gave himself, he forbids reason to ask at all, and answers all its questions curtly: "This does not concern you, you are not the master." The man who still has to ask before he moves, to inform himself, gather experience, look behind, is not yet awakened, has still to pass through the school of humility and of wisdom which Plotinus himself has left behind, to learn from his own experience what that reality is worth which admits only that which is ἐφ' ἡμῖν, where human "good" takes the place of real life. The horror of such a desolate world leads to the "awakening" and gives courage to disregard all proofs and evidence and speak with reason as Plotinus spoke.

The parts are reversed; it is not Plotinus who goes to reason to ask what is good and what evil, what true and what false, what is and what is not, what is possible and what impossible—it is reason which looks up to Plotinus like a slave and begs of him even a little part of its earlier rights. But Plotinus is inexorable. All reason's pleas remain unanswered; ἐν ἀφαιρέσει πάντα περὶ τοῦτο λεγόμενα (VI, viii, 11) (all that is said about it consists only in negation). Thus Plotinus fights against reason. And how can the truth of reason "compel" Plotinus when he has felt that he himself is κρείττονος μοίρας? Whatever reason may say, it only gets one answer: No. It tries to tempt him with the old words: καλός, ἀγαθός, οὐσία, εἶναι—words which always used to make an irresistible impression. Plotinus seems not even to hear them and calls out his ὑπέρκαλος, ὑπεράγαθος (beyond all measure lovely, beyond all measure good) as though anxious to be rid of this tiresome intrusion. Reason recalls the ἐπιστήμη, which Plotinus himself so respected, but he has long since come to the point of δραμεῖν ὑπὲρ ἐπιστήμην (escaping beyond scientific knowledge) (VI, ix, 4). For him science is now reason and reason is multiplicity—λόγος γὰρ ἡ ἐπιστήμη, πολλὰ δὲ ὁ λόγος (V, viii, 11). Finally reason appeals to necessity, which none can overcome. But Plotinus does not even fear necessity; even necessity "came later," and he rejects any definition which reason may propose. "It is in truth unspeakable. Whatever you may say you will yet only say one individual thing. But that which lies ἐπέκεινα πάντων, ἐπέκεινα τοῦ σεμνοτάτου νοῦ, which is separated from all things, has no other true name except that it is the Other and not of the All" (V, iii, 13). You must cast off everything (ἄφελε πάντα; leave all things aside; ib. 17). To grasp true reality "reason must, as it were, retreat backwards"—δεῖ τὸν νοῦν οἷον εἰς τοὐπίσσω ἀναχωρεῖν (III, viii, 9). "For what gives God His value (τὸ τίμιον)? Thought, or Himself? If thought, then He has no value of Himself, or at best only a small one; if Himself, then He is already perfect before any thought and is not made perfect by thinking" (VI, vii, 37). Something which seems quite impossible is passing under our eyes. "Awakened" Plotinus overthrew reason, which he, like all his predecessors, had thought invincible. *He overthrew it*, he carried the battle into a new field which had not, as it were, existed for us. The reasonable proofs which were self-evident for all the world lost their power over him. He released, as it were, the world and man from a spell which supernatural forces had cast over them. "It is not there because it had to be so (οὐ διότι ἐχρῆν), but rather because it is as it is, is it also beautiful: a conclusion not arising from the premises, for there things do not arise out of deductions and inquiries; all these things, like conclusions, proofs, and confirmation, came later" (ὕστερα γὰρ τὰ πάντα καὶ λόγος, καὶ ἀπόδειξις καὶ πίστις—V, viii, 7). So Plotinus speaks, but reason is silent; it has lost its strength and knows not what to reply. It feels that, say what it may, its words will not make the slightest impression. That which the One creates stands *above* reason. In fact, that which exists cannot be "deduced" from premises, but comes when and how it pleases. Plotinus, who has left reason far below him, now conceives the world in quite a different fashion. He tells us of his experiences in enigmatic, unaccustomed words. He himself did not get used at once to living and breathing in this atmosphere of the eternally ungrounded. The soul does not easily resolve to leave earth behind her. She yearns back, "she fears to stand before nothingness" (φοβεῖται μὴ οὐδὲν ἔχῃ—VI, ix, 3). But at last "then she leaves all knowledge . . . and as though carried on the same wave of the spirit and lifted up by its swell, she suddenly (ἐξαίφνης) sees without knowing how" (VI, vii, 36). We shall not meet the last, the supremely real, the supremely necessary on those ways which we can guess by conclusions. Τότε δὲ χρὴ ἑωρακέναι πιστεύειν, ὅταν ἡ ψυχὴ ἐξαίφνης φῶς λάβῃ. ("But then indeed we must believe that we have seen, when light *suddenly* dawns upon the soul"—V, iii, 17.) Reason led to the ways which could be foreseen, and led Plotinus to wisdom. He fled before wisdom, fled before reason and reached the "suddenly" which was grounded on nothing, had no roots in the earth. And this "suddenly" with everything which it brought seemed to him desirable and wondrous in comparison with wisdom and with that which wisdom had given him. What use has he for earth and firm ground who needs no support? What need has he of foresight and presuppositions who has approached God? For reason, truth was bound up for all eternity with the idea of necessity, of a certain compelling, immutable order. Reason fears the unexpected, fears freedom and the "suddenly" —and has every reason to fear. Plotinus knows this; reason dared forsake God (ὁ νοῦς . . . ἀποστῆναι δέ πως τοῦ ἑνὸς τολμήσας—VI, ix, 5), and after terrifying man with imagined horrors of chaos and with other threats (τοιούτῳ τὸ φθείρεσθαι, ᾧ καὶ τὸ πάσχειν) made him an apostate from that true reality created by the "suddenly" which is rich in grace and inexhaustible in creative power. Man, having trusted himself to reason, began to see his *summum bonum* in the fruits of reason, to esteem only that which came *ex sua potestate,* and to forget the gifts showered on him from on high. The awakening out of the spell came through the same "suddenly," and as unexpectedly as the best things in life always come.

VII

Zeller, unlike all other commentators on Plotinus, had the courage to say of him that his philosophy breaks with the Hellenic tradition, and that "the philosopher had lost absolute confidence in his thought." Zeller clearly did not observe what a fatal admission lurked in his words. Then one can trust one's thought, or one can also not trust it? Then reason has to justify itself, show its title, its *justus titulus?* Husserl says: "We shall not let ourselves be convinced that a thing which is logically and geometrically nonsensical is psychologically possible" (*Logical Inquiries,* II, 215). But here precisely that which is logically nonsensical, as Plotinus' example shows, has proved itself psychologically, i.e., really, possible: this is just what Zeller, conscientious as he is, is pointing out. In other words, the bounds of the possible and impossible are not fixed by reason. There is a judge and lawgiver above reason, and philosophy cannot remain a "rational" philosophy insofar as it seeks the ῥιζώματα πάντων (the roots of all things); it must be ἐπέκεινα νοῦ καὶ νοήσεως (beyond reason and knowledge). But how escape reason and its dominion? How arrive at the true sources of being?

We remember that Plotinus could not "depart from" reason. He had to δραμεῖν ὑπὲρ τὴν ἐπιστήμην, soar aloft above knowledge, leave the ground to which reason chains us. One cannot "soar aloft" with discussions and proofs. All attempts at "deductions from premises" hamper flight. We need something else of a quite different nature from proofs and the self-evident truths which lie behind proofs. We need a daring which knows no compromise, asks no questions, never looks behind. Only such a courage, only a mysterious faith in oneself and one's higher destiny (*me praestantioris sortis esse*), a faith which replaces the humble submission inculcated by wisdom, could give Plotinus the daring and the strength to begin his supreme and final battle, his ἀγὼν μέγιστος καὶ ἔσχατος, with the thousand years' tradition of philosophy. Sometimes his ego, terrorized, hypnotized, almost paralyzed by wisdom, sees in self-renunciation the highest ideal and, in order to gain praises from wisdom suppresses all vital impulses. It does not weep, it does not laugh, it is not wroth; reason and reason's truths seem to be eternal and invincible truths. But then comes the awakening, the spell woven by dream is broken, and man now speaks free and imperious. It is not that Plotinus has lost trust in reason—nay, he makes of reason his servant and slave.

Truth lies ἐπέκεινα νοῦ καὶ νοήσεως. This is no break with ancient philosophy, as Zeller says; it is a challenge to reason. This means that what really is, is not determined by reason's self-evidences, nor, indeed, by anything, but that it itself determines all things. The field of what really is, is a field of boundless freedom, not of a "rational" freedom such as man imposed on God Himself, but an unlimited, composed of those self-willed "suddenlies" which in Plotinus have taken the place of the former ἐξ ἀνάγκης. When reason "retreated" at Plotinus' demand it became clear that true being is not contained in that which lies "in our power," not in the "good," but in that which lies beyond the bounds of our possibilities, and that the morning and the evening stars are lovelier than moderation and justice. Or perhaps, indeed most probably, the opposite happened: when Plotinus felt that that which we create has only a conditional and relative value, while the real true value, τὸ τιμιώτατον—and this is the true reality—lies in that which is not created by us: then came the awakening, then he saw that in the sublime *sub specie aeternitatis* lay concealed the fundamental lie and fatal error of the human race. In renouncing wisdom he tore himself free from the earth to which all cling so convulsively. What need has he of earth under his feet, who now has wings?

Plotinus lost confidence in reason, in the *philosophia vera*, the truth which exercises compulsion; he saw in reason, which had dared forsake the One, the beginning of evil, ἀρχὴ τοῦ κακοῦ, and he proclaimed that a supreme, final battel awaited the soul. Can philosophy stand aside from this battle? Can it continue to seek refuge in the shadow of morality and soothe itself with the traditional *sub specie aeternitatis*? People have done so, and still do so today. Husserl is right: we are offered wisdom in the place of philosophy. Hegel himself, for whom nothing apparently existed outside objective truth, saw in morality the beginning of philosophy. He writes in his *Logic*, which is also an ontology: "The return from the particular, finite existence to existence as such, in all its abstract universality, is to be considered the first requisite of theory and even of practice. . . . Man must raise himself up to this abstract universality in which it is . . . indifferent to him, whether he is or is not: is, that is, in finite life (for a state, definite existence is meant) or not, etc.—even, *si fractus illabatur orbis, impavidum ferient ruinae*" (if the earth, falling to pieces, were to slip away, still the crashing ruins will strike him unafraid). This means: morality first, then philosophy. To "think" we must renounce ourselves, our own living entity. After all that we have quoted here it will hardly be necessary to explain that the truth which follows morality is not original but derived and secondary. When the philosopher begins with the imperative "that man shall raise himself up to this abstract universality" he will end by setting ethics in the place of ontology. The whole of nineteenth-century philosophy started from Spinoza's *sub specie aeternitatis* or Hegel's "man shall raise himself up." Nietzsche's appearance in Germany and Dostoevsky's in Russia was an echo of this. Nietzsche proclaimed, or "shouted aloud" if you will, his "beyond good and evil" and his "master morality." When he succeeded in shaking off Hegel's and Spinoza's "man shall," he, like Plotinus, lost confidence in reason; he saw that the philosopher cannot seek his truths in the quarter where the mathematician learns that the sum of the angles of a triangle is equal to two right angles. He saw that our synthetic *a priori* judgments, which are generally held as firmly established for all eternity, are the falsest imaginable. And as though in obedience to Plotinus' command φεύγωμεν δὴ φίλην ἐς πατρίδα (I, vi, 8), he fled, fled without a look behind, before the gifts of reason. He fled even before modern Christianity which, in order to live in understanding with reason, had changed itself of its free will into morality. Yes, it will be said, and he dashed to his "blonde beast"—and that is surely *atavism*? But are we not rather inclined to see atavism even in Plato's ἀνάμνησις?

The same outbreak came in Dostoevsky's soul; he tells us about it in his *Underground*. He too was carried away beyond good and evil, beyond Hegel's first "theoretical and practical requisite." *Sub specie aeternitatis* seems to him the embodiment of horror and nonsense. All "lovely and sublime things," he says, "have lain heavy enough on my back during my forty years of life." The moment he had convinced himself that there was no necessity whatever to "raise oneself up to universality" he answered all morality's demands with laughter and scorn. Not only has he not the slightest intention of fulfilling any demands whatever, but he begins to make them himself. "I want," he says, "my caprice to be guaranteed," I want "to live according to my stupid (irrational) will," etc. Accordingly his thought went another way. Even "twice two is four" ceased to impress him. "'Twice two is four' is in my opinion simply an impertinence! 'Twice two is four' is a lout; he plants himself across our path, arms akimbo, and spits on the ground." Like Nietzsche and Plotinus, Dostoevsky also ceased to "believe" that a living being can be dominated by a lifeless truth, when it was revealed to him that he was *praestantioris sortis.* The *Underground* is a critique of pure reason, if you will, but far more radical than Kant's. Kant started from the postulate that metaphysics must offer proofs, like geometry and other sciences. Dostoevsky goes further; he opens up the question whether there is any need for these proofs, whether mathematics gives the *norma veritatis.* Therefore he does not even argue, he does not answer, he does not think it worth an answer, he laughs, scorns, mocks. The moment he sees a very sublime truth or a quite unshakable principle, he makes a long nose, sticks out his tongue, and far surpasses Aristotle himself in boldness; for Aristotle, although, as we know, he used arguments of this sort against Plato and Heraclitus, never dared mention them in his logic. Dostoevsky felt that we should and can δραμεῖν ὑπὲρ τὴν ἐπιστήμην (soar above knowledge). Zeller could have said of him, too, that he lost confidence in reason.

But if it has come about, both in ancient days and in our own times, for men to lose confidence in reason, can we construct theories of knowledge on the basic principle that there is and can be no other power beside reason? Is it permissible to the philosopher to seek the *norma veritatis* in strict science? This brings us back to Hering's objection. In his estimation the "Awakening" of which I spoke in my *Memento Mori*—Plotinus', Nietzsche's, and Dostoevsky's ἐγρήγορσις, is no concern of the phenomenologist. "As for phenomenology and its doctrine of the *cogitationes,* in the well-known redaction its strength lies precisely in the fact that it takes for the theme of its inquiries the pure consciousness, for which the difference between *homo dormiens* (man asleep) and *homo vigilans* (man awake) in the sense used here does not exist. That which says *ego cogito, ego existo,* is Husserl's pure ego." If this were so, if the *ego cogito* meant one and the same thing in Plotinus and Spinoza, in Dostoevsky and Hegel, in him who sleeps and him who wakes, phenomenology could triumph. But to reach this end we should have, as we know, first to bring all these egos, to look on life *sub specie aeternitatis,* or "to rise to universality." Can phenomenology be sure of achieving this? We remember how Plotinus, Nietzsche, Dostoevsky, answer reasoned arguments. It will be objectod that scorn and coarse mockery are no rejoinder. But I repeat once again that Aristotle himself took refuge in such methods when he could find no other reply to Heraclitus and Plato, and that in Plotinus reason had to "retreat" in the end. This means that phenomenology has power only over an ego tamed and chastened by wisdom. It says *ego cogito* but operates on the *ego cogitat.* It seeks for the essence, i.e., it tries to entice the human egos into the "field of logical reason." With tyros this succeeds, but the more experienced egos take flight in all directions at the first attempt to pen them into a general conception. They know that once they accept the challenge to battle on the field of logical reason they are lost. Not only will mockery and scorn be illicit weapons there, but one will also not be allowed either *ridere* or *lugere,* and particularly not *detestari.* *Les vérités de la raison* or the *veritates aeternae* come into their rights, and that is the end forever of that "unexpected," of that "suddenly" of which Plotinus has given us such a glorious account. Men will then be subjected to the law of continuity, which, if we are to believe Leibniz, is as unshakable as the law of contradiction *—then the "suddenly" will be stamped once and for all with the reproach of being a *Deus ex machina.* Plo-

---

* *L' Entendement humain, avant-propos: C'est une de mes grandes maximes et des plus vérifiées, que la nature ne fait jamais de sauts. J'appellais cela la loi de la continuité.* ("It is one of my great and best established maxims that nature never makes any leaps. I shall call this the law of continuity").

tinus, who "tore himself loose from the earth," asks reason to follow him, and continues the battle not on the firm earth but above it. Will reason take up the challenge under such conditions? There can be only one answer. There is nothing more terrible in the world for reason than to have no ground. It is indeed *a priori* convinced that this is the supreme terror for every living creature. When Kant asked whether metaphysics was possible, he started from the presupposition, which seemed to him self-evident, that the aim of metaphysics, as of the other sciences, must be well-grounded, compelling truths, and his critique of pure reason turns into an apology of pure reason. Husserl, who diverges in many places from Kant, is absolutly at one with him in this respect. He *believes* that reason needs no justification; that, on the contrary, everything has to justify itself before reason. And the moment he loses this faith (and if that "happened" to Plotinus, there is no guarantee that some unexpected "memento" may not rob the most convinced of rationalists of the ground under his feet), then what is left of the theory of knowledge founded on self-evidences? Hering asks me, "Since Shestov knows German philosophy so well, can he really have failed to notice that throughout phenomenological literature . . . few philosophic terms occur so frequently as 'intuition,' 'view,' 'essence'? Is there any contemporary philosophy, that of Bergson alone excepted, which is so emphatic as phenomenology in basing all knowledge on processes which give rise to views?" Of course I noticed it; it would be impossible not to notice a thing which leaps to the eye. But intuition helps as little as the *ego cogito*, unless we agree to renounce ready-made presuppositions, or rather, if we still place these presuppositions before every *cogito* and all intuition; and this is what "illimitability of reason" surely means. Bergson permitted himself the most violent attacks on reason; he say somewhere: *Notre raison incurablement présomptueuse s'imagine posséder par droit de naissance ou par droit de conquête . . . tous les éléments de la vérité.*

(Our incurably presumptuous reason imagines that it possesses by right of birth or by right of conquest . . . all the elements of truth.) In another place he says, almost like Plotinus: *Le raisonnement me clouera toujours à la terre ferme.* (Reasoning will always nail me to firm ground.) But Bergson himself begins to waver and tries to retreat when the moment has come δραμεῖν ὑπὲρ τὴν ἐπιστήμην (to soar above knowledge) when he feels that the earth is giving way under his feet. He fears that a philosophy which trusts too much to its own resources, *tôt ou tard sera balayée par la science* (will sooner or later be swept away by science). With Bergson, just as with Husserl, intuition has no independent rights. It takes refuge, and must take refuge, under the protection of reason, for only reason, with its unshakable *a priori*, can save it from all sorts of arbitrary and "sudden" things. Read Bergson's *L'Évolution créatrice* where he discusses *ordre et désordre,* and you will convince yourself that this is another declaration of the sovereign rights of reason; not quite so solemn, but in essence little different from what Husserl says in his *Philosophy as Strict Science,* and what Plotinus expressed in the formula ἀρχὴ οὖν ὁ λόγος. The reproaches of hostile critics notwithstanding, reality in Bergson never emancipates itself from the watchful and strict guardianship of reason.

Here I can end. Hering had ground enough to return to the protection of the *sub specie aeternitatis* and to ask for help of the wisdom which Husserl rejected. Husserl, one may assume, will agree to no compromise and will continue to maintain that there is and can be no other power beside reason; that what is logically and geometrically nonsensical is psychologically, i.e., *realiter,* impossible; that reason has the right to summon truth before its forum, to call on truth to show its title, etc.; for only under such conditions can philosophy be a strict science. My task has consisted in showing that reason has not the power which it claims. That which is logically nonsensical is psychologically possible. Truth gets through life without showing any

sort of documentary titles. And individual living men who have
awakened from the enchanted sleep of thousands of years of
a priori (ἀληθινὴ ἐγρήγορσις) and have reached the desired freedom do not in their search for truth turn to that quarter whither
Spinoza turned to learn what is the sum of the angles of a triangle: οὐ γὰρ δεῖται ἱδρύσεως, ὥσπερ αὐτὸ φέρειν οὐ δυνάμενον—"It does
not need a support, as though it could not carry itself." The
ultimate truth, that for which philosophy seeks, that which is
τὸ τιμιώτατον for living men, comes "suddenly." It knows no compulsion and compels none. Τότε δὲ χρὴ ἑωρακέναι πιστεύειν, ὅταν ἡ
ψυχὴ ἐξαίφνης φῶς λάβῃ. (But then indeed we must believe that
we have seen it, when a light *suddenly* dawns on the soul.) This
is where Plotinus was brought by Greek philosophy, that philosophy which had tried for a thousand years to subdue the
human spirit to reason and necessity; that is why Plotinus began
his last and mighty battle. We can, of course, turn away from
Plotinus; we can renounce the last battle and continue to look
upon the world and life *sub specie aeternitatis,* and in our flight
before the arbitrary "suddenlies" shut ourselves up in the ideal
world of moral existence, and refuse to step forth into the freedom of real life. We can bow before necessity and compelling
truth and give out ethics for ontology. In that case, however,
we must not only forget Plotinus; we must also forget everything
that Husserl, in his brilliant works, has told us with such extraordinary animation about wisdom and specific relativism.

Appendix I

A Note on *Potestas Clavium*

Vlast Klioutchei (Potestas Clavium) was published in Russian by Skythen Verlag in Berlin in 1923 and constitutes Volume VII of the original Russian edition of Lev Shestov's works. Most of the essays found in *Potestas Clavium* had previously been published in Russian journals:

"A Thousand and One Nights", in *Voprossi filosofii i psikologuii*, CXXXIX (1917).

Part I, Thirty-nine Aphorisms, in *Rouskaia Misl* (January and February, 1916).

Part II, Aphorism No. 10, in *Filosofski Ejegodnik* (1916).

Part III, *Memento Mori* and *Viatcheslav Velikolepni* in *Rouskaia Misl* (1916).

In the French edition, which appeared in 1928, Shestov removed the essay "Viatcheslav Velikolepni," devoted to the Russian poet Viatcheslav Ivanov, and replaced it with the essay "What Is Truth?" The latter essay, written by Shestov in France in reply to an article of the German professor Albert Hering entitled *Sub Specie Aeternitatis* [*Philosophischer Anzeiger*, I (1927)] appeared in Russian in *Sovremennia Zapiski*, No. 30 (1927). In his article Professor Hering had attacked Shestov's essay on Husserl, *Memento Mori*, which had appeared in French in the *Revue Philosophique*, for January, 1925. *Memento Mori* had contributed considerably to publicizing Husserl's work in France.

In the Russian edition of Shestov's works the essay "What Is Truth?" is included in Volume VIII entitled *Na Vessakh Iova (In Job's Balances)* Paris, 1929.

The English translation of "What is Truth?" in the present edition was made by Camilla Coventry and C. A. Macartney and first appeared in Lev Shestov, *In Job's Balances*, published by J. M. Dent and Sons, London, 1932. It is reprinted here with the kind permission of the publisher.

Grateful acknowledgement is made to Mr. Tom Sullivan of Cleveland, Ohio who translated a large number of Shestov's Greek and Latin quotations for this edition of *Potestas Clavium*.

Appendix II
The Works of Lev Shestov

(Roman numerals refer to the Collected Russian Edition)

I. SHAKESPEARE I EGO KRITIK BRANDES
   (Shakespeare and His Critic Brandes)
   First Edition: St. Petersburg: Stasyulevitch, 1898. 282 pages
   Second Edition: St. Petersburg: Shipovnik, 1912. 285 pages.

II. DOBRO V UCHENII GR. TOLSTOGO I NIETZSCHE—FILOSOFIA I PROPOVED
   (Good in the Teaching of Count Tolstoi and Nietzsche—
   Philosophy and Preaching)
   First Edition: St. Petersburg: Stasyulevitch, 1900. 209 pages.
   Unnumbered Edition: St. Petersburg: Piroshkov, 1907. 133
   pages.
   Second Edition: St. Petersburg: Shipovnik, n.d. 182 pages.
   Third Edition: Berlin: Skythen-Verlag, 1928. 122 pages.

   In German: Tolstoi und Nietzsche
   Translated by Nadia Strasser,
   Köln: Marcan-Block-Verlag, 1923. 262 pages.

   In French: L'idée du bien chez Tolstoï et Nietzsche
   Translated by T. Beresovski-Chestov and Georges Bataille,
   First Edition: Paris: Ed. du Siècle, 1925. 254 pages.
   Second Edition: Paris: Vrin, 1949. 254 pages.

III. DOSTOEVSKI I NIETZSCHE—FILOSOFIA TRAGEDII
   (Dostoevsky and Nietzsche—The Philosophy of Tragedy)

First Edition: St. Petersburg: Stasyulevitch, 1903. 245 pages.
Second Edition: St. Petersburg: Shipovnik, 1911 (?). 245 pages.
Third Edition: Berlin: Skythen-Verlag, 1922. 157 pages.

In German: Dostojewski und Nietzsche
Translated by Reinhold von Walter,
Köln: Marcan-Verlag, 1924. 389 pages.

In French: La Philosophie de la Tragédie: Dostoiewsky et Nietzsche
Translated by B. de Schloezer,
First Edition: Paris: Schiffrin, 1926. 250 pages.
Second Edition: Paris: Flammarion, 1966. 187 pages.

In Spanish: La Filosofía de la Tragedia: Dostoievsky y Nietzsche
Translated by D. Vogelman,
Buenos-Aires: Emece, 1949. 267 pages.

In Japanese: Tokyo, 1952.

IV. APOFEOZ BESPOCHVENNOSTI
(The Apotheosis of Groundlessness)
First Edition: St. Petersburg: Obshestvenaya Polza, 1905. 285 pages.
Second Edition: St. Petersburg: Shipovnik, 1911. 294 pages.

In English: Parts I and II, containing 122 and 46 aphorisms, respectively, were published in 1920 by Secker, London, and by Robert M. McBride, New York, under the title *All Things Are Possible* (244 pages), with an introduction by D. H. Lawrence.

Appendix I, "The Ethical Problem in Julius Caesar," appeared in the review *The New Adelphi*, June, 1928 (pp. 348–356).

In French: Sur les confins de la Vie: L'apothéose du dépaysement
Translated by B. de Schloezer,
First Edition: Paris: Schriffrin, 1927. 246 pages.
Second Edition: Paris: Flammarion, 1966. 167 pages.

In German: Apotheose der Bodenlösigkeit
Two parts of the book were published:

Das ethische Problem bei Shakespeare
(*Europäische Revue*, September, 1926, pp. 371–381) and
Die Grenzen der Erkenntnis
(*Europäische Revue*, August, 1927, pp. 341–348).

V. NACHALA I KONSTY
(Beginnings and Endings) Collected Essays,
St. Petersburg: Stasyulevitch, 1908. 497 pages.

In English: Anton Chekhov and Other Essays
Introduction by John Middleton Murry,
Dublin and London: Maunsel, 1916. 205 pages.

In the U.S.A.: Penultimate Words and Other Essays,
Boston: Luce & Co., 1916.
Chekhov and Other Essays, Ann Arbor: University of Michigan Press, 1966.

In French: Les commencements et les fins
Part I, *Création ex nihilo: A. Tchekov,* published by Gallimard in 1931 as part of *Pages choisies* and by Plon in 1966 as part of *L'Homme pris au piège.*

In German: Chapter I, *Schöpfung aus dem Nichts: Anton Tschechov,*
Published in *Neue Schweizer Rundschau,* Zurich, February, 1928, pp. 121–140, and March, 1928, pp. 198–213.

VI. VELIKIE KANUNY
(Great Vigils)
St. Petersburg: Shipovnik, 1911. 314 pages.

In French: Les grandes veilles
A few chapters were published in French periodicals and the chapter entitled *Celui qui detruit et édifie les mondes (Tolstoi)* as part of *L'Homme pris au piège.*

In German: Die grossen Vorabende
Parts of the book were published as follows:

Die grossen Vorabende
Die Kreatur, 1930, No. 4, pp. 343–371, Lambert Schneider, Berlin.

Bruchstücke einer Konfession
[Nine aphorisms from the preface to the book]
(*Die Tat*, June, 1929, pp. 161–167, Kuckhoff, Deiderichs, Jena.)

Tolstoi, der Welten schafft und zerstört
(*Europäische Revue*, August, 1928, pp. 365–379, September, 1928, pp. 419–440).

VII. VLAST KLYUCHEI: POTESTAS CLAVIUM
(The Power of the Keys)
Berlin: Skythen-Verlag, 1923. 279 pages.

In German: Potestas Clavium oder die Schlüsselgewalt
Translated by Hans Ruoff,
Munich: Verlag der Nietzsche-Gesellschaft, 1926. 459 pages.

In French: Le pouvoir des clefs
Translated by Boris de Schloezer,
First Edition: Paris: Schiffrin, 1928. 458 pages.
Second Edition: [as *Potestas Clavium*] Paris: Flammarion, 1966 340 pages.

In English: Potestas Clavium
Translated by Bernard Martin,
Athens: Ohio University Press, 1968.

VIII. NA VESAKH IOVA
(In Job's Balances)
Paris: Annales Contemporaines, 1929. 371 pages.

In English: In Job's Balances
Translated by Camilla Coventry and C. A. Macartney,
London: Dent and Sons, 1932. 407 pages.

In German: Auf Hiob's Waage
Translated by H. Ruoff and R. von Walter,
Berlin: Lambert Schneider, 1929. 578 pages.
Part of the book, *Nacht zu Gethsemane*, had previously been published in 1929 in *Ariadne, Erstes Jahrbuch der Nietzsche-Gesellschaft*, Berlin.

In French: The following parts of the book were published, *Les révélations de la mort.*

First Edition: Plon, 1923. 230 pages.
Second Edition: Plon, 1958. 210 pages.
La nuit de Gethsemani: Essai sur la philosophie de Pascal
Paris: Grasset, 1923. 161 pages.

Other parts appeared in various periodicals.

In Dutch: Two chapters of this book and one from Volume VII
were published by Rosenbeek, Hilversum in 1934, under the
title, *Crises der Zekereden (Pascal-Dostojewsky-Husserl)*,
234 pages.

In Spanish: Two parts were published by Sur, Buenos-Aires, as
separate books:
Las revelationes de la muerte, 1938. 203 pages.
La noche de Gethsemane, 1958. 101 pages.

IX. KIERKEGAARD I EXSISTENTSIALNAYA FILOSOFIA
(Kierkegaard and Existential Philosophy)
Paris: La Maison de livres et Annales Contemporaines, 1939.
197 pages.

In French: Kierkegaard et la Philosophie Existentielle
Translated by T. Rageot and B. de Schloezer,
First Edition: Paris: Vrin, 1936. 384 pages.
Second Edition: Paris: Vrin, 1948. 384 pages.

In German: Kierkegaard und die Existenzphilosophie
Translated by H. Ruoff,
Graz: Schmidt-Dengler, 1949. 281 pages.

In Spanish: Kierkegaard y la filosofia existencial
Translated by Jose Ferrater Mora,
Buenos-Aires: Editorial Sudamerican, 1949. 327 pages.

In Danish: Kierkegaard og den Eksistentielle Taenking,
Copenhagen: Hagedur, 1947. 252 pages.

In English: Kierkegaard and Existential Philosophy
Translated by Elinor Hewitt,
Athens: Ohio University Press, 1968.

X. AFINY I JERUSALIM
(Athens and Jerusalem)
Paris: YMCA Press, 1951. 274 pages.

In English: Athens and Jerusalem
Translated by Bernard Martin,
Athens: Ohio University Press, 1966.

In German: Athen und Jerusalem: Versuch einer religiösen Philosophie
Translated by H. Ruoff,
Graz: Schmidt-Dengler-Verlag, 1938. 505 pages.

In French: Athènes et Jérusalem: Un essai de philosophie religieuse
Translated by B. de Schloezer,
First Edition: Paris: Vrin, 1938. 465 pages.
Second Edition: Paris: Flammarion, 1966.

In Italian: Part I, II, III published by Bocca, Milan, in three
separate volumes:
   Parmenide Incatenato, 1944. 141 pages.
   Il Sapere e la Liberta, 1943. 210 pages.
   Concupiscentia Irresistibilis: della filosofia medioevale,
   1946. 232 pages.

XI. UMOZRENIE I OKTROVENIE: RELIGIOZNAYA FILOSOFIA VLADIMIRA
   SOLOVIEVA I DRUGIE STATII
(Speculation and Revelation: The Religious Philosophy of
V. Solovyev and Other Essays) Posthumously Collected,
Paris: YMCA Press, 1964. 347 pages.

In German: Spekulation und Offenbarung: Essays und Betrachtungen nach dem Tode von L. Schestow gesammelt
Translated by H. Ruoff,
München: H. Ellermann Verlag, 1963. 415 pages.

In Dutch: Rede en Geloof (Reason and Faith)
This book contains three chapters from Volume XI (Tolstoi-
Husserl-Jaspers) and two extracts from Volume VII.
Bussum: F. G. Kroonder, 1950. 132 pages.

In French: The last chapter, *Pouchkine,* was published as part
of *L'Homme pris au piège.*

XII. TOLKO VEROI: SOLA FIDE
   (Unfinished Russian manuscript of a book written between
   1910 and 1914)
   Part I: "Greek Philosophy and the Philosophy of the Middle
   Ages"
   Part II: "Luther and the Church"
   Paris: YMCA Press, 1966. 295 pages.

In French: The second part has been published under the title:
   Sola Fide: Luther et L'Église
   Translated by Sophie Seve,
   Paris: Les Presses Universitaires, 1957.

In German: Translation is in preparation, to be published by
   Ellermann, Munich, in 1967.

XIII. A volume is in preparation. It will contain:

   —A biography of Shestov written by Herman Lowtzky and
   published in Russian in the Review *Grani,* Nos. 45 and 46,
   Frankfurt, 1960.

   —*An History of Greek Phiolsophy* (lectures given at Kiev University Extension, 1918–19—unfinished Russian manuscript).

   —Selected letters and fragments.

ANTHOLOGIES

   In French: Pages Choisies. Paris: Gallimard, 1932. 230 pages.
   L'Homme pris au piège (Pouchkine-Tolstoi-Tcheckov)
   Paris: Librairie Plon, 1966. 124 pages.